THE VISTA HIGHER LEARNING

Introductory Spanish

Pocket Dictionary & Language Guide

VISTA
HIGHER LEARNING

Boston, Massachusetts

ISBN 1-59334-387-6

Library of Congress Control Number: 2004106252

5 6 7 8 9 B 09 08 07 06 05

CONTENTS

Introduction 1

Spanish-English Dictionary 3

English-Spanish Dictionary 115

Useful Expressions 213

Verb Conjugation Tables 264

Reference Section

Academic Subjects	286
Animals	288
The Human Body and Health	290
Useful Classroom Expressions	296
Countries and Nationalities	298
Currencies	303
Expressions and Sayings	304
False Friends	309
Foods	312
Holidays	317
Weights and Measures	321
Spanish Names	325
Numbers	333
Occupations	334

Introduction

***The Vista Higher Learning Introductory Spanish Pocket
Dictionary & Language Guide*** was created to complement
your Vista Higher Learning introductory Spanish textbook. Its
Spanish-English and English-Spanish dictionaries contain all
of the active words and expressions taught in these texts:

- *VISTAS*
- *AVENTURAS*
- *PANORAMA*
- *INVITACIONES: Primera parte y Segunda parte*

Besides active vocabulary, the dictionaries also
incorporate several thousand additional words, expressions,
and idioms chosen because of their high-frequency and their
usefulness to students who are using these Vista Higher
Learning introductory textbooks to learn Spanish.

The dictionaries are followed by *Useful Expressions*, a
storehouse of contextualized sentences illustrating new
vocabulary, idioms, and grammatical structures that can help
you make your Spanish more natural and expressive. These
sentences are related to the themes presented in your Vista
Higher Learning textbook. Verb conjugation tables containing
all of the verbs taught in your textbook follow the *Useful
Expressions* section.

The Pocket Dictionary & Language Guide then closes with
the *Reference* section. It contains lists of specialized
vocabulary on a variety of topics, such as country names,
adjectives of nationality, academic subjects, foods, numbers,
sayings, false friends, and so forth.

We hope that you will find the ***Vista Higher Learning
Introductory Spanish Pocket Dictionary & Language Guide*** to
be a useful language learning resource and that it will help
you to increase your Spanish language skills in a productive,
enjoyable fashion.

The Vista Higher Learning Editorial Staff

Note on Alphabetization

For purposes of alphabetization, the Spanish language contains one more letter, **ñ**, than English. **Ñ** follows **n**; therefore, the word **dañar**, for example, appears after **danza**.

Abbreviations Used in This Dictionary

adj.	adjective	*L.A.*	Latin America
adv.	adverb	*loc.*	set expression
art.	article	*m.*	masculine
aux.	auxiliary	*n.*	noun
conj.	conjunction	*obj.*	object
def.	definite	*p.p.*	past participle
dem.	demonstrative	*pl.*	plural
d.o.	direct object	*poss.*	possessive
f.	feminine	*prep.*	preposition
fam.	familiar	*pron.*	pronoun/pronominal
form.	formal		
i.	intransitive	*recip.*	reciprocal
impers.	impersonal	*refl.*	reflexive
indef.	indefinite	*sing.*	singular
inf.	infinitive	*subj.*	subject/subjunctive
interj.	interjection	*t.*	transitive
i.o.	indirect object	*v.*	verb
irreg.	irregular		

Español-Inglés
Spanish–English

A

a *prep.* at; to
  a la(s) + (*time*) at + (*time*)
abadía *f.* abbey
abajo *adv.* down
  ¡Abajo! Down (with it/him/her/them)!
abatido/a *adj.* dejected
abeja *f.* bee
abeto *m.* fir tree
abierto *p.p.* of **abrir** opened
abierto/a *adj.* open
abogado/a *m. f.* lawyer
abonar *v.t.* (*soil*) to fertilize
abono *m.* fertilizer
abortar *v.i.* to have a miscarriage
  abortar de manera provocada to have an abortion
aborto *m.* (espontáneo) miscarriage; (provocado) abortion
abrazar *v.t.* to hug; to embrace
abrazarse *v. pron.* (*recip.*) to hug; to embrace each other
abrazo *m.* hug; embrace
abrebotellas *m.* bottle opener
abrelatas *m. sing.* can opener
abreviar *v.t.* to abbreviate
abreviatura *f.* abbreviation
abridor *m.* opener
abrigo *m.* coat; overcoat; jacket
abril *m.* April
abrillantador (para pisos/suelos) *m.* (*floor*) polish

abrillantar *v.t.* to polish
abrir *v.t.* to open
abrirse *v. pron.* to open
  La ventana se abrió de golpe. The window opened suddenly.
absorbente *adj.* absorbent
absorber *v.t.* to absorb
absurdo/a *adj.* absurd
abuelo/a *m.* grandfather; *f.* grandmother
abuelos *m., pl.* grandparents
aburrido/a *adj.* bored; boring
aburrir *v.t.* to bore
  Este libro me aburre. This book bores me.
aburrirse *v. pron.* to get bored
  Espero que hoy no se aburran. I hope you don't get bored today.
acá *adv.* here
  ¡Ven acá! Come here!
acabar *v.t.* to finish
  Acabé la tarea. I'm done with my homework.
acabar de (+ *inf.*) *v.i.* to have just done something
  Acabo de limpiar. I've just finished cleaning.
acampada *f.* camp; camping
  ir de acampada to go camping
acampar *v.i.* to camp
acantilado *m.* cliff
acariciar *v.t.* to caress; (*hair, pet*) to stroke, to pet
acaso: por si acaso *loc.* just in case
accesorio *m.* accessory
accidentado/a *adj.* (*terrain*) rugged; (*person*) hurt, injured

3

accidente *m.* accident
  accidente laboral industrial accident
acción *f.* action
  ...de acción action (*genre*)
accionar *v.t.* (*machine*) to operate; to activate
aceite *m.* oil
  aceite de oliva olive oil
aceituna *f.* olive
acelerador *m.* accelerator (*pedal*)
acelerar *v.t.* to accelerate
  ¡Acelera! Hurry up!
aceptar *v.t.* to accept
acera *f.* sidewalk
acerca de *prep.* about
  Leí un artículo acerca de Sevilla. I read an article about Seville.
acercarse (a) *v. pron.* to approach, to come closer (to)
acero *m.* steel
  acero inoxidable stainless steel
ácido *m.* acid
  ácido fólico folic acid
ácido/a *adj.* acid; (*flavor*) tart, tangy
acogedor(a) *adj.* cozy
acolchado/a *adj.* padded
acompañar *v.t.* to go with, to accompany
acondicionado *adj.* conditioned
aconsejar *v.t.* to advise
acontecimiento *m.* event
acordar (o:ue) *v.t.* to agree
acordarse (de) (o:ue) *v. pron.* to remember

acostarse (o:ue) *v. pron.* to go to bed
acostumbrarse (a) *v. pron.* to be accustomed to
acrobacia *f.* acrobatics
acróbata *m., f.* acrobat
activar *v.t.* to activate
actividad *f.* activity
activo/a *adj.* active
acto *m.* act
  en el acto *loc.* immediately, right away
  acto seguido *adv.* immediately after
actor *m.* actor
actriz *f.* actor
actual *adj.* current, present
actualidades *f., pl.* news; current events
acuarela *f.* watercolor (*painting*)
acuario *m.* aquarium
acuático/a *adj.* aquatic
acuerdo *m.* agreement
  de acuerdo con according to
  llegar a un acuerdo to reach an agreement
adaptación *f.* adaptation
adaptarse (a) *v. pron.* to adapt; to adjust (to)
adelantar (a un vehículo) *v.t.* to pass (*a vehicle*)
adelante *adv.* forward, ahead
  La librería Porté está un poco más adelante. The Porté Bookshop is a little farther ahead.
adelgazar *v.i.* to lose weight; to slim down
además (de) *adv.* furthermore; besides; in addition (to)

adentro *adv.* inside
aderezar *v.t.* (*food*) to season; (*salad*) to dress
aderezo *m.* seasoning; dressing
adicción *f.* addiction
adicional *adj.* additional
adicto/a *m., f.* addict; *adj.* addicted
adiós *m.* good-bye
aditivo *m.* additive
adivinanza *f.* riddle
adivinar *v.t.* to guess
adjetivo *m.* adjective
administración *f.* management, administration
　administración de empresas business administration
administrar *v.t.* (*business*) to manage; to run
adolescencia *f.* adolescence
adolescente *m., f.* teenager, adolescent
adolorido/a *adj.* sore
¿adónde? *adv.* (*destination*) (to) where?
adornar *v.t.* to decorate; (*food*) to garnish
adorno *m.* ornament, decoration
　de adorno for decoration
　Se puso un lazo de adorno en el pelo. She wore a ribbon in her hair for decoration.
adquirir (i:ie) *v.t.* to acquire
adquisición *f.* acquisition
adrede *adv.* intentionally, on purpose
aduana *f.* customs
adulación *f.* flattery

adulador(a) *m., f.* flatterer
adular *v.t.* to flatter
advertencia *f.* warning
advertir (i:ie) *v.t.* to warn; to notice
　Por fin alguien advirtió mi presencia. Finally someone noticed I was there.
aéreo/a *adj.* air
　correo aéreo air mail
aeróbico/a *adj.* aerobic
aerolínea *f.* airline
aeroplano *m.* airplane
aeropuerto *m.* airport
afectado/a *adj.* affected
afectar *v.t.* to affect
afeitarse *v. pron.* to shave (*oneself*)
afición *f.* hobby
aficionado/a *adj.* fan
aficionarse (a) *v. pron.* to become a fan (of); (*hobby*) to take up
afinar *v.t.* (*musical instrument*) to tune
afirmativo/a *adj.* affirmative
africano/a *adj./m., f.* African
afuera *adv.* outside
afueras *f., pl.* suburbs; outskirts
agachar *v.t.* (*head*) lower
agacharse *v. pron.* to squat
agencia *f.* office; agency
　agencia de viajes travel agency
agente *m., f.* agent
　agente de viajes travel agent
agosto *m.* August
agotado/a *adj.* (*person, supplies*) exhausted; (*commerce*) out of stock; (*tickets*) sold out

5

agotamiento *m.* exhaustion
agotarse *v. pron.* (*provisions, supplies*) to run out
agradable *adj.* (*person*) pleasant, nice; (*situation*) enjoyable
agradecer (c:zc) *v.t.* to thank, to be grateful
Te agradezco tu ayuda. Thank you for your help.
agradecido/a *adj.* grateful
agrícola *adj.* agricultural
labor agrícola farm labor
agricultor(a) *m., f.* farmer
agricultura *f.* agriculture, farming
agridulce *adj.* bittersweet
agrio/a *adj.* sour
agrupar *v.t.* to group
agruparse *v. pron.* to get into groups
agua (el) *f.* water
agua bendita holy water
agua dulce fresh water
agua mineral mineral water
agua potable drinking water
agua salada salt water
aguacate *m.* avocado
aguafiestas *m., f.* party pooper
aguantar *v.t.* to endure, to put up with; (*Spain*) to hold
aguante *m.* endurance
águila (el) *f.* eagle
aguja *f.* needle
agujerear *v.t.* (*material*) to make holes; (*ear*) to pierce
agujero *m.* hole
ahijado/a *m.* godson; *f.* goddaughter
ahogado/a *adj.* drowned

ahogar *v.t.* to drown
Ahoga sus dudas leyendo. He drowns his doubts by reading.
Ahoga sus penas trabajando. She drowns her sorrow with work.
ahogarse *v. pron.* to drown
Se ahogó en el río. He drowned in the river.
ahora *adv.* now
ahora mismo right now
de ahora en adelante from now on
ahorrador(a) *adj.* frugal
ahorrar (dinero) *v.t.* to save (*money*)
ahorros *m.* savings
aire *m.* air
aire acondicionado air conditioning
al aire libre in the open air
aislante *adj.* insulating
aislar *v.t.* to isolate; to insulate
ajedrecista *m., f.* chess player
ajedrez *m.* chess
ajo *m.* garlic
al (*contraction of* a + el) to the, at the
al contado in cash
al (+ *inf.*) upon, on
Al llegar a San Juan, fuimos a la playa. Upon arriving in San Juan, we went to the beach.
ala (el) *f.* wing
ala delta (*vehicle*) hang glider; (*sport*) hang gliding
practicar el ala delta to hang glide

alardear (de) *v.i.* (*Spain*) to boast (about)
  Alardeaba de haber ganado. He was boasting about having won.
alarmante *adj.* alarming
albahaca *f.* basil
albañil *m.* builder; bricklayer
albañilería *f.* (*profession*) building; bricklaying
albaricoque *m.* apricot
alberca *f.* (*Mexico*) swimming pool
albergue *m.* hostel
  albergue juvenil youth hostel
alcachofa *f.* artichoke
alcalde, alcaldesa *m., f.* mayor
alcaldía *f.* city hall
alcoba *f.* (*L.A.*) bedroom
alcohol *m.* alcohol
alcohólico/a *adj.* alcoholic
aldea *f.* village
alegrarse (de) *v. pron.* to be happy
alegre *adj.* happy; joyful
alegría *f.* joy; happiness
alejado/a *adj.* remote
alemán *m.* (*language*) German
alemán, alemana *adj./m., f.* German
alérgico/a *adj.* allergic
aleta *f.* (*fish*) fin; (*swiming*) flipper
alfabeto *m.* alphabet
alfombra *f.* carpet; rug
alga (el) *f.* seaweed
algarabía *f.* rejoicing, jubilation; noisy commotion
algo *pron.* something; anything
algodón *m.* cotton

de algodón (made of) cotton
alguien *pron.* someone; somebody; anyone
algún, alguno/a(s) *adj.* any; some
  alguna vez ever
aliento *m.* breath
  dar aliento to encourage
alimentación *f.* diet
alimentar *v.t.* to feed
alimentarse *v. pron.* to feed oneself
alimento *m.* food
aliñar *v.t.* (*food*) to season; (*salad*) to dress
aliño *m.* seasoning; dressing
aliviar *v.t.* to ease; alleviate; (*pain*) to relieve
  aliviar el estrés/la tensión to relieve/reduce stress/tension
aliviarse *v. pron.* (*pain*) to let up; (*person*) to get better
alivio *m.* relief
allí *adv.* there
  allí mismo right there
alma (el) *f.* soul
almacén *m.* department store
almacenamiento *m.* storage
almacenar *v.t.* to store
almeja *f.* clam
almendra *f.* almond
almendro *m.* almond tree
almíbar *m.* syrup
almohada *f.* pillow
almorzar (o:ue) *v.i.* to have lunch
almuerzo *m.* lunch
¿Aló? *interj.* Hello? (*on the telephone*)
alojado/a *adj.* guest
alojamiento *m.* lodging

alojar (a alguien) *v.t.* to lodge, to put up

alojarse *v. pron.* (*hotel*) to stay

alpinismo *m.* (*mountain*) climbing

alpinista *m., f.* (*mountain*) climber

alquilar *v.t.* to rent

alquiler *m.* rent (*payment*)

alrededor (de) *prep.* around
   Hay una muralla alrededor de la ciudad vieja. There is a wall around the old city.

alrededor *adv.* around
   una mesa con cuatro sillas alrededor a table with four chairs around it

alrededores *m., pl.* outskirts, surrounding area
   en los alrededores de Barcelona on the outskirts of Barcelona

altavoz *m.* loudspeaker

alternador *m.* alternator

alternativa *f.* alternative

altillo *m.* attic

alto/a *adj.* tall; high

alto *m.* halt, stop
   señal de alto stop (*sign*)

altura *f.* height

aluminio *m.* aluminum
   de aluminio (*made*) of aluminum

alumno/a *m., f.* (*elementary school*) pupil, student

ama: el ama *m., f.* **de casa** housekeeper; caretaker; housewife; home-maker

amable *adj.* nice; friendly; kind

amanecer *m.* dawn

al amanecer at dawn

amanecer (c:zc) *v. impers.* to dawn; (*person*) to wake up (*in the morning*)
   Amanecí con dolor de cabeza. I woke up with a headache.

amapola *f.* poppy

amante *m., f.* lover; fan; *adj.* loving
   amantes del jazz jazz lovers
   su amante esposa his loving wife
   amante de la buena conversación fond of good conversation

amar *v.t.* to love

amargo/a *adj.* bitter

amarillento/a *adj.* yellowish

amarillo/a *adj.* yellow

amarse *v. pron.* (*recip.*) to love each other

ambición *f.* ambition

ambicionar *v.t.* to aspire to

ambicioso/a *adj.* ambitious

ambientador *m.* air freshener

ambiente *m.* (*natural*) environment; (*created by people, decoration*) atmosphere

ambos/as *adj.* both
   Sujetó la pelota con ambas manos. He held down the ball with both hands.

ambulancia *f.* ambulance

amenaza *f.* threat

amenazar *v.t.* to threaten

amígdala *f.* tonsil

amigo/a *m., f.* friend
   hacer amigos to make friends

amistad *f.* friendship
amistades *m., pl.* friends
   **Martina tiene muchas
   amistades en Cartagena.**
   Martina has lots of friends
   in Cartagena.
amistoso/a *adj.* friendly
amor *m.* love
amortiguador *m.* shock
   absorber
amueblado/a *adj.* furnished
amueblar *v.t.* to furnish
analfabeto/a *m., f.* illiterate
   person; *adj.* illiterate
analista *m., f.* analyst
anaranjado/a *adj.* (*color*) orange
anarquía *f.* anarchy
anárquico/a *adj.* anarchic
anatomía *f.* anatomy
anatómico/a *adj.* anatomical
ancho/a *adj.* wide
anchoa *f.* anchovy
anciano/a *adj.* elderly; *m.*
   elderly man; *f.* elderly woman
andar en bicicleta to ride bikes
andar en patineta to skateboard
anestesia *f.* anesthesia
anestesiar *v.t.* anesthetize
anestesiólogo/a *m., f.*
   anesthesiologist
anfitrión *m.* host
anfitriona *f.* hostess
anglosajón, anglosajona
   adj./m., f. Anglo-Saxon
anguila *f.* eel
ángulo *m.* angle
anillo *m.* ring
   anillo de bodas wedding ring
   anillo de compromiso
   engagement ring

animado/a *adj.* (*person*) in
   good spirits; (*party*) lively
animal *m.* animal
animar *v.t.* to cheer up; to
   encourage
animarse *v. pron.* to cheer up
aniversario (de bodas) *m.*
   (wedding) anniversary
anoche *adv.* last night
anormal *adj.* abnormal
ansia *f.* longing
ansiar *v.t.* to crave for, to long
   for
anteayer *adv.* the day before
   yesterday
antepasado/a *m., f.* ancestor
antes *adv.* before
   antes de *prep.* before
   antes (de) que *conj.* before
antibiótico *m.* antibiotic
anticipación *f.* anticipation;
   (*business*) advance
   con anticipación ahead of
   time; beforehand
anticonceptivo *m.*
   contraceptive
anticuado/a *adj.* old-fashioned
antideportivo *adj.*
   unsportsmanlike
antídoto *m.* antidote
antifaz *m.* mask
antigüedades *f., pl.* antiques;
   antiquities
antiguo/a *adj.* old; ancient
antipatía *f.* dislike
antipático/a *adj.* unpleasant,
   irritating, hasty
antojo *m.* whim
antología *f.* anthology
antorcha *f.* torch

anular *v.t.* to cancel

anunciar *v.t.* to announce; to advertise

anuncio *m.* (*newspaper*) advertisement

anzuelo *m.* hook
  morder el anzuelo (*loc.*) to swallow the bait; to bite

añil *adj.* indigo

año *m.* year
  el año pasado last year

añoranza *f.* yearning

añorar (a alguien) *v.t.* to long for (someone); to miss (someone)

apagar *v.t.* (*TV, radio*) to turn off; (*fire*) to put out, to extinguish

apagón *m.* power failure, blackout

aparato *m.* appliance
  aparato circulatorio circulatory system
  aparato digestivo digestive system
  aparato doméstico household appliance
  aparato respiratorio respiratory system

aparecer (c:zc) *v.i.* to appear

apartamento *m.* apartment

apellido *m.* last name

apenas *adv.* hardly; scarcely; barely; just
  Apenas le conozco. I barely know him.
  Apenas te oigo. I can hardly hear you.

aperitivo *m.* appetizer

apilar *v.t.* to stack

apio *m.* celery

aplaudir *v.t./v.i.* to applaud, to clap

aplauso *m.* applause

aplazamiento *m.* postponement

aplazar *v.t.* to postpone, to put off

apodo *m.* nickname

apoyar *v.t.* to support

apoyo *m.* support

apreciar *v.t.* to appreciate

aprecio *m.* esteem

aprender (a + inf.) *v.t.* to learn

apresurarse *v. pron.* to hurry

aprobado *m.* passing grade, C

aprobar (o:ue) *v.i.* to pass

aprovechar *v.t.* to make good use of

aprovecharse (de) *v. pron.* to take advantage (of)

aptitud *f.* aptitude, competence

apto/a *adj.* fit (*to practice a profession*); suitable
  No es apto para ejercer la psicología. He's not fit to practice psychology.

apuñalar (a alguien) *v.t.* to stab (somebody)

apurarse *v. pron.* to hurry; to rush

aquel, aquella, aquellos/as *dem. adj.* that (over there); those (over there)

aquél, aquélla, aquéllos/as *dem. pron.* that (over there); those (over there)

aquello *dem. neuter pron.* that; that thing; that fact

aquí *adv.* here
  aquí está here (he/she/it) is

aquí estamos en... here we are in . . .

aquí mismo right here

árabe *m.* (*language*) Arabic

árabe *adj.* Arabian; *m., f.* Arab

araña *f.* spider; (*light*) chandelier

árbitro/a *m.* referee; umpire

árbol *m.* tree

árbol frutal fruit tree

árbol genealógico family tree

arboleda *f.* grove

arbusto *m.* shrub, bush

archipiélago *m.* archipelago

archivar *v.t.* to file

archivo *m.* file

arcilla *f.* clay

arco *m.* arch; (*sport*) bow

arco iris *m.* rainbow

ardilla *f.* squirrel

arena *f.* sand

arete *m.* (*L.A.*) earring

argumentar *v.t.* to argue

argumento *m.* (*reasoning*) argument; (*literature, film*) plot

arisco/a *adj.* unfriendly

aristocracia *f.* aristocracy

aristócrata *m., f.* aristocrat

arma (el) *f.* weapon, arm

armar (un rompecabezas) *v.t.* to assemble (a puzzle)

armario *m.* closet

aroma *m.* scent

arqueólogo/a *m., f.* archaeologist

arquitecto/a *m., f.* architect

arrancar *v.t.* (*car*) to start; (*sheet of paper*) to tear out

arrastrar *v.t.* to drag

arrastrarse (por el piso/suelo) *v. pron.* to crawl (on the ground)

arrecife *m.* reef

arreglado/a *adj.* tidy

arreglar *v.t.* to fix; to arrange; to neaten; to straighten up

El profesor arregló la situación. The professor fixed the situation.

La modista me arregló el vestido. My dressmaker fixed my dress.

arreglarse *v. pron.* to do oneself up; to get ready

Tarda mucho en arreglarse. He/She takes forever getting ready.

arrepentido/a *adj.* repentant, feeling sorry

arrepentirse *v. pron.* to be sorry; to regret

arrestado/a *adj.* arrested; under arrest

estar arrestado/a to be under arrest

arrestar *v.t.* to arrest

arresto *m.* arrest

arriba *adv.* up

¡Manos arriba! Hands up!

Me miró de arriba abajo. He/She looked me up and down.

arriesgarse *v. pron.* to take the risk

arroba *f.* @ symbol

arrogante *adj.* arrogant

arroz *m.* rice

arte *m.* art

arteria *f.* artery

artes *f., pl.* arts

artes marciales martial arts
artesanía f. craftsmanship; crafts
articulación f. joint, articulation
artículo m. article; item
artículos m., pl. (*business*) goods
  artículos de cocina kitchenware
  artículos de deporte sporting goods
  artículos de piel leather goods
  artículos de punto knitwear
artista m., f. artist
artístico/a adj. artistic
arveja m. pea
asa (el) f. (*cup, serving dish*) handle
asado m. roast
  asado de cordero roast lamb
asado p.p. of **asar** roasted;
  asado/a adj. roast(ed)
  castañas asadas roasted chesnuts
asador m. barbecue
asar v.t. to roast
ascender v.t. (*temperature, prices*) to rise; v.i. (*employee*) to be promoted
ascenso m. rise; (*at work*) promotion
ascensor m. elevator
asco m. nausea
  ¡Qué asco! How revolting! How disgusting!
asegurar v.t. to assure, to guarantee
asegurarse v. pron. to make sure

asesinato m. murder; assassination
asesino/a adj./m., f. murderer; assassin
asfalto m. asphalt
así adv. thus; so (*in such a way*); like this
  Debe hacerse así. It must be done like this.
  así así so-so
asiático/a adj. Asiatic; m., f. Asian
asiduo/a m., f. (*client*) regular; adj. frequent
asiento m. seat
  asiento delantero front seat
  asiento trasero rear seat
asignación f. (*Mexico*) homework
asistencia f. assistance
  asistencia médica health care
asistir (a) v.i. to attend
asociación f. association
asociar v.t. (*ideas, words*) to associate
asociarse (con) v. pron. to collaborate (with)
asombroso/a adj. amazing, astonishing
aspecto m. appearance
áspero/a adj. (*surface, skin*) rough
aspiradora f. vacuum cleaner
aspirante m., f. candidate; applicant
aspirina f. aspirin
asqueroso/a adj. (*food, smell*) disgusting, revolting; (*place*) filthy

Esta cocina está asquerosa.
This kitchen is filthy.
astrología *f.* astrology
astrólogo/a *m., f.* astrologist
astronauta *m., f.* astronaut
astronomía *f.* astronomy
astrónomo/a *m., f.* astronomer
astuto/a *adj.* shrewd
asumir *v.t.* to assume
atajo *m.* short cut
ataque *m.* attack
  ataque al corazón heart
  attack
  ataque cardíaco heart attack
  ataque de nervios panic
  attack
atardecer *m.* dusk
  al atardecer at dusk, at
  twilight
ataúd *m.* coffin
ateísmo *m.* atheism
atención *f.* attention; care
atender *v.i.* to pay attention
  atender a los clientes to
  take care of clients
atentado *m.* assault, attack;
crime
  atentado terrorista terrorist
  attack; assassination attempt
atentar (contra) *v.t.* to attempt
to assassinate (*somebody*);
to attack (*something*)
ateo/a *adj.* atheistic; *m., f.*
atheist
aterrizaje *m.* landing
aterrizar *v.i.* to land
atleta *m., f.* athlete
atlético/a *adj.* athletic
atletismo *m.* athletics; track
and field
atontado/a *adj.* stunned, dazed

atracar *v.t.* (*bank*) to hold up;
(*person*) to mug
atracción *f.* attraction
atraco *m.* robbery, holdup
atractivo/a *adj.* attractive
atractivo *m.* attraction; appeal,
charm
  No entiendo su atractivo. I
  don't understand his appeal.
atraer *v.t. irreg.* (**yo atraigo**) to
attract
atragantarse *v. pron.* to choke
atrás *adv.* behind
atravesar *v.t.* to cross
atreverse *v. pron.* to dare
atrevido/a *adj.* (*dress*) daring,
provocative; (*person*) brave;
daring, cheeky.
  ¿No te da miedo viajar sola?
  Eres muy atrevida.
  You're not afraid of traveling
  all by yourself? You're really
  brave.
atrevimiento *m.* nerve
atropellar (a alguien con un
vehículo) *v.t.* to run over
(someone with a vehicle)
atroz *adj.* atrocious, awful
atún *m.* tuna
audición *f.* hearing; (*test*)
audition
auditorio *m.* auditorium;
audience; theater
auge *m.* peak
  estar en auge to be on the
  increase
aula *f.* classroom; lecture hall
  aula magna main lecture hall
aumentar *v.t.* to increase
  aumentar de peso to gain
  weight

aumento *m.* increase
aumento de sueldo (*pay*) raise
aunque *conj.* although, even though
auricular *m.* headphone; (*telephone*) receiver
ausencia *f.* absence
ausentarse *v. pron.* to go away
ausente *adj.* absent
australiano/a *adj./m., f.* Australian
auténtico/a *adj.* real
autobús *m.* bus
autodidacta *m., f.* self-taught person; autodidact
auto(e)stop *m.* hitchhiking
hacer auto(e)stop to hitchhike
auto(e)stopista *m., f.* hitchhiker
autógrafo *m.* autograph
automático/a *adj.* automatic
automóvil *m.* automobile
automovilismo *m.* motor racing
automovilista *m., f.* motorist
autonomía *f.* autonomy
autónomo/a *adj.* (*government*) autonomous; *m., f.* (*work*) self-employed worker, freelancer
autopista *f.* highway; freeway, expressway
autor(a) *m., f.* author
autor intelectual (*L.A.*) mastermind (*of a crime*)
autoritario/a *adj.* authoritarian
autoritarismo *m.* authoritarianism
autorretrato *m.* self-portrait
auxiliar *v.t.* to help
¡Auxilio! *interj.* Help!

avance *m.* advance
avanzado/a *adj.* advanzed
avanzar *v.i.* to advance; to move forward
avaricia *f.* avarice
avaricioso/a *adj.* greedy, avaricious
avaro/a *m., f.* miser
ave (el) *f.* bird
avellana *f.* hazelnut
avellano *m.* hazel tree
avenida *f.* avenue
aventura *f.* adventure
...de aventuras adventure (*genre*)
aventurero/a *adj.* adventurous; *m., f.* adventurer
avergonzado/a *adj.* embarrassed
avergonzar (o:ue) *v.t.* to shame, to embarrass
avergonzarse (o:ue) *v. pron.* to be ashamed
avería *f.* (*Spain*) (*automobile, mechanical*) breakdown
averiado/a *adj.* (*Spain*) broken down, out of order
averiarse *v. pron.* (*Spain*) to break down
averiguar *v.t.* to find out; to check
aversión *f.* aversion, dislike
avestruz *m.* ostrich
avión *m.* airplane
viajar en avión to travel by plane
avioneta *f.* light aircraft
avisar *v.t.* to warn, to inform
aviso *m.* warning, notice
avispa *f.* wasp
axila *f.* armpit

¡Ay! *interj.* Oh!, Ouch!, Yikes!
  ¡Ay, qué dolor! Ouch, it
  hurts!/Oh, what pain!
ayer *adv.* yesterday
ayudar (a) *v.t.* to help (to)
ayudarse *v. pron. (recip.)* to
  help each other
ayunar *v.i.* to fast
ayuno *m.* fast
ayunas: salir en ayunas to go
  out without breakfast
ayuntamiento *m.* city hall
azafrán *m.* saffron
azar *m.* chance; coincidence
  al azar at random, randomly
azúcar *m.* sugar
azucarero *m.* sugar bowl
azul *adj./m.* blue
  azul celeste sky blue
  azul marino navy blue
azulado/a *adj.* bluish
azulejo *m.* (*ceramic*) tile

B

babero *m.* bib
bacalao *m.* cod, codfish
bahía *f.* bay
bailar *v.t.* to dance
bailarín, bailarina *m., f.* dancer
baile *m.* dance
bajar *v.i.* to go down
bajar(se) de (un vehículo) *v.
  pron.* to get off/out of (a
  vehicle)
bajo/a *adj.* (*person*) short;
  (*volume, light, temperature*)
  low
  Por favor, hablen más bajo.
  Please speak quietly.
bajo/a *prep.* under

bajo cero below zero
bajo control under control
bajo ningún pretexto under
  no circumstances
bajo juramento under oath
balanza *f.* (*for weighing*) scale
balcón *m.* balcony
baldosa *f.* (*floor*) tile
ballena *f.* whale
ballet *m.* ballet
balneario *m.* spa, resort
baloncesto *m.* basketball
balonmano *m.* handball
banana *f.* banana
banco *m.* bank; bench
banda *f.* (*music*) band
  banda sonora sound track
bandera *f.* flag
banquero/a *m., f.* banker
bañarse *v. pron. (refl.)* to
  bathe; to take a bath; to
  shower
bañera *f.* bathtub
baño *m.* bathroom
baraja (de cartas/naipes) *f.*
  deck (of cards)
barato/a *adj.* cheap
barba *f.* beard
barbero *m.* barber
barbudo/a *adj.* bearded
barco *m.* ship
barra (de pan) *f.* (*Spain*) loaf
  (of bread)
barrer (el suelo/el piso) *v.t.* to
  sweep the floor
barriga *f.* stomach
barrio *m.* neighborhood
barro *m.* mud
barroco/a *adj.* baroque
báscula *f.* scale

bastante *adj.* enough; sufficient; rather

bastar *v.i.* to be enough
Con esto basta y sobra. This is more than enough.
Con ocho basta. Eight is enough.
Dos semanas no bastan para completarlo. Two weeks are not enough to finish it.

bastón *m.* walking stick

basura *f.* trash

basurero *m.* garbage dump; garbage can

basurero/a *m., f.* garbage collector

bata *f.* robe
bata de baño bathrobe

batidor *m.* whisk

batidora *f.* (*Spain*) blender, mixer

batir *v.t.* to whisk; to beat
batir un récord mundial to break a world record

baúl *m.* trunk

bautizar *v.t.* to baptize; to name

bautizo *m.* baptism

bazo *m.* spleen

bebé *m., f.* baby

beber *v.t./v.i.* to drink

bebida *f.* drink
bebida alcohólica *f.* alcoholic beverage

beca *f.* grant; scholarship

béisbol *m.* baseball

belleza *f.* beauty

bello/a *adj.* beautiful
bellas artes *f., pl.* (fine) arts

bendecir *v.t. irreg.* (**yo bendigo**) to bless

bendición *f.* blessing

beneficiarse *v.t.* to benefit

beneficio *m.* benefit

beneficioso/a *adj.* beneficial

benigno *adj.* benign

berenjena *f.* eggplant

bermellón *m.* vermilion

berrinche *m.* tantrum

besar *v.t.* to kiss

besarse *v. pron.* (*recip.*) to kiss each other

beso *m.* kiss

betabel *f.* (*Mexico*) (*sugar*) beet

biblioteca *f.* library

bibliotecario/a *m., f.* librarian

bicarbonato *m.* baking soda

bicicleta *f.* bicycle

bien *adj.* good; well

bienes raíces *m., pl.* real estate

bienestar *m.* well-being

bienvenida *f.* welcome
dar la bienvenida to welcome

bienvenido/a *adj.* welcome

bigote(s) *m.* (*pl.*) moustache

bikini *m.* bikini

bilingüe *adj.* bilingual

bilingüismo *m.* bilingualism

billete *m.* (*Spain*) ticket; paper money
billete de ida y vuelta round-trip ticket
Vale muchos billetes. It costs a lot of money.

billón *m.* trillion
Un billón es un millón de millones. One trillion is a million millions.

biodiversidad *f.* biodiversity

biogenética *f.* genetic engineering

biografía *f.* biography
biográfico/a *adj.* biographical
biología *f.* biology
biólogo/a *m., f.* biologist
biosfera *f.* biosphere
bisabuelo/a *m.* great-grandfather; *f.* great-grandmother
bisagra *f.* hinge
bisnieto/a *m.* great-grandson; *f.* great-granddaughter
bistec *m.* steak
bisturí *m.* scalpel
blanco/a *adj.* white
bluejeans *m., pl.* (*L.A.*) jeans
blusa *f.* blouse
boca *f.* mouth
  boca abajo face-down
  boca arriba face-up
bocina *f.* (*automobile*) horn
boda *f.* wedding
  boda concertada arranged marriage
bodega *f.* (*house*) cellar; (*store*) wine cellar
boina *f.* beret
boletín *m.* bulletin, report
  boletín de notas school report
  boletín informativo newsletter
boleto *m.* (*L.A.*) ticket
boliche *m.* bowling
bolígrafo *m.* pen
bolsa *f.* purse; bag
  la Bolsa the stock market
bolsillo *m.* pocket
  libro de bolsillo paperback book
bolsista *m., f.* stockbroker
bolsita *f.* (*diminutive*) small bag

bolsita de té teabag
bolso *m.* shoulder bag
bomba *f.* bomb
bombero/a *m., f.* firefighter
bonito/a *adj.* pretty
bordar *v.t.* to embroider
bordo: a bordo aboard, on board
  ¡Todos a bordo! All aboard!
borracho/a *adj.* drunk
borrador *m.* eraser
borrar *v.t.* to erase
bosque *m.* forest
  bosque nuboso cloud forest
  bosque tropical tropical forest; rain forest
bota *f.* boot
  botas de agua rubber boots
  botas de montar riding boots
botánica *f.* botany
botánico/a *m., f.* botanist; *adj.* botanical
botar *v.t.* (*L.A.*) to throw away
botella *f.* bottle
  botella de vino bottle of wine
botiquín *m.* medicine cabinet
  botiquín de primeros auxilios first-aid kit
botón *m.* button
  botón de rebobinado rewind button
botones *m., sing.* bellhop
boxeador(a) *m., f.* boxer
boxear *v.i.* to box
boxeo *m.* boxing
bragas *f., pl.* (*Spain*) panties
brasier *m.* (*L.A.*) bra
brazo *m.* arm
  Es su brazo derecho. He's her right-hand man.
breve *adj.* brief; short

en breve *adv.* shortly, soon
brevedad *f.* brevity
brillar *v.i.* to shine
brillo (para zapatos) *m.* (*shoe*) polish
brindar *v.t. (drink)* to toast
brindis *m.* toast
brisa *f.* breeze
brócoli *m.* broccoli
broma *f.* joke
  broma pesada practical joke
  bromas aparte joking aside
  en broma in jest, as a joke
  hacer bromas to make jokes
bromista *m., f.* joker
bronce *m.* bronze
bronceado/a *adj.* sun-tanned
bronceador *m.* suntan lotion
broncear *v.t.* to tan
broncearse *v. pron.* to (get a) tan
buceador(a) *m., f.* (*underwater*) diver
bucear *v.i.* to scuba dive
budista *adj./m., f.* Buddhist
buen, bueno/a *adj.* good
  Buen viaje. Have a good trip.
  Buena idea. Good idea.
  Buenas noches. Good evening.; Good night.
  Buenas tardes. Good afternoon.
  buenísimo/a *adj.* (*superlative*) extremely good
  ¿Bueno? Hello? (*on telephone*)
  (No) Es bueno que … It's (not) good that …
  (No) Es bueno que corras. It's (not) good that you run.
  Buenos días. Good morning.

bueno *adv.* well
bufanda *f.* scarf
búho *m.* owl
buitre *m.* vulture
bujía *f.* spark plug
bulevar *m.* boulevard
bulto *m.* bundle, package
buque *m.* boat, ship
burbuja *f.* bubble
buscar *v.t.* to look for
búsqueda *f.* search
buzón *m.* mailbox

C

caballero *m.* gentleman
caballo *m.* horse
  montado/a a caballo on horseback
cabaña *f.* cabin
cabello *m.* hair
caber *v.i. irreg.* (**yo quepo**) to fit
  Esta mesa no cabe aquí. This table doesn't fit here.
  Esta falda no me cabe. This skirt doesn't fit me.
  no cabe duda (de) que… there's no doubt that…
cabeza *f.* head
cable *m.* cable
  echarle un cable a alguien *idiom.* to help somebody out
cada *adj.* each
cadáver *m.* corpse
cadena *f.* chain
  cadena perpetua life imprisonment; life sentence
cadena *f.* channel (TV)
cadera *f.* hip
caer *v.t. irreg.* (**yo caigo**) to fall
caerse *v. pron. irreg.* (**yo me caigo**) to fall (down)

café m. (place) café, coffee shop; (drink) coffee; (color) brown
cafeína f. caffeine
cafetera f. coffee maker
cafetería f. cafeteria
caída f. fall
  caída libre free fall
caído p.p. of **caer** fallen; **caído/a** adj. fallen
caja f. box; cash register
  caja de música music box
  caja fuerte safe
cajero/a m., f. cashier
  cajero automático automatic teller machine (ATM)
calabaza f. pumpkin
calamar m. squid
calavera m. skull
calcetín m. sock
calculadora f. calculator
calcular v.t. to calculate, to work out
cálculo m. calculation, estimate
caldo m. broth, soup
  caldo de patas (Ecuador) beef soup
  caldo de gallina chicken soup
  caldo de res beef soup
calefacción f. heating
calendario m. calendar
calentador m. heater
calentar (e:ie) v.t. to heat
calentarse (e:ie) v. pron. to warm up
calidad f. quality
caliente adj. hot
calificación f. grade
calificar v.t. to grade

calificarse v. pron. to qualify
callado/a adj. (person) quiet
calle m. street
callejón m. alley
  callejón sin salida dead end, blind alley
calor m. heat
caloría f. calorie
calvo/a adj. bald
calzado m. shoes
calzar v.t. to take size . . . shoes
  Calzo un 38. I take size 38.
calzarse v. pron. to put one's shoes on
calzoncillos m., pl. men's underwear
  calzoncillos largos long underwear
cama f. bed
cámara f. camera
  cámara digital f. digital camera
  cámara de video video camera
camarero/a m. waiter; f. waitress
camarón m. shrimp
camarote m. (ship) cabin
cambiar (de/en) v.t. to change
  cambiar de casa to move
  cambiar de marcha to shift gears
cambio m. change; exchange rate
  a cambio de in exchange for
  cambio de marchas gearshift
  cambio de moneda currency exchange
  cambio de velocidades gearshift

en cambio on the other hand
camello m. camel
camerino m. (*theater*) dressing room
camilla f. stretcher
caminar v.i. to walk
camino m. road, path
De camino a casa, me perdí. On my way home, I got lost.
camión m. truck
camionero/a m., f. truck driver
camioneta f. pickup truck
camisa f. shirt
camiseta f. t-shirt
campana f. bell
campeón, campeona m., f. champion
campeonato m. championship
campestre adj. rural
campo m. countryside; field
la gente del campo country people
campo de fútbol soccer field
campo de golf golf course
cana f. gray hair
echar una cana al aire idiom. to let one's hair down
canadiense adj./m., f. Canadian
canal m. (TV) channel
canario m. canary
cancha f. court, field
canción f. song
candidato/a m., f. candidate
candidato a la presidencia presidential candidate
canela f. cinnamon
cangrejo m. crab
canguro m. kangaroo
cansado/a (de + inf.) adj. tired (of + gerund)

Estoy cansado de esperar. I'm tired of waiting.
cansancio m. fatigue
cansarse v. pron. to tire oneself out
cantante m., f. singer
cantar v.t. to sing
cantidad f. amount
cantimplora f. water bottle, canteen
caña f. cane
caña de azúcar sugar cane
caña de pescar fishing rod
cañería f. pipe
capacitación f. training
capilla f. chapel
capital m. (*finance*) capital
capital f. capital city
capítulo m. chapter
capó m. (*car*) hood
capricho m. whim
cápsula f. capsule
capturar v.t. to capture
cara f. face
cara a cara face to face
¡Caramba! interj. Darn! Shoot! Gosh!
caracol m. snail
caradura adj./m., f. cheeky (*person*)
¡Qué cara más dura tienes! You've got some nerve!
caravana f. trailer
carbohidrato m. carbohydrate
carbón m. coal
carburador m. carburator
cárcel f. prison, jail
cardiología f. cardiology
carencia f. lack, (*supplies, food*) shortage

caribeño/a *adj./m., f.* Caribbean (person)

caricia *f.* caress

caries *f.* (*sing. or pl.*) cavity, cavities

cariño *m.* affection

cariñoso/a *adj.* affectionate, loving

carisma *m.* charisma

carne *f.* meat

  carne de res beef

  carne picada/molida ground beef

carnicería *f.* butcher shop

carnicero/a *m., f.* butcher

carnívoro/a *adj.* carnivorous; *m., f.* carnivore

caro/a *adj.* expensive

carpeta *f.* folder

carpintería *f.* carpenter's workshop; (*activity*) carpentry

carpintero/a *m., f.* carpenter

carrera *f.* (*profession*) career; (*sports*) race

  a la carrera on the run

  carrera ciclista bicycle race

  carrera contra reloj time trial

  carrera de caballos horse race

  carrera de fondo long-distance race

  carrera de obstáculos obstacle course

  carrera de relevos relay race

  carrera pedestre foot race

  Está en la cima de su carrera. She's at the peak of her career.

carretera *f.* highway

carretilla *f.* wheelbarrow

carril *m.* (*highway*) lane

carro *m.* (*L.A.*) automobile, car; (*Spain*) cart

  carro de bomberos fire engine

  carro de carreras racecar

  carro deportivo sports car

carroza *f.* (*carnival*) float

carta *f.* letter; (*playing*) card

cartel *m.* poster

cartera *f.* wallet

cartero/a *m., f.* mail carrier

casa *f.* house; home

  casa de apartamentos apartment building

  en casa at home

casado/a *adj.* married

casar *v.t.* to marry

casarse (con) *v. pron.* to get married (to)

cascanueces *m., sing.* nutcracker

casco *m.* helmet

casero/a *adj.* (*meal*) homemade, home style

casi *adv.* almost

caso *m.* case

  el caso es que the thing is that

  en caso de in case of

caspa *f.* dandruff

castaña *f.* chestnut

castaño/a *adj.* (*hair, eyes*) brown

castellano *m.* (*language*) Spanish, Castilian

castellano/a *adj./m., f.* Castilian

castigar *v.t.* to punish

castigo *m.* punishment

castillo *m.* castle

casualidad *f.* chance, coincidence

  por (pura) casualidad by (sheer) chance

  ¡Qué casualidad! What a coincidence!

catarata *f.* waterfall

catarro *m.* cold

catástrofe *f.* catastrophe

catastrófico/a *adj.* catastrophic

catedral *f.* cathedral

  como una catedral (*fam.*) huge, enormous

  una mentira como una catedral a whopper of a lie

catedrático/a *m., f.* professor; department head

categoría *f.* category

  de categoría fine, first-rate, excellent

  un restaurante de categoría a first-rate restaurant

  un escritor de poca categoría a second-rate writer

católico/a *adj./m., f.* Catholic

catorce fourteen

cava *m.* sparkling wine

caverna *f.* cavern

cavernícola *adj./m., f.* cave dweller; caveman

caza *f.* (*sport*) hunting

cazador(a) *m., f.* hunter

cazar *v.t.* to hunt

cazuela *f.* casserole

cebolla *f.* onion

cebra *f.* zebra

paso cebra (*Spain*) crosswalk

ceder *v.t.* to give in; to give way

  ceder el paso to yield (the right of way)

  Discutieron hasta que el más sensato cedió. They argued until the most sensible one gave in.

cederrón *m.* CD-ROM

cedro *m.* cedar

ceja *f.* eyebrow

celebrar *v.t.* to celebrate

celos *m., pl.* jealousy

  Tiene celos de su hermanita. She is jealous of her little sister.

celoso/a *adj.* jealous

célula *f.* cell

celular *adj.* (*phone*) cellular

celulitis *f.* cellulite

cementerio *m.* cemetery

cemento *m.* cement

cena *f.* dinner, supper

cenar *v.i.* to have dinner, to dine

  ¿Qué hay para cenar? What's for dinner?

cenicero *m.* ashtray

ceniza *f.* ash

censo *m.* census

censura *f.* censorship; censure

censurar *v.t.* to censor; to censure

centro *m.* center; (*city*) downtown

  centro comercial shopping mall/center

  centro de gravedad center of gravity

centro de atención center of attention

cepillar *v.t.* to brush

cepillarse (el pelo/los dientes) *v. pron.* to brush one's hair/teeth

cepillo *m.* brush
  cepillo de dientes toothbrush
  cepillo de pelo hairbrush

cera *f.* wax

cerámica *f.* pottery

ceramista *m., f.* ceramist

cerca de *adv.* near

cercano/a *adj.* near; (*relative*) close
  Cercano Oriente Near East

cerdo *m.* (*animal*) pig; (*meat*) pork

cereales *m., pl.* cereal; grains

cerebro *m.* brain

cereza *f.* cherry

cerezo *m.* cherry tree

cerilla *f.* match

cero *m.* zero

cerrado *p.p. of* cerrar closed

cerrado/a *adj.* closed

cerrajero/a *m., f.* locksmith

cerrajería *f.* locksmith's shop

cerrar (e:ie) *v.t.* to close

cerrarse (e:ie) *v. pron.* to close
  La puerta se cerró lentamente. The door closed slowly.

cerrojo *m.* (*lock*) bolt
  correr/echar el cerrojo to bolt the door

certeza *f.* certainty

cerveza *f.* beer

césped *m.* grass

cesta *f.* basket

ceviche *m.* marinated fish dish
  ceviche de camarón marinated shrimp

chal *m.* shawl

chaleco *m.* vest

champán *m.* champagne

champiñón *m.* mushroom

champú *m.* shampoo

chantaje *m.* blackmail

chantajear *v.t.* to blackmail

chantajista *m., f.* blackmailer

chaqueta *f.* jacket

charlatán, charlatana *m., f.* chatterbox; *adj.* talkative

chau *fam.* bye

cheque *m.* (*bank*) check
  cheque de viajero traveler's check
  cheque en blanco blank check

chequeo (médico) *m.* (*L.A.*) physical exam

chévere *adj., fam.* terrific, great, cool

chicle *m.* chewing gum

chico/a *m.* boy; *f.* girl

chimenea *f.* chimney; fireplace

chino *m.* (*language*) Chinese

chino/a *adj./m., f.* Chinese

chismes *m., pl.* gossip

chiste *m.* joke

chistoso/a *adj.* funny, amusing

chocar (con, contra) *v.i.* to crash, to collide; to run into; to hit (*a car*); to dislike (**me choca**)

chocolate *m.* chocolate

chofer/chófer *m.* chauffeur, driver

choque *m.* collision; (crash) car accident
chuleta *f. (food)* chop
  chuleta de cerdo pork chop
cibercafé *m.* cybercafé
cicatriz *f.* scar
cicatrizar *v.i.* to scar, to heal
ciclismo *m.* cycling
ciclista *m., f.* cyclist
ciego/a *adj.* blind
  a ciegas *adv.* blindly
cielo *m.* sky; heaven
  ¡Cielos! Good heavens!
cien(to) one hundred
  cientos de miles hundreds of thousands
  por ciento percent
  Es cien por cien(to) algodón. It's pure cotton.
ciénaga *f.* swamp
ciencia *f.* science
  (...de) ciencia ficción science-fiction *(genre)*
  ciencias exactas exact sciences
científico/a *adj.* scientific; *m., f.* scientist
cierto/a *adj.* certain; true
  (No) Es cierto. It's (not) true.
  por cierto by the way
ciervo *m.* deer
cifra *f. (arithmetic)* figure, number
cigüeña *f.* stork
cilindro *m.* cylinder
cima *f.* top, summit; peak
cimientos *m., pl. (house, building)* foundations
cinco five
cincuenta fifty

cine *m.* movie theater; movies
  cine mudo silent movies
  cine negro film noir
cineasta *m., f.* filmmaker, director
cinta *f. (audio)* tape; ribbon
  Siempre lleva una cinta en el pelo. She always wears a ribbon in her hair.
cinta caminadora *f.* treadmill
cintura *f.* waist
cinturón *m.* belt
  cinturón de seguridad seat belt
ciprés *m.* cypress
circo *m.* circus
circuito *m. (electric)* circuit
  circuito en serie series circuit
  circuito cerrado closed circuit
circulación *f.* circulation; traffic
  circulación sanguínea blood circulation
círculo *m.* circle
ciruela *f.* plum
cirugía *f.* surgery
cirujano/a *m., f.* surgeon
cisne *m.* swan
cita *f.* date; appointment
cítrico/a *adj.* citrus
ciudad *f.* city
  ciudad natal hometown
ciudadanía *f.* citizenship
ciudadano/a *m., f.* citizen
civilización *f.* civilization
civilizado/a *adj.* civilized
claro/a *adj.* clear; (color) light
  ¡Claro! *interj.* Of course!

¡**Claro que sí!** *(fam.)* Of course!

clase *f.* class

   clase de ejercicios aeróbicos aerobics class

   clase alta/baja upper/lower class

   clase media middle class

   clase trabajadora working class

clásico/a *adj.* classical

clausura *f.* closing

   ceremonia de clausura closing ceremony

clavado *m.* (*L.A.*) (*high*) dive

clavel *m.* carnation

clavícula *f.* clavicle

clavo *m.* nail

   dar en el clavo *idiom.* to hit the nail on the head

cliente/a *m., f.* customer

clientela *f.* clientele, customers

clima *m.* climate

climatizado/a *adj.* (*place, room*) air-conditioned

climatología *f.* climatology

clínica *f.* clinic

cloaca *f.* sewer

cloro *m.* chlorine

clorofila *f.* chlorophyll

clóset *m.* closet

coartada *f.* alibi

cobarde *adj.* coward

cobardía *f.* cowardice

cobertizo *m.* shed

cobija *f.* (*L.A.*) blanket

cobrar *v.t.* (*check*) to cash; (*rent*) to charge for; (*salary*) to earn

   El dueño de mi casa no me cobra la electricidad. My landlord doesn't charge me for electricity.

   Cobro una miseria. I earn a pittance.

cobre *m.* copper

cocer (o:ue) (c:z) *v.t.* to boil, to cook

   cocer a fuego lento to simmer

coche *m.* (*Spain*) car; automobile

   coche bomba car bomb

   coche cama sleeper, sleeping car

cocina *f.* kitchen; (*Spain*) stove

cocinar *v.t.* to cook

cocinero/a *m., f.* cook; chef

coco *m.* coconut

codo *m.* elbow

codorniz *f.* quail

cofre *m.* (*car*) hood

cohete *m.* rocket

   cohete espacial space rocket

coincidencia *f.* coincidence

   ¡**Qué coincidencia!** What a coincidence!

coincidir *v.i.* to coincide, to match up

cojín *m.* cushion

cojo/a *adj.* (*person*) lame

col *f.* (*Spain*) cabbage

cola *f.* line; (*animal*) tail

   cola de caballo pony tail

   hacer cola to line up; to stand in line

colaboración *f.* collaboration

colaborar *v.i.* to collaborate

colador *m.* colander

colar (o:ue)*v.t.* to strain, to drain; **colar café** (*L.A.*) to make coffee

colarse (o:ue) (**en una fiesta**) *v. pron.* to crash (a party)

colchón *m.* mattress
  colchón de agua water bed
  colchón de muelles spring mattress

coleccionar *v.t.* to collect (*as hobby*)

coleccionismo *m.* collecting

coleccionista *m., f.* collector

colegio *m.* school

colesterol *m.* cholesterol

colgar (o:ue) *v.t.* to hang

colibrí *m.* humming bird

cólico *m.* colic

collar *m.* necklace

colmillo *m.* fang; (*in humans*) eye tooth

colmo: ¡Esto es el colmo! *loc.* That's the last straw!

colocación *f.* placing; arrangement

colocar *v.t.* to place, to put; to arrange

colonia *f.* cologne

colonización *f.* colonization, settling

colonizar *v.t.* to colonize

colono *m.* colonist; settler

coloquio *m.* discussion, talk

color *m.* color

colorear *v.t.* to color

columna *f.* column
  columna vertebral spinal column, spine

combustible *m.* fuel

comedia *f.* comedy; play

comedor *m.* dining room

comenzar (e:ie) *v.t./v.i.* to begin

comer *v.t./v.i.* to eat; to have lunch

comercial *adj.* (*movie*) commercial; (*district, operation*) business-related; *m.* (*L.A.*) commercial, advertisement

comestible *adj.* edible

comestibles *m., pl.* groceries

cometa *f.* kite; *m.* comet

comida *f.* food; meal
  comida basura junk food
  comida rápida fast food

comienzo *m.* beginning
  a comienzos de at the beginning of
  al comienzo at first, in the beginning

comisaría (**de policía**) *f.* police station

como *prep.* like, as
  Anda despacio como una tortuga. She walks as slowly as a turtle.
  Es tan alto como su padre. He's as tall as his father.
  Quiero un carro como el tuyo. I want a car like yours.

¿cómo? *adv.* how?; what?
  ¿Cómo es...? What's . . . like?
  ¿Cómo está Ud.? *form.* How are you?
  ¿Cómo estás? *fam.* How are you?
  ¿Cómo les fue...? *pl.* How did . . . go for you?
  ¿Cómo se llama Ud.? (*form.*) What's your name?

¿Cómo te llamas (tú)? (*fam.*) What's your name?

cómoda *f.* chest of drawers, dresser

cómodo/a *adj.* comfortable

compañerismo *m.* camaraderie

compañero/a *m., f.* companion; partner; mate

compañero/a de clase classmate

compañero/a de cuarto roommate

compañía *f.* company; firm

El perro me hace compañía. My dog keeps me company.

comparación *f.* comparison

en comparación con compared to/with

comparar *v.t.* to compare

compartir *v.t.* to share

compás *m.* (*tool*) compass; (*music*) beat, rhythm

competencia *f.* (*L.A.*) competition, contest

competente *adj.* competent

competidor(a) *m., f.* competitor

competir (e:i) *v.i.* to compete

competitivo/a *adj.* competitive

complejo/a *adj.* complex

completamente *adv.* completely

complicar *v.t.* to complicate, to make difficult

cómplice *m., f.* accomplice

comportamiento *m.* behavior

comportarse *v. pron.* to behave oneself

compositor(a) *m., f.* composer

compra(s) *f.* buy, purchase

ir de compras to go shopping

la lista de la compra the shopping list

una buena/mala compra a good/bad buy

comprar *v.t.* to buy

comprender *v.t.* to understand

comprensión *f.* understanding

comprobar *v.t.* (o:ue) to check

comprometerse (a/con) *v. pron.* to promise (to); to get engaged (to)

Se comprometió a limpiar todas las ventanas. He promised to clean all the windows.

compromiso *m.* commitment; engagement

computación *f.* computer science

computadora *f.* computer

computadora portátil portable computer; laptop

común *adj.* common, shared

comunicación *f.* communication

comunicar *v.t.* to communicate

comunicarse (con) *v. pron.* to communicate (with)

comunidad *f.* community

con *prep.* with

Con él/ella habla. This is he/she. (*on the telephone*)

con tal (de) que provided (that)

conciencia *f.* conscience

a conciencia *adv.* conscientiously

concierto *m.* concert

concordar (con) *v.i.* to agree (with)

concreto *m.* (*L.A.*) concrete

concursar *v.i.* (*contest*) to participate, to take part

concurso *m.* contest; game show

condensar *v.t.* to condense

conducir (c:zc) *v.i.* to drive

conducta *f.* conduct, behavior

conductor(a) *m., f.* chauffeur; driver

conejo *m.* rabbit

conferencia *f.* lecture

confiado/a *adj.* (*person*) trusting

confianza *f.* confidence; trust
  en confianza *adv.* in confidence
  No le tengo mucha confianza. I don't trust him much.
  Es una persona de confianza. She's a trustworthy/reliable person.

confiar (en alguien) *v.t.* to trust (somebody)
  Confía en mí. Trust me.

confirmación *f.* confirmation

confirmar *v.t.* to confirm
  confirmar una reservación to confirm a reservation

confort *m.* comfort

confortable *adj.* comfortable

confundido/a *adj.* confused

confundir *v.t.* to confuse

confusión *f.* confusion

confuso/a *adj.* (*idea, text*) confused, hazy
  Su explicación fue muy confusa. His explanation was very confused.

congelador *m.* freezer

congestionado/a *adj.* (*medicine*) congested; stuffed-up

congreso *m.* conference

conmemoración *f.* commemoration, remembrance
  en conmemoración de in memory of

conmemorar *v.t.* to commemorate

conmigo with me

conocer (c:zc) *v.t.* to know; to be acquainted with; to meet

conocido/a *adj.* (well-)known; familiar

conquista *f.* conquest

conquistador(a) *m., f.* conqueror

conquistar *v.t.* to conquer

consecuencia *f.* consequence
  en consecuencia *adv.* consequently, as a result, therefore; (*to act*) accordingly

conseguir (e:i) *v.t.* to get; to obtain

consejero/a *m., f.* counselor; advisor

consejo *m.* advice
  dar consejos to give advice

consenso *m.* consensus

consentido/a *adj.* spoiled (person)

consentimiento *m.* consent, permission

consentir (e:ie) *v.t.* to consent to, to permit

conserje *m., f.* (*hotel*) receptionist

conservación *f.* (*culinary*) preserving; (*environment*) conservation, protection

conservador(a) *adj./m., f.* conservative

conservar *v.t.* (*culinary*) to preserve; to conserve

considerado/a *adj.* (*person*) considerate

constelación *f.* constellation

constitución *f.* constitution

constructor(a) (de obras) *m., f.* builder, building contractor

construir (y) *v.t.* to build

consulado *m.* consulate

consultar *v.t.* (*dictionary, facts*) to look up

consultorio *m.* doctor's office

consumidor(a) *m., f.* consumer

consumir *v.t.* consume
consumir alcohol to consume alcohol

consumo *m.* consumption, intake

contabilidad *f.* accounting

contador(a) *m., f.* accountant

contagiar *v.t.* (*disease*) to pass on

contagio *m.* contagion

contagioso/a *adj.* contagious

contaminación *f.* pollution; contamination
contaminación del aire/del agua air/water pollution

contaminado/a *m., f.* polluted

contaminar *v.t.* to pollute

contar (o:ue) *v.t.* to count; to tell
Contamos contigo. We count on you.

contemplar *v.t.* to contemplate, to gaze at

contemporáneo/a *adj.* contemporary

contentarse (con) *v. pron.* to be pleased (with), to be happy (with)

contento/a *adj.* happy; content

contestadora *f.* answering machine

contestar *v.t.* to answer

contigo with you
Contigo o sin ti. With or without you.

continuar *v.t.* (**yo continúo**) to continue
La novela continúa en el segundo tomo. The novel continues in the second volume.

contra *prep.* against
dos contra uno two against one
Estoy totalmente en contra. I'm totally against it.
Chocó contra un árbol. He crashed into a tree.

contradecir (a alguien) *v.t. irreg.* (**yo contradigo**) to contradict (somebody)

contradecirse *v. pron. irreg.* (**yo me contradigo**) to contradict oneself

contradicción *f.* contradiction

contraponer *v.t. irreg.* (**yo contrapongo**) to contrast

contrario *m.* contrary, opposite; *adj.* opposite
al contrario *adv.* on the contrary, quite the opposite

contrarreloj *adj.* timed
  a contrarreloj against the
  clock
contraseña *f.* password
contratar *v.t.* to hire
contrato *m.* contract; lease
contrincante *m., f.* opponent
control *m.* control
  control de natalidad birth
  control
  control remoto remote
  control
controlar *v.t.* to control
convencer (c:z) *v.t.* to convince
convento *m.* convent
conversación *f.* conversation
conversar *v.i.* to talk, to
  converse, to chat
convertirse (e:ie) (en) *v. pron.*
  to become; to turn into
  convertirse en rana to turn
  into a frog
  convertirse en realidad to
  come true
convicción *f.* conviction
convincente *adj.* convincing
convivencia *f.* coexistence
convivir *v.i.* (*people*) to live
  together; (*ideas, ideologies*)
  to coexist
copa *f.* wineglass; goblet
copiar *v.t.* to copy
coqueta *f.* flirt, coquette
coquetear *v.i.* to flirt
corazón *m.* heart
corbata *f.* tie
corcho *m.* cork
cordero *m.* lamb
cordillera (montañosa) *f.*
  (mountain) range

cordón *m.* shoelace
coro *m.* choir, chorus
corpulento/a *adj.* (*person*)
  hefty
correa *m.* belt
corrección *f.* correction;
  correctness
correcto/a *adj.* correct
corredor(a) (de bolsa) *m., f.*
  stockbroker
corregir (e:i) (g:j) *v.t.* to correct
correo *m.* post office; mail
  correo electrónico e-mail
correr *v.i.* to run; to jog
correspondencia *f.* mail
corrido *p.p.* of **correr** run
corrida (de toros) *f.* bullfight
corriente *f.* (*electricity*) current
  corriente alterna alternating
  current, AC
  corriente continua direct
  current, DC
  corriente eléctrica electric
  current
  contra corriente against the
  tide
  estar al corriente to be up to
  date
  ponerse al corriente to catch
  up
  **seguirle la corriente (a
  alguien)** to humor
  (somebody), to play along
  with (somebody)
cortacésped *f.* lawnmower
cortar *v.t.* to chop; to slice; to
  cut
  cortar el pasto to mow the
  lawn
corte *f.* cut; (*L.A.*) court (of law)

corte longitudinal lengthwise section

Corte Suprema Supreme Court

corte transversal cross section

cortés *adj.* courteous

cortesía *f.* courtesy

cortina *f.* curtain

correr las cortinas to draw the curtains

corto/a *adj.* short (*in length*)

cortocircuito *m.* short circuit

cosa *f.* thing

cosecha *f.* harvest

cosechar *v.t.* to harvest

coser *v.t.* to sew

costa *f.* coastline, coast

costar (o:ue) *f.* to cost

costar un ojo de la cara *idiom* to cost an arm and a leg

costero/a *adj.* coastal

costilla *f.* rib

costumbre *f.* habit, custom

cotillear *v.i.* (*Spain*) to gossip

cotilleo *m.* (*Spain*) gossip

cráneo *m.* skull

cráter *m.* crater

creador(a) *m., f.* creator

crear *v.t.* to create

creativo/a *adj.* creative

crecer (c:zc) *v.i.* to grow

creciente *adj.* increasing, growing

crecimiento *m.* growth

crédito *m.* credit

creer (en) *v.t.* to believe (in); to think

Creo que no. I don't think so.

no creer not to believe

creído *p.p. of* **creer** believed

crema *f.* cream

crema antiarrugas anti-wrinkle cream

crema de afeitar shaving cream

crema hidratante moisturizer

cremallera *f.* zipper

cremoso/a *adj.* creamy

crepúsculo *m.* (*evening*) twilight; (*morning*) dawn

criar *v.t.* (*children*) to raise, to bring up

crimen *m.* crime; murder

crisis *f.* crisis

crisis de los cuarenta midlife crisis

crisis nerviosa nervous breakdown

crisis respiratoria respiratory failure

cristal *m.* crystal; glass

cristalería *f.* glassware

cristiano/a *adj./m., f.* Christian

criticar *v.t.* to criticize

crítico/a *m., f.* critic

crítico de arte art critic

cronometrar *v.t.* to time

cronómetro *m.* chronometer; stopwatch

cruce *m.* crossroads

crucero *m.* cruise

crucigrama *m.* crossword

cruda *f.* (*Mexico*) hangover

tener cruda to have a hangover

crudo/a *adj.* (*food*) raw

crujiente *adj.* crunchy; (*bread*) crusty

cruz *f.* cross
Cruz Roja Red Cross
cruzar *v.t.* to cross
cuaderno *m.* notebook
cuadra *f.* (city) block
cuadrado *m.* square
cuadrilátero *m.* (*boxing*) ring; (*baseball*) home run
cuadro *m.* picture
cuadros, (de) *m., pl.* plaid
una falda de cuadros a plaid skirt
¿cuál(es)? *pron.* which?; which one(s)?; what?
¿Cuál te gusta más? Which one do you like best?
¿Cuál es la fecha (de hoy)? What is the date (today)?
cuando *conj.* when
Cuando estoy triste, canto. When I'm sad, I sing.
de cuando en cuando *loc.* every so often
de vez en cuando *loc.* now and then; from time to time
¿cuándo? *adv.* when?
¿Cuándo terminas? When do you finish?
No sé cuándo termina. I don't know when he finishes.
cuanto: cuanto antes as soon as possible
Envíemela cuanto antes. Send it to me as soon as possible.
¿cuánto/a? *adv.* how much?
¿Cuánto cuesta? How much does it cost?
¿Cuánto tiempo hace que esperas? How long have you been waiting?

¿cuántos/as? *adv.* how many?
¿Cuántos años tienes? How old are you?
cuarenta forty
cuarto *m.* room
cuarto de baño bathroom
cuarto/a *adj., m.* fourth
cuatro four
cuatrocientos/as four hundred
cubertería *f.* cutlery
cubierto *p.p. of* **cubrir** covered
cubiertos *m., pl.* silverware
cubrir *v.t.* to cover
cucaracha *f.* cockroach
cuchara *f.* (*table or large*) spoon
cucharita *f.* teaspoon
cucharón *m.* ladle
cuchillo *m.* knife
cuello *m.* neck
cuenta *f.* bill; account
a fin de cuentas all things considered, after all
A fin de cuentas, es mejor esperar que irse. All things considered, it's better to wait than to leave.
A fin de cuentas, ¿a quién le importa? After all, who cares?
cuenta corriente checking account
cuenta de ahorros savings account
en resumidas cuentas to make a long story short
por mi cuenta on my own
cuentakilómetros *m., sing.* odometer, speedometer
cuento *m.* short story

cuerda *f.* rope
cuero *m.* leather
cuerpo *m.* body
cuestión *f.* issue, matter
  Es un experto en cuestiones de historia medieval. He's an expert in matters of medieval history.
cuestionar *v.t.* to question
cuestionarse *v. pron.* to ask oneself
  Tenemos que cuestionarnos si es válida la conclusión. We have to ask ourselves if the conclusion is valid.
cuidado *m.* care; *interj.* Watch out!
cuidar *v.t.* to take care of
cuidarse *v. pron.* to take care of oneself
culpa *f.* fault
  echar la culpa a alguien to blame someone
  tener la culpa to be to blame
culpable *adj.* guilty; *m., f.* guilty person
culpar *v.t.* to blame
cultivar *v.t.* to grow
cultura *f.* culture
  Tiene mucha cultura. She's a highly educated person.
culturismo *m.* bodybuilding
cumpleaños *m., sing.* birthday
cumplir años *v.t.* to have a birthday
  ¿Cuántos años cumples? How old are you?
cumplir (con) *v.i.* (*duty*) to carry out
  Cumplí con mi deber. I did my duty.

cuna *f.* cradle
cuñado/a *m.* brother-in-law; *f.* sister-in-law
cura *f.* cure; *m.* priest
curar *v.t.* to cure
curita *f.* adhesive bandage
currículum *m.* (*Spain*) résumé; curriculum vitae
curso *m.* course
curva *f.* curve, bend
  curva peligrosa sharp bend
custodiar *v.t.* to guard
cutis *m.* skin, complexion
  limpieza de cutis skin cleansing

D

dados *m., pl.* (*game*) dice
dama *f.* lady
damas (chinas) *f., pl.* (*game*) checkers
danza *f.* dance
dañar *v.t.* to damage; to harm; to break down
dañarse *v. pron.* to get damaged; (*food*) to go bad
dañino/a *adj.* harmful
daño *m.* damage, harm
dar *v.t. irreg.* (**yo doy**) to give
  dar a luz (a) to give birth (to)
  dar de comer to feed
  dar direcciones to give directions
  dar en el clavo *idiom* to hit the nail on the head
  dar lo mismo to not matter
  dar un consejo to give advice
  dar un paseo to go for a walk
  dar vuelta to turn

Me da lo mismo si vienes o no. It doesn't matter to me if you come or not.

dardos *m., pl.* (*game*) darts

darse con *v. pron. irreg.* to bump into; to run into

  darse cuenta de (que) to realize, to become aware of

  Gustavo se dio cuenta de que tenía que salir por la puerta de atrás. Gustavo realized he would have to leave by the back door.

  darse prisa to hurry (up); to rush

  darse vuelta to turn

de *prep.* of; from

  ¿de quién(es)? whose?

  ¿De dónde eres? *fam.* Where are you from?

  ¿De dónde es Ud.? *form.* Where are you from?

  ¿De parte de quién? Who is calling? (*on telephone*)

  de ida y vuelta roundtrip

  de repente suddenly, all of a sudden

debajo de *prep.* below; under

debate *m.* debate

debatir *v.t.* to debate

deber (+ inf.) *v. aux.* to have to; should; must

  Deberías salir más temprano. You should leave earlier.

deber *m.* responsibility; obligation; duty

  Tu deber es esperar aquí. Your duty is to wait here.

deberes *m., pl.* homework

debido *adj.* appropriate

  a su debido tiempo in due course

  con el debido respeto with all due respect

  debido a (que) *loc.* due to, owing to (the fact that); because of

  No hubo partido debido a la lluvia. There was no match because of the rain.

débil *adj.* weak

década *f.* decade

  la década de los sesenta the sixties

decadencia *f.* decadence; decline

decaer *v. irreg.* (**yo decaigo**) to decay, to decline; to deteriorate

decano/a *m., f.* (*university*) dean

decepcionado/a *adj.* disappointed

decepcionarse *v.t.* to be disappointed

decidido *p.p. of* **decidir** decided

decidido/a *adj.* (*person*) determined

decidir (+ inf.) *v.t.* to decide

decidirse *v. pron.* to make up one's mind

  ¡Decídete de una vez! Come on, make up your mind!

décimo/a *adj.* tenth

decir *m.* a saying

  Es sólo un decir. It's just a manner of speaking.

decir *v.t.* (**e:i**) to say; to tell

¿Diga? Hello? (*on the telephone*)

No me diga(s). You don't say.

decisión *f.* decision

tomar una decisión to make a decision

declarar *v.t.* to declare; to say

decorado *m.* (*theater*) set

decorar *v.t.* to decorate; (*food*) to garnish

dedicación *f.* dedication

dedicar *v.t.* to dedicate

dedicatoria *f.* dedication

dedo *m.* finger; (*del pie*) toe

defecto *m.* fault, defect

defectuoso/a *adj.* faulty, defective

defender *v.t.* to defend, to protect

defensa *f.* defense

defensa personal self-defense

deficiencia *f.* deficiency, shortcoming

déficit *m.* deficit

definición *f.* definition

definir *v.t.* to define

deforestación *f.* deforestation

defunción *f.* death

dejar *v.t.* to let; to quit; to leave (behind); to drop off; to allow

dejar una propina to leave a tip

dejar de (+ *inf.*) *v.i.* to stop (*doing something*)

del (*contraction of* de + el) of the; from the

delantal *m.* apron

delante de *prep.* in front of

deleite *m.* delight

delfín *m.* dolphin

delgado/a *adj.* thin; slender

delicioso/a *adj.* delicious

delincuencia *f.* crime, delinquency

delincuente *m., f.* criminal

delineante *m.* draftsman, *f.* draftswoman

delinear *v.t.* to deliniate; to outline

delito *m.* crime, offense

demás (lo/los/las) *pron.* the rest

demasiado *adv.* too much

democracia *f.* democracy

demócrata *m., f.* democrat

democrático/a *adj.* democratic

demostración *f.* proof

demostrar *v.t.* to prove

densidad *f.* density

dentadura *f.* teeth

dentadura postiza false teeth

tener buena/mala dentadura to have good/bad teeth

dentista *m., f.* dentist

dentro *adv.* (*space*) inside

dentro de within

Llámame dentro de dos horas. Call me within two hours.

denuncia *f.* report

denunciar *v.t.* (*crime*) to report

departamento *m.* department

depender (de) *v.t.* to depend (on)

Eso no depende de mí. That doesn't depend on me.

dependiente/a *m., f.* clerk

depilarse *v.t.* (*eyebrows*) to pluck; (*legs*) to shave, to wax

deporte *m.* sport
deportista *m., f.* sports person
deportivo/a *adj.* sports-loving, sports-related
depositar *v.t.* to deposit
depósito *m.* tank
  depósito de gasolina gas tank
depredador(a) *adj.* predatory
depredador *m.* predator
depresión *f.* depression
deprimido/a *adj.* depressed
deprimirse *v. pron.* to get depressed
derecha *f.* right
  a la derecha (de) to the right (of)
derecho/a *adj.* straight
derecho *adv.* straight (ahead)
  (todo) derecho straight ahead
  Siga (todo) derecho. Keep on going straight.
derechos *m., pl.* rights
deriva *f.* drift
  a la deriva adrift
dermatólogo/a *m., f.* dermatologist
derramar *v.t.* (*liquid*) to spill
derramarse *v. pron.* (*liquid*) to spill over, to run over
derrame *m.* spillage; (*medical*) hemorrhage
derretir *v.t.* to melt
  El calor derritirá la mantequilla. The heat will melt the butter
derretirse *v. pron.* to melt
  El helado se derritió. The ice cream melted.

derrota *f.* defeat
derrotar *v.t.* to defeat, to beat (*an opponent*)
desactivar *v.t.* to defuse
desafiar *v.t.* to challenge
desafinado/a *adj.* out of tune
desafío *m.* challenge
desafortunadamente *adv.* unfortunately
desagradecido/a *adj.* ungrateful
desagüe *m.* wastepipe, drainpipe
desanimado/a *adj.* downhearted
desaparecer *v.t.* to disappear
desaparecido/a *adj.* missing
desaparición *f.* disappearance
desarreglado/a *adj.* unkempt, messy
desarrollar *v.t.* to develop
desarrollo *m.* development
desastre *m.* disaster
  desastre natural natural disaster
desastroso/a *adj.* disastrous
desatascar *v.t.* to unblock, to clear
desayunar *v.t.* to have breakfast
desayuno *m.* breakfast
descafeinado/a *adj.* decaffeinated
descalificación *f.* (*sports*) disqualification
descalificar *v.* (*sports*) to disqualify
descalzarse *v. pron.* to take off one's shoes
descampado *m.* open ground

en un descampado in/on open ground

descansar *v.i.* to rest

descanso *m.* rest

descapotable *adj./m.* (*automobile*) convertible

descarga *f.* (*electricity*) discharge

descarga eléctrica electric shock

descargar *v.t.* to download

descarrilamiento *m.* derailment

descarrilar *v.t.* to derail

descender *v.i.* to descend

descendiente *m., f.* descendant

descenso *m.* descend; (*temperatures, prices*) fall, decline, decrease

descifrar *v.t.* to decipher, to decode

descompuesto/a *adj.* (*L.A.*) not working; out of order

desconfiado/a *adj.* distrustful

desconfiar (de alguien) *v.i.* distrust

descontar *v.t.* to discount; to give a discount

descremado/a *adj.* (*dairy products*) skimmed

describir *v.t.* to describe

descrito/a *p.p.* of **describir** described

descubierto *p.p.* of **descubrir** discovered

descubrimiento *m.* discovery

descubrir *v.t.* to discover

descuento *m.* discount

desde *prep.* from; *conj.* since

Les llamé desde Japón. I called them from Japan.

¿Desde cuándo lo sabes? Since when have you known it?

desear *v.t.* to wish, to desire

desechable *adj.* disposable

desechar *v.t.* (*leftovers*) to throw away

desembocadura *f.* (*river*) mouth

desempacar *v.t./intrans.* to unpack

desempleo *m.* unemployment

desengañar *v.t.* to disillusion

desengaño *m.* disappointment

desenvolver (o:ue) *v.t.* to unwrap

deseo *m.* desire, wish

desértico/a *adj.* pertaining to the desert, desert-like

desesperación *f.* desperation

desesperado/a *adj.* desperate

desesperanza *f.* despair

desesperar *v.t.* to exasperate

La lentitud del tren le desesperó. The slowness of the train exasperated him.

desesperarse *v. pron.* to despair, to give up hope

No te desesperes; todo saldrá bien. Don't give up hope; everything will be fine.

desfavorable *adj.* unfavorable

desfile *m.* parade

desgraciado/a *adj.* unhappy, unfortunate; *m., f.* wretch

desgracia *f.* misfortune

desgraciadamente *adv.* unfortunately

deshelar (e:ie) *v.t.* to defrost

deshelarse (e:ie) *v. pron.* (*ice*) to melt; (*river, lake*) to thaw

deshidratar *v.t.* to dehydrate

deshielo *m.* thaw

deshonesto/a *adj.* dishonest

desierto *m.* desert

desigualdad *f.* inequality

desilusionado/a *adj.* disappointed

desinfectante *adj./m.* disinfectant

desinfectar *v.t.* to disinfect

desintoxicación *f.* detoxification

desintoxicar *v.t.* to detoxify

desmayarse *v. pron.* to faint

desnatado/a *adj.* (*dairy products*) skimmed

desobedecer *v.t.* to disobey

desodorante *m.* deodorant

desordenado/a *adj.* disorderly

despacio *adv.* slowly

despedida *f.* farewell; good-bye

despedir (e:i) *v.* to fire

despedirse (de) (e:i) *v. pron.* to say good-bye (to)

despegar *v.i.* (*airplane, rocket*) to take-off

despegue *m.* (*airplane, rocket*) takeoff

despeinado/a *adj.* disheveled, unkempt

despejado/a *adj.* (*sky*) clear

despensa *f.* pantry

despertador *m.* alarm clock

despertarse (e:ie) *v. pron.* to wake up

despistado/a *adj.* absent-minded, forgetful; *m., f.* scatterbrain

desplazamiento *m.* movement; trip

desplazarse *v. pron.* to move (*from one place to another*); to travel

después (de) *adv.* afterwards; then

   después de after

   después de que after

destacar *v.t.* to emphasize, to stress

destino *m.* destination, destiny

destornillador *m.* screwdriver

destrucción *f.* destruction

destruir (y) *v.t.* to destroy

desventaja *f.* disadvantage

desvestirse (e:i) *v. pron.* to get undressed, to undress

detalle *m.* detail

detallista *adj./m., f.* perfectionist

detención *f.* arrest

detener *v.t. irreg.* **(yo detengo)** (*vehicle*) to stop; (*person*) to arrest

detenido *p.p. of* **detener** arrested

detenido/a *adj.* detained; under arrest

   estar detenido to be under arrest

detractor(a) *m., f.* detractor; critic

detrás de *adv.* behind

devolución *f.* (*purchase*) return; (*money*) refund

devolver (o:ue) *v.t.* to take back; to return (*merchandise*)

día *m.* day

   día de fiesta holiday

día laborable work day
diabetes *f.* diabetes
diabético/a *adj./m., f.* diabetic
diagnosticar *v.t.* to diagnose
diagnóstico *m.* diagnostic
diálogo *m.* dialogue
diamante *m.* diamond
diapositiva *f.* slide
diario *m.* diary; newspaper
diario/a *adj.* daily
diarrea *f.* diarrhea
dibujar *v.t.* to draw
dibujo *m.* drawing
  dibujos animados *m., pl.*
  (*animated*) cartoons
diccionario *m.* dictionary
dicho *m.* saying
dicho *p.p. of* **decir** said
diciembre *m.* December
dictador(a) *m., f.* dictator
dictadura *f.* dictatorship
diecinueve nineteen
dieciocho eighteen
dieciséis sixteen
diecisiete seventeen
diente *m.* tooth
dieta *f.* diet
  a dieta on a diet
  comer una dieta equilibrada
  to eat a balanced diet
diez ten
diferencia *f.* difference
  a diferencia de in contrast
  to, unlike
diferente *adj.* different
difícil *adj.* hard; difficult
dificultad *f.* difficulty, hardship
dificultar *v.t.* to make difficult
difunto/a *m., f.* deceased
  (*person*)
Diga. Hello. (*on telephone*)

diligencia *f.* errand
dimisión *f.* resignation
dimitir *v.i.* to resign
dinamita *f.* dynamite
dinamitar *v.t.* to dynamite
dinastía *f.* dynasty
dinero *m.* money
dinosaurio *m.* dinosaur
Dios *m.* God
  ¡Dios me libre! *loc.* Heaven
  forbid!
diplomático/a *adj.* diplomatic,
  tactful; *m., f.* diplomat
dirección *f.* address
dirección electrónica *f.* e-mail
  address
direcciones *f., pl.* directions
directo *adj.* (*fly*) direct,
  nonstop
  en directo *adv.* (*radio, TV*)
  live
director(a) *m., f.* director;
  (*musical*) conductor
dirigir *v.t.* to direct
disciplina *f.* discipline;
  (*university*) subject
disco *m.* (computer) disk
  disco compacto compact
  disc; CD
discoteca *f.* disco(teque)
discreto/a *adj.* discreet,
  discrete
discriminación *f.*
  discrimination
disculpa *f.* apology
  pedir disculpas to apologize
disculpar *v.t.* to excuse
disculparse (por) *v. pron.* to
  apologize for
discurso *m.* speech
discusión *f.* argument

discutir *v.t.* to argue; to discuss

diseñador(a) *m., f.* designer

diseño *m.* design

disfraz *m.* costume

disfrazarse de… to wear a… costume

disfrutar (de) *v.t.* to enjoy; to reap the benefits (of)

disfunción *f.* dysfunction

disgusto: a disgusto *adv.* against one's will

Fui, pero a disgusto. I went, but against my will.

disimular *v.t.* to hide; to conceal; to pretend

disminución *f.* decrease

disminuir (y) *v.i.* (*number*) to decrease; *v.t.* (*price, speed*) to reduce

Ha disminuido el número de parados. The number of unemployed people has decreased.

Debes disminuir la velocidad. You have to reduce your speed.

disparar *v.t./v.i.* to shoot, to fire

disparo *m.* shot, gunshot

disponibilidad *f.* availability

disponible *adj.* available

distancia *f.* distance

distinguido/a *adj.* distinguished

distinguir *v.t.* **(yo distingo)** to distinguish

distribución *f.* distribution

distribuir (y) *v.t.* to distribute

divergencia *f.* difference

divergente *adj.* (*opinions*) differing

divergir (e:i) (g:j) *v.i.* to differ

diversión *f.* fun activity; entertainment; recreation

divertido/a *adj.* fun

divertir (e:ie) *v.t.* to entertain

Pepe nos divirtió con sus historias. Pepe entertained us with his stories.

divertirse (e:ie) *v. pron.* to have fun

divisar *v.t.* to sight

divorciado/a *adj.* divorced

divorciarse (de) *v. pron.* to get divorced (from)

divorcio *m.* divorce

divulgación *f.* spreading

divulgar *v.t.* (*news, information*) to spread

El chismoso divulgó la noticia por toda la universidad. The gossip spread the news around the whole university.

doblar *v.t.* (*paper, clothes*) to fold; (*corner*) to turn; (*movie*) to dub

doble *adj.* double

doce twelve

docena *f.* dozen

doctor(a) *m., f.* doctor; physician

doctorado *m.* doctorate; Ph.D.

documental *m.* documentary

documentar *v.t.* to document; to provide evidence for

Estos artículos no documentan nada. These do not provide any evidence.

documentarse *v. pron.* to do research

Tuve que documentarme muy bien para escribir la tesis. I had to do a lot of research to write the thesis.

documento *m.* document

documentos de viaje travel documents

dólar *f.* dollar

doler (o:ue) *v.i.* to hurt

Me duele mucho. It hurts a lot.

dolor *m.* ache; pain

dolor de cabeza headache

doméstico/a *adj.* domestic

dominar *v.t.* to dominate; to master

Aún no domino muy bien el español. I haven't quite mastered Spanish yet.

dominarse *v. pron.* to restrain, to control oneself

domingo *m.* Sunday

dominó *m.* (*game*) dominoes; (*game piece*) domino

don/doña *title of respect used with a person's first name* Mr.; sir/Mrs.; ma'am

dona *f.* donut

donante *m., f.* donor

donde *conj.* where

Están donde las dejaste. They are where you left them.

¿dónde? *adv.* where

¿Dónde está…? Where is…?

¿Dónde están las llaves? Where are the keys?

donjuán *m.* womanizer

dorado/a *adj.* gold, golden

dormir (o:ue) *v.i.* to sleep

dormirse (o:ue) *v. pron.* to go to sleep; to fall asleep; to oversleep

Llego un poco tarde; me dormí. I'm a bit late; I overslept.

dormitorio *m.* bedroom

dos two

dos veces twice; two times

doscientos/as two hundred

drama *m.* drama; play

dramático/a *adj.* dramatic

dramaturgo/a *m., f.* playwright

droga *f.* drug

drogadicto/a *adj.* drug-addicted; *m., f.* drug addict

ducha *f.* shower

ducharse *v. pron.* to shower; to take a shower

duda *f.* doubt

poner en duda to question, to doubt

Nadie pone en duda su talento. Nobody questions his talent.

sin duda undoubtedly, without a doubt

dudar *v.t.* to doubt

no dudar not to doubt

dueño/a *m., f.* owner; landlord

dulce *adj.* sweet

dulces *m., pl.* sweets; candy

duna *f.* dune

duradero/a *adj.* lasting

durante *prep.* during

durar *v.i.* to last

¿Cuánto dura la película? How long is the movie?

El dinero no duró mucho. The money didn't last long.

¿**Dura más la piel?** Does leather last longer?
durazno m. (L.A.) peach
duro/a adj. hard

E

e conj. (used instead of **y** before words beginning with **i** and **hi**) and
    Javier e Inés Javier and Inés
    masaje e hidratación massage and moisturizing
ebrio/a adj. inebriated, drunk
echar v.t. to throw
    echar chispas idiom to be hopping mad
    echar la casa por la ventana loc. to go overboard, to pull out all the stops
    echar una carta al buzón to put a letter in the mailbox; to mail
    echarle flores a alguien idiom to flatter someone
eclipse m. eclipse
ecología f. ecology
ecológico/a adj. ecological; (food) organic
ecologista m., f. environmentalist, ecologist
economía f. economics
ecosistema m. ecosystem
ecoturismo m. ecotourism
ecuador m. equator
    cruzar el ecuador to cross the equator
ecuatoriano/a adj. Ecuadorian
edad f. age
    edad de piedra Stone Age
    edad media Middle Ages

No nos dijo su edad. He didn't tell us his age.
edificio m. building
    edificio de apartamentos apartment building
educado/a adj. polite, well-mannered
educador(a) m., f. educator
efectivo m. (money) cash
    en efectivo (in) cash
efecto m. effect
    bajo los efectos del alcohol under the influence of alcohol
    efectos especiales special effects
    efecto invernadero greenhouse effect
    efecto secundario side effect
    en efecto in fact
eficacia f. effectiveness
eficaz adj. effective
eficiencia f. efficiency
eficiente adj. efficient
egoísmo m. selfishness
egoísta adj. selfish
ejemplo m. example
ejercicio m. exercise
    ejercicios aeróbicos aerobic exercise
    ejercicios de estiramiento stretching exercises
    ejercicios de portugués Portuguese exercises
    hacer ejercicio to exercise, to work out
ejército m. army
el m., sing., def. art. the
él pron. m. sing. he; him
elástico/a adj. elastic
elección, elecciones f. election

electorado *m.* electorate
electricista *m., f.* electrician
electrocutarse *v. pron.* to be electrocuted
electrodoméstico *m.* electric appliance
electrólisis *f.* electrolysis
electrónica *f.* electronics
elefante *m.* elephant
elegante *adj.* elegant
elegir (e:i) (g:j) *v.t.* to elect
elemental *adj.* (*course, level*) elementary
Elemental, amigo Watson. Elementary, my dear Watson.
elevado/a *adj.* (*quantity*) large; (*price*) high
un elevado número de personas a large number of people
un precio elevado a high price
eliminación *f.* elimination
eliminar *v.t.* to eliminate
ella *pron. fem. sing.* she; her
ellos/as *pron. m., f. pl.* they; them
Dáselo a ellos. Give it to them.
elocuencia *f.* eloquence
elocuente *adj.* eloquent
elogiar *v.t.* to praise
elogio *m.* praise
embajada *f.* embassy
embalse *m.* reservoir
embarazada *adj.* pregnant
embarcadero *m.* jetty, wharf
embarcar *v.i.* (*passengers*) to board (*a ship*)
embargo: sin embargo however; yet

embotellamiento (de tráfico) *m.* (*Spain*) traffic jam
embrague *m.* clutch (*pedal*)
embriagado/a *adj.* inebriated, drunk
embudo *m.* funnel
emergencia *f.* emergency
emigración *f.* emigration
emigrante *m., f.* emigrant
emigrar *v.i.* emigrate
emitir *v.t.* to broadcast
emocionado/a *adj.* excited
emocionante *adj.* exciting
empacar *v.t.* to pack
empacharse *v. pron.* to get an upset stomach
empatar *v.i.* (*sports*) to tie
empate *m.* (*sports*) tie
empeorar *v.t.* to get worse; to make worse
Esto empeora la situación. This makes the situation worse.
empezar (e:ie) *v.t.* to begin; to start
para empezar to begin
empleado/a *m., f.* employee
empleo *m.* job, employment
empobrecer (c:zc) *v.t.* to impoverish, to make poor
Las guerras empobrecen los países. Wars impoverish countries.
empobrecerse (c:zc) *v. pron.* to become impoverished, poor
empresa *f.* company; firm; business
empresario/a *m., f.* entrepreneur
empujar *v.t.* to push
en *prep.* in; on

43

en caso (de) que in case (that)

en cuanto *conj.* as soon as

en qué in what; how

¡En marcha! Forward ho/march!

¿En qué puedo servirles? How may I help you?

en resumidas cuentas *loc.* to make a long story short, in short

en un dos por tres *idiom* in a jiffy

enamorado/a (de) *adj.* in love (with); beloved

enamorarse (de) *v. pron.* to fall in love (with)

encantado/a *adj.* delighted; pleased to meet you

encantador(a) *adj.* charming

encantar *v.t.* to like very much; (*inanimate things*) to love; to enchant

encanto *m.* charm

encarcelar *v.t.* to imprison, to jail

encargar *v.t.* to order

encargo *m.* order

encendedor *m.* lighter

encender *v.t.* to light, to turn on

encerar *v.t.* to polish, to wax

encía *f.* (*dental*) gum

encima de *adv.* on top of
  por encima *adv.* (*read*) superficially

encontrar (o:ue) *v.t.* to find

encontrarse (o:ue) *v. pron.* to meet each other; to run into each other; to find each other

encuesta *f.* poll; survey

energía *f.* energy
  energía (nuclear/solar) (nuclear/solar) energy

enero *m.* January

énfasis *m.* emphasis

enfatizar *v.t.* to emphasize

enfermarse *v. pron.* to get sick

enfermedad *f.* illness

enfermería *f.* health center

enfermero/a *m., f.* nurse

enfermo/a *adj.* sick

enfocar *v.t.* (*a topic*) to focus on, to look at
  El programa enfoca el problema de la falta de vivienda. The program looks at the problem of homelessness.

enfoque *m.* approach

enfrentamiento *m.* clash

enfrentar *v.t.* to confront, to face
  Hay que enfrentar la realidad. It's necessary to face reality.

enfrentarse (con) *v. pron.* to confront
  El ejército se enfrentará con el enemigo. The army will confront the enemy.

enfrente *prep.* across from, in front of

enfrente de *adv.* opposite; facing
  El ayuntamiento está enfrente de la catedral. The town hall is opposite the cathedral.

enfriar *v.t.* to chill

engañar *v.t.* to deceive, to cheat on

engaño *m.* deception

engordar *v.i.* to gain weight
que no engorda *adj.* non-fattening

engreído/a *adj.* conceited

enigma *m.* enigma, mystery

enigmático/a *adj.* enigmatic, mysterious

enloquecer (c:zc) *v.i.* to go crazy

ennegrecer (c:zc) *v.t.* to blacken

ennegrecerse (c:zc) *v. pron.* to go black, (*sky, clouds*) to darken

enojado/a *adj.* mad; angry; upset

enojar *v.t.* to annoy, to make angry

enojarse (con) *v. pron.* to get angry (with)

enredadera *f.* climbing plant

enriquecer (c:zc) *v.t.* to enrich, to make rich
La lectura enriquece la imaginación. Reading enriches imagination.

enriquecerse (c:zc) *v. pron.* to get rich

ensalada *f.* salad

ensaladera *f.* salad bowl

ensayar *v.t.* to rehearse

ensayo *m.* essay; rehearsal

enseguida *adv.* right away

enseñanza *f.* learning

enseñar *v.t.* to teach; to show

ensuciar *v.t.* to dirty; to get (something) dirty

entender (e:ie) *v.t.* to understand

entierro *m.* burial

entonces *adv.* then

entrada *f.* entrance; (*Spain*) ticket

entrar (en) *v.i.* to enter, to come in

entre *prep.* between; among
entre tú y yo between you and me
entre la multitud among the crowd
entre semana on weekdays

entregar *v.t.* to turn in, to deliver

entremeses *m., pl.* hors d'oeuvres; appetizers

entrenador(a) *m., f.* trainer; coach

entrenamiento *m.* coaching; training
El boxeo requiere mucho entrenamiento. Boxing requires a lot of training.
El entrenamiento duró seis horas. The training lasted six hours.

entrenarse *v. pron.* to practice; to train

entretener *v.t. irreg.* (**yo entretengo**) to entertain

entretenerse *v. pron. irreg.* (**yo me entretengo**) to amuse oneself; to hang about
No te entretengas camino a la escuela. Don't mess around on the way to school.

entretenido/a *adj.* entertaining

entrevista *f.* interview

entrevistador(a) *m., f.* interviewer

entrevistar *v.t.* to interview

entusiasmado/a *adj.* enthusiastic

entusiasmo *m.* enthusiasm

envase *m.* container

envejecer (c:zc) *v.i.* to age, to grow old

envejecimiento *m.* aging

enviar *v.t.* to send; to mail
  Te enviaré los libros por correo. I'll mail you the books.

envidioso/a *adj.* envious, jealous

envolver (o:ue) *v.t.* to wrap
  papel de envolver wrapping paper

enyesar *v.t.* (*medicine*) to put in a cast
  El médico me enyesó el brazo. The doctor put my arm in a cast.
  Tengo el brazo enyesado. My arm is in a cast.

equilibrado/a *adj.* balanced

equipado/a *adj.* equipped

equipaje *m.* luggage

equipo *m.* team
  equipo local home team
  equipo visitante visiting team
  equipo de técnicos team of technicians

equitación *f.* (horse) riding

equivalencia *f.* equivalence

equivaler *v.i.* to be equivalent to

equivocación *f.* mistake

equivocado/a *adj.* mistaken; wrong

equivocarse *v. pron.* to make a mistake, to be mistaken
  ¿Me equivoco al pensar que mientes? Am I mistaken in thinking you're lying?
  Nos equivocamos de camino. We went the wrong way.

eres *fam.* you are

ermita *f.* chapel

ermitaño/a *m., f.* hermit

eructar *v.i.* to belch, to burp

eructo *m.* belch, burp

erupción *f.* eruption
  hacer erupción (*volcano*) to erupt

es he/she/it is; *form.* you
  Es de… He/She is from…
  Es la una. It's one o'clock.
  Es obvio que… It's obvious that…

escalada *f.* (*mountaineering*) climb, ascent

escalador(a) *m., f.* (*mountaineering*) climber

escalar *v.t.* to climb
  escalar montañas to climb mountains

escalera *f.* stairs; stairway
  escalera de incendios fire escape
  escalera mecánica escalator

escalofrío *m.* shiver
  tener escalofríos to be shivering; to have the chills

escalón *m.* step, stair

escandaloso/a *adj.* loud; outrageous

escapada f. getaway

escaparate m. (*Spain*) shop window

escarcha f. frost

escayola f. (*Spain*) plaster cast

escayolar v. (*Spain*) *trans.* to put in a cast

escenario m. stage

escoba f. broom

escoger (g:j) v.t. choose

esconder v.t. to hide

escondidillas f. hide-and-seek

escondite, (al) m. hide-and-seek

escorpión m. scorpion

escribir v.t./v.i. to write
  escribir a máquina to type
  escribir un mensaje electrónico to write an e-mail message
  escribir una (tarjeta) postal to write a postcard
  escribir una carta to write a letter

escrito *p.p.* of **escribir** written
  por escrito *adv.* in writing

escritor(a) m., f. writer

escritorio m. desk

escuchar v.t. to listen (to)
  escuchar la radio to listen to the radio
  escuchar música to listen to music

escuela f. school

escuela pública f. public school

escuela de niños/as f. all-boys/girls school

esculpir v.t. to sculpt

escultor(a) m., f. sculptor

escultura f. sculpture

escurrir v.t. (*dishes*) to drain; (*clothes*) to wring out

ese, esa, esos, esas *dem. adj.* that (by you); those (by you)

ése, ésa, ésos, ésas *dem. pron.* that (one by you); those (by you)

esfera f. sphere

esforzarse (o:ue) v. pron. to try hard
  Debes esforzarte más. You must try harder.

esfuerzo m. effort

esgrima f. (*sport*) fencing

esgrimidor(a) m., f. fencer

esmeralda f. emerald

esnob *adj.* snobby; m., f. snob

esnobismo m. snobbery

esnórkel m. snorkel

eso *dem. pron. neuter.* that (by you)

esófago m. esophagus

espacio m. space

espagueti m. spaghetti

espalda f. back
  No me importa que hablen a mis espaldas. I don't mind them talking behind my back.

España f. Spain

español m. (*language*) Spanish

español(a) *adj./m., f.* Spanish

espárrago m. asparagus

espátula f. spatula

especialista m., f. specialist

especialización f. major (field of study or interest); specialization

especializarse v. pron. to specialize

especie f. (*biology*) species; type

especie en peligro de extinción endangered species

especie protegida protected species

espectacular *adj.* spectacular

espectáculo *m.* show

espectador(a) *m., f.* spectator

espejo *m.* mirror

esperanza *f.* hope

esperanza de vida life expectancy

esperar (+ *inf.*) *v.t.* to wait (for); to hope; to wish; to expect

espina *f.* (*fish*) bone; (*plant*) thorn

espinaca *f.* spinach

espolvorear *v.t.* (*sugar*) to sprinkle

esponja *f.* sponge

esponjoso/a *adj.* (*pastry*) spongy, soft; (*fabric*) fluffy

espontáneo/a *adj.* spontaneous

esposo/a *m.* husband; *f.* wife; *m., f.* spouse

espuma *f.* foam

esqueleto *m.* skeleton

esquema *m.* outline

esquí (acuático) *m.* (water) skiing

esquiador(a) *m., f.* skier

esquiar *v.i.* to ski

esquina *f.* corner

establecer (c:zc) *v.t.* to establish

establecer una marca mundial to set a world record

establo *m.* stable

estación *f.* station; season

estación de autobuses bus station

estación del metro subway station

estación de tren train station

estacionamiento *m.* parking lot; parking; parking space

estacionar *v.t.* to park

estacionarse *v. pron.* to park

estadio *m.* stadium

estado *m.* state

estado civil marital status

Estados Unidos *m. pl.* (EE.UU.; E.U.) United States

estadounidense *adj./m., f.* from the United States

estafador(a) *m., f.* fraud, con artist

estafar *v.t.* to defraud

estampado/a *adj.* print(ed), patterned

estampilla *f.* stamp

estancia *f.* stay

Nuestra estancia en La Coruña fue magnífica. Our stay in La Coruña was magnificent.

estanque *m.* pond (*man-made*)

estante *m.* bookcase; bookshelf, bookshelves

estar *v.i.* to be

Está bien. That's fine. It's okay.

(no) está nada mal it's not at all bad

estar a (veinte kilómetros) de aquí to be (twenty kilometers) from here

estar a dieta to be on a diet

estar a régimen to be on a diet

estar aburrido/a to be bored
estar afectado/a (por) to be affected (by)
estar bajo control to be under control
estar cansado/a to be tired
estar contaminado/a to be polluted
estar de acuerdo (con) to be in agreement with
estar de acuerdo to agree
no estar de acuerdo to disagree
estar de moda to be in fashion
estar de vacaciones *f., pl.* to be on vacation
estar de vuelta to be back
estar en buena forma to be in good shape
estar en las nubes to be daydreaming
estar enfermo/a to be sick
estar listo/a to be ready
estar perdido/a to be lost
estar roto/a to be broken
estar seguro/a to be sure
estar torcido/a to be twisted; to be sprained
estatua *f.* statue
este *m.* east
al este to the east
este, esta, estos, estas *dem. adj.* this; these
éste, ésta, éstos, éstas *dem. pron.* this (one); these
 Éste/Ésta es... This is... *(introducing someone)*
estéreo *m.* stereo
estéril *adj.* sterile
esterilizar *v.t.* to sterilize

esteticista *m., f.* beautician
estetoscopio *m.* stethoscope
estiércol *m.* manure
estilo *m.* style; *(swimming)* stroke, style
 algo por el estilo something like that
 estilo braza *(Spain)* breaststroke
 estilo espalda backstroke
 estilo libre freestyle
 estilo mariposa butterfly
 estilo pecho *(L.A.)* breaststroke
estiramiento *m.* stretching
estirar *v.t.* to stretch
esto *dem. pron. neuter* this; this thing
estómago *m.* stomach
estornudar *v.i.* to sneeze
estrecho/a *adj.* narrow, tight
estrella *f.* star
 estrella *m., f.* **de cine** movie star
 estrella fugaz shooting star
estrellado/a *adj.* starry
estrenar *v.t.* to wear for the first time; to début
estreno *m.* *(film, play)* premiere
estreñido/a *adj.* constipated
estreñimiento *m.* constipation
estrés *m.* stress
estresado/a adj. under stress
estresante *adj.* *(situation)* stressful
estropear *v.t.* to damage
estropearse *v. pron.* *(automobile)* to break down
estudiante *m., f.* student
estudiantil *adj.* student
estudiar *v.t.* to study

estudioso/a *adj.* studious
estufa *f. (L.A.)* stove
estupendo/a *adj.* stupendous
etapa *f.* stage; step
  las etapas de la vida the stages of life
ética *f.* ethics
ético/a *adj.* ethical
euforia *f.* euphoria, elation
eufórico/a *adj.* euphoric
Europa *f.* Europe
europeo/a *adj.* European
evadir *v.t.* (*danger, problem*) to avoid; (*taxes*) to evade
evadirse *v. pron.* (*responsibility, prison*) to escape
  Luis se evadió de la responsabilidad. Luis escaped responsibility.
evaluación *f.* assessment; test
evaluar *v.t.* to assess; to test
evasión *f.* escape
evitar *v.t.* to avoid
evolución *f.* evolution
evolucionar *v.i.* to evolve
exageración *f.* exaggeration
exagerar *v.t.* to exaggerate
  No exageres el valor de las cosas. Do not exagerate the value of things.
examen *m.* test; exam
  examen médico physical exam
excavadora *f.* power shovel, excavator
excavar *v.t.* to dig, to excavate
excelente *adj.* excellent
exceso *m.* excess; too much
  en exceso in excess, too much

excursión *f.* hike; tour; excursion
  Vamos de excursión. We're going hiking.
excursionista *m., f.* hiker
exhibición de arte *f.* art exhibition
exigir (g:j) *v.t.* to demand
éxito *m.* success
  tener éxito to succeed
éxodo *m.* exodus
experiencia *f.* experience
experimentar *v.t.* to experiment; to try out
expiración *f.* expiration
expirar *v.t.* (*time period, contract*) to expire
explicar *v.t.* to explain
explorar *v.t.* to explore
  explorar un pueblo to explore a town
  explorar una ciudad to explore a city
explosivo/a *adj.* explosive
exponer *v.t. irreg.* **(yo expongo)** (*art*) to exhibit
exportación *f.* exportation
exportar *v.t.* to export
exposición *f.* exhibition
expresión *f.* expression
expresivo/a *adj.* expressive
exprimidor *m.* juicer
expulsar *v.t.* to expel
expulsión *m.* expulsion
extinción *f.* extinction
extinguir *v.t.* **(yo extingo)** (*fire*) to extinguish, to put out
  Los bomberos extinguieron el incendio. The firefighters put out the blaze.

extinguirse *v. pron.* **(yo me extingo)** to become extinct; to die out
Su entusiasmo se está extinguiendo poco a poco. Her enthusiasm is dying little by little.
extranjero/a *adj.* foreign; *m., f.* foreigner
en el extranjero abroad
extrañar (algo o a alguien) *v.t.* to miss
extrañarse (de) *v. pron.* to be surprised, to find strange
Me extraña que no te hayas quejado. I'm surprised that you haven't complained.
extraño/a *adj.* strange, odd
Es extraño (que…) It's strange (that…)
Es extraño que tosas tanto. It's strange that you cough so much.
extravagante *adj.* flamboyant
extremidades *f., pl.* (*anatomy*) extremities
extrovertido/a *adj.* extroverted

F

fábrica *f.* factory
fabricación *f.* manufacture
fabricación en serie mass production
fabricante *m., f.* manufacturer
fabricar *v.t.* to manufacture, to produce
fabricar en serie to mass produce
fabuloso/a *adj.* fabulous
fachada *f.* façade

fácil *adj.* easy
facilitar *v.t.* to facilitate, to make easier
faisán *m.* pheasant
falda *f.* skirt
fallecer (c:zc) *v.i.* to pass away
fallecido/a *m., f.* deceased
fallecimiento *m.* death
falta *f.* lack; (*spelling*) mistake
falta de recursos lack of resources
falta de ortografía spelling mistake
faltar *v.t.* to lack; to need
familia *f.* family
familiar *adj.* family; (*known*) familiar
Este lugar me resulta familiar. This place looks familiar.
familiares *m., pl.* relatives
famoso/a *adj.* famous; *m., f.* famous person, celebrity
fango *m.* mud
faringe *f.* pharynx
farmacia *f.* pharmacy
farmacia de guardia 24-hour pharmacy
faro *m.* (*automobile*) headlight
fascinar *v.t.* to fascinate; to love; to be fascinated by
fatigado/a *adj.* weary
fatigarse *v. pron.* to wear oneself out
favorable *adj.* favorable
favorito/a *adj.* favorite
fax *m.* fax (*machine*)
fe *f.* faith
febrero *m.* February
fecha *f.* date

fecha de caducidad expiration date

fecundación *f.* fertilization

fecundar *v.t.* to fertilize

felicidad *f.* happiness

¡Felicidades! Congratulations! (*for an event such as a birthday or anniversary*)

felicitar *v.t.* to congratulate

¡Felicitaciones! Congratulations! (*for an event such as an engagement or a good grade on a test*)

feliz *adj.* happy

¡Feliz cumpleaños! Happy birthday!

fenomenal *adj.* fantastic, great, phenomenal

fenómeno *m.* phenomenon

feo/a *adj.* ugly

ferrocarril *m.* railroad

fértil *adj.* fertile

fertilidad *f.* fertility

fertilizante *m.* fertilizer

festejar *v.t.* to celebrate

festejo *m.* celebration

festival *m.* festival

fiambre *m.* cold cut

fiambrera *f.* (*Spain*) lunch box

fianza *f.* bail

ficha *f.* (*game*) counter, game piece

fidelidad *f.* fidelity; faithfulness

fiebre *f.* fever

fiel *adj.* faithful; loyal

fiesta *f.* party

dar una fiesta to throw a party

fijo/a *adj.* set; fixed; permanent; steady

precio fijo fixed price

trabajo fijo permanent job

fila *f.* row

filatelia *f.* philately, stamp collecting

filmoteca *f.* film library

filología *f.* philology

filólogo/a *m., f.* philologist

filosofar *v.i.* to philosophize

filosofía *f.* philosophy

filósofo/a *m., f.* philosopher

fin *m.* end

fin de semana weekend

a fin de *conj.* in order to

a fines de at the end of

al fin *loc.* at last

al fin y al cabo *loc.* after all

por fin *adv.* at last

final *m.* end

al final at the end

a finales de at/toward the end of

finalmente *adv.* finally

financiar *v.t.* to finance

fingir (g:j) *v.t.* to pretend

Fingía no saberlo. She pretended not to know it.

firma *f.* signature

firmar *v.t.* to sign (*a document*)

física *f.* physics

físico/a *m., f.* physicist

flaco/a *adj.* skinny

flamenco/a *adj., m.* (*music*) flamenco

flan (de caramelo) *m.* baked (caramel) custard

flecha *f.* arrow

flexible *adj.* flexible

flexionar *v.t.* to flex
flor *f.* flower
florería *f.* (*L.A.*) flower shop
florero *m.* vase
florero/a *m., f.* (*L.A.*) florist
florista *m., f.* (*Spain*) florist
floristería *f.* (*Spain*) flower shop
flotar *v.i.* to float
fluir (y) *v.i.* to flow
foca *f.* seal
folklórico/a *adj.* folk; folkloric
folleto *m.* brochure
fondo *m.* (*street, corridor*) end; (*sea*) bottom
  a fondo *adv.* completely
  al fondo (de) *adv.* at the end (of)
fondos *m., pl.* (*money*) funds
fonética *f.* phonetics
fonología *f.* phonology
fontanería *f.* (*Spain*) *f.* plumbing
fontanero/a *m., f.* (*Spain*) plumber
forense *m., f.* forensic scientist
forma *f.* shape
  estar en buena/mala forma to be in good/bad shape
formación *f.* training
  formación profesional vocational training
formal *adj.* formal
formar *v.t.* to train
formulario *m.* form
  (re)llenar el formulario fill out the form
fortaleza *f.* fortress
fortuna *f.* fortune
  por fortuna *adv.* fortunately

fósforo *m.* match
fósil *m.* fossil
fosilizarse *v. pron.* to fossilize, to become fossilized
foto(grafía) *f.* photograph
fotocopiadora *f.* photocopier
fotocopiar *v.t.* to photocopy
fotosíntesis *f.* photosynthesis
fracasado/a *adj.* failed, unsuccessful
fracasar *v.i.* to fail
fracaso *m.* failure
frambuesa *f.* raspberry
francés *m.* (*language*) French
francés, francesa *adj./m., f.* French
Francia *f.* France
frase *f.* phrase; sentence
frazada *f.* (*L.A.*) blanket
frecuencia *f.* frequency
  con (mucha) frecuencia frequently, regularly
frecuentemente *adv.* frequently
fregadero (de la cocina) *m.* (kitchen) sink
fregar *v.* (*Spain*) *trans.* to mop
fregona *f.* (*Spain*) mop
frenar *v.i.* to brake
freno *m.* brake
  freno de mano handbrake
frente *f.* (*anatomy*) forehead
fresa *f.* strawberry
fresco/a *adj.* cool, fresh
frijol *m.* bean
frío/a *adj.* cold; chilled
  Sírvase frío. Serve chilled.
fritada *f.* fried dish (*pork, fish, etc.*)
frito/a *adj.* fried
frontera *f.* border, frontier

fronterizo/a *adj.* border
fruta *f.* fruit
frutería *f.* fruit store
frutilla *f.* (*L.A.*) strawberry
fucsia *adj.* fuchsia
fuego *m.* fire
  fuegos artificiales *m., pl.*
  fireworks
fuente *f.* platter, serving dish;
  fountain
  fuente de fritada platter of
  fried food
fuera *adv.* outside
fuerte *adj.* strong
fuga *f.* (*prison*) escape; (*gas,
water*) leak
fugarse *v. pron.* to escape, to
flee, to run away
fugitivo/a *m., f.* fugitive
fumar *v.t.* to smoke
  no fumar not to smoke
  Prohibido fumar. No
  smoking.
función *f.* show, function
funcionar *v.i.* to work; to
function
  Funciona a la perfección. It
  works perfectly.
funeral *m.* funeral
furioso/a *adj.* furious
fusible *m.* (*electricity*) fuse
fútbol *m.* soccer
  fútbol americano football
futbolista *m., f.* soccer player;
football player
futuro/a *adj./m.* future
  en el futuro (cercano) in the
  (near) future
  futura mamá mother-to-be
  un trabajo sin futuro a job

with no prospects

G

gacela *f.* gazelle
gafas (oscuras/de sol) *f. pl.*
(sun)glasses
galardón *m.* award, prize
galardonado/a *m., f.* award-
winner
galardonar *v.t.* to award
galaxia *f.* galaxy
galería *f.* gallery
galleta *f.* cookie
gallo *m.* rooster
gana *f.* desire
  de buena/mala gana *adv.*
  willingly/unwillingly
ganadería *f.* ranching, cattle
raising
ganadero/a *m., f.* rancher,
cattle farmer
ganar *v.t.* to win; (*money*) to
earn
  ganarse la vida *idiom* to
  make a living, to earn one's
  living **Mario se gana la vida
  escribiendo guiones de
  telenovela.** Mario makes his
  living writing soap opera
  scripts.
ganga *f.* bargain
garaje *m.* garage
garantía *f.* guarantee, warranty
garantizar *v.t.* to guarantee
garbanzo *m.* chickpea
gardenia *f.* gardenia
garganta *f.* throat
gas *m.* gas
  gas lacrimógeno tear gas
gasolina *f.* gasoline

gasolinera *f.* gas station
gastar *v.t.* (*money*) to spend
gasto *m.* expense
gastronomía *f.* gastronomy
gatillo *m.* (*firearm*) trigger
  apretar el gatillo to pull the trigger
gato/a *m., f.* cat
géiser *m.* geyser
gelatina *f.* gelatine
gemelo/a *m., f.* twin
generoso/a *adj.* generous
genética *f.* genetics
genético/a *adj.* genetic
gente *f.* people
  buena gente *idiom* nice person, nice guy, nice gal
geografía *f.* geography
geólogo/a *m., f.* geologist
geometría *f.* geometry
geométrico/a *adj.* geometric(al)
geranio *m.* geranium
gerente *m., f.* manager
gimnasia *f.* gymnastics
  gimnasia rítmica rhythmic gymnastics
gimnasio *m.* gymnasium
gimnasta *m., f.* gymnast
ginecólogo/a *m., f.* gynecologist
girar *v.t./intrans.* to turn
  Gire a la izquierda en la próxima esquina. Turn left at the next corner.
  No gires la cabeza. Don't turn your head.
girasol *m.* sunflower
giro *m.* turn
  giro bancario bank draft

  giro postal money order
globo *m.* balloon
glotón, glotona *adj.* gluttonous; greedy
gobernar (e:ie) *v.t.* to govern, to rule
gobierno *m.* government
golf *m.* golf
golfista *m., f.* golfer
golpe *m.* blow; coup; hit
  Dio unos golpes en la mesa. He pounded on the table several times.
  de golpe *adv.* suddenly
  Ocurrió de golpe. It happened suddenly.
goma *f.* (*pencil*) eraser
  de goma (made of) rubber
gordo/a *adj.* fat
gorra *f.* cap (*with a visor*)
  gorra de béisbol baseball cap
gorrión *m.* sparrow
gorro *m.* cap (*without a visor*)
  gorro de lana wool cap, ski cap
gota *f.* drop
gótico/a *adj.* Gothic
gozar (de) *v.t.* to enjoy
  Mi padre goza de una salud de hierro. My father has a strong constitution.
grabadora *f.* tape recorder
grabar *v.t.* to record
gracias *f., pl.* thank you; thanks
  Gracias por todo. Thanks for everything.
  Gracias una vez más. Thanks again.
  (Muchas) gracias. Thank you (very much). Thanks (a lot).

gracioso/a *adj.* funny

graduación *f.* graduation

graduar *v.t.* (*temperature, etc.*) to adjust, to regulate

graduarse (en/de) *v. pron.* (*university*) to graduate (from/in)

gran, grande *adj.* big; great; large

   Es un gran amigo. He's a great friend.

granada *f.* (*fruit*) pomegranate; (*military*) grenade

granero *m.* barn

grano *m.* grain, seed, bean; (*medical*) blemish, pimple

   ir al grano *idiom* to get to the point

grasa *f.* fat

gratis *adj.* free of charge

grave *adj.* (*illness, wound, problem*) serious

gravedad *f.* gravity

gravísimo/a *adj.* (*superlative*) extremely serious; grave

griego *m.* (*language*) Greek

griego *adj./m., f.* Greek

grifo *m.* faucet

grillo *m.* cricket

gripe *f.* flu

gris *adj./m.* gray

gritar *v.i.* to scream

grito *m.* yell, shout

grosero/a *adj.* rude, ill-mannered, impolite, rough

grúa *f.* (*machinery*) crane

grupo *m.* group

guagua *f.* bus

guantes *m., pl.* gloves

guapo/a *adj.* handsome; good-looking

guarda forestal *m., f.* ranger

guardabarros *m.* (*automobile*) fender

guardar *v.t.* to save (on a computer)

guardería *f.* nursery school, day-care center

guardia *m., f.* guard, police officer

   estar de guardia (*doctor*) to be on duty, to be on call

   guardia de seguridad security guard

guerra *f.* war

guía *m., f.* guide

   guía de teléfonos phone book

   Lo puedo usar de guía. I can use it as a guide.

guiñar (el ojo) *v.t.* to wink

guión *m.* script, screenplay

guionista *m., f.* scriptwriter, screenwriter

guisante *m.* pea

guisar *v.i.* (*Spain*) to cook

guiso *m.* stew

guitarra *f.* guitar

gusano *m.* worm

gustar *v.i.* to be pleasing to; to like

   Me gusta. I like it.

   Me gustaría. I would like it.

   ¿Te gusta(n)…? Do you like…?

   ¿Te gustaría (+ *inf.*)…? Would you like to…?

gusto *m.* pleasure; (*senses*) taste

   El gusto es mío. The pleasure is mine.

   Gusto de (+ *inf.*)… It's a pleasure to . . .

H

haber *v. impers. irreg.* **(no) hay**
sing. there is (not); *pl.* there
are (not)
  Hay (mucha) contaminación.
It's (very) smoggy.
  Hay (mucha) niebla. It's
(very) foggy.
  hay que it is necessary (that)
  **Hay que pensar antes de
hablar.** Think before you
speak.
  No hay de qué. You're
welcome.
  No hay duda (de) que…
There's no doubt that…
haber *v. aux. irreg.* (*in
compound verbs*) to have
  Yo no lo he hecho. I haven't
done it.
hábil *adj.* skillful
habilidad *f.* skill
habitación *f.* room
  habitación doble double room
  habitación individual single
room
hablar *v.i.* to talk; to speak
hacer *v.t. irreg.* **(yo hago)** to do;
to make
  hacer amigos to make
friends
  hacer berrinches to throw
tantrums
  hacer cola to stand in line
  hacer diligencias to do
errands; to run errands
  hacer ejercicio to exercise,
to work out
  hacer ejercicios aeróbicos
to do aerobics
  hacer ejercicios de

estiramiento to do stretching
exercises
  hacer el papel (de) to play
the role of
  hacer gimnasia to work out;
to exercise,
  hacer juego (con) (*clothing*)
to match (with), to go well
(with)
  hacer la cama to make the
bed
  hacer las maletas to pack
(one's suitcases)
  **hacer quehaceres
domésticos** to do household
chores
  hacer travesuras to get into
trouble
  hacer turismo to go
sightseeing
  hacer un picnic to have a
picnic
  hacer un viaje to go on/take
a trip
  hacer una excursión to go
on a hike; to go on a tour
  hacer una fiesta to throw a
party
  hacer una maestría to
pursue a Master's degree
hacer *v. impers.* (*weather*)
  Hace buen/mal tiempo. The
weather is good/bad. It's
good/bad weather.
  Hace (mucho) calor. It's
(very) hot.
  Hace fresco. It's cool.
  Hace (mucho) frío. It's (very)
cold.
  Hace (mucho) sol. It's (very)
sunny.

Hace (mucho) viento. It's (very) windy.

hacer v. impers. (time)
  hace dos semanas two weeks ago

hacerse v. pron. irreg. **(yo me hago)** to become
  hacerse daño to hurt oneself
  hacerse el sordo to pretend not to hear
  hacerse rico to become rich

hacha (el) f. ax

hacia prep. toward

hada (el) f. fairy
  hada madrina fairy godmother

hallar v.t. to find

hallazgo m. find, discovery
  Aquel restaurante fue un verdadero hallazgo. That restaurant was a real find.

halterofilia f. (sport) weightlifting

hamaca f. hammock

hambre (el) f. hunger

hambriento/a adj. hungry

hamburguesa f. hamburger

harina f. flour
  harina de otro costal idiom another kettle of fish

hartarse v. pron. to get fed up; (food) to fill oneself

hasta prep. until, toward
  hasta ahora until now
  Hasta la vista. See you later.
  Hasta luego. See you later.
  Hasta mañana. See you tomorrow.
  Hasta pronto. See you soon.

hasta (que) conj. until

hasta que lleguen until they arrive

hebreo m. (language) Hebrew

hebreo adj./m., f. Hebrew

hecho p.p. of **hacer** done
  de hecho in fact

heladería f. ice cream shop

helado m. ice cream

helado/a adj. iced

helicóptero m. helicopter

hembra f. female

hemisferio m. hemisphere

hemorragia f. hemorrhage

herbívoro/a adj. herbivorous; m., f. herbivore

heredar v.t. to inherit

heredera f. heiress

heredero m. heir

hereditario/a adj. hereditary

herencia f. inheritance

herida f. wound

herido/a adj./m., f. injured
  Hubo un herido de gravedad. One person was seriously injured.

hermanastro/a m. stepbrother; f. stepsister

hermano/a m. brother, f. sister
  hermano/a mayor/menor older/younger brother/sister

hermanos m., pl. brothers and sisters

hermético/a adj. airtight

hermoso/a adj. beautiful

héroe m. hero

heroína f. heroine

herramienta f. tool

hervido/a adj. boiled

hervir (e:ie) v.t. to boil

hidráulico/a adj. hydraulic

hiedra *f.* ivy

hielo *m.* ice

  quebrar/romper el hielo *loc.* break the ice

hierba *f.* grass

hierbas *f., pl.* herbs

hierro *m.* iron

hígado *m.* liver

higo *m.* fig

higuera *f.* fig tree

hijastro/a *m.* stepson; *f.* stepdaughter

hijo/a *m.* son; *f.* daughter

  hijo/a único/a only child

hijos *m., pl.* children

hilera *f.* row

hilo *m.* thread

  de hilo (made of) linen

  hilo dental dental floss

hindú *adj./m., f.* Hindu

hipérbole *f.* hyperbole

hípica *f.* equestrian sports

hipo *m.* hiccups

hipódromo *m.* hippodrome

hipoteca *f.* mortgage

hipotecar *v.t.* to mortgage

hipótesis *f.* hypothesis

hipotético/a *adj.* hypothetical

hispano/a *adj./m., f.* Hispanic

historia *f.* history; story

historiador(a) *m., f.* historian

hockey *m.* hockey

  hockey sobre césped (*L.A.*) field hockey

  hockey sobre hielo ice hockey

  hockey sobre hierba (*Spain*) field hockey

hoguera *f.* bonfire

hoja *f.* (*plant*) leaf; (*paper*) sheet

hoja de vida (*Colombia*) résumé

hola *interj.* hello; hi

hombre *m.* man

  hombre de negocios businessman

  hombre del tiempo weatherman

  hombre lobo werewolf

  hombre rana frogman, diver

hombrera *f.* shoulder pad

hombro *m.* shoulder

homenaje *m.* tribute, homage

homenajear *v.t.* to pay homage

honesto/a *adj.* honest

hora *f.* hour

  ¿A qué hora…? At what time…?

horario *m.* schedule

  horario fijo fixed schedule

  horario flexible flexible schedule

horizonte *m.* horizon

hormiga *f.* ant

hormigón *m.* (*Spain*) concrete

hormona *f.* hormone

hornear *v.t.* to bake

  pan recién horneado freshly baked bread

hornillo *m.* portable electric stove

horno *m.* oven

  horno de microondas microwave oven

horror *m.* horror

  …de horror horror

hortensia *f.* hydrangea

horticultor(a) *m., f.* horticulturalist

horticultura *f.* horticulture

hospedar *v.t.* to provide accommodation
hospital *m.* hospital
hospitalario/a *adj.* hospitable
hospitalidad *f.* hospitality
hostal *m.* inn; hostel
hotel *m.* hotel
hoy *adv.* today
  hoy día *adv.* nowadays
  Hoy es... Today is . . .
huelga *f.* strike
huelguista *m., f.* striker
huella *f.* footprint; mark
  huella dactilar fingerprint
huerta *f.* orchard
huerto *m.* vegetable garden
hueso *m.* bone; (*fruit*) pit
huésped *m., f.* guest
huevo *m.* egg
huida *f.* escape
huir (y) *v.i.* to flee, to escape
  Huir de la injusticia. Escape injustice.
humanidades *f., pl.* humanities
humanismo *m.* humanism
humanista *m., f.* humanist
humectante *m.* moisturizer
humedad *f.* humidity
húmedo *adj.* humid; damp
humilde *adj.* humble
  en mi humilde opinión in my humble opinion
humillado/a *adj.* humiliated
humo *m.* smoke
humor *m.* mood
  de buen/mal humor in a good/bad mood
huracán *m.* hurricane

I

iceberg *m.* iceberg

ida *f.* (*travel*) one way
  boleto/billete de ida one-way ticket
idea *f.* idea
idealista *adj.* idealist
idioma *m.* language
iglesia *f.* church
ignorancia *f.* ignorance
ignorante *adj.* ignorant
igual *adj.* equal, same, like
  dos y dos igual a cuatro two and two equals four
  Es igual que su madre. She's like her mother.
  Son las dos iguales. They are both the same.
  ¿Blanco o negro? –Me da igual. ¿Black or white? – It's all the same to me.
igualdad *f.* equality
igualmente *adv.* likewise
  ¡Que te diviertas! **–Igualmente.** Have fun! –Likewise.
ilegible *adj.* illegible
ilusionado/a *adj.* thrilled
ilustrar *v.t.* to illustrate
imaginar *v.t.* to imagine
imaginarse *v. pron.* to imagine
imán *m.* magnet
imitación *f.* imitation
imitar *v.t.* to imitate
impaciencia *f.* impatience
impacientarse *v. pron.* to get impatient
  Se impacientó con el retraso del autobús. She got impatient over the delay of the bus.
impaciente *adj.* impatient
impedir (e:i) *v.t.* to prevent

impensable *adj.* unthinkable

imperio *m.* empire

impermeable *adj.* waterproof

impermeable *m.* raincoat

importación *f.* importation

importante *adj.* important

(No) Es importante que… It's (not) important that…

Es importante que vengas a clase. It's important that you come to class.

importar *v.i.* to be important to; to matter

No importa. It doesn't matter.

imposible *adj.* impossible

(No) Es imposible (que…) It's (not) impossible (that…)

Es imposible que tenga sed. It's impossible that she's thirsty.

impostor(a) *m., f.* impostor

imprenta *f.* print shop

impresora *f.* printer

imprimir *v.t.* to print

improbable *adj.* improbable

(No) Es improbable (que…) It's (not) improbable (that…)

Es improbable que llueva. It probably won't rain.

impuesto *m.* tax

inadvertido/a *adj.* unnoticed

inauguración *f.* inauguration

inaugurar *v.t.* to inaugurate

incendio *m.* fire

incertidumbre *f.* uncertainty

incógnito *adj.* unknown

de incógnito *adv.* incognito

incomprensible *adj.* incomprehensible

incomprensión *f.* lack of understanding

inconcebible *adj.* inconceivable

inconveniente *m.* drawback

increíble *adj.* incredible

incremento *m.* increase

independiente *adj.* independent

independizarse *v. pron.* to become independent

indicar *v.t.* to indicate, to show

índice *m.* rate

índice de mortalidad mortality rate

índice de natalidad birth rate

indicio *m.* evidence

indígena *adj.* indigenous, native

indiscreto/a *adj.* indiscreet, tactless

individual *adj.* individual; (*room*) private; *m.* (*sport*) singles

individualidad *f.* individuality

inefable *adj.* indescribable

inesperado/a *adj.* unexpected

inexplicable *adj.* inexplicable

infarto *m.* heart attack

infección *f.* infection

influir (en) (y) *v.i.* to influence

Los poemas de Darío influyeron en otros poetas. Darío's poems influenced other poets.

información *f.* information

informal *adj.* casual

informar *v.t.* to inform

informarse *v. pron.* to get information

informe *m.* report; (*written work*) paper

infusión (de hierbas) *f.* herbal tea

ingeniero/a *m., f.* engineer
ingerir (e:ie) *v.t.* to ingest
ingestión *f.* ingestion
Inglaterra *f.* England
ingle *f.* groin
inglés *m.* (*language*) English
inglés, inglesa *adj./m., f.*
English
ingrávido/a *adj.* weightless
injusto/a *adj.* unfair
inmaduro/a *adj.* (*person*)
immature
inmediatamente *adv.*
immediately
inmigración *f.* immigration
inmigrante *m., f.* immigrant
inmigrar *v.i.* to immigrate
**inmunizar (a alguien contra
algo)** *v.t.* to immunize
inmunológico/a *adj.*
immunological
innovación *f.* innovation
innovador(a) *adj.* innovative;
m., f. innovator
innovar *v.t.* to innovate
inodoro *m.* toilet
inolvidable *adj.* unforgettable
inquietante *adj.* worrying
inquietar(se) *v. pron.* to worry
inquieto/a *adj.* worried
inscribirse *v. pron.* to register,
to enroll
**Quiere inscribirse en la
clase de astronomía.** She
intends to register for the
astronomy class.
inscripción *f.* registration,
enrollment
insecto *m.* insect
insípido/a *adj.* (*food*) bland;

(*person, work*) insipid
insistencia *f.* insistence
insistir (en) *v.i.* to insist (on)
(**insistir en +***inf.***) Insistió en
invitarme.** He insisted on
inviting me.
(**insistir en que +***subj.***)
Insiste en que vayamos
todos.** He insists on all of us
going.
insociable *adj.* unsociable
insólito/a *adj.* unusual
insomnio *m.* insomnia
insoportable *adj.* unbearable
inspector(a) *m., f.* inspector
inspector(a) de aduanas
customs inspector
inspirar *v.t.* to inspire
instalación *f.* installation
instalaciones deportivas
sports facilities
instalar *v.t.* (*equipment*) to
install
instalarse *v. pron.* to settle,
install oneself
**Se instaló delante de la tele
y no se movió.** He settled in
front of the TV and didn't
budge.
institución *f.* institution
instrumento *m.* (*medical,
musical*) instrument
insulina *f.* insulin
inteligente *adj.* intelligent
intentar *v.* to try
intento *m.* attempt; try
intercambiar *v.t.* exchange
intercambio *m.* exchange
interés *m.* interest
interesante *adj.* interesting

interesar *v.i.* to be interesting to; to interest

interesarse (en) *v. pron.* to take an interest (in)
Siempre se interesa en los resultados. He's always interested in the results.

intermedio *adj.* intermediate

intermitente *m.* (*automobile*) turn signal

internacional *adj.* international

Internet *m.* Internet

interpretación *f.* (*oral translation*) interpreting

interpretar *v.t.* to play (a role), to perform

intérprete *m., f.* interpreter

interrumpir *v.t.* to interrupt

intersección *f.* intersection

intervención *f.* intervention, participation
intervención quirúrgica operation

intestino *m.* intestine
intestino delgado small intestine
intestino grueso large intestine

intimar (con alguien) *v.i.* to get close (to someone)

intimidad *f.* privacy

intolerante *adj.* intolerant

intriga *f.* intrigue

intrigado/a *adj.* intrigued, in suspense

inundación *f.* flood

inundar *v.t.* to flood

inútil *adj.* useless

inválido/a *adj.* (*person*) disabled

invernadero *m.* greenhouse

inverosímil *adj.* unlikely, improbable; unrealistic

invertebrado/a *adj./m.* invertebrate

invertir (e:ie) *v.t.* to invest

investigador(a) *m., f.* researcher; investigator

investigar *v.t.* to research

invierno *m.* winter

invitado/a *m., f.* guest

invitar *v.t.* to invite

involuntario *adj.* involuntary

inyección *f.* injection

inyectar *v.t.* to inject

ir *v.i. irreg.* to go
ir a (+ inf.) to be going to (do something) **Voy a leer un rato.** I'm going to read for a while.
ir a exceso de velocidad to speed
ir a la playa to go to the beach
ir de campamento to go camping
ir de compras to go shopping
ir de excursión (a las montañas) to (go on a) hike (in the mountains)
ir de pesca to go fishing
ir de vacaciones to go on vacation
ir en auto(móvil) to go by auto(mobile); to go by car
ir en autobús to go by bus
ir en avión to go by plane
ir en barco to go by ship/boat
ir en metro to go by subway
ir en motocicleta to go by motorcycle

ir en taxi to go by taxi
ir en tren to go by train
¡Vamos! Let's go!; Come on!
ironía *f.* irony
irónico/a *adj.* ironic
irresponsable *adj.* irresponsible
irse *v. pron. irreg.* to go away; to leave **No te vayas, aún es temprano.** Don't leave; it's still early.
  irse de pinta (*idiom*) (*Mexico*) to play hooky
  irse de vacaciones to go on vacation
italiano *m. (language)* Italian
italiano/a *adj./m., f.* Italian
itinerario *m.* itinerary
izquierdo/a *adj.* left; *m., f.* left
  a la izquierda (de) to the left (of)

J

jabón *m.* soap
jabonera *f.* soap dish
jamás *adv.* never; not ever
jamón *m.* ham
Januká *m.* Chanukah
japonés *m.* (*language*) Japanese
japonés, japonesa *adj./m., f.* Japanese
jarabe para la tos *m.* cough syrup
jardín *m.* garden, (back) yard
jardinería *f.* gardening
jardinero/a *m., f.* gardener
jarra *f.* pitcher
jarrón *m.* vase
jeans *m., pl.* jeans

jefe/a *m., f.* boss
jerarquía *f.* hierarchy
jerárquico/a *adj.* hierarchical
jerarquizado/a *adj.* hierarchical
jerez *m.* (*wine*) sherry
jeringa *f.* syringe
jirafa *f.* giraffe
joroba *f.* hump
jorobado/a *adj.* hunchbacked
jota *f.* (*playing cards*) jack
joven *adj.* young; *m., f.* youth, young person
joyas *f.* jewels
joyería *f.* jewelry store
joyero/a *m., f.* jeweler; *m.* jewelry box
jubilado/a *m., f.* retired person
jubilarse *v. pron.* to retire (from work)
judío/a *adj.* Jewish; *m., f.* Jew
juego *m.* game
  juego limpio/sucio fair/foul play
juegos *m. pl.* games
  juegos de azar gambling
  juegos de mesa board games
  Juegos Olímpicos Olympic Games
  Juegos Paralímpicos Paralympics
jueves *m., sing.* Thursday
juez *m., f.* judge
jugador(a) *m., f.* player; gambler
jugar (u:ue) *v.t./v.i.* to play
  jugar a las cartas to play cards
jugo *m.* juice

jugo de fruta fruit juice
jugoso/a *adj.* juicy
juguete *m.* toy
juguetería *f.* toy store
juicio *m.* judgment; trial
julio *m.* July
junio *m.* June
jungla *f.* jungle
junta *f.* board, committee
  junta directiva board of
  directors
juntarse *v. pron.* to get
  together
juntos/as *adj./adv.* together
jurado *m.* jury
jurar *v.i.* to swear
justicia *f.* justice
justo/a *adj.* fair
juvenil *adj.* youthful
juventud *f.* youth
juzgar *v.t.* to judge

K

kilo(gramo) *m.* kilo(gram)
kilómetro *m.* kilometer

L

la *f., sing. art., def.* the
la *d.o. pron. f., sing.* her, it, you
labio *m.* lip
laboratorio *m.* laboratory
lacio/a *adj.* (*hair*) straight
ladera *f.* hillside, mountainside,
  slope
  **El primer grupo subió por la
  ladera norte.** The first group
  ascended the northern slope.
lado *m.* side
  al lado de beside; next to
  por un lado…, por otro

lado… on (the) one hand…,
  on the other hand . . .
ladrar *v.i.* to bark
ladrido *m.* bark
ladrillo *m.* brick
ladrón, ladrona *m., f.* thief;
  robber; burglar
lagarto *f.* lizard
lago *m.* lake
lágrima *f.* tear
lamentar *v.t.* to regret
lámpara *f.* lamp
lana *f.* wool
  de lana (made of) wool
lancha *f.* motorboat
langosta *f.* lobster
langostino *m.* prawn
lanzado *p.p. of* **lanzar** thrown
lanzado/a *adj.* (*person*)
  impulsive, impetuous
lanzamiento *m.* launch, throw
  lanzamiento de bala *(L. A.)*
  shotput
  lanzamiento de disco discus
  throw
  lanzamiento de jabalina
  javelin throw
  lanzamiento de peso *(Spain)*
  shotput
lanzar *v.t.* to throw; to launch
  **La NASA lanzó un cohete a
  Saturno.** NASA launched a
  rocket to Saturn.
lápiz *m.* pencil
  lápiz labial lipstick
largo/a *adj.* long (*in length*)
  a la larga in the long run
laringe *f.* larynx
larva *f.* larva
las *f., pl. art., def.* the

DICTIONARY: SPANISH/ENGLISH

las *d.o. pron. f., pl.* them
lástima *f.* shame, pity
  Es una lástima (que…) It's too bad (that…); It's a shame (that…)
  Es una lástima que no te puedas quedar. It's a pity that you can't stay.
lastimar *v.t.* to hurt
lastimarse *v. pron.* to injure oneself; to get hurt
  lastimarse el pie to injure one's foot
lata *f.* (*tin*) can
  ¡Qué lata! *loc.* What a drag!
latido *m.* heartbeat
latín *m.* (*language*) Latin
latino/a *adj./m., f.* Latin
latir *v.i.* (*heart*) to beat
lavabo *m.* (bathroom) sink
lavadora *f.* washing machine
lavandería *f.* laundromat
lavaplatos *m., sing.* dishwasher
lavar (el suelo) *v.t.* to wash (the floor)
  lavar los platos to do (wash) the dishes
lavarse *v. pron.* to wash (oneself)
  lavarse la cara to wash one's face
  lavarse las manos to wash one's hands
  lavarse los dientes to brush one's teeth
lazo *m.* bow; ribbon
lazos *m., pl.* ties
  lazos familiares family ties
le *i.o. pron. sing.* to/for him, her, *form.* you

lección *f.* lesson
leche *f.* milk
lechuga *f.* lettuce
lector *m., f.* reader
leer *v.t.* to read
  leer correo electrónico to read e-mail
  leer un periódico to read a newspaper
  leer una revista to read a magazine
legado *m.* legacy
legal *adj.* legal
legalizar *v.t.* to legalize
leído *p.p. of* **leer** read
lejano/a *adj.* distant; remote; far-off
  un pariente lejano a distant relative
lejía *f.* bleach
lejos de *adv.* far from
lengua *f.* tongue; language
  lenguas extranjeras *f., pl.* foreign languages
lentamente *adv.* slowly
lenteja *f.* lentil
lentes *m., pl.* eyeglasses, lenses
  lentes de contacto contact lenses
  lentes (de sol/oscuros/ negros) (sun)glasses
lento/a *adj.* slow
leña *f.* firewood
leño *m.* log
león *m.* lion
leopardo *m.* leopard
les *i.o. pron. pl.* to/for them, *form.* you

letra *f.* (*alphabet*) letter; handwriting; (*song*) lyrics
Tienes una letra ilegible. Your handwriting is illegible.
letra de imprenta printing
Escriba su nombre completo en letra de imprenta. Print your full name.

letra mayúscula capital letter
letra minúscula lowercase letter
letrero *m.* sign
levadura *f.* yeast
levantar *v.t.* to lift
levantar pesas to lift weights
levantarse *v. pron.* to get up
ley *f.* law
la ley del más fuerte the survival of the fittest
leyenda *f.* legend
liberación *f.* liberation
liberal *adj./m., f.* liberal
liberar *v.t.* to free, to release
libertad *f.* liberty, freedom
la Estatua de la Libertad the Statue of Liberty
libertad condicional parole
libertad de expresión freedom of speech
libra *f.* pound
libre *adj.* free
librería *f.* bookstore
libro *m.* book
libro de bolsillo paperback
libro de consulta reference book
licencia *f.* license
licencia de

conducir/manejar driver's license
licor *m.* liqueur, liquor
licuadora *f.* (*L.A.*) blender
licuar *v.t.* to blend
líder *m., f.* leader
liderar *v.t.* to lead
liderazgo *m.* leadership
ligar *v.i.* (*Spain*) to pick up boys/girls
ligero/a *adj.* (*weight/food*) light
lima *f.* (*tool*) file; nail file
limitar *v.t.* to limit; to restrict
límite *m.* limit
limón *m.* lemon, lime
limonada *f.* lemonade
limonero *m.* lemon tree
limosna *f.* alms, charity
vivir de limosnas to live by begging
limpiaparabrisas *m. sing.* windshield wiper
limpiar *v.t.* to clean
limpiar la casa to clean the house
limpio/a *adj.* clean
limusina *f.* limousine
lindo/a *adj.* pretty
línea *f.* line
en línea in-line
línea discontinua broken line
lingüista *m., f.* linguist
lingüística *f.* linguistics
lingüístico/a *adj.* linguistic
linterna *f.* flashlight
líquido/a *adj./m.* liquid
lirio *m.* lily
lista *f.* list
lista de espera waiting list
lista de éxitos best-seller list

pasar lista to call roll
listo/a *adj.* smart; ready
  estar listo/a to be ready
  ser listo/a to be smart
literal *adj.* literal
  Es una traducción demasiado literal; no suena natural. It's too literal a translation; it doesn't sound natural.
literario/a *adj.* literary
literatura *f.* literature
litro *m.* liter
liviano/a *adj.* light
llamada *f.* call
  llamada telefónica telephone call
llamar *v.t.* to call
  llamar a cobro revertido to call collect
  llamar la atención (a) to attract attention (to)
  llamar por teléfono to call on the phone
llamarse *v. pron.* to be called; to be named
  Me llamo… My name is…
llanta *f.* tire
llanura *f.* prairie
llave *f.* key
  llave maestra master key
llavero *m.* key chain
llegada *f.* arrival
llegar *v.i.* to arrive
  llegar a ser to become
  llegar tarde to be late
llenar *v.t.* to fill; (*form*) (*L.A.*) to fill out
  llenar el tanque to fill the tank

llenar un formulario to fill out a form
lleno/a *adj.* full
llevar *v.t.* to carry, to take (someone somewhere); (*clothes*) to wear **¿Qué es eso que llevas puesto?** What's that you're wearing?
  llevar una vida sana to lead a healthy lifestyle
llevarse *v. pron.* to take
  Puedes llevártelo. You can take it.
  llevarse bien/mal (con) to get along well/badly/poorly (with)
llorar *v.i.* to cry
lloriquear *v.i.* to whine
llorón, llorona *adj./m., f.* crybaby
llover (o:ue) *v. impers.* to rain
  llover a cántaros *idiom* to pour, to rain cats and dogs
  Llueve. It's raining.
lluvia *f.* rain
  lluvia ácida acid rain
lo *d.o. pron.* it, him, *form.* you
  Dilo. Say it.
  Díselo. Say it to him.
  lo pasamos de película we had a great time
  lo que what; that which
lobo *m.* wolf
loco/a *adj.* crazy
  loco de remate stark raving mad
locomotora *f.* locomotive
locura *f.* madness
locutor(a) *m., f.* (*TV, radio*) announcer

lograr *v.t.* to achieve
logro *m.* achievement
lombriz *f.* earthworm
lomo *m.* flank steak
  lomo a la plancha grilled flank steak
lona *f.* canvas
lonchera *f.* (*L.A.*) lunch box
longevidad *f.* longevity
loro *m.* parrot
los *m.*, *pl. art.*, *def.* the
los *d.o. pron. m. pl.* them, *form.* you
lucha *f.* fight, struggle
luchar (por/contra) *v.i.* to fight, to struggle (for/against)
lucir (c:zc) *v.* to look good
luego *adv.* afterwards, then; later
  desde luego *idiom* of course
  ¡Hasta luego! See you later.
  Y luego qué. And then what?
lugar *m.* place
lujo *m.* luxury
lujoso/a *adj.* luxurious
luna *f.* moon
  luna de miel honeymoon
lunar *m.* mole, beauty mark; polka dot
  una corbata de lunares a polka-dot tie
lunes *m.*, *sing.* Monday
lupa *f.* magnifying glass
luz *f.* light, electricity
  Apaga la luz. Turn out the light.
  la luz del sol sunlight

M

maceta *f.* flower pot

macho *m.* male
madera *f.* wood
madrastra *f.* stepmother
madre *f.* mother
madrina *f.* godmother
madrugada *f.* early morning
madrugar *v.i.* to get up early
madurez *f.* maturity; middle age
maduro/a *adj.* (*person*) mature; (*fruit*) ripe
maestría *f.* (*L.A.*) Master's degree
maestro/a *m.*, *f.* (*elementary school*) teacher
magia *f.* magic
mágico/a *adj.* magical
magma *m.* magma
magnesio *m.* magnesium
magnífico/a *adj.* magnificent
mago/a *m.*, *f.* magician
maíz *m.* corn
mal *adv.* bad, ill
maleducado/a *adj.* rude, bad-mannered
maleta *f.* suitcase
maletero *m.* (*Spain*) (*automobile*) trunk
malgastar *v.t.* to waste
  No malgastes tu tiempo en tonterías. Don't waste your time with stupid little things.
maligno *adj.* (*tumor*) malignant
malo/a *adj.* bad; mean
  ¡Mala suerte! Unlucky!
  ¡Qué película más mala! What a terrible movie!
  (No) Es malo que... It's (not) bad that...

No es malo que lo digas. It's not bad that you say it.

mamá *f.* mom

mami *f.* mom

mamífero *m.* mammal

manantial *m.* (*water*) spring

mandar *v.t.* to order; to send; to mail

mandarina *f.* tangerine

manejar *v.i.* to drive

manera *f.* way

de ninguna manera by no means; no way

manga *f.* sleeve

manguera *f.* hose

manicomio *m.* mental hospital

manicura *f.* manicure

manifestación *f.* demonstration

manifestante *m., f.* demonstrator

manillar *m.* (*Spain*) (*bike*) handlebars

maniquí *m.* mannequin

mano *f.* hand

manta *f.* blanket

mantel *m.* tablecloth

mantener (e:ie) *v.t. irreg.* **(yo mantengo)** to maintain, to support; to keep

Mantengan la calma. Stay calm.

Mantener las apariencias. Keep up appearances.

¿Quién va a mantener a la familia? Who's going to support the family?

mantenerse en forma (e:ie) *v. pron. irreg.* **(yo me mantengo)** to stay in shape

mantequilla *f.* butter

manzana *f.* apple

mañana *f.* morning, a.m.; *adv.* tomorrow

a las dos de la mañana at two in the morning, at two a.m.

mañanitas *f. pl.* birthday song

mapa *m.* map

mapa de carreteras road map

maquillador(a) *m., f.* makeup artist

maquillaje *m.* makeup

maquillar *v.t.* to apply makeup

maquillarse *v. pron.* to put on makeup

máquina *f.* machine

máquina de afeitar razor

máquina de coser sewing machine

máquina de escribir typewriter

mar *m.* sea, ocean

en alta mar on the high sea

maratón *m.* marathon

maravillosamente *adv.* marvelously

maravilloso/a *adj.* marvelous

marca *f.* mark; (*commerce*) brand, brand name; (*sport*) record

Es una marca de prestigio. It's a well-known brand.

Superó su marca. She beat her own record.

marcador *m.* (*sports*) scoreboard

marcapasos *m., sing.* pacemaker

marcar *v.t.* (*telephone*) to dial; (*sports*) to score

Marca el 007. Dial 007.
¿Quién marcó el gol de la victoria? Who scored the winning goal?
marea *f.* tide
  marea alta/baja high/low tide
  marea negra oil slick
mareado/a *adj.* dizzy; nauseated
marearse *v. pron.* to get dizzy
  ¿Te mareas en barco? Do you get seasick?
maremoto *m.* seaquake; tidal wave
margarina *f.* margarine
margarita *f.* daisy
marinero *m.* sailor
mariposa *f.* butterfly
mariscada *f.* assorted seafood
mariscos *m., pl.* shellfish; seafood
mármol *m.* marble
marrón *adj./m.* brown
martes *m., sing.* Tuesday
martillo *m.* hammer
marzo *m.* March
más *adv./ pron.* more **¿Quieres más?** Would you like some more?
  más de (+ *number*) more than **Hay más de diez personas.** There are more than ten people.
  más o menos so so
  más… que more… than **más grande que una casa** bigger than a house
  más tarde later
masa *f.* dough

masaje *m.* massage
masajista *m.* masseur; *f.* masseuse
máscara *f.* mask
mascarilla *f.* mask
masticar *v.t.* to chew
matar *v.t.* to kill
  matar dos pájaros de un tiro *loc.* to kill two birds with one stone
matarse *v. pron.* to kill oneself
  Se mata estudiando. She studies like crazy.
matemáticas *f., pl.* mathematics
matemático/a *m., f.* mathematician
materia *f.* matter; (*school*) subject; course
  materia inorgánica inorganic matter
  ¿Qué materia enseña la Srta. López? What subject does Miss López teach?
materialista *adj.* materialistic
materno/a *adj.* (*relative*) maternal
matrícula *f.* (*education*) registration, matriculation; (*automobile*) registration number, license plate
  matrícula de honor (*grade*) distinction, magna cum laude
matricularse *v. pron.* (*education*) to register, to enroll
matrimonio *m.* marriage
máximo/a *m.* maximum, top
mayo *m.* May
mayonesa *f.* mayonnaise

mayor *adj.* older
el/la mayor the oldest; the eldest
mayordomo *m.* butler
mayoría *f.* majority
me *pron.* me
Dámelo. Give it to me.
mecánico/a *m., f.* mechanic
mecanismo *m.* mechanism
mecanógrafo/a *m., f.* typist
mecedora *f.* rocking chair
mecer (c:z) *v.t.* to rock
medalla *f.* medal
mediano/a *adj.* medium
medianoche *f.* midnight
medias *f., pl.* pantyhose, stockings
medicamento *m.* medication
medicina *f.* medicine
medición *f.* measurement
médico/a *m., f.* doctor; physician
médico de cabecera family doctor
médico de familia family doctor
médico/a de guardia doctor on call, doctor on duty
médico/a *adj.* medical
tratamiento médico medical treatment
medida *f.* measurement, size
medio/a *m.* half
medio ambiente *m.* environment
medio/a hermano/a *m.* half-brother; *f.* half-sister
mediocre *adj.* mediocre
mediodía *m.* noon, midday
medios *m., pl.* means; resources

los medios de comunicación (the) media; means of comunication
medir (e:i) *v.t.* to measure
meditación *f.* meditation
meditar *v.i.* to meditate
médula *f.* marrow
medusa *f.* jellyfish
megáfono *m.* megaphone
mejilla *f.* cheek
mejillón *m.* mussel
mejor *adj.* better; best
el/la mejor *m., f.* the best
lo mejor the best (thing)
Es mejor que… It's better that…
Es mejor que vayas. It's better that you go.
mejor que *adj.* better than
mejora *f.* improvement
mejorar *v.t.* to improve
mejorarse *v. pron.* to get better
mellizo/a *m., f.* twin
melocotón *m.* (*Spain*) peach
melón *m.* melon
membrana *f.* membrane
memoria *f.* memory
de memoria *adv.* by heart
Se sabe el poema de memoria. He knows the poem by heart.
memorizar *v.t.* to memorize
mendigo/a *m., f.* beggar
menopausia *f.* menopause
menor *adj.* younger
el/la menor *m., f.* the youngest
menos *adv.* less
a menos que *conj.* unless **Iré a menos que llueva.** I'll go unless it rains.

menos cuarto/quince quarter to/of **Son las dos menos cuarto/quince.** It's a quarter to/of two.

menos de (+ *number***)** less/fewer than **Tengo menos de una hora.** I have less than an hour.

menos… que less… than **¿Qué es menos interesante que hablar?** What's less interesting than talking?

por lo menos at least

mensaje *m.* message

mensaje electrónico e-mail message

mensualidad *f.* (*monthly payment*) installment

menta *f.* mint

mentalidad *f.* mentality

mentir (e:ie) *v.i.* to lie

mentira *f.* lie

parecer mentira *idiom* to be hard to believe; to be incredible

Aunque parezca mentira, sólo tiene diez años. It's hard to believe, but he's only ten.

mentiroso/a *adj.* liar

menú *m.* menu

menudo/a *adj.* tiny, minute

a menudo *adv.* frequently, often

mercadillo *m.* street market

mercado *m.* market

mercado al aire libre open-air market

mercurio *m.* mercury

merecer (c:zc) *v.t.* to deserve

merendar (e:ie) *v.i.* to snack (in the afternoon); to have an afternoon snack

merienda *f.* afternoon snack

mérito *m.* merit

merluza *f.* (*fish*) hake

mermelada *f.* jam

mes *m.* month

mesa *f.* table

mesa de noche night table

mesero/a *m.* waiter; *f.* waitress

meseta *f.* plateau

mesita *f.* end table

mesita de noche night stand

meta *f.* objective, goal

metabolismo *m.* metabolism

metabolizar *v.t.* to metabolize

metáfora *f.* metaphor

metafórico/a *adj.* metaphoric

metal *m.* metal

metamorfosis *f.* metamorphosis

meteorito *m.* meteorite

meteorólogo/a *m., f.* meteorologist

meter *v.t.* to put (into)

meter la pata put one's foot in one's mouth

metereología *f.* meteorology

metódico/a *adj.* methodical

método *m.* method

metro *m.* meter; subway

mexicano/a *adj./m., f.* Mexican

México *m.* Mexico

mezclar *v.t.* to mix, to toss

mezquita *f.* mosque

mí *pron.* me

¿Para mí? For me?

mi(s) *poss.* my

micrófono *m.* microphone

microonda *f.* microwave

microondas, (el) *m.* microwave (oven)

73

microscopio *m.* microscope
miedo *m.* fear
  No tengas miedo. Don't be
  afraid.
miel *f.* honey
miembro *m.* member; (*body*)
  limb
mientras *adv.* while
  mientras tanto meanwhile
miércoles *m., sing.*
  Wednesday
mil *m.* one thousand
  a las mil y una very late
  Anoche llegó a las mil y una.
  Last night he arrived very late.
  Mil perdones. I'm extremely
  sorry.
milagro *m.* miracle
milla *f.* mile
millón *m.* million
  mil millones a billion (*US*)
  millones (de) millions (of)
mimbre *m.* wicker
mina *f.* mine
mineral *m.* mineral
minería *f.* mining industry
minero/a *m., f.* miner
minifalda *f.* miniskirt
mínimo/a *adj./m.* minimum
  como mínimo at least
ministro/a *m., f.* (*government*)
  minister
minoría *f.* minority
minúsculo/a *adj.* minute, tiny
minuto *m.* minute
mío/a(s) *poss.* my, (of) mine
miope *adj.* myopic
miopía *f.* myopia
mirar *v.t.* to watch, to see, to
  look at

mirar (la) televisión to watch
  television
misil *m.* missile
mismo/a *adj.* same
misterioso/a *adj.* mysterious
mitad *f.* half, middle
mitin *m.* political meeting
mochila *f.* backpack
moda *f.* fashion
  ir a la moda *v.* to be
  fashionably dressed or
  trendy
  de moda in fashion
módem *m.* modem
modernizar *v.t.* to modernize
moderno/a *adj.* modern, trendy
modificar *v.t.* to modify
modista *f.* dressmaker
modo *m.* way, manner; (*verb
  tense*) mood **¿el modo
  subjuntivo o el indicativo?**
  the subjunctive or the
  indicative mood?
  de ningún modo by no
  means
  de todos modos anyway; in
  any case
moho *m.* mold
mojado/a *adj.* wet
mojar *v.t.* to wet, to get wet
mojarse *v. pron.* to get
  (oneself) wet
  **Salí sin paraguas y me mojé
  toda.** I went out without an
  umbrella and I got all wet.
molestar *v.t.* to bother, to
  annoy; to disturb
  **No le molestes, está
  estudiando.** Don't disturb
  him, he's studying.

Deja de molestarme, estoy pensando. Stop bothering me, I'm thinking.

Este ruido me molesta. This noise annoys me.

molestia *f.* inconvenience, bother

No es ninguna molestia. It's no bother at all.

molesto/a *adj.* upset

molino *m.* (*machine, factory*) mill

momento *m.* moment

monarca *m., f.* monarch

monarquía *f.* monarchy

monasterio *m.* monastery

mondadientes *m.* toothpick

moneda *f.* coin

monedero *m.* coin purse

monitor *m.* (*computer*) monitor

monitor(a) *m., f.* trainer, coach, instructor

monitor de esquí ski instructor

monja *f.* nun

monje *m.* monk

mono *m.* monkey

monólogo *m.* monologue

montacargas *m.* forklift

montaña *f.* mountain

montar *v.t.* (*bike*) to ride; (*machine, furniture*) to assemble

montar a caballo to ride a horse

¿Aún no has montado el escritorio? You still haven't assembled the desk?

monumento *m.* monument

mora *f.* blackberry

morado/a *adj.* purple

moral *f.* moral

moralidad *f.* morality

morder (o:ue) *v.t.* to bite

mordisco *m.* bite

moreno/a *adj.* brunet(te), dark-skinned, tanned

morfología *f.* morphology

moribundo/a *adj.* moribund, dying

morir (o:ue) *v.i.* to die

Me muero por ir. I'm dying to go.

Me muero por un beso. I'm dying for a kiss.

mortalidad *f.* mortality

mosca *f.* fly

mosquitero *m.* mosquito net

mostaza *f.* mustard

mostrar (o:ue) *v.t.* to show

moto *f.* motorcycle

motocicleta *f.* motorcycle

motociclismo *m.* motorcycling

motociclista *m., f.* motorcyclist

motor *m.* motor, engine

móvil *adj.* mobile

movilidad *f.* mobility

mozo/a (*L.A.*) *m.* waiter; *f.* waitress

muchacho/a *m., f.* boy; *f.* girl

muchísimo/a *adj. (superlative)* very much

Muchísimas gracias. Thank you very much.

mucho/a(s) *adj.* many; a lot of; much; *adv.* a lot

muchas veces many times; a lot

Mucho gusto. Pleased/Nice to meet you.

mudanza *f.* move
mudar *v.t.* to move, to change
Las serpientes mudan de piel cada año. Snakes change their skin each year.
mudarse *v. pron.* to move (from one house to another)
¿Cuántas veces te has mudado este año? How many times have you moved this year?
mudo/a *adj.* mute
muebles *m., pl.* furniture
muela *f.* molar, back tooth; (*generic*) tooth **Me sacaron una muela.** I had a tooth pulled.
muela del juicio wisdom tooth
muelle *m.* spring
muerte *f.* death
muerto/a *p.p. of* **morir** died; *adj.* dead
Estoy muerto de hambre. I'm starving.
muestra *f.* sample
mujer *f.* woman
mujer de negocios businesswoman
mujer policía female police officer
mujeriego *m.* womanizer
multa *f.* fine, ticket
multitud *f.* crowd
mundial *adj.* worldwide
mundo *m.* world
municipal *m.* municipal
muñeca/o *m., f.* doll; *f.* wrist
muralla *f.* wall
murciélago *m.* (*animal*) bat

muro *m.* wall
músculo *m.* muscle
musculoso/a *adj.* muscular
museo *m.* museum
música *f.* music
poner la música muy alta to play loud music
musical *adj.* musical
músico/a *m., f.* musician
muslo *m.* thigh
musulmán, musulmana *adj./m., f.* Muslim
muy *adv.* very
Muy amable. That's very kind of you.
Muy bien, gracias. Very well, thank you/thanks

N

nacer (c:zc) *v.i.* to be born
nacimiento *m.* birth
nación *f.* nation
Naciones Unidas United Nations **Ése es el edificio de las Naciones Unidas.** That's the UN building.
nacional *adj.* national
nacionalidad *f.* nationality
nacionalismo *m.* nationalism
nacionalista *adj.* nationalist
nada *pron./adv.* nothing, (not) anything
De nada. You're welcome.
No está nada mal. It's not bad at all.
No me gustan nada. I don't like them at all.
nada mal not bad at all
nadador(a) *m., f.* swimmer
nadar *v.i.* to swim

nadie *pron.* no one, nobody, not anyone, anybody
  No lo sabe nadie. Nobody knows it.
naipe *m.* playing card
naranja *f.* orange
naranjo *m.* orange tree
nariz *f.* nose
narrador(a) *m., f.* narrator
nata *f.* (*Spain*) cream; (*on boiled milk*) skin
natación *f.* swimming
  natación sincronizada synchronized swimming
natalidad *f.* birthrate
natural *adj.* natural
naturaleza *f.* nature
naturalmente *adv.* naturally; of course
navaja *f.* jackknife, penknife
navegar *v.i.* to sail
  navegar (en Internet/la red) to surf (the Internet/Web)
Navidad *f.* Christmas
necesario/a *adj.* necessary
  (No) Es necesario que... It's (not) necessary that...
  No es necesario que te quedes. It's not necessary that you stay.
neceser *m.* toilet kit
necesidad *f.* necessity
necesitar (+ *inf.*) *v.t.* to need
nectarina *f.* nectarine
negación *f.* refusal
negar (e:ie) *v.t.* to deny
  no negar not to deny
negarse (e:ie) *v. pron.* to refuse
negativo/a *m.* negative

negocios *m., pl.* business, commerce
negro/a *adj./m.* (*color*) black
nervio *m.* nerve
nervioso/a *adj.* nervous
neumático *m.* tire
neurona *f.* neuron
nevar (e:ie) *v. impers.* to snow
  Nieva. It's snowing.
ni *conj.* nor
  ni... ni *conj.* neither... nor
  Ni tú ni yo. Neither you nor I.
niebla *f.* fog
nieto/a *m.* grandson; *f.* granddaughter
nieve *f.* snow
ningún, ninguno/a(s) *adj.* no; none; not any
  ningún problema no problem
  ninguna parte, (a) nowhere
niñero/a *m., f.* baby-sitter
niñez *f.* childhood
niño/a *m., f.* child, kid
  de niño/a as a child
  niño/a mimado/a spoiled child, brat
nitrógeno *m.* nitrogen
nivel *m.* level
no *adv.* no; not
  No es así. That's not the way it is.
  No muy bien. Not very well.
  No, no vengo. No, I'm not coming.
  Vienes, ¿no? You're coming, right?
  ¿Vienes o no? Are you coming or not?
noche *f.* night, evening
  de la noche in the evening,

at night, P.M. **a las diez de la noche** at ten P.M.
  por la noche at night
nogal *m.* walnut tree
nombre *m.* name
  en mi nombre in my name
  en nombre de on behalf of, in the name of
  nombre de pila first name
nórdico/a *adj.* Nordic; *m., f.* Northern European
norte *m.* north
  al norte to the north
norteamericano/a *adj./m., f.* (North) American
nos *pron.* us, ourselves, each other
  Nos vemos. See you.
nosotros/as *pron.* we, us
  entre nosotros/as between us; off the record
nota *f.* (*school*) grade, mark, note
notar *v.t.* to notice
noticias *f., pl.* news
noticiero *m.* newscast
novatada *f.* practical joke
  hacer una novatada (a alguien) *v.* to haze (somebody)
novato/a *adj.* inexperienced, new
novecientos/as nine hundred
noveno/a *adj./m.* ninth
noventa ninety
noviembre *m.* November
novillo *m.* steer
  hacer novillos *(Spain)* to play hooky
novio/a *m.,* boyfriend; *f.* girlfriend

nube *f.* cloud
nublado/a *adj.* cloudy
  Está (muy) nublado. It's (very) cloudy.
nuclear *adj.* nuclear
núcleo *m.* nucleus
nuera *f.* daughter-in-law
nuestro/a(s) *poss.* our
nueve nine
nuevo/a *adj.* new
  de nuevo again
nuez *f.* walnut
número *m.* number; (*shoe*) size
nunca *adv.* never; not ever
nutrición *f.* nutrition
nutricionista *m., f.* nutritionist

Ñ

ñame *m.* yam

O

o *conj.* or
  o... o *conj.* either... or
  O te quedas o te vas. Either you stay or you go.
obedecer (c:zc) *v.t.* to obey
obesidad *f.* obesity
obeso/a *adj.* obese
objetivo/a *m.* objective; aim, goal
objeto *m.* object; purpose
  ¿Cuál es el objeto de esta discusión? What's the purpose of this argument?
obligar *v.t.* to force, to oblige; to make
  (a alguien a + *inf.***)**
  No le obligues a estudiar. Don't force him to study.

(a alguien a que + *subj*.)
**No me obligues a que lo
diga.** Don't make me say it.
obra *f.* (*of art, literature, music,
etc.*) work
obra maestra masterpiece
observación *f.* observation
observador(a) *adj.* observant
observatorio *m.* observatory
observar *v.t.* to observe
obtener (e:ie) *v.t. irreg.* **(yo
obtengo)** to obtain; to get
obvio/a *adj.* obvious
Es obvio (que...) It's obvious
(that...)
océano *m.* ocean; sea
ochenta eighty
ocho eight
ochocientos/as eight hundred
ocio *m.* leisure time
ocioso/a *adj.* idle
ocre *m.* ocher
octavo/a *adj./m.* eighth
octubre *m.* October
oculista *m., f.* optician
ocupación *f.* occupation
ocupado/a *adj.* busy
ocurrir *v. impers.* to occur; to
happen
Ocurrió lo inesperado. The
unexpected happened.
odiar *v.t.* to hate
oeste *m.* west
al oeste to the west
ofender *v.t.* to offend
ofenderse *v. pron.* to take
offense
ofensa *f.* insult
oferta *f.* offer
oficina *f.* office

oficio *m.* trade
ofrecer (c:zc) *v.t.* to offer
ofrenda *f.* offering
oftalmólogo/a *m., f.*
ophthalmologist
oído *m.* (*sense of*) hearing;
inner ear
oído *p.p. of* **oír** heard
oír (y) *v.t./v.i. irreg.* **(yo oigo)** to
hear
oiga(n) *form., sing. pl.* listen
(*in conversation*)
oír decir que *idiom* to have
heard that **He oído decir que
te casas.** I've heard that you
are getting married.
oye *fam., sing.* listen (*in
conversation*)
¡Ojalá! *interj.* I hope so!
Ojalá (que) I hope (that); I
wish (that)
Ojalá que vuelva pronto.
I hope/Hopefully he comes
back soon.
Ojalá no llueva mañana.
I hope/wish it doesn't rain
tomorrow.
ojo *m.* eye
ola *f.* wave
oler (a) *v.i. irreg.* to smell (like)
Huele a humo aquí. It smells
like smoke here.
olfato *m.* (*sense*) smell
olimpiada/olimpiadas *f./f., pl.*
Olympic Games, Olympics
Olimpiadas Especiales
Special Olympics
olímpico/a *adj.* Olympic
olla *f.* cooking pot
olla a presión pressure
cooker

79

olor *m.* smell, odor
  el olor de la primavera the smell of spring
  olor corporal body odor
olvidar *v.t.* to forget
ombligo *m.* navel
omoplato *m.* scapula
once eleven
oncólogo/a *m., f.* oncologist
onda *f.* (*physics, radio*) wave
onza *f.* ounce
opaco/a *adj.* opaque
ópera *f.* opera
operación *f.* operation
opinar *v.t.* to express an opinion
opinión *f.* opinion
  en mi opinión in my opinion
oportunidad *f.* opportunity
optimista *adj./m., f.* optimist, optimistic
orden *m.* order, sequence; *f.* order, command
  A sus órdenes. At your service.
ordenado/a *adj.* orderly; well-organized
ordenador *m.* (*Spain*) computer
ordinal *adj.* ordinal
orégano *m.* oregano
oreja *f.* (*outer*) ear
organización *f.* organization; arrangement
organizar *v.t.* to organize; to arrange
órgano *m.* organ
  órganos de los sentidos sensory organs
orgullo *m.* pride
orgulloso/a *adj.* proud

original *adj.* original
originalidad *f.* originality
orilla *f.* shore, (river)bank
  La casa está a orillas del mar. The house is on the seashore.
orina *f.* urine
orinar *v.i.* to urinate
oro *m.* gold
orquesta *f.* orchestra
ortografía *f.* spelling
ortográfico/a *adj.* spelling
os *fam., pl.* you
  ¿Os gusta? Do you like it?
osito *m.* teddy bear
oso/a *m., f.* bear
  Osa Mayor Big Dipper
  Osa Menor Little Dipper
ostra *f.* oyster
otoño *m.* autumn, fall
otro/a *adj.* other; another
  otra vez again
oveja *f.* sheep
OVNI (Objeto Volador No Identificado) *m.* UFO (Unidentified Flying Object)
oxidarse *v. pron.* to rust
óxido *m.* rust
oxígeno *m.* oxygen
oyentes *m., pl.* listeners

P

paciencia *f.* patience
paciente *adj./m., f.* patient
pacifista *adj./m., f.* pacifist
padecer de (c:zc) *v.i.* (*disease*) to suffer from
  Padece del corazón. He has heart problems.
padecimiento *m.* suffering

padrastro *m.* stepfather
padre *m.* father; priest
padres *m., pl.* parents
padrino *m.* godfather
pagar *v.t.* to pay
  pagar a plazos to pay in installments
  pagar al contado to pay in cash
  pagar en efectivo to pay in cash
  pagar la cuenta to pay the bill
página *f.* page
  página principal home page
país *m.* country
  país desarrollado developed country
  país en vías de desarrollo developing country
paisaje *m.* landscape; countryside
pájaro *m.* bird
pala *f.* shovel
palabra *f.* word
palacio *m.* palace
paladar *m.* palate
palanca *f.* lever
paleontología *f.* paleontology
paleontólogo/a *m., f.* paleontologist
pálido/a *adj.* pale, pallid
palmera *f.* palm tree
palo *m.* stick; (*golf*) club
  de tal palo, tal astilla *loc.* like father, like son
paloma *f.* dove
pan *m.* bread
  pan integral whole-wheat bread

  pan tostado toasted bread; toast
panadería *f.* bakery
páncreas *m.* pancreas
pandilla *f.* gang
pandillero/a *m., f.* gang member
pantaletas *f., pl.* (*Venezuela*) panties
pantalla *f.* screen
pantalones *m., pl.* pants
  pantalones cortos shorts
pantano *m.* (*natural*) marsh, swamp; (*man-made*) reservoir
pantorrilla *f.* (anatomy) calf
pantuflas *f., pl.* slippers
pañuelo *m.* handkerchief
papa *f.* (*L.A.*) potato
  papas fritas fried potatoes; French fries
papá *m.* dad
papás *m., pl.* parents
papel *m.* paper; *m.* role
  papel de aluminio tinfoil
  papel higiénico toilet paper
  hacer un buen/mal papel *idiom* to make a good/bad impression
papelera *f.* wastebasket
papi *m.* daddy
paquete *m.* package
par *m.* pair
  un par de días a couple of days
  un par de zapatos a pair of shoes
para *prep.* for; in order to
  para que so that
parabrisas *m., sing.* windshield

paracaídas *m., sing.* parachute
paracaidismo *m.* parachuting
paracaidista *m., f.* parachutist
parachoques *m., sing.* bumper
parada *f.* (*train, bus*) stop
parador *m.* lodging
paraguas *m.* umbrella
paragüero *m.* umbrella stand
parar(se) *v.i.* to stop
pararrayos *m.* lightning rod
parásito *m.* parasite
parecer (c:zc) *v.i.* to seem; to appear
  al parecer *adv.* apparently, seemingly
parecerse (c:zc) (a alguien/a algo) *v. pron.* to look like (*somebody/something*); to be alike
  ¿A quién se parece? Who does he/she look like?
pared *f.* wall
pareja *f.* partner; (married) couple
  ¿Cuántas parejas vienen a cenar? How many couples are coming for dinner?
parientes *m., pl.* relatives
párpado *m.* eyelid
parque *m.* park
  parque acuático water park
  parque de atracciones (*Spain*) amusement park
  parque de diversiones (*L.A.*) amusement park
  parque natural nature reserve
párrafo *m.* paragraph
parrilla *f.* grill
  a la parrilla grilled, broiled

parte *f.* part
  de parte de on behalf of
participación *f.* participation
participante *m., f.* competitor
participar *v.t.* to participate
particular *adj.* private
partida *f.* departure
partido *m.* (*sports*) game, match; (*politics*) party
partir *v.t.* to cut; *v.i.* to leave
  a partir de from, starting (on)
pasa *f.* raisin
pasado *p.p. of* **pasar** passed
pasado/a *adj.* last; past
  el pasado lunes last Monday
pasaje *m.* ticket
  pasaje de ida y vuelta roundtrip ticket
pasajero/a *m., f.* passenger
pasamanos *m.* handrail, bannister
pasaporte *m.* passport
pasar *v.i.* to go by; to pass
  pasar la aspiradora to vacuum
  pasar por el banco to go by the bank
  pasar por la aduana to go through customs
  pasar tiempo to spend time
  pasarlo bien/mal to have a good/bad time
  pasar de película to have a great time
pasarse (el alto/el semáforo en rojo) *v. pron.* to run a red light
pasatiempo *m.* pastime; hobby
pasear *v.i.* to take a walk; to stroll

pasear en bicicleta to ride a bicycle
pasear por la ciudad/el pueblo to walk around the city/town
paseo *m.* stroll, walk
pasillo *m.* hallway
paso *m.* step; way
  paso a nivel railroad crossing
  paso de peatones (*L.A.*) crosswalk
  ceder el paso to yield (the right of way)
pasta de dientes *f.* toothpaste
pastel *m.* cake; pie
  pastel de chocolate chocolate cake
  pastel de cumpleaños birthday cake
pastelería *f.* pastry shop
pastilla *f.* pill; tablet
pasto *m.* lawn, grass
patata *f.* (*Spain*) potato
  patatas fritas fried potatoes, French fries
  tortilla de patatas potato omelet
paterno/a *adj.* (*relative*) paternal
patilla *f.* sideburn
patinaje *m.* skating
  patinaje artístico figure skating
  patinaje sobre hielo ice skating
  patinaje sobre ruedas roller skating
patinar *v.i.* to skate
  patinar en hielo to ice skate

  patinar en línea to rollerblade; to skate in-line
patio *m.* patio; yard
patrimonio *m.* heritage
patrocinador(a) *m., f.* sponsor
patrocinar *v.t.* to sponsor
patrón *m.* boss, owner
pavo *m.* turkey
payaso/a *m., f.* clown
paz *f.* peace
peatón *m.* pedestrian
peca *f.* freckle
pecho *m.* chest; breast
pechuga (de pollo) *f.* (chicken) breast
pecoso/a *adj.* freckled
pedagogía *f.* pedagogy
pedagógico/a *adj.* pedagogical
pedagogo/a *m., f.* pedagogue
pedal *m.* pedal
  pedal del acelerador gas pedal
  pedal del embrague clutch pedal
  pedal del freno brake pedal
pedante *adj.* pedantic
pedazo *m.* piece
pedicura *f.* pedicure
pedir (e:i) *v.t.* to ask (for); to request; (*food*) to order
  pedir prestado to borrow
  pedir un préstamo to apply for a loan
pegar *v.t.* to hit; to glue; to stick
peinado *m.* hairstyle; hairdo
  Su nuevo peinado le sienta bien. Her new hairdo suits her.
peinarse *v. pron.* to comb one's hair

peine *m.* comb
pelapapas *m.* peeler
pelar *v.t.* to peel
peldaño *m.* step, stair
pelea *f.* quarrel, fight
pelearse *v. pron.* to quarrel, to fight
  Siempre se pelean por lo mismo. They always quarrel over the same thing.
película *f.* movie
peligro *m.* danger
peligroso/a *adj.* dangerous
pelirrojo/a *adj.* red-headed, red-hair
pelo *m.* hair
pelota *f.* ball; baseball
peluca *f.* wig
peludo/a *adj.* hairy
peluquería *f.* beauty salon
peluquero/a *m., f.* hairdresser
pena *f.* ache, grief, pity
  No vale la pena. It's not worth the trouble.
pendiente *adj.* (*problem, matter*) unresolved
  estar pendiente to be waiting
  Estoy pendiente de que el jefe me llame. I'm waiting for the boss to call me.
  tener (un asunto) pendiente to have (an) unfinished (matter)
pendientes *m.* (*Spain*) earrings
penicilina *f.* penicillin
península *f.* peninsula
penitenciaría *f.* penitentiary
pensar (e:ie) (en) *v.t.* to think (about)
  pensar (+ inf.) to intend/plan

(*to do something*)
  Pienso llamarle mañana. I intend to call him tomorrow.
pensión *f.* boardinghouse; retirement pension
pensionista *m., f.* pensioner, retired person
peor *adj.* worse; worst
  el/la peor the worst
  lo peor the worst (thing)
peor que *adv.* worse than
pepino *m.* cucumber
pequeño/a *adj.* small
pera *f.* pear
percha *f.* hanger
perchero *m.* coat hanger
perder (e:ie) *v.t.* to lose; to miss
perdido *p.p. of* **perder** lost;
  perdido/a *adj.* lost
Perdón. Pardon me.; Excuse me.
perdonar *v.t.* to forgive
peregrinación *f.* pilgrimage
peregrino/a *m., f.* pilgrim
perejil *m.* parsley
pereza *f.* laziness
perezoso/a *adj.* lazy
perfecto/a *adj.* perfect
perfil *m.* profile
perforadora *f.* (*tool*) drill
perforar *v.t.* to drill; to perforate
perfume *m.* perfume
perfumería *f.* perfumery
perico *m.* parakeet
perímetro *m.* perimeter
periódico *m.* newspaper
periodismo *m.* journalism
periodista *m., f.* journalist
periquito *m.* parakeet

permanecer (c:zc) *v.i.* to remain; to stay

permiso *m.* permission
 Con permiso. Pardon me., Excuse me.
 Con su permiso, tengo que irme. If you'll excuse me, I have to leave.
 permiso de trabajo work permit

permitir *v.t.* to permit, to allow

pero *conj.* but

perro/a *m., f.* dog

perseguir (e:i) *v.t. irreg.* **(yo persigo)** to pursue; to chase

persiana *f.* blind

persistente *adj.* persistent

persistir *v.i.* to persist

persona *f.* person

personaje *m.* character
 personaje principal main character

personalidad *f.* personality

pertenecer (c:zc) (a) *v.t.* to belong to

pertenencias *f., pl.* belongings

pesa *f.* weight

pesadilla *f.* nightmare

pesado/a *adj.* heavy; annoying

pesar *m.* sorrow
 a pesar de despite, in spite of

pesar *v.t.* to weigh

pesarse *v. pron.* to weigh oneself

pesca *f.* fishing

pescadería *f.* fish market

pescado *m.* (*cooked*) fish

pescador(a) *m., f.* fisherman/fisherwoman

pescar *v.i.* to fish

pesimista *adj.* pessimist, pessimistic

peso *m.* weight

pestaña *f.* eyelash

pesticida *m.* pesticide

pétalo *m.* petal

petrificado/a *adj.* petrified

pez *m.* (*live*) fish
 pez gordo big shot

picante *adj.* spicy

pico *m.* beak

pie *m.* foot

piedra *f.* stone

piel *f.* skin
 de piel (made) of leather

pierna *f.* leg

pijama *m., f.* pajamas

píldora *f.* pill

pimienta *f.* black pepper

pimiento *m.* bell pepper

pinacoteca *f.* art gallery

pinar *m.* pine forest

pinchar *v.t.* (*tire*) to go flat

pingüino *m.* penguin

pino *m.* pine tree

pintada *f.* graffiti
 Hay pintadas de pandillas en la pared. There is gang graffiti on the wall.

pintalabios *m.* lipstick

pintar *v.t.* to paint

pintarse *v. pron.* to put on makeup

pintor(a) *m., f.* painter

pintoresco/a *adj.* picturesque

pintura *f.* painting; picture

piña *f.* pineapple

piñata *f.* container filled with candies

piragua f. canoe
piragüismo m. (sport) canoeing
piragüista m., f. canoeist
pirámide f. pyramid
piropear v.t. to make flattering comments
piropo m. flattering comment
piscina f. swimming pool
  piscina climatizada indoor pool
piso m. (of a building) floor, story; (L.A.) floor; (Spain) apartment
pista f. track; clue
  Dame una pista. Give me a clue.
  pista cubierta indoor track
  pista de aterrizaje landing strip
  pista de atletismo sports track
  pista de baile dance floor
  pista de esquí ski slope
  pista de hielo ice rink
  pista de hierba grass court
  pista de patinaje skating rink
  pista de tenis tennis court
  pista de tierra batida clay court
pizarra f. blackboard
pizarrón m. blackboard
pizca f. (quantity) pinch, little bit
placa (de matrícula) f. license plate
placer m. pleasure; delight
  Ha sido un placer. It's been a pleasure.
plagiar v.t. to plagiarize
plagio m. plagiarism

plancha f. (appliance) iron; griddle
  a la plancha grilled
planchar (la ropa) v.t. to iron (clothes)
plan m. plan
planeta m. planet
planetario m. planetarium
plano m. (architecture) blueprint; city map
plano/a adj. (surface) flat
planta f. plant; (building) floor
  planta baja ground floor
plantado/a: dejar plantado/a (a alguien) to stand (somebody) up
plástico m. plastic
  de plástico (made) of plastic
plata f. silver
plátano m. banana; plantain
plateado/a adj. silver
platillo m. dish
plato m. plate; (meal) dish, course
  plato principal main dish/main course
playa f. beach
plaza f. city or town square
  plaza de toros bullring
  plaza mayor town square
plazo m. (time) period, (payments) installment
plegable adj. folding
plegar v.t. to fold
plomería f. (L.A.) plumbing
plomero/a m., f. (L.A.) plumber
plomo m. lead
pluma f. pen; feather
pluralidad f. plurality
pluralismo m. plurarism

población *f.* population
poblar (o:ue) *v.t.* to populate
pobre *adj.* poor
pobreza *f.* poverty
poco/a *adj.* little; few
poder *m.* power
poder (o:ue) *v. aux.* to be able to; can
poderoso/a *adj.* powerful
podio *m.* podium
poema *m.* poem
poesía *f.* poetry
poeta *m., f.* poet
polémica *f.* controversy
polémico/a *adj.* controversial, polemical
　El aborto es aún un tema polémico. Abortion is still a controversial topic.
polen *m.* pollen
policía *f.* police (force); *m., f.* police officer
polideportivo *m.* sports center
política *f.* politics
político/a *m., f.* politician; *adj.* political
pollo *m.* chicken
　pollo asado roast chicken
polvo *m.* dust
pomelo *m.* (*Argentina, Spain*) grapefruit
ponchar *v.t.* to go flat
poncharse (una llanta) *v. pron.* to have a flat tire
ponchera *f.* punchbowl
poner *v.t. irreg.* (**yo pongo**) to put; to place; *v.i.* to turn on (*electrical appliances*)
　poner a uno al día/al corriente *idiom* to bring

someone up to date
　poner el árbol to decorate the tree
　poner en libertad (a alguien) to release (*somebody*)
　poner la mesa to set the table
　poner una inyección to give an injection
ponerse *v. pron. irreg.* (**yo me pongo**) to put on; to wear
ponerse (+ *adj.*) *v. pron. irreg.* (**yo me pongo**) to become (+ *adj.*)
　ponerse elegante to dress up
　Te has puesto muy elegante esta noche. You have dressed up tonight.
　ponerse rojo/a to blush
por *prep.* for; for the sake of; for; by; in; through; due to; in exchange for
　por aquí around here
　por avión by plane
　por ejemplo for example
　por eso that's why; therefore
　por favor please
　por fin finally
　por la mañana in the morning
　por la noche at night
　por la tarde in the afternoon; in the evening
　por lo menos at least
　por lo visto apparently
　¿por qué? why?
　por supuesto of course
　por teléfono by phone; on the phone
　por último finally

porcentaje *m.* percentage
porche *m.* porch
porción *f.* serving
porque *conj.* because
portaaviones *m., sing.* aircraft carrier
portarse *v. pron.* to behave oneself
  portarse bien/mal to behave well/badly, to behave/misbehave
portátil *adj.* portable
portavoz *m., f.* spokesperson
portero/a *m., f.* doorman, porter
porvenir *m.* future
poseer *v.t.* to own
posesión *f.* possession
posesivo/a *adj.* possessive
posible *adj.* possible
  lo antes posible as soon as possible
  (no) es posible it's (not) possible
postal *f.* postcard
postre *m.* dessert
potencia *f.* power
pozo *m.* well
práctica *f.* practice
practicar *v.i.* to practice
  practicar deportes to play sports
práctico/a *adj.* handy; useful
precaución *f.* precaution
precio *m.* price
precio fijo fixed/set price
predecir (e:i) *v.t. irreg.* **(yo predigo)** to predict, to foretell
predicción *f.* prediction
  predicción del tiempo weather forecast
prefabricado/a *adj.* prefabricated
prefabricar *v.t.* to prefabricate
preferir (e:ie) *v.t.* to prefer
pregunta *f.* question
preguntar *v.t.* to ask (*a question*)
premiar *v.t.* to award
premio *m.* prize; award
prenda *f.* garment
  Colgaron las prendas en el armario. They hung up the garments in the wardrobe.
prender *v.t.* to turn on
prensa *f.* press
preocupado/a (por) *adj.* worried (about)
preocuparse (por) *v. pron.* to worry (about)
  No se/te preocupe(s). Don't worry.
preparar *v.t.* to prepare
prepararse *v. pron.* to get ready
preparativos *m., pl.* preparations
  los preparativos del viaje/para la boda the travel/wedding preparations
preparatoria *f.* high school
preposición *f.* preposition
presa *f.* prey
presentación *f.* introduction
presentador(a) *m., f.* presenter
presentar *v.t.* to introduce; (*performance*) to put on; to present
  Le presento a… *form.* I would like to introduce (*name*) to you.

Te presento a... *fam.* I would like to introduce (*name*) to you.
presidiario/a *m., f.* convict
presión *f.* pressure
  las presiones de la vida diaria pressures of daily life
  presión sanguínea blood pressure
preso/a *m., f.* prisoner
prestación *f.* fringe benefits
prestado/a *adj.* borrowed
préstamo *m.* loan
prestar *v.t.* to lend; to loan
presumido/a *adj.* vain
presupuesto *m.* budget
pretencioso/a *adj.* pretentious
pretexto *m.* excuse
prevención *f.* prevention
prevenir (e:ie) *v.t. irreg.* **(yo prevengo)** to prevent
primaria *f.* grammar school
primavera *f.* spring
primer, primero/a *adj.* first
  en primer lugar *adv.* first of all
primitivo/a *adj.* primitive
primo/a *m., f.* cousin
primogénito/a *m., f.* firstborn
principal *adj.* main
príncipe *m.* prince
princesa *f.* princess
prisa *f.* haste; hurry
  a toda prisa as fast as possible
  ¡De prisa! Hurry!
  sin prisa pero sin pausa slowly but surely
prisión *f.* prison
probable *adj.* probable

(no) es probable it's (not) probable
probador *m.* dressing room
probar (o:ue) *v.t.* to taste; to try
probarse (o:ue) *v. pron.* (*clothes*) to try on
problema *m.* problem
prodigio/a *m., f.* prodigy
prodigioso/a *adj.* exceptional
productos *m., pl.* products
  productos alimenticios foodstuffs
  productos lácteos dairy (products)
profesión *f.* profession
profesor(a) *m., f.* teacher; professor
  profesor(a) particular tutor
profundidad *f.* depth
profundo/a *adj.* deep
programa *m.* program
  programa de computación software
  programa de entrevistas talk show
programador(a) *m., f.* computer programmer
prohibido *p.p. of* **prohibir** prohibited
  prohibido adelantar (*traffic sign*) no passing
  prohibido el paso (*traffic sign*) no entry
prohibir *v.t.* to prohibit; to forbid
prolífico/a *adj.* prolific
promedio *m.* average
promesa *f.* promise
prometer *v.t.* to promise
pronombre *m.* pronoun

pronto *adj.* soon
propagar *v.t.* to propagate, to spread, to disseminate
Algunos periódicos propagan rumores. Some papers disseminate rumors.
propagarse *v. pron.* to propagate, to spread
El rumor se propagaba rápidamente. The rumor was propagating rapidly.
propenso/a a *adj.* prone to
propiedad *f.* property
propietario/a *m., f.* owner, proprietor
propina *f.* tip
propio/a *adj.* own
proponer *v.t. irreg.* **(yo propongo)** to propose
propósito *m.* intention; purpose
a propósito *adv.* on purpose, deliberately
a propósito by the way
buenos propósitos good intentions
propuesta *f.* proposal
protección *f.* protection
proteger (g:j) *v.t.* to protect
proteína *f.* protein
protesta *f.* protest
protestante *adj./m., f.* Protestant
protestar *v.i.* to protest
provecho *m.* benefit
¡Buen provecho! Enjoy your meal!
provisiones *f., pl.* provisions, supplies
provocación *f.* provocation
provocado/a *adj.* induced

provocar *v.t.* to cause; to provoke
próximo/a *adj.* next
proyección *f.* projection
proyectar *v.t.* to project
proyectil *m.* missile
proyecto *m.* project
prueba *f.* test; quiz
prueba de aptitud aptitude test
prueba de la alcoholemia sobriety test
prueba de nivel placement test
(p)sicología *f.* psychology
(p)sicólogo/a *m., f.* psychologist
(p)siquiatra *m., f.* psychiatrist
pubertad *f.* puberty
publicar *v.t.* to publish
público *m.* audience
pueblo *m.* town
puente *m.* bridge
puente colgante suspension bridge
puerta *f.* door
puerta principal front door
puerta trasera back door
puerto *m.* port, harbor
Puerto Rico *m.* Puerto Rico
puertorriqueño/a *adj./m., f.* Puerto Rican
pues *conj.* well; *adv.* then
puesto *m.* position; job; *p.p. of* **poner** put
puesta *f.* **de sol** sunset
pulgar *m.* thumb
pulmón *m.* lung
pulpo *m.* octopus
pulsera *f.* bracelet

punto *m.* point, period
  en punto (*time*) on the dot, exactly, sharp
puntual *adj.* punctual
puñal *m.* dagger
puñalada *f.* stab
puño *m.* fist
pupila *f.* pupil
pupitre *m.* student desk
puro/a *adj.* pure; *adv.* sheer; *m.* cigar
  aceite puro de oliva pure olive oil
  pura casualidad sheer coincidence

Q

que *pron.* that; who; *conj.* that; (*in exclamations*) what; how
  ¡Qué alto eres! How tall you are!
  ¡Qué dolor! What pain!
  ¡Qué extraño! How strange!
  ¡Qué grande! How big!
  ¡Qué gusto (+ *inf.*)! What a pleasure to . . . !
  ¡Qué lata! *loc.* What a drag!
  ¡Qué ropa más bonita! What pretty clothes!
  ¡Qué sorpresa! What a surprise!
¿qué? *adv.* what?
  ¿Qué día es hoy? What day is it?
  ¿Qué hay de nuevo? What's new?; What's happening?
  ¿Qué hora es? What time is it?
  ¿Qué les parece? What do you (*pl.*) think?

  ¿Qué pasa? What's happening?; What's going on?
  ¿Qué pasó? What happened?; What's wrong?
  ¿Qué precio tiene? What is the price?
  ¿Qué tal? How are you?; How is it going?
  ¿Qué tal...? How is/are . . . ?
  ¿Qué talla lleva/usa? What size do you take?
  ¿Qué tiempo hace? What's the weather like?
quedar *v.i.* to be left over; (*clothing*) to fit; to be located; to be left behind
  Ese vestido te queda muy bien. That dress fits you nicely.
  ¿Dónde queda la panadería? Where's the bakery (located)?
  quedar embarazada to get pregnant
quedarse *v. pron.* to stay
  ¡Quédate! Stay!
  quedarse calvo to go bald
  quedarse embarazada to get pregnant
  quedarse soltero/a to stay single
  quedarse viudo/a to be widowed
quehaceres *m., pl.* chores
  quehaceres domésticos household chores
queja *f.* complaint
quejarse (de) *v. pron.* to complain (about)

quemado/a *adj.* burned;
(*figurative*) burned out
quemados *m., pl.* dodge ball
quemar *v.t.* to burn
  No quemes la ropa vieja.
  Don't burn old clothes.
querer (e:ie) *v.t.* to want; to
love
  Quisiera un café. I would like
  a coffee.
  No quiero. I don't want to.
querido/a *adj.* beloved
queso *m.* cheese
quien *pron.* who; whom
  Ella es quien me lo dijo.
  She's the one who told me.
¿quién(es)? who?; whom?
  ¿Quién es...? Who is . . . ?
  ¿Quién habla? Who is
  speaking? (*telephone*)
química *f.* chemistry
químico/a *adj.* chemical; *m., f.*
chemist
quince fifteen
quinceañero/a *m., f.* fifteen-
year-old; teenager
  (fiesta de) quinceañera
  young woman's fifteenth
  birthday celebration
quincena *f.* two weeks,
fortnight
quinientos/as five hundred
quinto/a *adj./m.* fifth
quirófano *m.* operating room
quitar *v.t.* to take away
  **El policía me quitó los
  documentos.** The police
  officer took away my
  documents.
  quitar la mesa to clear the
table
quitarse *v. pron.* (*clothes*) to
take off
  Quítate esos zapatos. Take
  those shoes off.
quizás *adv.* perhaps

R

rábano *m.* radish
rabino/a *m., f.* rabbi
racismo *m.* racism
racista *adj./m., f.* racist
radio *f.* (*medium*) radio; *m.* (*set*)
radio
radiografía *f.* X-ray
radioyente *m., f.* radio listener
raíz *f.* root
rallador *m.* grater
rama *f.* branch
rana *f.* frog
rápido/a *adj.* fast
  comida rápida fast food
rápido *adv.* quickly
  ¡Ven rápido! Come quickly!
raqueta *f.* (*sports*) racket
rascacielos *m.* skyscraper
rastrillo *m.* rake
rasuradora *f.* razor
rato *m.* while **Espera un rato,
por favor.** Wait a while,
please.
  ratos libres *m., pl.* spare/free
  time
ratón *m.* mouse
  ratón de biblioteca
  bookworm
raya *f.* stripe
  de rayas striped
  una camisa de rayas a
  striped shirt

rayo *m.* lightning bolt
raza *f.* race
razón *f.* reason
  Lo hice por dos razones.
  I did it for two reasons.
  Tienes razón. You're right.
  No tienes razón. You're
  wrong.
reacción *f.* reaction
reaccionar *v.i.* to react
real *adj.* royal
realeza *f.* royalty
realizar *v.t.* to carry out; to
  make
rebaja *f.* sale
  de rebaja reduced
rebanada *f.* slice
  una rebanada de pan a slice
  of bread
rebelde *adj.* rebellious
rebobinar *v.t.* to rewind
  **Apriete el botón de
  rebobinar.** Push the rewind
  button.
recado *m.* (*phone*) message
  dejar un recado to leave a
  message
recaudar (fondos) *v.t.* to raise
  (money)
receloso/a *adj.* distrustful
recepción *f.* front desk
receta *f.* prescription;
  (*cooking*) recipe
recetar *v.t.* (*medication*) to
  prescribe
rechazar *v.t.* to reject
rechazo *m.* rejection
recibir *v.t.* to receive; to get
recibirse *v. pron.* to graduate
recibo *m.* receipt; bill

el recibo del teléfono the
  phone bill
reciclaje *m.* recycling
reciclar *v.t.* to recycle
recién *adv.* just
  recién casado/a newlywed
  recién nacido/a newborn
  (baby)
  recién pintado/a wet paint
recipiente *m.* container
recital *m.* (*music, poetry*)
  recital
recoger (g:j) *v.t.* to pick up
recoger la mesa *v.t.* to clear
  the table
recomendable *adj.* advisable
recomendar (e:ie) *v.t.* to
  recommend
reconocer (c:zc) *v.t.* to
  recognize
reconocimiento *m.* recognition
récord *m.* (*sports*) record
recordar (o:ue) *v.t.* to
  remember
recorrer *v.t.* to tour around an
  area
recreo *m.* recess
rectángulo *m.* rectangle
rectificar *v.t.* to rectify
recuerdo *m.* souvenir
recuerdos *m., pl.* regards
recurso *m.* resource
  recurso natural natural
  resource
red *f.* net; network;
  Web
reducir (c:zc) *v.t.* to reduce
reemplazar *v.t.* to replace
reflexionar *v.i.* to reflect
reforma *f.* reform

reformar *v.t.* to reform
reforzar (o:ue) *v.t.* to reinforce
refrán *m.* saying
refrescante *adj.* refreshing
refresco *m.* soft drink, soda
refrigerador *m.* refrigerator
refrigerar *v.t.* to refrigerate
refuerzo *m.* reinforcement
regadera *f.* watering can
regalar *v.t.* to give (a gift)
regalo *m.* gift, present
regañar *v.t.* to scold, to reprimand
regar *v.t.* (*plants*) to water
regatear *v.i.* to bargain
régimen *m.* diet
  Está a régimen. She's on a diet.
región *f.* region; area
regla *f.* rule; ruler
regresar *v.i.* to return
regular *adj.* regular; so so; OK
regular *v.t.* to regulate
regularización *f.* regularization
reído *p.p.* of **reír** laughed
reina *f.* queen
reinar *v.i.* to reign
reino *m.* kingdom
reírse (e:i) *v.i.* (**yo río**) to laugh
reírse (e:i) (de) *v. pron.* (**yo me río**) to laugh (about)
rejuvenecer (c:zc) *v.t.* to rejuvenate
rejuvenecimiento *m.* rejuvenation
relación *f.* relationship
relajación *f.* relaxation
relajarse *v. pron.* to relax
relámpago *m.* lightning bolt
religión *f.* religion

religioso/a *adj.* religious
rellenar *v.t.* (*culinary*) to stuff; (*document*) (*Spain*) to fill out
relleno *m.* stuffing
relleno/a (de) *adj.* stuffed (with)
  Me encantan los chiles rellenos de queso rallado. I love chilies stuffed with grated cheese.
reloj *m.* clock; watch
remar *v.i.* to row
remedio *m.* remedy
remero/a *m., f.* rower
remo *m.* oar
remolacha *f.* beet
remolino *m.* whirlpool; whirlwind
remover (o:ue) *v.t.* to stir
renacentista *adj.* Renaissance
renacimiento *m.* Renaissance
rencor *m.* grudge, resentment, hard feelings
  Todavía siente rencor por lo que le hicieron. She still resents what they did to her.
rencoroso/a *adj.* resentful
renglón *m.* line
  papel con renglones lined paper
renovación *f.* renewal, updating, renovation
renovar (o:ue) *v.t.* to renew, to change, to renovate
renunciar (a) *v.t.* to resign (from)
repelente *m.* (*for insects*) repellent
repente: de repente *adv.* suddenly

repetir (e:i) *v.t.* to repeat

repollo *m.* (*L.A.*) cabbage

reportaje *m.* report

reportero/a *m., f.* reporter; journalist

reposar *v.i.* to rest
  Tenía que reposar por varias semanas después de la operación. He had to rest for several weeks after the operation.

reposo *m.* rest

represa *f.* dam

representante *m., f.* representative

represión *f.* repression

reprimir *v.t.* to repress
  Tuvo que reprimir la emoción. He had to repress his emotion.

reprimirse *v. pron.* (*refl.*) to control oneself

reproducir (c:zc) *v.t.* to repeat, to reproduce
  Es difícil reproducir los resultados. It's difficult to reproduce the results.

reproducirse (c:zc) *v. pron.* (*biology*) to reproduce; to happen again
  Es improbable que se reproduzcan tales circunstancias. It's unlikely that such circumstances will happen again.

reproductor de DVD DVD player

reptil *m.* reptile

resaca *f.* (*Spain*) hangover
  tener resaca to have a hangover

rescatar *v.t.* to rescue

rescate *m.* rescue

reservación *f.* reservation
  hacer una reservación to book

reservado/a *adj.* reserved

resfriado *m.* (*illness*) cold

residencia *f.* residence
  residencia de ancianos home for the elderly
  residencia estudiantil dormitory

residente *adj./m., f.* resident

residir *v.i.* to live, to reside

resistencia *f.* resistance

resistir *v.t.* to resist

resolución *f.* (*problem*) solution; (*conflict*) settlement

resolver (o:ue) *v.t.* to resolve; to solve

respaldar *v.t.* (*person, decision*) to back, to support

respecto: con respecto a with regard to, regarding

respetar *v.t.* to respect

respeto *m.* respect

respiración *f.* breathing, respiration
  respiración boca a boca mouth-to-mouth resuscitation

respirar *v.i.* to breathe

responder *v.t.* to respond, to answer

responsable *adj.* responsible

respuesta *f.* answer

restaurante *m.* restaurant

restaurar *v.t.* to restore

restos *m., pl.* leftovers

resuelto *p.p. of* **resolver** resolved

resultado *m.* result

resumen *m.* summary
en resumen in summary

resumir *v.t.* to summarize
resumiendo summarizing

retar (a alguien a + inf.) *v.t.* to challenge (somebody to + *inf.*)
Me retó a imitarle. He challenged me to imitate him.

reto *m.* challenge
El gran reto de nuestro siglo es acabar con la pobreza. The great challenge of our century is to end poverty.

retórica *f.* rhetoric

retórico/a *adj.* rhetorical

retraído/a *adj.* withdrawn

retrasarse *v.i.* to be late

retraso *m.* delay

retrato *m.* portrait, photograph of people

retrovisor *m.* rearview mirror

reumatismo *m.* rheumatism

reunión *f.* meeting

revelar *v.t.* to reveal; (*photography*) to develop

revés: al revés *adv.* the other way around; backward(s)

revisar *v.t.* to check
revisar el aceite to check the oil

revisión *f.* (*Spain*) (medical) checkup

revista *f.* magazine

rey *m.* king

rezar *v.i.* to pray

riachuelo *m.* stream, brook

rico/a *adj.* rich; (*food*) tasty, delicious

ridículo/a *adj.* ridiculous
Es ridículo (que…) It's ridiculous (that…)
Es ridículo que llores. It's ridiculous that you cry.

rincón *m.* (*inside*) corner

rinoceronte *m.* rhinoceros

riñón *m.* kidney

río *m.* river

riquísimo/a *adj.* (*superlative*) extremely delicious

risa *f.* laughter
morirse/partirse de risa to die laughing

robar *v.t.* to rob; to steal

roble *m.* oak tree

robo *m.* robbery; theft

rocío *m.* dew

rodaja *f.* slice
hamburguesa con queso y rodajas de cebolla a hamburger with cheese and sliced onions

rodaje *m.* (*cinema*) filming, shooting

rodar *v.t.* (*cinema*) to shoot, to film

rodilla *f.* knee

rogar (o:ue) *v.t.* to beg; to plead

rojizo/a *adj.* reddish

rojo/a *adj./m.* red
al rojo vivo red-hot
La situación está al rojo vivo. The situation is at the boiling point.

románico/a *adj.* Romanesque

romano/a *adj./m., f.* Roman

romanticismo *m.* Romanticism

romántico/a *adj./m., f.* romantic
romero *m.* rosemary
rompecabezas *m., sing.* (jigsaw) puzzle
rompeolas *m.* breakwater
romper (con) *v.t./v.i.* to break; to break up (with)
  romper el hielo *loc.* break the ice
  ¿Han roto? Have they broken up?
romperse *v. pron.* to break
  Se rompió la pierna. He broke his leg.
ron *m.* rum
roncar *v.i.* to snore
ronquido *m.* snore
ropa *f.* clothing; clothes
  ropa deportiva sportswear
  ropa interior underwear
ropero *m.* wardrobe
rosa *f.* rose
rosado/a *adj./m.* pink
rosal *m.* rosebush
roto/a *adj.* broken
rubí *m.* ruby
rubio/a *m., f.* blond(e)
rueda *f.* wheel
  rueda de recambio spare tire
  rueda de repuesto spare tire
rugido *m.* roar
rugir (g:j) *v.i.* to roar
ruido *m.* noise
ruidoso/a *adj.* noisy
ruleta *f.* roulette
rumor *m.* rumor
ruta *f.* route
rutina *f.* routine
  rutina diaria daily routine

S

sábado *m.* Saturday
sábana *f.* sheet
saber *v.t. irreg.* **(yo sé)** to know; to know how (to); *m.* knowledge
  no sé I don't know
  saber (a) to taste like
  Sabe a limón. It tastes like lemon.
sabiduría *f.* wisdom
sabihondo/a *adj./m., f.* know-it-all
sabio/a *adj.* learned, wise; *m., f.* wise person
sabor *m.* flavor
sabrosísimo/a *adj.* (*superlative*) extremely delicious
sabroso/a *adj.* tasty; delicious
sacacorchos *m.* corkscrew
sacar *v.t.* to take out
  sacar buenas notas to get good grades
  sacar fotos to take pictures/photographs
  sacar la basura to take out the trash
  sacar al perro a pasear to take out (walk) the dog
  sacar(se) una muela to extract a tooth; to pull a tooth
saco *m.* bag, sack
  saco de dormir sleeping bag
sacudir *v.t.* to shake; to dust
  sacudir el polvo to dust
  sacudir los muebles to dust the furniture
saga *f.* saga

sagrado/a *adj.* sacred

sal *f.* salt

sala *f.* living room; room
  sala de emergencia
  emergency room

salado/a *adj.* salty

salario *m.* salary

salchicha *f.* sausage

salero *m.* salt shaker

salida *f.* departure; exit
  callejón sin salida dead-end
  street
  salida del sol sunrise

salir *v.i. irreg.* **(yo salgo)** to
  leave; to go out
  salir con to go out with; to
  date (*someone*)
  salir de to leave from
  salir para to leave for (*a*
  place)

salirse (en) *v. pron.* to get off
  (at)

salmón *m.* salmon

salón *m.* hall; salon; classroom
  salón de actos auditorium
  salón de belleza beauty
  salon

salsa *f.* sauce

saltar *v.i.* to jump

saltear *v.t.* to sauté

salto *m.* jump
  salto alto (*L.A.*) high jump
  salto de altura (*Spain*) high
  jump
  salto de longitud (*Spain*)
  long jump
  salto largo (*L.A.*) long jump
  salto mortal somersault

salud *f.* health

saludable *adj.* healthy

saludar *v.t.* to greet, to say
  hello

saludarse *v. pron.* to greet
  each other, to say hello to
  each other
  ¿No se saludan? They don't
  say hello to each other?

saludo *m.* greeting
  Saludos. (*in a letter*) Best
  wishes.
  saludos a… greetings to…
  Saludos a tu padre. Give my
  regards to your father.

salvaje *adj.* (*animal, flower*)
  wild

salvamento *m.* rescue

salvar *v.t.* to save

salvavidas *m., f.* lifeguard; *m.*
  life jacket

salvia *f.* sage

sandalia *f.* sandal

sandía *f.* watermelon

sándwich *m.* sandwich

sangre *f.* blood

sanguíneo/a *adj.* blood

sano/a *adj.* healthy

sapo *m.* toad

sarampión *m.* measles

sardina *f.* sardine

sartén *f.* frying pan

sastre *m.* tailor

satisfecho/a *adj.* satisfied

sauna *f.* sauna

savia *f.* (*botany*) sap

se *pron.* himself, herself, itself,
  form. yourself, themselves,
  yourselves

se one; on one; on us
  Se hizo… He/She/It
  became…

Se nos dañó el auto. The car broke down on us.
Se nos ponchó/pinchó una llanta. We got a flat tire.
Se pueden comprar boletos aquí. One can buy tickets here.
secador *m.* hairdryer
secadora *f.* clothes dryer
secar *v.t.* to dry
secarse *v. pron.* to dry (oneself)
sección *f.* section
   sección de (no) fumar *f.* (non) smoking section
seco/a *adj.* dry
secretario/a *m., f.* secretary
secuencia *f.* sequence
secuestrar *v.t.* (*person*) to kidnap; (*airplane*) to hijack
secuestro *m.* kidnapping; hijack
secundaria, (escuela) *f.* high school
sed *f.* thirst
seda *f.* silk
   de seda (made of) silk
sedentario/a *adj.* sedentary; related to sitting
sediento/a *adj.* thirsty
sedimentación *f.* sedimentation
sedimento *m.* sediment
seducir (c:zc) *v.t.* to seduce; to captivate
seductor(a) *adj.* seductive; *m.* seducer, *f.* seductress
seguir (e:i) *v.t.* **(yo sigo)** to follow; to continue
según *prep.* according to

segundo/a *adj./m.* second
   en segundo lugar *adv.* secondly
seguro *m.* insurance; safe
   seguro médico medical insurance
seguro/a *adj.* sure; safe
   (No) Es seguro (que)… It's (not) sure (that)…
   No es seguro que lo tenga. He may not have it.
   No estoy seguro. I'm not sure
seis six
seiscientos/as six hundred
seleccionar *v.t.* to select
selecto/a *adj.* select
sello *m.* stamp
selva *f.* jungle
semáforo *m.* traffic signal; street light
semana *f.* week
   semana entrante/que viene next week
   la semana pasada last week
   Semana Santa Holy Week
semántica *f.* semantics
semejante *adj.* similar
semestre *m.* semester
semilla *f.* seed
seminario *m.* seminar
senado *m.* senate
sencillo/a *adj.* simple; (*person*) modest
sendero *m.* trail; trailhead
sensatez *f.* good sense
sensato/a *adj.* sensible
sensibilidad *f.* sensitivity
sensible *adj.* sensitive
sentar (e:ie) *v.i.* (*clothes*) to suit

Esa chaqueta te sienta bien.
That jacket suits you.
sentarse (e:ie) *v. pron.* to sit
down
sentido *m.* sense
sentido común common
sense
sentido del orden sense of
order
sentimental *adj.* sentimental
sentir (e:ie) *v.t.* to feel; to be
sorry; to regret
Lo siento. I'm sorry.
sentirse (e:ie) *v. pron.* to feel
Me siento bien/mal. I feel
good/bad.
señal *f.* sign
señal de alto stop sign
señal de tráfico traffic sign
señor (Sr.) *m.* Mr.; sir
señora (Sra.) *f.* Mrs.; ma'am
señorita (Srta.) *f.* Miss
separado/a *adj.* separated
separar *v.t.* to separate
separarse (de) *v. pron.* to
separate (from)
septiembre *m.* September
séptimo/a *adj./m.* seventh
sequía *f.* drought
ser *m.* being
ser humano human being
ser vivo living being
ser *v. irreg.* to be
Es la una. It's one o'clock.
sea lo que sea *loc.* be that
as it may
ser aficionado/a (a) to be a
fan (of)
ser alérgico/a (a) to be
allergic (to)

ser gratis to be free of
charge
Son las… It's… o'clock.
serio/a *adj.* serious
serpentina *f.* streamer
serpiente *f.* snake
serpiente de cascabel
rattlesnake
serrar *v.t.* to saw
servicio *m.* service
servilleta *f.* napkin
servir (e:i) *v.i.* to serve; to help
sesenta sixty
setecientos/as seven hundred
setenta seventy
seto *m.* hedge
seudónimo *m.* pseudonym, pen
name
sexismo *m.* sexism
sexto/a *adj./m.* sixth
sí *adv.* yes
si *(conj.)* if
**SIDA (síndrome de
inmunodeficiencia
adquirida)** *m.* AIDS
sido *p.p. of* **ser** been
sidra *f.* cider
siempre *adv.* always
siempre que (+ *subj.*)
whenever **Voy siempre que
puedo.** I go whenever I can.
siempre y cuando (+ *subj.*)
provided (that) **Iré siempre y
cuando vengas conmigo.** I'll
go provided you come with
me.
sien *f.* (*anatomy*) temple
sierra *f.* saw
siesta *f.* afternoon nap
siete seven

siglo *m.* century
significar *v.t.* to mean
siguiente *adj.* next, following
silbar *v.i.* to whistle
silbato *m.* whistle
silenciador *m.* (*automobile*) muffler
silencio *m.* silence
silla *f.* seat; chair
  silla de ruedas wheel chair
sillón *m.* armchair
silvestre *adj.* (*flower, plant*) wild
simbiosis *f.* symbiosis
simbolizar *v.t.* symbolize
similar *adj.* similar
simpático/a *adj.* (*person*) nice; likeable
sin *prep.* without
  sin (+ inf.) without (+ -ing)
  sin hablar without talking
  sin que *conj.* without
  sin ton ni son *adv.* without rhyme or reason
sinagoga *f.* sinagogue
sinfín *m.* a great many, a lot
  Aún tiene un sinfín de cosas que hacer. He still has a lot of things to do.
sinfonía *f.* symphony
sinfónica *f.* symphony orchestra
sinfónico/a *adj.* symphonic
sino *conj.* but
  No una sino dos. Not one but two.
sinónimo/a *m.* synonym; *adj.* synonymous
sintaxis *f.* syntax
síntoma *m.* symptom
sinvergüenza *m., f.* shameless

person; scoundrel
sistema *m.* system
  sistema inmunológico immune system
sitio *m.* place; site
  sitio web website
situado/a *p.p.* of **situar** located
sobrar *v.t.* to be left over
  Sobró mucho dinero. There was a lot of money left over.
sobras *m., pl.* leftovers
sobre *m.* envelope; *prep.* on; over
sobreestimar *v.t.* overestimate
sobrehumano/a *adj.* superhuman
sobrenombre *m.* nickname
sobresaliente *adj.* outstanding; *m.* (*grade*) excellent
sobresalir *v.i. irreg.* **(yo sobresalgo)** to excel, to stand out
sobrevalorar *v.t.* to overvalue; to overrate
sobrino/a *m.* nephew; *f.* niece
sobrio/a *adj.* sober
sociable *adj.* sociable
socializar *v.i.* to socialize
sociedad *f.* society
sociología *f.* sociology
sociólogo/a *m., f.* sociologist
socorrer *v.t.* to help
socorro *m.* help; *interj.* Help!
sodio *m.* sodium
sofá *m.* couch; sofa
sofocar *v.t.* (*fire*) to suffocate, to put out; (*weather*) to be stifling
  El calor me sofoca. The heat is stifling.

101

sofoco *m.* suffocation

sol *m.* sun

solamente *adv.* only

solar *adj.* solar

solario *m.* solarium

soldado *m., f.* soldier

soldadura *f.* weld

soldar (o:ue) *v.t.* to weld

soleado/a *adj.* sunny

soler (o:ue) + inf. *v.i.* usually; to be accustomed to
Suelo desayunar sólo café con leche. I usually just have coffee with milk for breakfast.
Suelo ir los domingos. I usually go on Sundays.

solicitar (empleo) *v.t.* to apply (for a job)

solicitud (de trabajo) *f.* (job) application

sollozar *v.i.* to sob

sollozo *m.* sob

solo *adj.* alone

sólo *adv.* only
Sólo sé que estoy solo. I only know that I'm alone.

soltar (o:ue) *v.t.* to release; to let go

soltero/a *adj.* single; unmarried

soltura *f.* ease, agility

solución *f.* solution

solucionar *v.t.* to solve

sombra *f.* shade, shadow

sombrero *m.* hat

sombrilla *f.* sunshade, beach umbrella

someterse a *v. pron.* (*test, examination*) to undergo

sonar (o:ue) *v.t.* to ring; (*alarm*) to go off

sonreído *p.p. of* **sonreír** smiled

sonreír (e:i) *v.i.* to smile

sonrisa *f.* smile

soñar (o:ue) *v.t.* to dream; *v.i.*
soñar con algo to dream about something
soñar despierto to daydream

sopa *f.* soup

soportar *v.t.* to support, to withstand, to endure
No lo soporto más. I can't take it any more.

soprano *m., f.* soprano

sorbete *m.* sorbet

sorbo *m.* sip

sordo/a *adj.* deaf

sorprender *v.t.* to surprise

sorprenderse *v. pron.* to be surprised
Se sorprendió al verme. He was surprised to see me.

sorpresa *f.* surprise
por sorpresa *adv.* by surprise

sortija *f.* ring

soso/a *adj.* (*culinary*) bland, tasteless; (*person*) boring, dull

sospecha *f.* suspicion

sospechar (algo) *v.t.;* (**de alguien**) *v.i.* to suspect

sospechoso/a *adj.* suspicious

sostener (e:ie) *v.t. irreg.* (**yo sostengo**) support

sótano *m.* basement; cellar

soy I am
Soy yo. It's me. That's me.
soy de… I'm from…

su(s) *poss.* his; her; *form.* your; their

suave *adj.* (*to the touch*) soft; (*taste*) mild
subir *v.t.* to go up
subir(se) a *v.t.* to get on/into (a vehicle)
  subirse a los árboles *v.* to climb trees
  subirse a los columpios *v.* to go on the swings
  subirse a los juegos *v.* to go on rides
subjetivo/a *adj.* subjective
submarino/a *m.* submarine
subrayado/a *adj.* underlined
subrayar *v.t.* to underline
subterráneo/a *adj.* underground, subterranean
sucesivamente *adv.* successively
  y así sucesivamente and so forth
sucio/a *adj.* dirty
sucre *m.* Ecuadorian currency
sudado/a *adj.* sweaty
sudamericano/a *adj./m., f.* South American
sudar *v.i.* to sweat
suegro/a *m.* father-in-law; *f.* mother-in-law
sueldo *m.* salary, wage
suelo *m.* floor
sueño *m.* sleep
suerte *f.* luck
suéter *m.* sweater
sufrir *v.t.* to suffer **Sufre muchas presiones.** He's under a lot of pressure. **sufrir una enfermedad** to suffer an illness **Sufre una grave enfermedad.** He has a serious illness.

sugerencia *f.* suggestion
sugerir (e:ie) *v.t.* to suggest
suicidarse *v. pron.* to commit suicide
suicidio *m.* suicide
sujetador *m.* (*Spain*) *m.* bra
sumamente *adv.* extremely
suministrador(a) *m., f.* supplier
suministrar *v.t.* to supply
suministro *m.* supply; *m., pl.* supplies
suntuoso/a *adj.* sumptuous
superar *v.t.* to exceed, to go beyond; to overcome **La realidad supera la ficción.** Truth is stranger than fiction.
superarse *v. pron.* to better oneself
supermercado *m.* (super)market
superstición *f.* superstition
supersticioso/a *adj.* superstitious
supervisar *v.t.* to supervise
supervivencia *f.* survival
superviviente *m., f.* survivor
suponer *v.t. irreg.* (**yo supongo**) to suppose; to assume
sur *m.* south
  al sur to the south
surtido *m.* assortment; variety
suspender *v.t.* (*examination*) to fail; (*performance*) to cancel
suspenso *m.* (*grade*) fail, F
sustancia *f.* substance
sustantivo *m.* noun
sustituir (y) *v.t.* to replace **Sustituyeron el azúcar por la miel.** They replaced the sugar with honey.
sustituto/a *m., f.* substitute

suyo/a(s) *adj./pron. poss.* (of) his; her; (of) hers; (of) its; *form.* your, (of) yours; their (of)

T

tabaco *m.* tobacco

tablero *m.* blackboard; board
  tablero de anuncios bulletin board
  tablero de control control panel

taburete *m.* stool

tacaño/a *adj.* stingy

tachadura *f.* crossing out, correction

tachar *v.t.* to cross out, to delete

tacto *m.* (*sense*) touch

tal *adv.* such **Nunca te dije tal cosa.** I never told you any such thing.
  Son tal para cual. They are two of a kind.
  tal vez *adv.* maybe
  tales como such as

talentoso/a *adj.* talented

talla *f.* size
  talla grande large

tallar *v.t.* (*wood, stone*) to carve

taller *m.* workshop
  taller de mecánica mechanic's workshop
  taller mecánico mechanic's repairshop

talón *m.* heel

tamaño *m.* size

también *adv.* also; too

tampoco *adv.* neither; not either

tan *adv.* so
  tan pronto como as soon as
  tan… como as . . . as

tanque *m.* tank

tanto *adv.* so much
  No es para tanto. It's no big deal.
  por lo tanto therefore
  tanto… como as much … as

tantos/as… como as many . . . as

tapa *f.* lid; (*Spain*) bar snack
  ir de tapas (*Spain*) to go out and have a snack in a bar

tapar *v.t.* to cover

tapete (**verde**) *m.* (*games*) card table

tapiz *m.* tapestry

taquilla *f.* box office, ticket office

tardar (en) *v.i.* to be late (in) **El autobús tardó en llegar.** The bus was late (in arriving).
  a más tardar at the very latest **Llévamelo el jueves a más tardar.** Bring it to me on Thursday at the very latest.

tarde *adv.* late

tarde *f.* afternoon; evening; p.m.
  a las tres de la tarde at three in the afternoon, at three p.m.

tarea *f.* homework

tarjeta *f.* (post)card
  tarjeta de crédito credit card
  tarjeta de invitación invitation
  tarjeta de Navidad Christmas card

tarjeta postal postcard
tartamudear *v.i.* to stutter, to stammer
tatarabuelo/a *m.* great-great grandfather; *f.* great-great grandmother
tauromaquia *f.* bullfighting
taxi *m.* taxi(cab)
taza *f.* cup; mug
tazón *m.* bowl
te *pron. fam.* you
  Te presento a... Let me/I would like to introduce you to . . .
té *m.* tea
  té helado iced tea
teatro *m.* theater
techo *m.* (*L.A.*) roof, ceiling; (*Spain*) ceiling
teclado *m.* keyboard
técnico/a *m., f.* technician
teja *f.* (*roof*) tile
tejado *m.* (*Spain*) roof
tejido *m.* weaving; (*anatomy*) tissue
tela *f.* fabric
  tela metálica wire netting
telaraña *f.* spiderweb
teleadicto/a *m., f.* couch potato
teléfono (celular) *m.* (cellular) telephone
telenovela *f.* soap opera
telescopio *m.* telescope
teletrabajo *m.* telecommuting
televisión *f.* television
  televisión por cable cable television
televisor *m.* television set
tema *m.* subject; theme

temática *f.* subject matter
temático/a *adj.* thematic, according to subject
temer *v.t.* to fear
temperamento *m.* temperament
temperatura *f.* temperature
templo *m.* temple
temporada *f.* season
temprano *adj.* early
tenazas *f., pl.* tongs
tendedero *m.* clothesline
  colgar la ropa en el tendedero to hang clothes on the line
tendencia *f.* tendency
tender (e:ie) *v.t.* (*clothes*) to hang out
tendón *m.* tendon
tenedor *m.* fork
tener (e:ie) *v.t. irreg.* (**yo tengo**) to have
  tener algo en la punta de la lengua *loc.* to have something on the tip of one's tongue
  tener calor to be hot
  tener cuidado to be careful
  tener dolor to have a pain
  tener dolor de... to have a(n) ...ache
  tener en cuenta to keep in mind
  tener éxito to be successful
  tener fama de to be well-known for, to have a reputation for
  tener buena/mala fama to have a good/bad reputation
  tener fiebre to have a fever

tener frío to be cold
tener ganas de (+ inf.) to feel like (*doing something*); would like to **Tengo ganas de visitar Diamantina.** I would like to visit Diamantina.
tener hambre to be hungry
tener malas pulgas *idiom* to be bad tempered
tener miedo de to be afraid of, to be scared of
tener miedo (de) que to be afraid that
tener planes to have plans
tener prisa to be in a hurry
tener razón to be right
tener sed to be thirsty
tener sueño to be sleepy
tener suerte to be lucky
tener tiempo to have time
tener una cita to have a date; to have an appointment
tener… años to be . . . years old
Tengo… años. I'm . . . years old.
tener (e:ie) *v.aux. irreg.* (**yo tengo**) to have
tener que (+ inf.) to have to (*do something*) **Tengo que irme.** I have to go.
tener que ver con *loc.* to have to do with **La carta no tiene nada que ver con el problema.** The letter doesn't have anything to do with the problem.
tenis *m.* tennis(sport); tennis(sneakers)
tenista *m., f.* tennis player

tenor *m.* tenor
tensión *f.* tension
tentáculo *m.* tentacle
teñir (e:i) *v.t.* to dye
teoría *f.* theory
teorizar (sobre algo) *v.i.* to theorize (about something)
terapeútico/a *adj.* therapeutic
terapia *f.* therapy
tercer, tercero/a *adj.* third
en tercer lugar *adv.* thirdly
tercio *m.* third
terciopelo *m.* velvet
terminar *v.t.* to end; to finish
terminar de (+inf.) *v.i.* to finish (*doing something*) **¿Has terminado de leer el libro?** Have you finished reading the book?
termostato *m.* thermostat
ternera *f.* veal
terraza *f.* terrace
terremoto *m.* earthquake
terreno *m.* plot of land, lot; terrain
terrible *adj.* terrible
Es terrible (que…) It's terrible (that…)
Es terrible que diga eso. It's terrible that he says that.
terrorista *adj./m., f.* terrorist
tertulia *f.* gathering (*to discuss literature, politics, etc.*)
tesis *f.* thesis
tesoro *m.* treasure
testarudo/a *adj.* stubborn
testigo *m., f.* witness; *m.* (*relay race*) baton
tetera *f.* teapot
ti *obj. of prep., fam.* you

tiburón *m.* shark
tiempo *m.* time; weather; occasion
  a tiempo on time
  tiempo completo/parcial full-time, part-time
  tiempo libre free/spare time
tienda *f.* shop, store
  tienda de campaña tent
tierno/a *adj.* tender; (*person*) affectionate
tierra *f.* land; ground; soil; Earth
tigre *m.* tiger
tijeras *f., pl.* scissors
timbre *m.* doorbell
tímido/a *adj.* timid, shy
timón *m.* (*ship*) rudder
tina *f.* (*L.A.*) bathtub
tinta *f.* ink
tinto *m.* red (wine)
tío/a *m.* uncle; *f.* aunt
  tíos *m. pl.* aunts and uncles
típico/a *adj.* typical, traditional
tipo *m.* type, kind, sort; (*person*) figure
  No es mi tipo. He's not my type.
  ¿Qué tipo de música te gusta? What kind of music do you like?
  Tiene muy buen tipo. She has a lovely figure.
tirantes *m., pl.* suspenders
tirar *v.t.* to throw
tiro *m.* shot
  tiro al blanco target shooting
  tiro al plato trapshooting
  tiro con arco archery
título *m.* title
tiza *f.* chalk

toalla *f.* towel
toallero *m.* towel bar
tobillo *m.* ankle
tobogán *m.* (*child's toy*) slide
tocadiscos compacto *m., sing.* compact disc player
tocar *v.t.* to touch
  tocar (un instrumento musical) to play (a musical instrument)
todavía *adv.* yet; still; already
todo *m.* everything
  Todo está bajo control. Everything is under control.
todo/a *adj.* whole, entire; all
  del todo *adv.* entirely **No está del todo equivocada.** She is not entirely mistaken.
  por todo el mundo all over the world
  todo el mundo the whole world
  todos los días every day
todos *m., pl.* all of us; everybody; everyone
tolerancia *f.* tolerance
tolerante *adj.* tolerant
tolerar *v.t.* to tolerate
tomar *v.t.* to take; to drink
  algo de tomar something to drink
  tomar clases to take classes
  tomar el sol to sunbathe
  tomar en cuenta take into account
  tomar fotos to take photos
  tomar la temperatura to take someone's temperature
  tomarle el pelo a alguien *idiom* to pull someone's leg, to kid someone

tomate *m.* tomato
tomillo *m.* thyme
tonto/a *adj.* silly; foolish; dumb
torcer (o:ue) (c:z) *v.t.* to twist
torcerse (o:ue) (c:z) (el tobillo)
  v. pron. to sprain (one's
  ankle)
torcido/a *adj.* twisted; sprained
torero/a *m., f.* bullfighter
tormenta *f.* storm
tornado *m.* tornado
tornillo *m.* screw
toro *m.* bull
toronja *f.* (*L.A.*) grapefruit
torpe *adj.* clumsy, awkward
torre *f.* tower
  torre de control control
  tower
tortilla *f.* (*egg*) omelet; (*corn*)
  kind of flat bread
  tortilla de maíz flat bread
  made of corn flour
  tortilla de patatas potato
  omelet
tortuga *f.* turtle
tos *f., sing.* cough
toser *v.i.* to cough
tostado/a *adj.* toasted
tostadora *f.* toaster
trabajador(a) *m., f.* hard-
  working person
trabajar *v.i.* to work
trabajo *m.* job; work; (*paper*)
  written work
tradición *f.* tradition
traducción *f.* translation
traducir (c:zc) *v.t.* to translate
traductor(a) *m., f.* translator
traer *v.t. irreg.* (**yo traigo**) to
  bring; to take

traficante *m., f.* (*arms, drugs*)
  dealer
traficar (en/con) *v.i.* to traffic in
tráfico *m.* traffic
tragaluz *m.* skylight
tragaperras *f., sing.* slot
  machine
tragar *v.t.* to swallow
tragedia *f.* tragedy
trágico/a *adj.* tragic
traición *f.* treason, betrayal,
  treachery
traicionar (algo o a alguien)
  v.t. to betray (something or
  someone)
traicionero/a *adj.* treacherous
traído *p.p. of* **traer** brought
traje *m.* suit
  traje de baño
  bathing/swimming suit
traidor(a) *m., f.* traitor; *adj.*
  treacherous
tramar *v.t.* to plot, to scheme
trampa *f.* trap; trick; catch
  ¿Cuál es la trampa? What's
  the catch?
  hacer trampa(s) to cheat
trampolín *m.* diving board
tranquilidad *f.* calm, tranquility
tranquilizar *v.t.* to calm down
tranquilizarse *v. pron.* to calm
  down
tranquilo/a *adj.* (*person*)
  easygoing; quiet; calm
  ¡Tranquilo! Stay calm!
transatlántico *m.* ocean liner
transbordador *m.* ferry; (*space*)
  shuttle
transeúnte *m., f.* passer-by;
  non-resident

transferencia *f.* transfer
transfusión *f.* transfusion
transmitir *v.t.* to broadcast
transparente *adj.* transparent;
see-through
transpiración *f.* perspiration
transpirar *v.i.* to perspire
transplante *m.* transplant
transportar *v.t.* to transport; to
carry
transporte *m.* transportation
trapeador *m.* (*L.A.*) mop
trapear *v.t.* (*L.A.*) to mop
trapo *m.* dishcloth
trasnochar *v.i.* to stay up all
night
trastorno *m.* (*medicine*)
disorder
  trastorno estomacal
  stomach disorder
  trastorno mental mental
  disorder
trasvasar *v.t.* (*computer*) to
download
tratar *v.i.* to try
  tratar de (+ inf.) to try (*to do
  something*)
  Trata de resolverlo. Try to
  solve it.
trato *m.* deal
  Trato hecho. It's a deal.
travesura *f.* prank; mischief
travieso/a *adj.* naughty,
mischievous
trayectoria *f.* (*rocket, ball*)
path, trajectory
trece thirteen
treinta thirty
tren *m.* train
  tren de alta velocidad high-
speed train
trenza *f.* braid
tres three
trescientos/as three hundred
triángulo *m.* triangle
tribunal *m.* (*Spain*) court
  Tribunal Supremo (*Spain*)
  Supreme Court
triciclo *m.* tricycle
trigo *m.* wheat
trigonometría *f.* trigonometry
trimestre *m.* trimester; quarter
  **El año tiene cuatro
  trimestres.** The year has four
  quarters.
trípode *m.* tripod
triste *adj.* sad
  Es triste (que…) It's sad
  (that…)
  **Es triste que esté tan
  enfermo.** It's sad that he's so
  sick.
tristeza *f.* sadness
triturar *v.t.* to crush
  triturador de basura garbage
  disposal
triunfar *v.t.* to succeed; to win
trivialidad *f.* triviality
trivializar *v.t.* to trivialize
tronco *m.* (*living tree*) trunk;
(*lumber*) log
  dormir como un tronco
  idiom. to sleep like a log
tropezar (e:ie) *v.i.* to stumble
tropezarse (e:ie) (con alguien)
v. pron. to run/bump into
(*somebody*)
trozo *m.* piece, bit, slice
trucha *f.* trout
trueno *m.* thunder

tú *pron. fam.* you
  Tú eres... You are . . .
tu(s) *poss. fam.* your
tuberculosis *f.* tuberculosis
tubería *f.* pipe
tubo *m.* tube
  tubo de ensayo test tube
  tubo de escape exhaust pipe
tulipán *m.* tulip
tumbarse *v. pron.* to lie down
  tumbarse al sol lie down in
  the sun, sunbathe
tumbona *f.* lounge chair, deck
  chair
túnel *m.* tunnel
turbina *f.* turbine
turismo *m.* tourism
turista *m., f.* tourist
turístico/a *adj.* touristic
turno *m.* turn; (*work*) shift
turquesa *f.* turquoise
tuyo/a(s) *poss. fam.* your; (of)
  yours

U

Ud. *pron. form. sing.* you
Uds. *pron. form. pl.* you
últimamente *adv.* lately
último/a *adj.* last
  por último *adv.* finally
un, uno/a *indef. art.* a; one
  uno/a *m., f., sing. pron.* one
  a la una at one o'clock
único/a *adj.* only
  **...y ese es el único
  problema** ...and that's the
  only problem
unido/a *adj.* close
  una familia muy unida a
  close family

universidad *f.* university;
  college
universo *m.* universe
unos/as *m., f., pl., indef. art.*
  some
  unos/as *pron.* some
untar *v.t.* to spread (*butter,
  honey*)
  untar pan con mantequilla to
  butter a piece of bread
uña *f.* (*finger, toe*) nail
urbanización *f.* (*housing*)
  development
urgente *adj.* urgent
  (No) Es urgente (que...) It's
  (not) urgent (that...)
  Es urgente que termines. It's
  urgent that you finish.
usar *v.t.* to use; to wear
  Esta camisa está sin usar.
  This shirt hasn't been worn.
usted *pron. form. sing.* you
ustedes *pron. form. pl.* you
utensilio *m.* utensil
útero *m.* womb, uterus
útil *adj.* useful
uva *f.* grape

V

vaca *f.* cow
vacaciones *f., pl.* vacation
  de vacaciones on vacation
vacío/a *adj.* empty
vainilla *f.* vanilla
vajilla *f.* dishes, crockery,
  china
vale *interj.* (*Spain*) okay
  Ven a la una, ¿vale? Come at
  one o'clock, okay?
  ¡Sí, vale! Yes, sure!

valentía *f.* bravery, courage

valer *v.t. irreg.* **(yo valgo)** to be worth, to cost
  No vale la pena. It's not worth the trouble.

valiente *adj.* brave

valla *f.* fence

vallas *f., pl.* (*sport*) hurdles

valle *m.* valley

valor *m.* value; courage

valorar *v.t.* to value

vapor *m.* vapor, steam

vaquero/a *m.* cowboy; *f.* cowgirl
  (una película) de vaqueros a western (movie)

variación *f.* variation

variado/a *adj.* varied, diverse

variar *v.t./v.i.* **(yo varío)** to vary

varios/as *pron.* several; various
  Irán varios de ustedes. Several of you will go.

vaso *m.* glass

veces *f., pl.* times
  a veces *adv.* sometimes

vecino/a *m., f.* neighbor

vegetación *f.* vegetation

vehículo *m.* vehicle
  vehículos pesados heavy vehicles

veinte twenty

veinticinco twenty-five

veinticuatro twenty-four

veintidós twenty-two

veintinueve twenty-nine

veintiocho twenty-eight

veintiséis twenty-six

veintisiete twenty-seven

veintitrés twenty-three

veintiún, veintiuno/a twenty-one

vejez *f.* old age

vejiga *f.* bladder

vela *f.* (*ship*) sail; (*sport*) sailing; candle

velero *m.* sailboat

velocidad *f.* speed
  velocidad máxima speed limit

velódromo *m.* velodrome

vena *f.* vein

venda *f.* bandage

vendaje *m.* dressing

vendar *v.t.* to bandage

vendedor(a) *m., f.* salesperson

vender *v.t.* to sell

venido *p.p. of* **venir** come; arrived

venir (e:ie) *v.i. irreg.* **(yo vengo)** to come
  venir al mundo to be born; to come into the world

ventaja *f.* advantage

ventana *f.* window

ventilador *m.* fan

ver *v.t./v.i. irreg.* **(yo veo)** to see; to watch
  ¡A ver! Let's see!
  ver películas to see movies

veraneante *m., f.* summer vacationer

veranear *v.i.* to spend the summer
  Veraneo en las montañas. I summer in the mountains.

verano *m.* summer

veras: de veras *loc.* really

verbena *f.* festival; open-air dance

verbo *m.* verb
verdad *f.* truth
  Es cierto, ¿verdad? It's true, right?
  (No) Es verdad que (+ *ind.*) It's (not) true that… **¿Es verdad que eres millonario?** Is it true that you're a millionaire?
verdadero/a *adj.* true
verde *adj./m.* green
  verde claro light green
  verde oscuro dark green
verduras *f., pl.* vegetables
vergonzoso/a *adj.* disgraceful; shameful
vergüenza *f.* embarrassment; shame
verosímil *adj.* credible; realistic, true-to-life
  Sus personajes no son verosímiles. His characters aren't realistic.
verruga *f.* wart
versátil *adj.* versatile
vértebra *f.* vertebra
vertebrado/a *adj./m.* vertebrate
vertedero *m.* garbage dump
vesícula (biliar) *f.* gall bladder
vestido *m.* dress
vestirse (e:i) *v. pron.* to get dressed
vestuario *m.* locker room
veterinaria *f.* veterinary science
veterinario/a *m., f.* veterinarian
vez *f.* time
  a veces sometimes
  dos veces twice
  en vez de instead of

tres veces three times
una vez once; one time
una vez más one more time
vía *f.* (railroad) track
  Vía Láctea Milky Way
viajar *v.i.* to travel
viaje *m.* trip
viajero/a *m., f.* traveler
vibración *f.* vibration
vibrar *v.i.* to vibrate
vicio *m.* vice
  El trabajo es su único vicio. Work is his only vice.
vicioso/a *m., f.* dissolute person
vid *f.* (grape) vine
vida *f.* life
  de mi vida of my life
video(casete) *m.* video (cassette)
videocasetera *f.* VCR
videoconferencia *f.* videoconference; teleconference
vidrio *m.* glass
  de vidrio (*made*) of glass
vieira *f.* scallop
viejo/a *adj.* old
viento *m.* wind
viernes *m., sing.* Friday
villancicos *m., pl.* carols
vinagre *m.* vinegar
vínculo *m.* tie, bond
vino *m.* wine
  vino blanco white wine
  vino tinto red wine
violencia *f.* violence
viruela *f.* smallpox
visera *f.* eyeshade
visitante *m., f.* visitor

visitar *v.t.* to visit
  visitar monumentos to visit monuments
vista *f.* (*senses*) sight; view
  amor a primera vista love at first sight
  habitación con vistas a room with a view
  Hasta la vista. See you.
  Tener vista de águila. To have eyes like a hawk.
  Tierra a la vista. Land ho!
visto/a *p.p.* of **ver** seen
  por lo visto *adv.* apparently
vitamina *f.* vitamin
vitrina *f.* (*L.A.*) shop window
viudo/a *m.* widower; *f.* widow; widowed
víveres *m., pl.* provisions, supplies
vivienda *f.* housing
vivir *v.i.* to live
vivo/a *adj.* bright; lively; living
volante *m.* steering wheel
volar (o:ue) *v.i.* to fly
volcán *m.* volcano
vóleibol *m.* volleyball
voltear *v.t.* (*L.A.*) to turn (over)
volumen *m.* volume
voluntario *adj.* voluntary; *m., f.* volunteer
volver (o:ue) *v.i.* to return; to come back
  volver a ver(te, lo, la) to see (you/him/her) again
  ¿Cuándo te volveré a ver? When will I see you again?
vomitar *v.t./v.i.* to vomit
vos (*Argentina*) *pron.* you
vosotros/as *pron. fam. pl.* you

votar *v.t./v.i.* to vote
voto *m.* vote
voz *f.* voice
vuelta *f.* lap
vuelta *f.* return trip; (*sports*) lap; turn
  de vuelta back
  Estará de vuelta a la una. She will be back at one.
vuelto *p.p.* of **volver** returned
vuestro/a(s) *poss. fam.* your

W

walkman *m.* Walkman

X

xenofobia *f.* xenophobia
xenófobo/a *adj.* xenophobic; *m., f.* xenophobe

Y

y *conj.* and
  y cuarto quarter after/past (time)
  y media half-past (time)
  y quince quarter after/past (time)
  y treinta thirty (minutes past the hour)
  ¿Y Ud.? *form.* And you?
  ¿Y tú? *fam.* And you?
ya *adv.* already; still
  Ya fui. I already went.
yerno *m.* son-in-law
yeso *f.* (*L.A.*) plaster cast
yo *pron.* I
  Yo soy… I'm . . .
yoga *m.* yoga
yogur *m.* yogurt

z

zanahoria *f.* carrot

zapatería *f.* shoe store

zapatilla *f.* slipper
zapatillas de deporte tennis shoes; sneakers

zapato *m.* shoe
zapato de tacón alto high-heeled shoe
zapatos de tenis tennis shoes; sneakers

zona *f.* area
zona verde green space

zoológico *m.* zoo

zoólogo/a *m., f.* zoologist

zorro *m.* fox

zueco *m.* clog

zumo *m.* (*Spain*) juice

A

@ (symbol) arroba *f.*
a un, uno/a *m., f., sing., indef. art.*
A.M. en la mañana, de la mañana
abbey *n.* abadía *f.*
abbreviate *v.t.* abreviar
abbreviation *n.* abreviatura *f.*
able: be able to poder (o:ue)
abnormal *adj.* anormal
aboard *adv.* a bordo
  All aboard! ¡Todos a bordo!
abortion *n.* aborto *m.* provocado
  have an abortion abortar de manera provocada
abroad *adv.* en el extranjero
absence *n.* ausencia *f.*
absent *adj.* ausente
absorb *v.t.* absorber
absorbent *adj.* absorbente
absurd *adj.* absurdo/a
accelerate *v.t.* acelerar
accelerator (pedal) *n.* acelerador *m.*
accept *v.t.* aceptar
accessory *n.* accesorio *m.*
accident *n.* accidente *m.*
  industrial accident accidente laboral
accommodation: provide accommodation hospedar
accompany *v.t.* acompañar
according to *prep.* de acuerdo a; según
account *n.* cuenta *f.*

checking account cuenta corriente
  take into account tomar en cuenta
accountant *n.* contador(a) *m., f.*
accounting *n.* contabilidad *f.*
accustomed *adj.* acostumbrado/a
  be accustomed to acostumbrarse (a)
ache *n.* dolor *m.*
achieve *v.t.* lograr
achievement *n.* logro *m.*
acid *n.* ácido *m.*; ácido/a *adj.*
  acid rain lluvia *f.* ácida
acquainted: be acquainted with conocer
acquire *v.t.* adquirir
acquisition *n.* adquisición *f.*
acrobat *n.* acróbata *m., f.*
acrobatics *n.* acrobacia *f.*
across from *prep.* enfrente
action *n.* acción *f.*; …de acción
activate *v.t.* activar
active *adj.* activo/a
activity *n.* actividad *f.*
actor *n.* actor *m.*, actriz *f.*
adapt *v.i.* adaptarse
adaptation *n.* adaptación *f.*
addict *n.* adicto/a *m., f.*
  drug addict drogadicto/a
addicted *adj.* adicto/a
  drug-addicted drogadicto/a
addiction *n.* adicción *f.*
additional *adj.* adicional
additive *n.* aditivo *m.*
address *n.* dirección *f.*
adhesive bandage *n.* curita *f.*

adjective *n.* adjetivo *m.*

adjust *v.t. (temperature, etc.)* graduar; *v.i.* adaptarse

administration *n.* administración *f.*

adolescence *n.* adolescencia *f.*

adolescent *n.* adolescente *m., f.*

advance *n.* avance *m.*

advance *v.i.* avanzar

advanced *adj.* avanzado/a

advantage *n.* ventaja *f.*

adventure *n.* aventura *f.*; …de aventuras

adventurer *n.* aventurero/a *m., f.*

adventurous *adj.* aventurero/a

advertise *v.t.* anunciar

advertisement *n.* anuncio *m.*

advice *n.* consejo *m.*
  give advice dar un consejo

advisable *adj.* aconsejable, recomendable

advise *v.t.* aconsejar; recomendar

advisor *n.* consejero/a *m., f.*

aerobic *adj.* aeróbico/a
  aerobic exercise *n.,* ejercicios *m., pl.* aeróbicos
  do aerobics hacer ejercicios aeróbicos
  aerobics class *n.* clase *f.* de ejercicios aeróbicos

affected *adj.* afectado/a
  be affected (by) estar afectado/a (por)

affectionate *adj.* cariñoso/a, tierno/a

affirmative *adj.* afirmativo/a

afraid: be afraid (of) tener miedo (de); **be afraid that** tener miedo (de) que

African *n., adj.* africano/a *m., f.*

after *prep.* después de; después de que

afternoon *n.* tarde *f.*
  in the afternoon de la tarde; por la tarde

afterwards *adv.* después (de); luego

again *adv.* otra vez

age *n.* edad *f.*

age *v.i.* envejecer

agility *n.* soltura *f.*

aging *n.* envejecimiento *m.*

agree (about) *v.* concordar (con), estar de acuerdo (sobre)

agreement *n.* acuerdo *m.*
  be in agreement with estar de acuerdo (con)
  reach an agreement llegar a un acuerdo

agricultural *adj.* agrícola

agriculture *n.* agricultura *f.*

AIDS (Acquired Immune Deficiency Syndrome) *n.* SIDA *m.* (Síndrome de Inmunodeficiencia Adquirida)

aim *n.* objetivo *m.*, meta *f.*

air *n.* aire *m.*

air-conditioned *adj.* climatizado/a

air conditioning *n.* aire acondicionado

air freshener *n.* ambientador *m.*

aircraft carrier *n.* portaaviones *m., sing.*

airline n. aerolínea f.
airplane n. aeroplano m.;
avión m.
  by plane en avión
  go by plane ir en avión
airport n. aeropuerto m.
airtight adj. hermético/a
alarm n. alarma f.
alarming adj. alarmante
alcohol n. alcohol m.
alcoholic adj. alcohólico/a
  alcoholic beverage bebida f.
  alcohólica
all adj. todo/a
  all of a sudden de repente
  all of us n. todos m., pl.
  all over the world en todo el
  mundo
  all-boys/girls school n.
  escuela f. de niños/as
allergic adj. alérgico/a
  be allergic (to) ser alérgico/a
  (a)
alleviate v.t. aliviar
alley n. callejón m.
allow v. dejar
almond n. almendra f.
almond tree n. almendro m.
almost adv. casi
alms n. limosna f.
alone adj. solo/a
along prep. por
alphabet n. alfabeto m.,
  abecedario m.
already adv. ya; todavía
also adv. también
alternating current: AC
  corriente f. alterna
alternative n. alternativa f.
alternator n. alternador m.

although conj. aunque
aluminum n. aluminio m.
  made of aluminum de
  aluminio
always adv. siempre
amazing adj. asombroso/a
ambition n. ambición f.
ambitious adj. ambicioso/a
ambulance n. ambulancia f.
American n., adj.
  norteamericano/a, m., f.;
  estadounidense m., f.
among prep. entre
amount n. cantidad f.
amuse oneself v. entretenerse
amusement n. diversión f.
  amusement park n. parque
  m. de atracciones (Spain);
  parque de diversiones (L.A.)
amusing adj. chistoso/a,
  gracioso/a, divertido/a
analyst n. analista m., f.
anarchic adj. anárquico/a
anarchy n. anarquía f.
anatomy n. anatomía f.
ancestor n. antepasado/a m., f.
anchovy n. anchoa f.
and conj. y (e before words
  beginning with i or hi)
  and so forth y así
  sucesivamente
  And you? ¿Y tú? fam.; ¿Y
  usted? form.
anesthesia n. anestesia f.
anesthesiologist n.
  anestesiólogo/a m., f.
anesthetize v.t. anestesiar
angle n. ángulo m.
Anglo-Saxon n,. adj.
  anglosajón m., anglosajona f.

angry *adj.* enojado/a
get angry (with) enojarse (con)
animal *n.* animal *m.*
ankle *n.* tobillo *m.*
anniversary *n.* aniversario *m.; (wedding)* aniversario de bodas
announce *v.t.* anunciar
announcer *n. (TV/radio)* locutor(a) *m., f.*
annoy *v.t.* molestar
The noise is annoying me. Me molesta el ruido.
another *adj.* otro/a
answer *n.* respuesta *f.*
answer *v.t.* contestar
ant *n.* hormiga *f.*
anthology *n.* antología *f.*
antibiotic *n.* antibiótico *m.*
anticipation *n.* expectativa *f.*
antidote *n.* antídoto *m.*
antiques *n., pl.* antigüedades *f., pl.*
antiquities *n., pl.* antigüedades *f., pl.*
any *adj.* algún, alguno/a(s)
anybody *pron.* nadie
anyone *pron.* alguien
anything *pron.* algo; *n.* nada *f.*
apartment *n.* apartamento *m.*
apartment building *n.* edificio *m.* de apartamentos
apologize *v.i.* disculparse
apology *n.* disculpa *f.*
apparently *adv.* por lo visto
appear *v.i. (come into view)* aparecer; *(seem)* parecer
appearance *n. (looks)* aspecto *m.*

appetizers *n., pl.* aperitivos *m., pl.;* entremeses *(Spain) m., pl.*
applaud *v.t./v.i.* aplaudir
applause *n.* aplauso *m.*
apple *n.* manzana *f.*
appliance *n.* aparato *m.*
electric appliance *n.* electrodoméstico *m.*
household appliance aparato doméstico
applicant *n.* aspirante *m., f.*
application *n.* solicitud *f.*
job application solicitud de trabajo
apply *v.t. (for a job)* solicitar *(empleo); (for a loan)* pedir un préstamo; *(oneself)* aplicarse
appointment *n.* cita *f.*
have an appointment tener una cita
appreciate *v.t.* apreciar
approach *n.* enfoque *m.*
apricot *n.* albaricoque *m.*
April *n.* abril *m.*
apron *n.* delantal *m.*
aptitude test *n.* prueba *f.* de aptitud
aquarium *n.* acuario *m.*
aquatic *adj.* acuático/a
Arab *n.* árabe *m., f.; (language)* árabe
Arabic *adj.* árabe
archaeologist *n.* arqueólogo/a *m., f.*
archery *n.* tiro *m.* con arco
archipelago *n.* archipiélago *m.*
architect *n.* arquitecto/a *m., f.*
area *n.* región *f.;* zona *f.*

argue *v.t.* discutir; argumentar

argument *n.* (*reasoning*) argumento *m.*; (*dispute*) discusión *f.*

aristocracy *n.* aristocracia *f.*

aristocrat *n.* aristócrata *m., f.*

arm *n.* (*limb*) brazo *m.*; (*weapon*) arma (el) *f.*

armchair *n.* sillón *m.*

armpit *n.* axila *f.*

army *n.* ejército *m.*

around *prep.* alrededor (de)
  There is a wall around the old city. Hay una muralla alrededor de la ciudad vieja.
  adv. alrededor **a table with four chairs around it** una mesa con cuatro sillas alrededor
  around here por aquí

arrange *v.t.* colocar; organizar; arreglar **arranged marriage** *n.* boda *f.* concertada

arrangement *n.* (*position*) colocación *f.*

arrest *n.* detención *f.*, arresto *m.*

arrest *v.t.* arrestar
  under arrest detenido/a; arrestado/a
  be under arrest estar arrestado; estar detenido

arrested *p.p.* arrestado (*of* arrestar)

arrival *n.* llegada *f.*

arrive *v.i.* llegar

arrogant *adj.* arrogante

arrow *n.* flecha *f.*

art *n.* arte *m.*; las artes *f., pl.*

art exhibition *n.* exhibición *f.* de arte

artery *n.* arteria *f.*

artichoke *n.* alcachofa *f.*

article *n.* artículo *m.*

artist *n.* artista *m., f.*

artistic *adj.* artístico/a

arts *n., pl.* artes *f., pl.*

as como
  as . . . as tan… como
  as a child de niño/a
  as many . . . as tantos/as… como
  as much . . . as tanto… como
  as soon as en cuanto; tan pronto como

ascent *n.* (*hill, mountain*) escalada *f.*

ash *n.* ceniza *f.*

ashamed: be ashamed avergonzarse

ashtray *n.* cenicero *m.*

Asian *n., adj.* asiático/a *m., f.*

ask *v.t.* (*a question*) preguntar
  ask (for) pedir (e:i)

ask oneself *v.ref.* preguntarse; cuestionarse; **We have to ask ourselves if the conclusion is valid.** Tenemos que cuestionarnos si es válida la conclusión.

asparagus *n.* espárrago *m.*

asphalt *n.* asfalto *m.*

aspire (to) *v.i.* ambicionar

aspirin *n.* aspirina *f.*

assassin *n.* asesino/a *m., f.*

assassination *n.* asesinato *m.*

assemble (a puzzle) *v.t.* armar (un rompecabezas)

assess *v.t.* evaluar

assessment *n.* evaluación *f.*

assistance *n.* asistencia *f.*

association *n.* asociación *f.*

assortment *n.* surtido *m.*

assume *v.t.* asumir; suponer

assure *v.t.* asegurar

astonishing *adj.* asombroso/a

astrologist *n.* astrólogo/a *m., f.*

astrology *n.* astrología *f.*

astronaut *n.* astronauta *m., f.*

astronomer *n.* astrónomo/a *m., f.*

astronomy *n.* astronomía *f.*

at *prep.* a

  at + time a la(s) **+ time**

  At what time . . . ? ¿A qué hora…?

  At your service. A sus órdenes.

atheism *n.* ateísmo *m.*

atheist *n.* ateo/a *m., f.*

atheistic *adj.* ateo/a

athlete *n.* atleta *m., f.*

athletic *adj.* atlético/a

ATM *n.* cajero *m.* automático

atmosphere *n.* (*created by people, decoration*) ambiente *m.* (*metheorology*) atmósfera *f.*

atrocious *adj.* atroz

attack *n.* ataque *m.*

attack *v.t.* atacar

attempt *n.* intento *m.*

  assassination attempt atentado *m.* terrorista

attempt to assassinate *v.t.* atentar (contra)

attend *v.t.* asistir (a)

attention *n.* atención *f.*

attic *n.* altillo *m.*

attract *v.t.* atraer

attraction *n.* atracción *f.*

attractive *adj.* atractivo/a

audience *n.* público *m.*

audiotape *n.* cinta *f.*

audition *n.* (*try-out*) audición *f.*

auditorium *n.* auditorio *m.;* salón *m.* de actos

August *n.* agosto *m.*

aunt *n.* tía *f.*

aunts and uncles *n., pl.* tíos *m., pl.*

Australian *n., adj.* australiano/a *m., f.*

author *n.* autor(a) *m., f.*

authoritarian *adj.* autoritario/a

authoritarianism *n.* autoritarismo *m.*

autograph *n.* autógrafo *m.*

automatic *adj.* automático/a

  automatic teller machine *n.* **(ATM)** cajero *m.* automático

automobile *n.* automóvil *m.;* carro *m.;* coche *m.*

  auto racing *n.* automovilismo *m.*

autonomous *adj.* autónomo/a

autonomy *n.* autonomía *f.*

autumn *n.* otoño *m.*

availability *n.* disponibilidad *f.*

available *adj.* disponible

avarice *n.* avaricia *f.*

avaricious *adj.* avaricioso/a

avenue *n.* avenida *f.*

average *n.* promedio *m.*

aversion *n.* aversión *f.*

avocado *n.* aguacate *m.*

avoid *v.t.* evitar; (*danger, problem*) evadir

award *n.* premio *m.;* galardón *m.*

award *v.t.* galardonar; premiar

award-winner *n.* galardonado/a *m., f.*

aware: become aware of darse cuenta de
awful *adj.* atroz, horrible
awkward *adj.* torpe
ax *n.* hacha (el) *f.*

B

baby *n.* bebé *m., f.*
baby-sitter *n.* niñero/a *m., f.*
back *n.* espalda *f.*
back *v.t.* respaldar
  be back estar de vuelta
backpack *n.* mochila *f.*
backseat *n.* asiento *m.* trasero
backstroke *n.* estilo *m.* espalda
backyard *n.* jardín *m.*
bad *adj. adv.* mal, malo/a
  It's (not) bad that… (No) Es malo que…
  It's not at all bad. No está nada mal.
bad-mannered *adj.* maleducado/a
bad-tempered: be bad-tempered *idiom* tener malas pulgas
bag *n.* bolsa *f.*
bail *n.* fianza *f.*
bake *v.t.* hornear
bakery *n.* panadería *f.*
baking soda *n.* bicarbonato *m.*
balanced *adj.* equilibrado/a
balcony *n.* balcón *m.*
bald *adj.* calvo/a
ball *n.* pelota *f.;* bola *f.*
ballet *n.* ballet *m.*
balloon *n.* globo *m.*
banana *n.* banana *f.;* plátano *m.*
band *n.* banda *f.*
bandage *n.* venda *f.*

bandage *v.t.* vendar
bank *n.* banco *m.*
  bank draft *n.* giro *m.* bancario
banker *n.* banquero/a *m., f.*
banister *n.* pasamanos *m., sing.*
baptism *n.* bautizo *m.*
baptize *v.t.* bautizar
barbecue *n.* asador *m.*
barber *n.* barbero *m.*
bargain *n.* ganga *f.*
bargain *v.i.* regatear
bark *n.* ladrido *m.*
bark *v.i.* ladrar
barn *n.* granero *m.*
baroque *adj.* barroco/a
baseball *n. (sport)* béisbol *m.; (ball)* pelota *f.*
basement *n.* sótano *m.*
basil *n.* albahaca *f.*
basketball *n. (sport)* baloncesto *m.*
bat *n. (sport)* bate *m.; (animal)* murciélago *m.*
bath *n.* baño *m.*
  take a bath bañarse
bathe *v.i.* bañarse
bathing suit *n.* traje *m.* de baño
bathrobe *n.* bata *f.* de baño
bathroom *n.* baño *m.;* cuarto *m.* de baño
bathtub *n.* bañera *f.;* tina *(L.A.) f.*
baton *n. (sport)* testigo *m.*
bay *n.* bahía *f.*
be *v.* ser; estar
  be at/in/on estar en
  be that as it may *loc.* sea lo que sea

He/She/It is from . . . Es de…
I'm from… Soy de…
beach *n.* playa *f.*
beach umbrella *n.* sombrilla *f.*
beak *n.* pico *m.*
bean *n. (coffee)* grano *m.;*
frijol *m.*
bear *n.* oso/a *m., f.*
beard *n.* barba *f.*
bearded *adj.* barbudo/a
beat *n. (music)* compás *m.*
beat *v.t.* batir; *(an opponent)*
derrotar; *(heart)* latir
beautician *n.* esteticista *m., f.*
beautiful *adj.* hermoso/a
beauty *n.* belleza *f.*
beauty salon *n.* peluquería *f.;*
salón *m.* de belleza
because *conj.* porque
because of *prep.* debido a
become *v.i.* hacerse **He**
became famous. Se hizo
famoso.; llegar a ser **She**
wants to become president.
Ella quiere llegar a ser
presidente.; ponerse (+ *adj.*)
He becomes sad sometimes.
A veces él se pone triste.;
convertirse (en) **The church**
became a museum. La
iglesia se convirtió en
museo.
bed *n.* cama *f.*
go to bed acostarse (o:ue)
make the bed hacer la cama
bedroom *n.* alcoba *f.;*
recámara *f.;* cuarto *m.;*
dormitorio
bee *n.* abeja *f.*
beef *n.* carne *f.* de res

been *p.p.* sido *(of* ser)
beer *n.* cerveza *f.*
beet *n.* remolacha *f.;* betabel
(Mexico.) *f.*
before *adv., conj., prep.* antes;
antes (de) que; antes de
beg *v.t.* rogar (o:ue)
beggar *n.* mendigo/a *m., f.*
begin *v.t.* comenzar (e:ie);
empezar (e:ie)
behalf: on behalf of de parte
de; en nombre de
behave (oneself) *v.* portarse
(bien), comportarse
behave well/badly portarse
bien/mal
behavior *n.* comportamiento
m., conducta *f.*
behind *prep.* detrás de; atrás
being *n.* ser *m.*
belch *v.i.* eructar
belch *n.* eructo *m.*
believe (in) *v.t.* creer (en)
be hard to believe parecer
mentira **It's hard to believe,**
but he's only ten. Aunque
parezca mentira, tiene sólo
diez años.
not to believe no creer
bellhop *n.* botones *m., sing.*
belly *n.* barriga *f.,* vientre *m.*
belong to *v.t.* pertenecer (a)
belongings *n., pl.* pertenencias
f., pl.
beloved *adj.* querido/a;
enamorado/a
below *adv., prep.* abajo;
debajo de
belt *n.* correa *f.;* cinturón *m.*
bench *n.* banco *m.*

bend *n.* curva *f.*
beneficial *adj.* beneficioso/a
benefit *n.* beneficio *m.*
  fringe benefits *n.* prestaciones *f., pl*
benefit *v.i.* beneficiarse
benign *adj.* benigno
beret *n.* boina *f.*
beside *prep.* al lado de
besides *adv.* además (de)
best *adj.* mejor
  the best el/la mejor *m., f.; (neuter)* lo mejor
betray *v.t.* traicionar
betrayal *n.* traición *f.*
better *adj.* mejor
  better than *adj.* mejor que
  It's better that . . . Es mejor que…
  get better mejorarse; *(health)* aliviarse
better (oneself) *v.t.* superarse
  Better late than never. *loc.* Más vale tarde que nunca.
between *prep.* entre
bib *n.* babero *m.*
bicycle *n.* bicicleta *f.*
  ride a bicycle pasear/montar en bicicleta
big *adj.* gran, grande
Big Dipper *n.* Osa *f.* Mayor
big shot *n.* pez *m.* gordo
bikini *n.* bikini *m.*
bill *n.* cuenta *f.;* factura *f.*
billion *n.* mil *m.* millones (de)
biodiversity *n.* biodiversidad *f.*
biographical *adj.* biográfico/a
biography *n.* biografía *f.*
biologist *n.* biólogo/a *m., f.*
biology *n.* biología *f.*

biosphere *n.* biosfera *f.*
bird *n.* ave (el) *f.,* pájaro *m.*
birth *n.* nacimiento *m.*
birth control *n.* control *m.* de natalidad
birthday *n.* cumpleaños *m., sing.*
  birthday cake pastel *m.* de cumpleaños
  birthday song *n.* mañanitas *f., pl.*
  Happy birthday! ¡Feliz cumpleaños!
  have a birthday cumplir años
birthrate *n.* (índice *m.* de) natalidad *f.*
bite *n.* mordisco *m.*
bite *v.t.* morder
bitter *adj.* amargo/a
bittersweet *adj.* agridulce
black *n., adj.* negro/a
blackberry *n.* mora *f.*
blackboard *n.* pizarra *f.; m.* pizarrón
blackout *n.* apagón *m.*
bladder *n.* vejiga *f.*
bland *adj.* insípido/a; soso/a
blanket *n.* cobija *(L.A.) f.;* frazada *(L.A.) f.;* manta *f.*
bleach *n.* lejía *f.*
blend *v.t.* licuar
blender *n.* licuadora *(L.A.) f.;* batidora *(Spain) f.*
bless *v.t.* bendecir
blind *adj.* ciego/a
blind *n.* persiana *f.*
block *n. (city)* cuadra *(L.A.) f.;* manzana *(Spain)*
blond(e) *adj.* rubio/a
blood *n.* sangre *f.*

blood circulation *n.* circulación *f.* (sanguínea)

blood pressure *n.* presión *f.* sanguínea

blouse *n.* blusa *f.*

blue *n., adj.* azul

blueprint *n.* plano *m.*

bluish *adj.* azulado/a

blush *v.i.* ponerse rojo/a, sonrojarse

board *n. (organizational)* junta *f.;* tablero *m.*

board *v.i. (ship)* embarcar

board games *n., pl.* juegos *m., pl.* de mesa

board of directors *n.* junta *f.* directiva

boardinghouse *n.* pensión *f.*

boast (about) *v.t.* alardear (de) *(Spain)*
   He was boasting about having won. Alardeaba de haber ganado.

boat *n.* barco *m.*
   go by boat ir en barco

body *n.* cuerpo *m.*

boil *v.t.* hervir

boiled *adj.* hervido/a

bolt *n.* (*lock*) cerrojo *m.*

bolt (the door) *v.t.* correr el cerrojo

bomb *n.* bomba *f.*

bond *n.* vínculo *m.*

bone *n.* hueso *m.;* (*fish*) espina *f.*

bonfire *n.* hoguera *f.*

book *n.* libro *m.*

book *v.t.* hacer una reservación

bookcase *n.* estantería *f.;* estante *m.*

bookshelf, bookshelves *n.* estante *m.*

bookstore *n.* librería *f.*

bookworm *n.* ratón *m.* de biblioteca

boot *n.* bota *f.*
   rubber boot bota de agua

bore *v.t.* aburrir

bored *adj.* aburrido/a
   be bored estar aburrido/a
   get bored aburrirse

boring *adj.* aburrido/a; soso/a

born: be born nacer

borrow *v.t.* pedir prestado

borrowed *adj.* prestado/a

boss *n.* jefe *m.,* jefa *f.*

botanical *adj.* botánico/a

botanist *n.* botánico/a *m., f.*

botany *n.* botánica *f.*

bother *v.t.* molestar **Does the music bother you?** ¿Te molesta la música?

bottle *n.* botella *f.*

bottle opener *n.* abrebotellas *m., sing.*

bottom *n.* fondo *m.*

boulevard *n.* bulevar *m.*

bow *n.* lazo *m.;* (*sport*) arco *m.*

bowl *n.* tazón *m.*

bowling *n.* boliche *m.*

box *v.i.* boxear

boxer *n.* boxeador(a) *m., f.*

boxer shorts *n., pl.* calzoncillos *m., pl.*

boxing *n.* boxeo *m.*

boy *n.* chico *m.;* muchacho *m.;* niño *m.*

boyfriend *n.* novio *m.*

bra *n.* sostén *m.;* sujetador *(Spain) m.;* brasier *(L.A.) m.*

braid *n.* trenza *f.*

brain *n.* cerebro *m.*

brake *v.i.* frenar

brake *n.* freno *m.*

   brake pedal *n.* pedal *m.* del freno

branch *n.* rama *f.*

brand (name) *n.* marca *f.*

   It's a well-known brand. Es una marca de prestigio.

brat *n.* niño/a *m., f.* mimado/a

brave *adj.* valiente

bravery *n.* valentía *f.*

bread *n.* pan *m.*

   freshly-baked bread pan recién horneado

break *v.t.* romper **She breaks the glass.** Ella rompe el vaso.; romperse **He broke his leg.** Se rompió la pierna.

   break a world record batir un récord mundial

break down *v.i. (auto)* descomponerse *(L.A.),* dañarse *(L.A.);* averiarse *(Spain)* estropearse, sufrir una avería

   The . . . broke down on us. Se nos dañó el/la…

   break the ice *loc.* romper el hielo

break up (with) *v.i.* romper (con)

breakdown *n. (mechanical)* avería *(Spain) f.*

breakfast *n.* desayuno *m.*

   have breakfast desayunar

breakwater *n.* rompeolas *m., sing.*

breast *n.* pecho *m.*

chicken breast pechuga *f.* (de pollo)

breaststroke *n.* estilo *m.* braza *(Spain);* estilo *m.* pecho *(L.A.)*

breath *n.* aliento *m.*

breathe *v.i.* respirar

breathing *n.* respiración *f.*

breeze *n.* brisa *f.*

brick *n.* ladrillo *m.*

bricklayer *n.* albañil *m.*

bricklaying *n.* albañilería *f.*

bridge *n.* puente *m.*

bright *adj. (color)* vivo/a

bring *v.t.* traer

bring up *v.t. (children)* criar

broadcast *v.t.* transmitir; emitir

broccoli *n.* brócoli *m.*

brochure *n.* folleto *m.*

broiled *adj.* a la parrilla

broken *adj.* roto/a

   be broken estar roto/a

broken down *adj.* averiado/a *(Spain)*

bronze *n.* bronce *m.*

brook *n.* riachuelo *m.*

broom *n.* escoba *f.*

broth *n.* caldo *m.*

brother *n.* hermano *m*

   brothers and sisters *n., pl.* hermanos *m., pl.*

   younger brother *n.* hermano *m.* menor

brother-in-law *n.* cuñado *m.*

brought *p.p.* traído *(of* traer)

brown *n., adj. (color)* café; marrón; *(eyes, hair)* castaño/a

brunet(te) *adj.* moreno/a

brush *n.* cepillo *m.*

brush *v.t.* cepillar

brush one's hair cepillarse el pelo
brush one's teeth cepillarse/lavarse los dientes
bubble n. burbuja f.
Buddhist n., adj. budista m., f.
build v.t. construir
builder n. albañil m.; constructor(a) m., f. (de obras)
building n. edificio m.; (profession) albañilería f.
apartment building casa f. de apartamentos/edificio m. de apartamentos
building contractor n. constructor(a) m., f. (de obras)
bull n. toro m.
bulletin n. boletín m.
bulletin board n. tablero m. de anuncios
bullfight n. corrida f. de toros
bullfighter n. torero/a m., f.
bullfighting n. tauromaquia f.
bullring n. plaza f. de toros
bump into v. (meet accidentally) darse con
bumper n. parachoques m., sing.
burglar n. ladrón m., ladrona f.
burial n. entierro m.
burn v.t. quemar
burned (out) adj. quemado/a
burp n. eructo m.
burp v.i. eructar
bus n. autobús m.; camión m. (Mexico)
go by bus ir en autobús
bus station n. estación f. de autobuses
bush n. arbusto m.
business n. negocios m., pl.; empresa f.
business administration n. administración f. de empresas
businessman n. hombre m. de negocios
business-related adj. comercial
businesswoman n. mujer f. de negocios
busy adj. ocupado/a
but conj. pero; (in negative sentences) sino
butcher shop n. carnicería f.
butler n. mayordomo m.
butter n. mantequilla f.
butter a piece of toast untar una tostada con mantequilla
butterfly n. mariposa f.
butterfly stroke n. estilo m. mariposa
button n. botón m.
buy v.t. comprar
by prep. por
by the way a propósito, por cierto
bye fam. chau; adiós

C

cabbage n. col (Spain) f.; repollo (L.A.) m.
cabin n. cabaña f.
cable n. cable m.
cable television n. televisión f. por cable
café n. café m.
cafeteria n. cafetería f.

caffeine *n.* cafeína *f.*

cake *n.* pastel *m.*

calculate *v.t.* calcular

calculation *n.* cálculo *m.*

calculator *n.* calculadora *f.*

calendar *n.* calendario *m.*

calf *n.* *(anat.)* pantorrilla *f.*

call *v.t.* llamar
   be called llamarse
   be on call estar de guardia
   call on the phone llamar por teléfono

calm *n., adj.* tranquilidad *f.;* tranquilo/a
   Stay calm! ¡Tranquilo/a!

calm down *v.* tranquilizarse

calorie *n.* caloría *f.*

camaraderie *n.* compañerismo *m.*

camel *n.* camello *m.*

camera *n.* cámara *f.*

camp *n.* acampada *f.*

camp *v.i.* acampar
   go camping ir de acampada/campamento

can *n.* *(tin)* lata *f.*
   can opener *n.* abrelatas *m., sing.*

can *v.aux.* poder (o:ue)
   I can't take it any more! *loc.* ¡No puedo más!/¡No soporto más!

Canadian *n., adj.* canadiense *m., f.*

canary *n.* canario *m.*

cancel *v.t.* cancelar; anular; *(performance)* suspender

candidate *n.* aspirante *m., f.;* candidato/a *m., f.*

candle *n.* vela *f.*

candy *n.* dulces *m., pl.*

cane *n.* caña *f.*

canoe *n.* piragua *f.*

canoeing *n.* piragüismo *m.*

canoeist *n.* piragüista *m., f.*

canvas *n.* lona *f.*

cap *n.* *(with a visor)* gorra *f.;* *(without a visor)* gorro *m.*

capital *n.* capital *f.*
   capital letter *n.* mayúscula *f.*

capsule *n.* cápsula *f.*

capture *v.t.* capturar

car *n.* carro *(L.A.)* *m.;* coche *(Spain)* *m.;* automóvil *m.*
   go by car ir en auto(móvil)

car accident *n.* *(crash)* choque *m.*

carbohydrate *n.* carbohidrato *m.*

carburator *n.* carburador *m.*

card *n.* tarjeta *f.;* *(playing)* carta *f.,* naipe *m.*

card table *n.* tapete (verde) *m.*

cardiology *n.* cardiología *f.*

care *n.* cuidado *m.,* atención *f.*
   take care of cuidar
   take care of oneself cuidarse

careful: be careful tener cuidado; ¡Cuidado!

career *n.* carrera *f.*

caretaker *n.* el ama *(m., f.)* de casa

Caribbean *adj.* caribeño/a

carnation *n.* clavel *m.*

carnivore *n.* carnívoro/a *m., f.*

carnivorous *adj.* carnívoro/a

carols *n.* villancicos *m., pl.*

carpenter *n.* carpintero/a *m., f.*

carpet *n.* alfombra *f.*

carrot *n.* zanahoria *f.*
carry *v.t.* llevar; transportar
cart *n.* carro *(Spain) m.*
cartoons *n., pl. (animated)* dibujos *m., pl.* animados; *(political)* caricaturas *f., pl.* (políticas)
carve *v.t.* tallar
case *n.* caso *m.*
  in case of en caso de que
  in case (that) en caso (de) que
cash *n.* (en) efectivo *m.*
cash (a check) *v.t.* cobrar
cash register *n.* caja *f.*
cashier *n.* cajero/a *m., f.*
casserole *n.* cazuela *f.*
cast *n.* yeso *(L.A.) m.*; escayola *(Spain) f.*
castle *n.* castillo *m.*
casual *adj.* informal
cat *n.* gato/a *m., f.*
catastrophe *n.* catástrofe *f.*
catastrophic *adj.* catastrófico/a
catch *v.t. (illness)* pegar
category *n.* categoría *f.*
cathedral *n.* catedral *f.*
Catholic *n., adj.* católico/a *m., f.*
cattle *n.* ganado *m.*
cattle farmer *n.* ganadero/a *m., f.*
cattle raising *n.* ganadería *f.*
cause *v.t.* causar; provocar
cavern *n.* caverna *f.*
CD-ROM *n.* cederrón *m.*
cedar *n.* cedro *m.*
celebrate *v.t.* celebrar; festejar
celebration *n.* festejo *m.*
celery *n.* apio *m.*
cell *n.* célula *f.*

cellar *n.* sótano *m.; (wine)* bodega *f.*
cellular *adj.* celular
cement *n.* cemento *m.*
cemetery *n.* cementerio *m.*
censor *v.t.* censurar
censorship *n.* censura *f.*
censure *n.* censura *f.*
censure *v.t.* censurar
census *n.* censo *m.*
century *n.* siglo *m.*
cereal *n.* cereales *m., pl.*
certain *adj.* cierto/a; seguro/a
  it's (not) certain (no) es cierto/seguro
certainty *n.* certeza *f.*
chain *n.* cadena *f.*
chair *n.* silla *f.*
chalk *n.* tiza *f.*
challenge *n.* reto *m.;* desafío *m.*
challenge *v.t.* desafiar; retar
champagne *n.* champán *m.*
champion *n.* campeón *m.,* campeona *f.*
championship *n.* campeonato *m.*
chance *n.* azar *m.*
chandelier *n.* araña *f.* (de luces)
change *v.t.* cambiar (de/en); renovar
change *n.* cambio *m.*
change purse *n.* monedero *m.*
channel *n. (TV, radio)* canal *m.;* cadena *f.*
Chanukah *n.* Januká *m.*
chapel *n.* capilla *f.;* ermita *f.*
character *n.* carácter *m.; (fictional)* personaje *m.*

main character personaje principal

charisma *n.* carisma *m.*

charity *n.* caridad *f.; (money)* limosna *f.; (organization)* sociedad *f.* benéfica

charm *n.* encanto *m.*

charming *adj.* encantador(a)

chase *v.t.* perseguir

chat *v.* conversar

chatterbox *n.* charlatán *m.,* charlatana *f.*

chauffeur *n.* conductor(a) *m., f.*

cheap *adj.* barato/a

cheat *v.i.* hacer trampa(s); *(money)* engañar

cheat on *v.t. (relationship)* engañar

check *n. (bank)* cheque *m.*

check *v.t.* comprobar; revisar; averiguar

check the oil revisar el aceite

checkers *n., pl. (game)* damas (chinas) *f., pl.*

checkup *n.* revisión *(Spain) f.;* chequeo (médico) *(L.A.) m.*

cheek *n.* mejilla *f.*

cheeky *adj.* caradura

cheeky person *n.* caradura *m., f.*

cheer up *v.* animar(se)

cheese *n.* queso *m.*

chef *n.* cocinero/a *m., f.*

chemical *adj.* químico/a

chemist *n.* químico/a *m., f.*

chemistry *n.* química *f.*

cherry *n.* cereza *f.*

cherry tree *n.* cerezo *m.*

chess *n.* ajedrez *m.*

chess player *n.* ajedrecista *m., f.*

chest *n. (anatomy)* pecho *m.*

chest of drawers *n.* cómoda *f.*

chew *v.t.* masticar

chicken *n.* pollo *m.*

chickpea *n.* garbanzo *m.*

child *n.* niño/a *m., f. (son, daughter)* hijo/a *m., f.*

only child hijo/a único/a

childhood *n.* niñez *f.*

children *n., pl. (sons and daughters)* hijos *m., pl.*

chill *v.t.* enfriar

chilled *adj.* frío/a

chimney *n.* chimenea *f.*

china *n. (fine)* porcelana *f.*

Chinese *n., adj.* chino/a *m., f.; (language)* chino

chlorine *n.* cloro *m.*

chlorophyll *n.* clorofila *f.*

chocolate *n.* chocolate *m.*

chocolate cake *n.* pastel *m.* de chocolate

choir *n.* coro *m.*

choke *v.i.* atragantarse

cholesterol *n.* colesterol *m.*

choose *v.t.* escoger

chop *n. (meat)* chuleta *f.*

chop *v.t.* cortar

chores *n., pl.* quehaceres *m., pl.*

household chores quehaceres domésticos

do household chores hacer quehaceres domésticos

chorus *n.* coro *m.*

Christian *n., adj.* cristiano/a *m., f.*

Christmas *n.* Navidad *f.*

Christmas card n. tarjeta f. de Navidad

church n. iglesia f.

cider n. sidra f.

cinnamon n. canela f.

circle n. círculo m.

circuit n. (electric) circuito m.

circus n. circo m.

citizen n. ciudadano/a m., f.

citrus adj. cítrico/a

city n. ciudad f.

　　city hall n. ayuntamiento m.

clam n. almeja f.

clap v.t./v.i. aplaudir

clash n. enfrentamiento m.

class n. clase f.

　　take classes tomar clases

classical adj. clásico/a

classmate n. compañero/a m., f. de clase

classroom n. aula f.; salón m.

clavicle n. clavícula f.

clay n. arcilla f.

clean adj. limpio/a

clean v.t. limpiar

　　clean the house limpiar la casa

clear adj. claro/a; (weather) despejado/a

　　It's (very) clear. (weather) Está (muy) despejado.

clear v.t. (pipes) desatascar

　　clear the table quitar/recoger la mesa

clerk n. dependiente/a m., f.

cliff n. acantilado m.

climate n. clima m.

climatology n. climatología f.

climb n. (mountain) escalada f.

climb v.t. escalar

climb mountains escalar montañas

climb trees v. subirse a los árboles

climber n. (mountain) alpinista m., f., escalador(a) m., f.

climbing n. (mountain) alpinismo m.

clinic n. clínica f.

clock n. reloj m.

　　alarm clock despertador m.

clog n. zueco m.

close adj. (relative) cercano/a; (people) unido/a

　　get close (to someone) intimar (con alguien)

close v.t. cerrar (e:ie)

closed adj. cerrado/a

closet n. armario m.; clóset m.

closing n. clausura f.

clothes n., pl. ropa f.

　　What pretty clothes! ¡Qué ropa más bonita!

　　clothes dryer n. secadora f.

clothesline n. tendedero m.

clothing n. ropa f.

cloud n. nube f.

　　have one's head in the clouds estar en las nubes

cloudy adj. nublado/a

　　It's (very) cloudy. Está (muy) nublado.

clown n. payaso/a m., f.

clue n. pista f.

　　Give me a clue. Dame una pista.

clumsy adj. torpe

clutch n. embrague m.

　　clutch pedal n. pedal m. del embrague

coach *n.* entrenador(a) *m., f.*
coaching *n.* entrenamiento *m.*
coal *n.* carbón *m.*
coast *n.* costa *f.*
coastal *adj.* costero/a
coastline *n.* costa *f.*
coat *n.* abrigo *m.*
  coat hanger *n.* perchero *m.*
cockroach *n.* cucaracha *f.*
coconut *n.* coco *m.*
cod *n.* bacalao *m.*
coffee *n.* café *m.*
  coffee maker *n.* cafetera *f.*
coffin *n.* ataúd *m.*
coincide *v.i.* coincidir
coincidence *n.* azar *m.;*
  coincidencia *f.*
colander *n.* colador *m.*
cold *n. (temperature)* frío *m.;*
  (illness) catarro *m.,* resfriado
  m.
  be cold *(thing)* estar frío/a
  be (feel) cold tener frío
  It's (very) cold. *(weather)*
  Hace (mucho) frío.
collaborate *v.i.* colaborar
  collaborate (with) *v. pron.*
  asociarse (con)
collaboration *n.* colaboración
  f.
collect *v.t.* coleccionar
collecting *n.* coleccionismo *m.*
collector *n.* coleccionista *m., f.*
college *n.* universidad *f.*
collision *n.* choque *m.*
cologne *n.* colonia *f.*
colonist *n.* colono *m.*
colonization *n.* colonización *f.*
colonize *v.t.* colonizar
colony *n.* colonia *f.*

color *n.* color *m.*
color *v.t.* colorear
column *n.* columna *f.*
comb *n.* peine *m.*
comb one's hair *v. refl.*
  peinarse
come *v.i.* venir
come back *v.* volver; regresar
comedy *n.* comedia *f.*
comfort *n.* confort *m.*
comfortable *adj.* confortable;
  cómodo/a
comic strip *n.* tira *f.* cómica,
  historieta *f.*
commemorate *v.t.* conmemorar
commemoration *n.*
  conmemoración *f.*
commerce *n.* negocios *m., pl.*
commercial *adj.* comercial
committee *n.* junta *f.*
common *adj.* común
communicate *v.t.* comunicar;
  (speak with) comunicarse
  (con)
communication *n.*
  comunicación *f.*
community *n.* comunidad *f.*
compact disc (CD) *n.* disco *m.*
  compacto
compact disc player *n.*
  tocadiscos *m., sing.*
  compacto
companion *n.* compañero/a
  m., f.
company *n.* compañía *f.;*
  empresa *f.*
comparison *n.* comparación *f.*
compete *v.i.* competir
competence *n.* aptitud *f.*
competent *adj.* competente

competition n. competencia (L.A.) f.; competición (Spain) f.

competitive adj. competitivo/a

competitor n. competidor(a) m., f.; participante m., f.

complain v.i. quejarse

complaint n. queja f.

completely adv. completamente; a fondo

complex adj. complejo

complexion n. cutis m.

complicate v.t. complicar

composer n. compositor(a) m., f.

computer n. computadora f.

computer disk n. disco m.

computer monitor n. monitor m.

computer programmer n. programador(a) m., f.

computer science n. computación f.

con artist n. estafador(a) m., f.

conceal v.t. disimular

conceited adj. engreído/a

concert n. concierto m.

concrete n. concreto (L.A.) m.; hormigón (Spain) m.

condense v.t. condensar

conditioned adj. acondicionado/a

conduct n. conducta f.

conductor n. (musical) director(a) m., f.

conference n. congreso m.

confirm v.t. confirmar

confirm a reservation confirmar una reservación

confirmation n. confirmación f.

confront v.t. enfrentar; enfrentarse (con)

The army will confront the enemy. El ejército se enfrentará con el enemigo.

confuse v.t. confundir

confused adj. confundido/a

confusion n. confusión f.

congested adj. congestionado/a

congratulate v.t. felicitar

Congratulations! (for an event such as a birthday or anniversary) ¡Felicidades! f., pl.; (for an event such as an engagement or a good grade on a test) ¡Felicitaciones! f., pl.

conquer v.t. conquistar

conqueror n. conquistador(a) m., f.

conquest n. conquista f.

conscience n. conciencia f.

consensus n. consenso m.

consent n. consentimiento m.

consent to v. consentir

conservation n. conservación f.

conservative n., adj. conservador(a) m., f.

conserve v.t. conservar

considerate adj. considerado/a

constellation n. constelación f.

constipated adj. estreñido/a

constipation n. estreñimiento m.

constitution n. constitución f.

consume v.t. consumir

consume alcohol consumir alcohol

consumer *n.* consumidor(a) *m., f.*

consumption *n.* consumo *m.*

contact lenses *n., pl.* lentes *m., pl.* de contacto

contagion *n.* contagio *m.*

contagious *adj.* contagioso/a

container *n.* recipiente *m.*; envase *m.*

contamination *n.* contaminación *f.*

content *adj.* contento/a

contest *n.* competencia *(L.A.) f.*; concurso *m.*

continue *v.t.* seguir (e:i)

contraceptive *n.* anticonceptivo *m.*

contract *n.* contrato *m.*

contradict *v.t.* contradecir

contradiction *n.* contradicción *f.*

contrast *v.t.* contraponer

control *n.* control *m.*
  control panel *n.* tablero *m.* de control
  control tower *n.* torre *f.* de control

control *v.t.* controlar
  be under control estar bajo control

control oneself *v.* dominarse

controversial *adj.* polémico/a

controversy *n.* polémica *f.*

convent *n.* convento *m.*

conversation *n.* conversación *f.*

converse *v.* conversar

convertible *n., adj. (car)* descapotable *m.*

convict *n.* presidiario/a *m., f.*

conviction *n.* convicción *f.*

convince *v.t.* convencer

convincing *adj.* convincente

cook *n.* cocinero/a *m., f.*

cook *v.t./v.i.* cocinar

cookie *n.* galleta *f.*

cool *adj.* fresco/a; *(slang)* chévere
  It's cool. *(weather)* Hace fresco.

copper *n.* cobre *m.*

copy *v.t.* copiar

cork *n.* corcho *m.*

corkscrew *n.* sacacorchos *m, sing.*

corn *n.* maíz *m.*

corner *n.* esquina *m.*

corpse *n.* cadáver *m.*

correct *v.t.* corregir

correction *n.* corrección *f.*

correctness *n.* corrección *f.*

cost *v.t.* costar (o:ue)
  cost an arm and a leg *idiom.* costar un ojo de la cara

costume *n.* disfraz *m.*

cotton *n.* algodón *m.*
  made of cotton de algoldón

couch *n.* sofá *m.*
  couch potato *n.* teleadicto/a *m., f.*

cough *n.* tos *f.*

cough syrup *n.* jarabe *m.* para la tos

cough *v.i.* toser

counselor *n.* consejero/a *m., f.*

count (o:ue) *v.t.* contar

counter *n. (game)* ficha *f.*

country *n. (nation)* país *m.*; *(rural)* campo *m.*
  developed country país desarrollado

developing country país en vías de desarrollo

countryside n. campo m.; paisaje m.

couple, (married) n. pareja f.
a couple of days un par de días

courage n. valentía f.; valor m.

course n. curso m.; materia f.

court n. (of law) corte (L.A.) f., tribunal (Spain) m.; (sport) cancha f.
clay court pista f. de tierra batida
grass court pista f. de hierba

courtesy n. cortesía f.

cousin n. primo/a m., f.

cover v.t. cubrir; (container, pan) tapar

covered p.p. cubierto (of cubrir)

cow n. vaca f.

coward adj. cobarde

cowardice n. cobardía f.

cowboy n. vaquero m.

cowgirl n. vaquera f.

cozy adj. acogedor(a)

crab n. cangrejo m.

cracker n. galleta f. (salada)

cradle n. cuna f.

crafts n. artesanía f.

craftsmanship n. artesanía f.

crane n. (machinery) grúa f.

crash (into sthg.) v.i. chocar (contra algo)
crash a party colarse en una fiesta

crater n. cráter m.

crave v.t. ansiar

crawl v.i. arrastrarse (por el suelo)

crazy adj. loco/a

cream n. crema f.; (dairy) nata f.
anti-wrinkle cream crema antiarrugas

creamy adj. cremoso/a

create v.t. crear

creative adj. creativo/a

creator n. creador(a) m., f.

credible adj. verosímil

credit n. crédito m.
credit card n. tarjeta f. de crédito

cricket n. grillo m.

crime n. crimen m.; delincuencia f.

criminal n. delincuente m., f.

crisis n. crisis f.
mid-life crisis crisis de los cuarenta

critic n. detractor(a) m., f.

crockery n. vajilla f.

cross v.t. cruzar; atravesar

cross section n. (Tech.) corte m. transversal

crossroads n., pl. cruce m.

crosswalk n. paso m. de peatones

crossword (puzzle) n. crucigrama m.

cruise n. crucero m.

crunchy adj. crujiente

crusty adj. (bread) crujiente

cry v.i. llorar

crybaby n. llorón m., llorona f.

crystal n. cristal m.

cucumber n. pepino m.

culture n. cultura f.

cup n. taza f.

cure n. cura f.
cure v.t. curar
currency exchange n. cambio m. de moneda
current n. corriente f.
　alternating current (AC) corriente alterna
　direct current (CD) corriente continua
　current events n., pl. actualidades f., pl.
curriculum vitae n. currículum m.
curtain n. cortina f.
curve n. curva f.
cushion n. cojín m.
custard n. (baked) flan m.; natillas f., pl.
　baked caramel custard flan de caramelo
custom n. costumbre f.
customer n. cliente/a m., f.
customs n. aduana f.
　go through customs pasar por la aduana
　customs inspector n. inspector(a) m., f. de aduanas
cut n. corte f.
cut v.t. cortar; partir (un pastel)
　cut class idiom irse de pinta (Mexico); hacer novillos (Spain)
cutlery n. cubertería f.
cybercafé n. cibercafé m.
cycling n. ciclismo m.
cycling race n. carrera f. ciclista
cyclist n. ciclista m., f.
cylinder n. cilindro m.

cypress n. ciprés m.

D

dad n. papá m.
daily adj. diario/a
daily routine n. rutina f. diaria
dairy n. productos m., pl. lácteos
daisy n. margarita f.
dam n. represa f.
damage v.t. dañar; estropear
damp adj. húmedo/a
dance n. baile m.; danza f.
dance v.t. bailar
dance floor n. pista f. de baile
dancer n. bailarín m., bailarina f.
danger n. peligro m.
dangerous adj. peligroso/a
dare (to + inf.) v.t. atreverse (a + inf.)
daring adj. atrevido/a
dark-skinned adj. moreno/a
darken v.t. (sky, clouds) ennegrecerse
darts n., pl. (game) dardos m., pl.
date (someone) v.t. salir con (alguien)
date n. (appointment) cita f.; (calendar) fecha f.
　have a date tener una cita
　What is the date (today)? ¿Cuál es la fecha (de hoy)?
　What is today's date? ¿Cuál es la fecha de hoy?
daughter n. hija f.
daughter-in-law n. nuera f.
dawn n. amanecer m.
dawn v.i. amanecer

day *n.* día *m.*
  What day is it? ¿Qué día es hoy?
day before yesterday *adv.* anteayer
day-care center *n.* guardería *f.*
daydream *v.i.* soñar despierto
dazed *adj.* atontado/a
dead-end street *n.* callejón *m.* sin salida
deaf *adj.* sordo/a
deal *n.* trato *m.*
  It's a deal. Trato hecho.
  It's no big deal. No es para tanto.
dealer *n. (arms, drugs)* traficante *m., f.*
dean *n. (university)* decano/a *m., f.*
death *n.* muerte *f.;* defunción *f.;* fallecimiento *m.*
debate *n.* debate *m.*
debate *v.t.* debatir
debut *v.t. (movie, play)* estrenar
decadence *n.* decadencia *f.*
decaffeinated *adj.* descafeinado/a
deceased *n., adj.* fallecido/a *m., f.,* difunto/a *m., f.*
deceive *v.t.* engañar
December *n.* diciembre *m.*
deception *n.* engaño *m.*
decide *v.t.* decidir (+ inf.)
decided *adj.* decidido/a
decipher *v.t.* descifrar
decision *n.* decisión *f.*
  make a decision tomar una decisión
deck (of cards) *n.* baraja *f.* (de cartas/naipes)
deck chair *n.* tumbona *f.*
declare *v.t.* declarar
decline *n.* descenso *m.;* decadencia *f.*
decode *v.t.* descifrar
decorate *v.t.* decorar; adornar
  decorate the tree poner el árbol
decrease *n.* descenso *m.;* disminución *f.*
decrease *v.t.* disminuir
dedicate *v.t.* dedicar
dedication *n.* dedicación; dedicatoria *f.*
deer *n.* ciervo *m.*
defeat *n.* derrota *f.*
defeat *v.t.* derrotar
deficiency *n.* deficiencia *f.*
deficit *n.* déficit *m.*
define *v.t.* definir
definition *n.* definición *f.*
deforestation *n.* deforestación *f.*
defraud *v.t.* estafar
defuse *v.t.* desactivar
dejected *adj.* abatido/a
delay *n.* retraso *m.,* atraso *m.*
delicious *adj.* delicioso/a, rico/a, sabroso/a
  be delicious *loc.* estar para chuparse los dedos
delight *n.* deleite *m.,* placer *m.*
delighted *adj.* encantado/a
delineate *v.t.* delinear
delinquency *n.* delincuencia *f.*
democracy *n.* democracia *f.*
democrat *n.* demócrata *m., f.*
democratic *adj.* democrático/a
demonstrate *v.i.* manifestarse

demonstration *n.*
  manifestación *f.*
demonstrator *n.* manifestante
  m., f.
density *n.* densidad *f.*
dental floss *n.* hilo *m.* dental
dentist *n.* dentista *m., f.*
deny *v.t.* negar (e:ie)
  not to deny no negar
deodorant *n.* desodorante *m.*
department *n.* departamento
  m.
department head *n.*
  catedrático/a *m., f.*
department store *n.* almacén
  m.
departure *n.* partida *f.*; salida *f.*
deposit *v.t.* depositar
depressed *adj.* deprimido/a
depression *n.* depresión *f.*
depth *n.* profundidad *f.*
derail *v.t.* descarrilar
derailment *n.* descarrilamiento
  m.
dermatologist *n.*
  dermatólogo/a *m., f.*
descend *v.i.* descender
descendant *n.* descendiente
  m., f.
descent *n.* descenso *m.*
describe *v.t.* describir
described *pp.* descrito (*of*
  describir)
desert *n., adj.* desierto *m.*;
  desértico/a
deserve *v.t.* merecer
design *n.* diseño *m.*
designer *n.* diseñador(a) *m., f.*
desire *n.* deseo *m.*
desire *v.t.* desear

desk *n.* escritorio *m.*
despair *n.* desesperanza *f.*
despair *v.i.* desesperar(se);
  perder las esperanzas
desperate *adj.* desesperado/a
desperation *n.* desesperación
  f.
dessert *n.* postre *m.*
destroy *v.t.* destruir
destruction *n.* destrucción *f.*
detail *n.* detalle *m.*
detained *adj.* detenido/a
deteriorate *v.* decaer
determined *adj.*
  condicionado/a
detoxification *n.*
  desintoxicación *f.*
detoxify *v.t.* desintoxicar
detractor *n.* detractor(a) *m., f.*
develop *v.t.* desarrollar
development *n.* desarrollo *m.*;
  (housing) urbanización *f.*
dew *n.* rocío *m.*
diabetes *n.* diabetes *f.*
diabetic *n., adj.* diabético/a *m.,*
  f.
diagnose *v.t.* diagnosticar
diagnostic *n.* diagnóstico *m.*
dial (the number) *v.t.* marcar
  (el número)
dialogue *n.* diálogo *m.*
diamond *n.* diamante *m.*
diarrhea *n.* diarrea *f.*
diary *n.* diario *m.*
dice *n., pl.* dados *m., pl.*
dictator *n.* dictador(a) *m., f.*
dictatorship *n.* dictadura *f.*
dictionary *n.* diccionario *m.*
die out *v.t.* extinguirse
die *v.i.* morir (o:ue)

died *p.p.* muerto (*of* morir)

diet *n.* dieta *f.*; alimentación *f.*
  eat a balanced diet comer una dieta equilibrada
  be on a diet estar a dieta

differ *v.i.* divergir

difference *n.* diferencia *f.*, divergencia *f.*

different *adj.* diferente

differing *adj.* (*opinions*) divergente

difficult *adj.* difícil
  make difficult dificultar; complicar

difficulty *n.* dificultad *f.*

dig *v.t.* excavar

digital camera cámara digital

dine *v.i.* cenar

dining room *n.* comedor *m.*

dinner *n.* cena *f.*
  have dinner cenar

dinosaur *n.* dinosaurio *m.*

diplomat *n.* diplomático/a *m., f.*

diplomatic *adj.* diplomático/a

direct *v.t.* dirigir

directions *n., pl.* direcciones *f.*, *pl.* indicaciones (*Spain*) *f., pl.*
  give directions dar direcciones

director *n.* director(a) *m., f.*

dirty *adj.* sucio/a

dirty *v.t.* ensuciar
  get (something) dirty ensuciar

disabled *adj.* (*person*) inválido/a

disadvantage *n.* desventaja *f.*

disagree *v.i.* no estar de acuerdo

disappear *v.i.* desaparecer

disappearance *n.* desaparición *f.*

disappointed *adj.* decepcionado/a; desilusionado/a
  be disappointed decepcionarse

disaster *n.* desastre *m.*
  natural disaster desastre natural

disastrous *adj.* desastroso/a

discipline *n.* disciplina *f.*

discoteque *n.* discoteca *f.*

discount *n.* descuento *m.*

discount *v.t.* descontar
  give a discount descontar

discover *v.t.* descubrir

discovered *p.p.* descubierto (*of* descubrir)

discovery *n.* descubrimiento *m.*; hallazgo *m.*

discreet *adj.* discreto/a

discrete *adj.* discreto/a

discrimination *n.* discriminación *f.*

discuss *v.t.* discutir

discus throw *n.* lanzamiento *m.* de disco

disgraceful *adj.* vergonzoso/a

disgusting *adj.* asqueroso/a

dish *n.* plato *m.*; platillo
  main dish plato principal
  serving dish fuente *f.*

dishcloth *n.* trapo *m.*

dishes (set) *n., pl.* vajilla *f.*

disheveled *adj.* despeinado/a

dishonest *adj.* deshonesto/a

dishwasher *n.* lavaplatos *m., sing.*

disinfect *v.t.* desinfectar

disinfectant *n., adj.* desinfectante

disk *n.* disco *m.*

dislike *n.* antipatía *f.;* aversión *f.*

dislike *v.i.* chocar

disobey *v.t.* desobedecer

disorder *n.* desorden *m.; (medical)* trastorno *m.*

disorderly *adj.* desordenado/a

disposable *adj.* desechable

disqualification *n. (sport)* descalificación *f.*

disqualify *v.t. (sports)* descalificar

disseminate *v.t.* propagar

distant *adj.* lejano/a

distinction *n. (grade)* matrícula *f.* de honor

distinguish *v.t.* distinguir

distinguished *adj.* distinguido/a

distribute *v.t.* distribuir

distribution *n.* distribución *f.*

distrustful *adj.* receloso/a

dive *n.* salto *m.;* clavado *(L.A.) m.*

dive, (scuba) *v.i. (underwater)* bucear

diving board *n.* trampolín *m.*

diver *n. (scuba)* buceador(a) *m., f.*

diverse *adj.* variado/a

divorce *n.* divorcio *m.*

divorced *adj.* divorciado/a
  get divorced (from) divorciarse (de)

dizzy *adj.* mareado/a
  feel dizzy marearse

do *v.t.* hacer

do the dishes lavar los platos

do oneself up *v.* arreglarse

doctor *n.* doctor(a) *m., f.;* médico/a *m., f.*
  doctor on call/duty médico/a de guardia

doctorate *n.* doctorado *m.*

document *n.* documento *m.*

document *v.t.* documentar

documentary *n.* documental *m.*

dodge ball *n.* quemados *m., pl.*

dog *n.* perro/a *m., f.*

doll *n.* muñeco/a *m., f.*

dolphin *n.* delfín *m.*

domestic *adj.* doméstico/a
  domestic appliance electrodoméstico *m.*

dominate *v.t.* dominar

domino *n.* dominó *m.*

done *p.p.* hecho *(of* hacer)

donor *n.* donante *m., f.*

donut *n.* dona *f.*

door *n.* puerta *f.*
  back door puerta trasera
  front door puerta principal

doorbell *n.* timbre *m.*

doorman *n.* portero/a *m., f.*

dormitory *n.* residencia *f.* estudiantil

double *adj.* doble

doubt *n.* duda *f.*
  There is no doubt that . . . No cabe duda (de) que… ; No hay duda (de) que…
  without a doubt sin duda

doubt *v.t.* dudar
  not to doubt no dudar

dough *n.* masa *f.*

dove *n.* paloma *f.*

down *adv.* abajo, debajo (de)

Down with...! ¡Abajo el/la...!
downhearted *adj.* desanimado/a
download *v.t. (computer)* descargar
downtown *n.* centro *m.*
draftsman *n.* delineante *m.*
draftswoman *n.* delineante *f.*
drag *v.t.* arrastrar
drain *v.t.* colar *(L.A.); (the dishes)* escurrir (los platos)
drainpipe *n.* desagüe *m.*
drama *n.* drama *m.*
dramatic *adj.* dramático/a
draw *v.t.* dibujar
drawback *n.* inconveniente *m.*
drawing *n.* dibujo *m.*
dream *v.i.* soñar
dress *n.* vestido *m.*
dress *v.t.* vestirse (e:i); *(salad)* aderezar; aliñar
   get dressed vestirse (e:i)
dress up *v.* ponerse elegante
   You have dressed up tonight. Te has puesto muy elegante esta noche.
dresser *n.* cómoda *f.*
dressing *n. (culinary)* aderezo *m.*, aliño *m.; (medical)* vendaje *m.*
dressing room *n.* probador *m.*
dressmaker *n.* modista *f.*
drill *n. (tool)* perforadora *f.*
drill *v.t.* perforar
drink *n.* bebida *f.*
drink *v.t.* beber; tomar
   Do you want something to drink? ¿Quieres algo de tomar?
drive *v.t.* conducir *(Spain);*

manejar *(L.A.)*
driver *n.* conductor(a) *m., f.*
driveway *n.* entrada *f.*
drop *n.* gota *f.; (temperature, price)* descenso *m.*
drop off *v.t.* dejar
drought *n.* sequía *f.*
drown *v.t.* ahogar **Ahoga sus penas cantando.** She drowns her sorrows by singing. *v.i.* ahogarse **Te ahogas en un vaso de agua.** You get worked up about nothing.
drowned *adj.* ahogado/a
drug *n.* droga *f.*
   drug addict *n., adj.* drogadicto/a *m., f.*
drunk *adj.* borracho/a; ebrio/a; embriagado/a
dry *adj.* seco/a
dry (oneself) *v. pron.* secarse
due to *prep.* debido a; por
   due to the fact that debido a
dull *adj.* sin brillo; *(person)* aburrido/a, soso/a
dumb *adj.* tonto/a
dune *n.* duna *f.*
during *prep.* durante; por
dusk *n.* atardecer *m.*
dust *n.* polvo *m.*
dust *v.t.* sacudir
   dust the furniture sacudir los muebles
duty: be on duty estar de guardia
DVD player reproductor de DVD
dye *v.t.* teñir
dying *adj.* moribundo/a
   I'm dying to/for . . . Me muero por (+ *inf.*)/*n.* . . .

dynamite n. dinamita f.
dynamite v.t. dinamitar
dynasty n. dinastía f.
dysfunction n. disfunción f.

E

each adj. cada
eagle n. águila (el) f.
ear, (outer) n. oreja f.
  inner ear n. oído m.
early adj., adv. temprano/a
  early morning n. madrugada f.
earn v.t. ganar
  earn one's living idiom ganarse la vida
earring n. arete (L.A) m.; pendiente m. (Spain)
earth n. tierra f.
earthquake n. terremoto m.
earthworm n. lombriz f.
ease n. soltura f.
ease v.t. aliviar
east n. este m.
  to the east al este
easy adj. fácil
  make easier facilitar
  Easier said than done. idiom Del dicho al hecho hay gran trecho.
easygoing adj. tranquilo/a
eat v.t. comer
eclipse n. eclipse m.
ecological adj. ecológico/a
ecologist n. ecologista m., f.
ecology n. ecología f.
economics n. economía f.
ecosystem n. ecosistema m.
ecotourism n. ecoturismo m.
Ecuadorian n., adj.

ecuatoriano/a m., f.
edible adj. comestible
educator n. educador(a) m., f.
eel n. anguila f.
effective adj. eficaz
effectiveness n. eficacia f.
efficiency n. eficiencia f.
efficient adj. eficiente, eficaz
effort n. esfuerzo m.
egg n. huevo m.
eggplant n. berenjena f.
eight ocho
eight hundred ochocientos/as
eighteen dieciocho
eighth octavo m.; adj. octavo/a
eighty ochenta
either . . . or conj. o… o
elastic adj. elástico/a
elbow n. codo m.
elderly adj. anciano/a
eldest el/la mayor
elect v.t. elegir
election n. elección f., elecciones f., pl.
electorate n. electorado m.
electric adj. eléctrico/a
electric current n. corriente f. eléctrica
electric shock n. descarga f. eléctrica
electrician n. electricista m., f.
electricity n. electricidad f.; luz f.
electrocuted: be electrocuted electrocutarse
electrolysis n. electrólisis f.
electronics n. electrónica f.
elegant adj. elegante
elementary adj. elemental; (school) primario/a

elephant *n.* elefante *m.*
elevator *n.* ascensor *m.*
eleven once
eliminate *v.t.* eliminar
elimination *n.* eliminación *f.*
eloquence *n.* elocuencia *f.*
eloquent *adj.* elocuente
e-mail *n.* correo *m.* electrónico
  e-mail address dirección electrónica
  e-mail message *n.* mensaje *m.* electrónico
embarrass *v.t.* avergonzar
embarrassed *adj.* avergonzado/a
embarrassment *n.* vergüenza *f.*
embrace *v.t.* abrazar; *(each other)* abrazarse
embroider *v.t.* bordar
emerald *n.* esmeralda *f.*
emergency *n.* emergencia *f.*
emergency room *n.* sala *f.* de emergencia
emigrant *n.* emigrante *m., f.*
emigrate *v.i.* emigrar
emigration *n.* emigración *f.*
emphasis *n.* énfasis *m.*
emphasize *v.t.* destacar; enfatizar
empire *n.* imperio *m.*
employee *n.* empleado/a *m., f.*
employment *n.* empleo *m.*
enchant *v.t.* encantar
encourage *v.t.* dar aliento; animar
end *n.* fin *m.*
  at the end (of) *(physical location)* al fondo (de); *(month, century)* a fines de
end *v.t.* terminar

end table *n.* mesita *f.*
endangered species *n., pl.* especie(s) *f. (pl.)* en peligro de extinción
endurance *n.* resistencia *f.;* aguante *m.;*
endure *v.t.* soportar; aguantar
energy *n.* energía *f.*
  (nuclear/solar) energy energía (nuclear/solar)
engaged: get engaged (to) comprometerse (con)
engagement *n.* compromiso *m.,* noviazgo *m.*
engagement ring *n.* anillo *m.* de compromiso
engineer *n.* ingeniero/a *m., f.*
English *adj., n.* inglés *m.,* inglesa *f.; (language)* inglés
enigma *n.* enigma *m.*
enigmatic *adj.* enigmático/a
enjoy *v.t.* disfrutar (de)
enjoyable *adj.* agradable; divertido/a
enough *adj.* bastante
enrich *v.t.* enriquecer
enroll *v.i.* matricularse; inscribirse
enrollment *n.* inscripción *f.*
enter *v.* entrar
entertaining *adj.* entretenido/a
entertainment *n.* diversión *f.*
enthusiasm *n.* entusiasmo *m.*
enthusiastic *adj.* entusiasmado/a
entirely *adv.* totalmente; del todo **He is not entirely mistaken.** No está del todo equivocado.
entrance *n.* entrada *f.*

entrance hall n. (residence) recibidor m.
entrepreneur n. empresario/a m., f.
envelope n. sobre m.
envious adj. envidioso/a
environment n. medio ambiente m.; (natural) ambiente m.
environmentalist n. ecologista m., f.
equality n. igualdad f.
equestrian sports n., pl. hípica f.
equipped adj. equipado/a
equivalence n. equivalencia f.
equivalent: be equivalent to equivaler
erase v.t. borrar
eraser n. borrador m.; (pencil) goma f.
errand n. diligencia f.
 do/run errands hacer diligencias
erupt v.i. (volcano) hacer erupción
eruption n. erupción f.
escalator n. escalera f. mecánica
escape n. evasión f.; huida f.; (prison) fuga f.
escape v.i. huir; fugarse; evadirse **Luis escaped responsibility.** Luis se evadió de la responsabilidad.
esophagus n. esófago m.
establish v.t. establecer
esteem n. aprecio m.
estimate n. cálculo m.
ethical adj. ético/a

ethics n. ética f.
euphoria n. euforia f.
euphoric adj. eufórico/a
European n., adj. europeo/a m., f.
evade v.t. evadir
evening n. tarde f.; noche f.
 in the evening de la noche; por la noche
event n. acontecimiento m.
ever alguna vez
every adj. cada
 every day cada día, todos los días
everybody n. todos m., pl.
everything n. todo m.
 Everything is under control. Todo está bajo control.
evidence n. indicio m.; pruebas f., pl.
 lack of evidence falta f. de pruebas
evolution n. evolución f.
evolve v.i. evolucionar
exactly adv. exactamente; (time) en punto
exaggerate v.t. exagerar
exaggeration n. exageración f.
exam n. examen m.
example: for example por ejemplo
exasperate v.t. desesperar
 The slowness of the train exasperated him. La lentitud del tren le desesperó.
excavate v.t. excavar
excavator n. excavadora f.
exceed v.t. superar
excel v.i. sobresalir

excellent *adj.* excelente; *(grade)* sobresaliente
exceptional *adj.* prodigioso/a
excess *n.* exceso *m.*
   in excess en exceso
exchange *n.* intercambio *m.*
   in exchange for a cambio de; por
exchange *v.t.* intercambiar
excited *adj.* emocionado/a
exciting *adj.* emocionante
excursion *n.* excursión *f.*
excuse *v.t.* disculpar
   Excuse me. *(May I?)* Con permiso.; *(Pardon me.)* Perdón.; *(interrupting)* Disculpe. **Excuse me, can you tell me…** Disculpe, puede decirme…
exercise *n.* ejercicio *m.*
   exercise *v.i.* hacer ejercicio
   do stretching exercises hacer ejercicios de estiramiento
exhaust pipe *n.* tubo *m.* de escape
exhausted *adj.* agotado/a
exhaustion *n.* agotamiento *m.*
exhibit *v.t. (paintings, goods)* exponer; *(skill)* demostrar
exhibition *n.* exposición *f.*
exit *n.* salida *f.*
exodus *n.* éxodo *m.*
expect *v.t.* esperar
expel *v.t.* expulsar
expense *n.* gasto *m.*
expensive *adj.* caro/a
experience *n.* experiencia *f.*
experiment *v.i.* experimentar
expiration *n.* expiración *f.*

expiration date *n.* fecha *f.* de caducidad
expire *v.i.* expirar
explain *v.t.* explicar
explore *v.t.* explorar
   explore a city/town explorar una ciudad/un pueblo
explosive *adj.* explosivo/a
export *v.t.* exportar
exportation *n.* exportación *f.*
expression *n.* expresión *f.*
expressive *adj.* expresivo/a
expressway *n.* autopista *f.*
expulsion *n.* expulsión *m.*
extinction *n.* extinción *f.*
   become extinct extinguirse
extinguish *v.t.* extinguir
extremely *adv.* sumamente
extremities *n., pl.* extremidades *f., pl.*
extroverted *adj.* extrovertido/a
eye *n.* ojo *m.*
eyebrow *n.* ceja *f.*
eyelash *n.* pestaña *f.*
eyelid *n.* párpado *m.*

F

fabric *n.* tela *f.*
fabulous *adj.* fabuloso/a
façade *n.* fachada *f.*
face *n.* cara *f.*
face *v.t.* enfrentar **It's necessary to face the problem immediately.** Hay que enfrentar el problema en seguida.
facedown *adv.* boca abajo
faceup *adv.* boca arriba
facilitate *v.t.* facilitar
facing *prep.* enfrente de

fact n. hecho m.
  in fact de hecho; en efecto
factory n. fábrica f.
fail v.t. (exam) suspender; fracasar
fail n. (grade) suspenso m.
failed adj. fracasado/a
failure n. fracaso m.
fair adj. justo/a
fairy n. hada (el) f.
fairy godmother n. hada madrina
faithful adj. fiel
fall n. (season) otoño m.
faithfulness n. fidelidad f.
fall v.i. caer; (down) caerse
  fall asleep v. dormirse (o:ue)
fallen p.p. caído (of caer)
familiar adj. conocido/a
family n., adj. familia f.; familiar
family doctor n. médico/a m., f. de cabecera; médico/a de familia
family tree n. árbol m. genealógico
famine n. hambre m.
famous adj. famoso/a
fan n., adj. aficionado/a m., f.; ventilador m.
  be a fan of ser aficionado/a a
fang n. colmillo m.
far from adv. lejos de
farewell n. despedida f.
farmer n. agricultor(a) m., f.
farming n. agricultura f.
far-off adj. lejano/a
fascinate v.t. fascinar
  be fascinated by fascinar
fashion n. moda f.
  be in fashion estar de moda

  be fashionably dressed ir a la moda
fast adj. rápido/a
fast n. ayuno m.
fast v.i. ayunar
fast adj. rápido/a, veloz
  fast food n. comida f. rápida
fat adj. gordo/a
fat n. grasa f.
father n. padre m.
father-in-law n. suegro m.
fatigue n. cansancio m.
fatten v.t. engordar
faucet n. grifo m.
fault n. culpa f.
favorable adj. favorable
favorite adj. favorito/a
fax (machine) n. fax m.
fear n. miedo m.
fear v.t. temer
February n. febrero m.
feed v.t. alimentar, dar de comer
  get fed up hartarse
feel v.t. sentir, sentirse
  feel like (doing something) tener ganas de (+ inf.)
feeling sorry adj. arrepentido/a
female n. hembra f.
fence n. valla f.
fencer n. esgrimidor(a) m., f.
fencing n. (sport) esgrima f.
fender n. guardabarros m., sing.
ferry n. transbordador m.
fertile adj. fértil
fertility n. fertilidad f.
fertilization n. fecundación f.
fertilize v.t. fecundar; (the soil) abonar (la tierra)

fertilizer n. abono m.; fertilizante m.

festival n. festival m.; verbena f.

fever n. fiebre f.
have a fever tener fiebre

few adj. pocos/as
fewer than menos de (+ number)

fidelity n. fidelidad f.

field n. campo m.; (sport) cancha f.
major field of study n. especialización f.

field hockey n. hockey m. sobre césped (L.A.); hockey sobre hierba (Spain)

fifteen quince

fifth quinto m.; adj. quinto/a

fifty cincuenta

fig n. higo m.

fig tree n. higuera f.

fight n. pelea f.; lucha f.

fight v.i. luchar (por/contra); pelear; pelearse

figure n. figura f.; (number) n. cifra f.

figure skating n. patinaje m. artístico

file n. archivo m.; (tool) lima f.

file v.t. archivar

fill v.t. llenar
fill the tank llenar el tanque

fill out v.t. (document) rellenar (Spain); llenar (L.A.)
fill out a form llenar un formulario

film v.t. rodar

film n. película

film library n. filmoteca f.

filming n. rodaje m.

filmmaker n. cineasta m., f.

fin n. aleta f.

finally adv. finalmente; por último; por fin

finance v.t. financiar

find n. hallazgo m. **That restaurant was a real find.** Ese restaurante fue un verdadero hallazgo.

find v.t. encontrar (o:ue); (each other) encontrarse **I can't find my shoe.** No encuentro el zapato. **Finally, they found each other.** Al fin se encontraron.

find out v.t. averiguar

fine n. multa f.

fine adj. bien **That's fine.** Está bien.

fine arts n., pl. bellas artes f., pl.

finger n. dedo m. (de la mano)

fingerprint n. huella f. dactilar

finish v.t. terminar; (doing something) terminar de (+ inf.)

fir tree n. abeto m.

fire n. fuego m.; incendio m.
fire engine n. carro m. de bomberos
fire escape n. escalera f. de incendios

fire v. despedir (e:i)

firefighter n. bombero/a m., f.

fireplace n. chimenea f.

firewood n. leña f.

fireworks n., pl. fuegos m., pl. artificiales

firm n. compañía f.; empresa f.

first *adj.* primer, primero/a
first of all *adv.* en primer lugar
first name *n.* nombre *m.* de pila
first-aid kit *n.* botiquín *m.* de primeros auxilios
firstborn *n.* primogénito/a *m., f.*
fish *n. (food)* pescado *m.; (live)* pez *m.*
marinated fish *n.* ceviche *m.*
fish *v.t.* pescar
fish market *n.* pescadería *f.*
fisherman *n.* pescador *m.*
fisherwoman *n.* pescadora *f.*
fishing *n.* pesca *f.*
go fishing ir de pesca
fit *adj. (suitable)* apto/a **He's not fit to practice psychology.** No es apto para ejercer la psicología.; *(physically)* en forma
fit *v.i. (clothing)* quedar
Does it fit me? ¿Me queda bien?
five cinco
five hundred quinientos/as
fix *v.t. (put in working order)* arreglar
fixed *adj. (set)* fijo/a
fixed price *n.* precio *m.* fijo
fixed schedule horario fijo
flag *n.* bandera *f.*
flamboyant *adj.* extravagante
flank steak *n.* lomo *m.*
flashlight *n.* linterna *f.;* foco *m.*
flat: go flat *v.t.* ponchar *(Mexico);* pinchar **We got a flat tire.** Se nos ponchó/pinchó una llanta.
flatter *v.t.* adular

flatter someone *idiom* echarle flores a alguien
flatterer *n.* adulador(a) *m., f.*
flattery *n.* adulación *f.*
flavor *n.* sabor *m.*
flee *v.i.* fugarse; huir
flex *v.t.* flexionar
flexible *adj.* flexible
flexible schedule horario flexible
flight *n.* vuelo *m.; (escape)* huida *f.*
flipper *n.* aleta *f.*
flirt *n.* coqueta *f.*
flirt *v.i.* coquetear
float *n.* carroza *f.*
float *v.i.* flotar
flood *n.* inundación *f.*
flood *v.t.* inundar
floor *n. (story in a building)* piso *m.; (ground)* suelo *(Spain) m.,* piso *(L.A.) m.*
ground floor planta *f.* baja
top floor planta alta
florist *n.* florista *(Spain) m., f.;* florero/a *(L.A.) m., f.*
flour *n.* harina *f.*
flow *v.i.* fluir
flower *n.* flor *f.*
flower pot *n.* maceta *f.*
flower shop *n.* florería *(L.A.) f.;* floristería *(Spain) f.*
flu *n.* gripe *f.*
fluffy *adj. (fabric, baked goods)* esponjoso/a
fly *n.* mosca *f.*
foam *n.* espuma *f.*
focus on *v.t.* enfocar
fog *n.* niebla *f.*

It's (very) foggy. Hay (mucha) niebla.
fold *v.t.* plegar
folder *n.* carpeta *f.*
folding *adj.* plegable
folic acid *n.* ácido *m.* fólico
folk *adj.* folklórico/a
follow *v.t.* seguir (e:i)
food *n.* comida *f.;* alimento *m.*
foolish *adj.* tonto/a
foot *n.* pie *m.*
football *n.* fútbol *m.* americano
footprint *n.* huella *f.*
foot race *n.* carrera *f.* pedestre
for *prep.* para; por
  for me para mí
forbid *v.t.* prohibir
forehead *n.* frente *f.*
foreign *adj.* extranjero/a
forensic scientist *n.* forense *m., f.*
forest *n.* bosque *m.*
  tropical forest bosque tropical
forget *v.t.* olvidar
forgive *v.t.* perdonar
forgiveness *n.* perdón *m.*
fork *n.* tenedor *m.*
forklift *n.* montacargas *m., sing.*
form *n. (shape)* forma *f.; (document)* formulario *m.*
formal *adj.* formal
fortnight *n.* quincena *f.*
fortress *n.* fortaleza *f.*
forty cuarenta
forward *adv.* hacia adelante; en marcha
fossil *n.* fósil *m.*
fossilize *v.i.* fosilizarse

become fossilized fosilizarse
foundation *n. (building)* cimientos *m., pl.*
fountain *n.* fuente *f.*
four cuatro
four hundred cuatrocientos/as
fourteen catorce
fourth cuarto *m.; adj.* cuarto/a
fox *n.* zorro *m.*
fraud *n.* estafador(a) *m., f.*
freckle *n.* peca *f.*
freckled *adj.* pecoso/a
free *adj.* libre; *(price)* gratis
  be free of charge ser gratis
  free fall *n.* caída *f.* libre
  free time *n.* tiempo *m.* libre; ratos *m., pl.* libres
free *v.t.* liberar
freedom *n.* libertad *f.*
freedom of speech *n.* libertad de expresión
freelancer *n.* [trabajador(a)] autónomo/a *m., f.*
freestyle *n.* estilo *m.* libre
freeway *n.* autopista *f.*
freezer *n.* congelador *m.*
French *n., adj.* francés *m.,* francesa *f.; (language)* francés
French fries *n., pl.* papas *f., pl.* fritas; patatas *f., pl.* fritas
frequently *adv.* frecuentemente; con frecuencia; a menudo
fresh *adj.* fresco/a
Friday *n.* viernes *m., sing.*
fried *adj.* frito/a
fried food *n.* fritada *f.*
fried potatoes *n., pl.* papas (L.A.) *f., pl.* fritas; patatas

(Spain) f., pl. fritas
friend n. amigo/a m., f.
  make friends hacer amigos
friendly adj. amable;
  amistoso/a
friendship n. amistad f.
frog n. rana f.
from prep. de; desde
  from the United States
  estadounidense
  from time to time adv. de vez
  en cuando
front desk n. recepción f.
front door n. puerta f. principal
front seat n. asiento m.
  delantero
frost n. escarcha f.
frugal adj. ahorrador(a)
fruit n. fruta f.
  fruit juice jugo m. de fruta
  fruit store n. frutería f.
  fruit tree n. árbol m. frutal
fuchsia adj. fucsia
fuel n. combustible m.
fugitive n. fugitivo/a m., f.
full adj. lleno/a
fun adj. divertido/a
  have fun divertirse (e:ie)
fun activity n. diversión f.
function v.i. funcionar
funds n., pl. (money) fondos m.,
  pl.
funeral n. funeral m.
funnel n. embudo m.
funny adj. chistoso/a;
  gracioso/a
furious adj. furioso/a
furnish v.t. amueblar
furnished adj. amueblado/a
furniture n. muebles m., pl.

furthermore adv. además (de)
fuse n. fusible m.
future n., adj. futuro/a; futuro
  m.; porvenir m.
  in the (near) future en el
  futuro (cercano)

G

gain v.t. ganar; obtener
  gain weight aumentar de
  peso; engordar
galaxy n. galaxia f.
gallbladder n. vesícula f.
  (biliar)
gallery n. galería f.
  art gallery pinacoteca f.
gambler n. jugador(a) m., f.
gambling n. juegos m., pl. de
  azar
game n. juego m.; (match)
  partido m.
game piece n. ficha f.
game show n. concurso m.
gang n. pandilla f.
gang member n. pandillero/a
  m., f.
garage n. garaje m.
garbage n. basura f.
garbage can n. basurero m.
garbage collector n.
  basurero/a m., f.
garbage disposal n. triturador
  m. de basura
garbage dump n. basurero m.;
  vertedero m.
garden n. jardín m.; huerto m.
  large garden n. huerta f.
gardener n. jardinero/a m., f.
gardenia n. gardenia f.
gardening n. jardinería f.

garlic *n.* ajo *m.*
garment *n.* prenda *f.*
garnish *v.t.* decorar; adornar
gas pedal *n.* pedal *m.* del acelerador
gas station *n.* gasolinera *f.*
gas tank *n.* depósito *m.* de gasolina
gasoline *n.* gasolina *f.*
gastronomy *n.* gastronomía *f.*
gathering *n.* *(to discuss politics, literature, etc.)* tertulia *f.*
gaze at *v.* contemplar
gazelle *n.* gacela *f.*
gearshift *n.* *(car)* cambio *m.* de marchas/velocidades
gelatin *n.* gelatina *f.*
generous *adj.* generoso/a
genetic *adj.* genético/a
genetic engineering *n.* biogenética *f.*
genetics *n.* genética *f.*
geography *n.* geografía *f.*
geologist *n.* geólogo/a *m., f.*
geometric(al) *adj.* geométrico/a
geometry *n.* geometría *f.*
geranium *n.* geranio *m.*
German *n., adj.* alemán *m.,* alemana *f.; (language)* alemán
get *v.t.* conseguir (e:i); obtener
  get along well/badly with llevarse bien/mal con
  get good grades *v.* sacar buenas notas
  get hurt *v. pron.* lastimarse
  get into trouble *v.* hacer travesuras

get pregnant *v.* quedar embarazada
get together *v. pron.* juntarse
get off (at) *v.* salirse (en)
get off of (a vehicle) *v.* bajar(se) de
get on/in to (a vehicle) *v.* subir(se) a
get up *v.* levantarse
  get up early madrugar
getaway *n.* escapada *f.*
geyser *n.* géiser *m.*
gift *n.* regalo *m.*
giraffe *n.* jirafa *f.*
girl *n.* chica *f.;* muchacha *f.;* niña
girlfriend *n.* novia *f.*
give *v.t.* dar; *(gift)* regalar
give in *v.* ceder
give up (doing something) *v.* dejar de (+ *inf.*)
give up hope *v.* desesperarse
give way *v.* ceder (el paso)
glass *n.* *(drinking)* vaso *m.,* *(material)* vidrio *m.,* cristal *m.*
  made of glass de vidrio
glasses *n., pl.* gafas *f., pl.*
glassware *n.* cristalería *f.*
gloves *n.* guantes *m.*
glue *v.t.* pegar
gluttonous *adj.* glotón *m.,* glotona *f.*
go *v.i.* ir
  go on rides *v.* subirse a los juegos
  go on the swings *v.* subirse a los columpios
  go shopping ir de compras
  Let's go. Vamos.
go away *v.* irse; ausentarse

go beyond *v.* superar
go by *v.* pasar por
  go by the bank pasar por el banco
go down *v.* bajar(se)
go off *v. (alarm)* sonar
go out (with) *v.* salir (con)
  go out and have a snack in a bar ir de tapas *(Spain)*
go overboard *loc.* echar la casa por la ventana
go up *v.* subir
go with *v.* acompañar
goal *n.* meta *f.;* objetivo *m.*
goblet *n.* copa *f.*
God *n.* Dios *m.*
god *n. (deity)* dios
goddaughter *n.* ahijada *f.*
godfather *n.* padrino *m.*
godmother *n.* madrina *f.*
godson *n.* ahijado *m.*
going to: be going to *(do something)* ir a (+ *inf.)*
gold *adj.* dorado/a
gold *n.* oro *m.*
golden *adj.* dorado/a
golf *n.* golf *m.*
golf club *n.* palo *m.* de golf
golf course *n.* campo *m.* de golf
golfer *n.* golfista *m., f.*
good *adj.* buen, bueno/a
  Good afternoon. Buenas tardes.
  Good evening. Buenas noches.
  Good morning. Buenos días.
  Good night. Buenas noches.
  I'm good, thanks. Bien, gracias.

in good spirits *adj.* animado/a
  It's good that... Es bueno que…
good sense *n.* sensatez *f.*
good-bye *n.* adiós *m.;* despedida *f.*
  say good-bye despedirse
good-looking *adj.* guapo/a
goods *n.* artículos *m., pl.*
gossip *n.* chismes *m., pl.;* cotilleo *(Spain) m.*
gossip *v.i.* cotillear *(Spain);* chismear
Gothic *adj.* gótico/a
govern *v.t.* gobernar
government *n.* gobierno *m.*
grade *n.* calificación *f.;* nota *f.*
grade *v.t.* calificar
graduate (from, in) *v.i.* graduarse (de), recibirse
graduation *n.* graduación *f.*
graffiti *n.* pintada *f.*
  There was gang graffiti on the wall. Había pintadas de pandillas en la pared.
grain *n.* grano *m.*
grains *n., pl.* cereales *m., pl.*
grammar school *n.* primaria *f.*
grandchildren *n., pl.* nietos *m., pl.*
granddaughter *n.* nieta *f.*
grandfather *n.* abuelo *m.*
grandmother *n.* abuela *f.*
grandparents *n., pl.* abuelos *m., pl.*
grandson *n.* nieto *m.*
grant *n.* beca *f.*
grape *n.* uva *f.*
grapefruit *n.* pomelo

(*Argentina, Spain*) *m.;* toronja
(*L.A.*) *f.*
grass *n.* césped *m.;* hierba *f.;*
pasto (*L.A.*) *m.*
grateful *adj.* agradecido/a
grater *n.* rallador *m.*
grave *n.* tumba *f.*
grave *adj.* grave
gravity *n.* gravedad *f.*
gray *n., adj.* gris *m.*
gray hair *n.* cana *f.*
great *adj.* fenomenal
great-grandchildren *n., pl.*
bisnietos *m., pl.*
great-granddaughter *n.*
bisnieta *f.*
great-grandfather *n.* bisabuelo
m.
great-grandmother *n.*
bisabuela *f.*
great-grandparents *n., pl.*
bisabuelos *m., pl.*
great-grandson *n.* bisnieto *m.*
great-great-grandfather *n.*
tatarabuelo *m.*
great-great-grandmother *n.*
tatarabuela *f.*
great-great-grandparents *n.,*
pl. tatarabuelos *m., pl.*
greedy *adj.* avaricioso/a
Greek *n., adj.* griego/a *m., f.;*
(*language*) griego
green *n., adj.* verde *m.*
dark green verde oscuro
green space *n.* zona *f.* verde
greet *v.t.* saludar **He greets his**
friend. Él saluda a su amigo.;
(*each other*) saludarse **They**
greet each other. Ellos se
saludan.

greeting *n.* saludo *m.*
Greetings to . . . Saludos a…
grenade *n.* (*military*) granada *f.*
grill *n.* parrilla *f.;* plancha *f.*
grilled *adj.* (*food*) a la plancha;
a la parrilla **grilled flank**
steak lomo a la plancha
groceries *n., pl.* comestibles
m., pl.
group *n.* grupo *m.*
group *v.t.* agrupar
get into groups agruparse
grove *n.* arboleda *f.*
grow *v.t.* cultivar; *v.i.* crecer
growing *adj.* creciente
growth *n.* crecimiento *m.*
grudge *n.* rencor *m.*
guarantee *n.* garantía *f.*
guarantee *v.t.* garantizar;
asegurar
guard *v.t.* custodiar
guess *v.t.* adivinar
guest *n.* (*at a house/hotel*)
huésped *m., f.;* (*at a function*)
invitado/a *m., f.*
guide *n.* guía *m., f.*
guitar *n.* guitarra *f.*
gum *n.* (*chewing*) chicle *m.;*
(*anat.*) encía *f.*
gunshot *n.* disparo *m.*
gymnasium *n.* gimnasio *m.*
gymnast *n.* gimnasta *m., f.*
gymnastics *n.* gimnasia *f.*
rhythmic gymnastics
gimnasia rítmica
gynecologist *n.* ginecólogo/a
m., f.

H

hair *n.* pelo *m.;* cabello *m.*

hairbrush n. cepillo m. de pelo
hairdo n. peinado m. **Her new hairdo suits/suited her.** Su nuevo peinado le sienta/le sentaba bien.
hairdresser n. peluquero/a m., f.
hairdryer n. secador m.
hairstyle n. peinado m.
hairy adj. peludo/a
hake n. merluza f.
half n., adj. medio m.; medio/a
half-brother n. medio hermano m.
half-past . . . . . .y media
half-sister n. media hermana f.
hall n. salón m.
hallway n. pasillo m.
ham n. jamón m.
hamburger n. hamburguesa f.
hammer n. martillo m.
hammock n. hamaca f.
hand n. mano f.
  Hands up! ¡Manos arriba!
handball n. balonmano m.
handbrake n. freno m. de mano
handkerchief n. pañuelo m.
handle n. asa m.
handlebars n., pl. manillar (Spain) m.; manubrio (L.A.) m.
handrail n. pasamanos m., sing.
handsome adj. guapo/a
handy adj. práctico/a
hang v.t. colgar
  hang clothes on the line colgar la ropa en el tendedero
hang glider n. ala (el) f. delta
hang gliding v. practicar el ala

delta
hang out (clothes) v. tender (ropa)
hanger n. percha f.
hangover n. resaca (Spain) f.; cruda (Mexico) f.
  have a hangover tener cruda; tener resaca
happen v.t. ocurrir
  What happened? ¿Qué pasó?
  What's happening? ¿Qué pasa?
happiness n. alegría f.
happy adj. alegre; contento/a; feliz
  be happy alegrarse (de)
  be happy (with) contentarse (con)
harbor n. puerto m.
hard adj. difícil; duro/a
  hard to believe idiom parece mentira
hard feelings n., pl. rencor m.
hardly adv. apenas
hardship n. dificultad f.
hard-working adj. trabajador(a)
harmful adj. dañino/a
harvest n. cosecha f.
harvest v.t. cosechar
haste n. prisa f.
hat n. sombrero m.
hate v.i. odiar
have v.t. tener
  have a(n) ...ache tener dolor de...
  have a good/bad time pasarlo bien/mal
  have a flat tire poncharse una llanta

have a picnic hacer un picnic

have an unfinished (matter) tener (un asunto) pendiente

have just done something acabar de (+ inf.)

have something on the tip of one's tongue loc. tener algo en la punta de la lengua

have to (do something) tener que (+ inf.); deber (+ inf.)

have to do with loc. tener que ver con **The letter doesn't have anything to do with the problem.** La carta no tiene nada que ver con el problema.

haze (someone) v.t. hacer una novatada (a alguien)

hazel tree n. avellano m.

hazelnut n. avellana f.

head n. cabeza f.

headache n. dolor m. de cabeza

headlight n. faro m.

headphone n. auricular m.

health n. salud f.

health care n. asistencia f. médica

health center n. enfermería f.

healthful adj. saludable

healthy adj. sano/a, saludable

hear v.t. oír

heard p.p. oído (of oír)

have heard idiom oír decir que

I've heard that Mapi and Kiko are getting married. He oído decir que Mapi y Kiko se van a casar.

hearing: (sense of) hearing n. oído m.

heart n. corazón m.

by heart de memoria **He knows the poem by heart.** Se sabe el poema de memoria.

heart attack n. infarto m.; ataque m. al corazón; ataque cardíaco

heartbeat n. latido m.

heat n. calor m.

heat v.t. calentar

heater n. calentador m.

heating n. calefacción f.

heaven n. cielo m.

Heaven forbid! loc. ¡Dios me libre!

heavy vehicles n., pl. vehículos m., pl. pesados

Hebrew n., adj. hebreo/a m., f; (language) hebreo

hedge n. seto m.

heel n. talón m.

hefty adj. corpulento/a

height n. altura f.

heir n. heredero m.

heiress n. heredera f.

helicopter n. helicóptero m.

hello interj. hola; (on the telephone) ¿Aló?, ¿Bueno?, ¿Diga?

helmet n. casco m.

help (to) v.t. ayudar (a); servir (e:i); (each other) ayudarse (a)

Help! interj. ¡Auxilio!; ¡Socorro!

hemisphere n. hemisferio m.

hemorrhage n. hemorragia f.

her poss. adj. su(s)

herbivore n. herbívoro/a m., f.
herbivorous adj. herbívoro/a
herbs n., pl. hierbas f., pl.
here adv. aquí
  Here it is. Aquí está.
  Here we are in . . . Aquí
  estamos en…
hereditary adj. hereditario/a
heritage n. patrimonio m.
hermit n. ermitaño/a m., f.
hero n. héroe m.
heroine n. heroína f.
hers poss. pron.
  suyo(s)/suya(s)
hi interj. hola
hiccups n., pl. hipo m.
hide v.t. esconder; disimular
hide-and-seek n. escondidillas
  f.; al escondite m.
hierarchical adj. jerárquico/a;
  jerarquizado/a
hierarchy n. jerarquía f.
high adj. alto/a
high jump n. salto m. alto
  (L.A.); salto m. de altura
  (Spain)
high school n. escuela f.
  secundaria; preparatoria f.
highway n. autopista f.;
  carretera f.
hijack n. secuestro m.
hijack v.t (aircraft) secuestrar
hike n. excursión f.
  **go for a hike (in the
  mountains)** ir de excursión (a
  las montañas)
  go hiking ir de excursión
  go on a hike hacer una
  excursión
hiker n. excursionista m., f.

hillside n. ladera f.
Hindu n., adj. hindú m., f
hint n. consejo m.; indicación f.
hip n. cadera f.
hippodrome n. hipódromo m.
hire v. contratar
his su(s) poss. adj.;
  suyo(s)/suya(s) poss. pron.
Hispanic n., adj. hispano/a m.,
  f.
historian n. historiador(a) m., f.
history n. historia f.
hit n. golpe m.
hit v.i. pegar
  hit (a car) v.i. chocar
hitchhike v.i. hacer auto(e)stop
hitchhiker n. auto(e)stopista
  m., f.
hobby n. afición f.; pasatiempo
  m.
hockey n. hockey m.
hold v.t. aguantar (Spain)
hold up v.t. (bank) atracar
holdup n. atraco m.
hole n. agujero m.; hueco m.;
  (in the ground) hoyo
  make holes in agujerear
holiday n. día m. de fiesta
Holy Week n. Semana f. Santa
homage n. homenaje m.
  pay homage to homenajear
home n. casa f.; hogar m.
  at home en casa
  home for the elderly n.
  residencia f. de ancianos
homemade adj. casero/a
home-maker n. el ama (m., f.)
  de casa
home page n. página f.
  principal

155

home run *n.* cuadrilátero *m.*
home style *adj.* casero/a
home team *n. (sports)* equipo *m.* local
hometown *n.* ciudad *f.* natal; *(my…)* mi pueblo *m.*, mi ciudad *f.*
homework *n.* deberes *m., pl.*; asignación *f.*; tarea *f.*
honest *adj.* honesto/a
honey *n.* miel *f.*
honeymoon *n.* luna *f.* de miel
hood *n. (car)* capó *m.*, cofre *m.*; *(jacket)* capucha *f.*
hope *n.* esperanza *f.*
hope *v.t.* esperar
I hope (that) *interj.* Ojalá (que)
hopefully ojalá que…
horizon *n.* horizonte *m.*
hormone *n.* hormona *f.*
horn *n.* cuerno *m.*; *(car)* bocina *f.*
horror *n.* horror *m.*; …de horror
hors d'oeuvres *n., pl.* entremeses *m., pl.*
horse *n.* caballo *m.*
ride a horse montar a caballo
horse race *n.* carrera *f.* de caballos
horseback riding *n.* equitación *f.*
horticulturalist *n.* horticultor(a) *m., f.*
horticulture *n.* horticultura *f.*
hose *n.* manguera *f.*
hospitable *adj.* hospitalario/a
hospital *n.* hospital *m.*

hospitality *n.* hospitalidad *f.*
host *n.* anfitrión *m.*
hostel *n.* albergue *m.*; hostal *m.*
hostess *n.* anfitriona *f.*
hot *adj.* caliente
be hot *(weather)* hacer calor; *(feel)* tener calor; *(thing)* estar caliente
It's (very) hot. *(weather)* Hace (mucho) calor.
hotel *n.* hotel *m.*
hour *n.* hora *f.*
house *n.* casa *f.*
housekeeper *n.* el ama (*m., f.*) de casa
housewife *n.* ama *f.* de casa
housing *n.* vivienda *f.*
how? *adv.* ¿cómo?
How are you? *fam.* ¿Cómo estás?; ¿Qué tal? *form.* ¿Cómo está usted?
How did it go for you . . .? ¿Cómo le/les fue…?
How is it going? ¿Qué tal?
How is/are . . . ? ¿Qué tal…?
How many? ¿Cuánto/a(s)?
How may I help you? ¿En qué puedo servirle(s)?
how much? *adv.* ¿cuanto/a?
How much does it cost? ¿Cuánto cuesta…?
How…! ¡Qué…!
How big! ¡Qué grande!
How nice to see you. *loc.* Dichosos los ojos (que te ven).
however *conj.* sin embargo
hug *v.t.* abrazar; *(each other)* abrazarse

human *adj.* humano/a

human being *n.* ser *m.* humano

humanism *n.* humanismo *m.*

humanist *n.* humanista *m., f.*

humanities *n., pl.* humanidades *f., pl.*

humble *adj.* humilde

humid *adj.* húmedo/a

humidity *n.* humedad *f.*

humiliated *adj.* humillado/a

humming bird *n.* colibrí *m.*

hump *n.* joroba *f.*

hunchbacked *adj.* jorobado/a

hunger *n.* hambre *f.*

　　be hungry tener hambre

hungry *adj.* hambriento/a

hunt *v.t.* cazar

hunter *n.* cazador(a) *m., f.*

hunting *n.* caza *f.*

hurdles *n., pl. (sport)* vallas *f., pl.*

hurricane *n.* huracán *m.*

hurry *v.i.* apurarse; darse prisa; apresurarse

　　be in a hurry tener prisa

hurt *v.t.* doler (o:ue); lastimar

　　hurt oneself hacerse daño

　　It hurts me a lot . Me duele mucho.

husband *n.* esposo *m.;* marido *m.*

hydrangea *n.* hortensia *f.*

hydraulic *adj.* hidráulico/a

hyperbole *n.* hipérbole *f.*

hypothesis *n.* hipótesis *f.*

hypothetical *adj.* hipotético/a

I

I am… Yo soy…

ice *n.* hielo *m.*

ice cream *n.* helado *m.*

ice cream shop *n.* heladería *f.*

ice hockey *n.* hockey *m.* sobre hielo

ice rink *n.* pista *f.* de hielo

ice skate patinar en hielo

ice skating *n.* patinaje *m.* sobre hielo

iceberg *n.* iceberg *m.*

iced *adj.* helado/a

iced tea *n.* té *m.* helado

idea *n.* idea *f.*

idealist *adj.* idealista

idle *adj.* ocioso/a

if *conj.* si

ignorance *n.* ignorancia *f.*

ignorant *adj.* ignorante

ill *adv.* mal

illiterate (person) *n., adj.* analfabeto/a *m., f.*

ill-mannered *adj.* grosero/a; maleducado/a

illness *n.* enfermedad *f.*

imagine *v.t.* imaginar

imitate *v.t.* imitar

imitation *n.* imitación *f.*

immediately *adv.* inmediatamente; en el acto

immigrant *n., adj.* inmigrante *m., f.*

immigrate *v.i.* inmigrar

immigration *n.* inmigración *f.*

immune system *n.* sistema *m.* inmunológico

immunize *v.t.* inmunizar

immunological *adj.* inmunológico/a

impatience *n.* impaciencia *f.*

impatient *adj.* impaciente

　　get impatient impacientarse

She got impatient over the delay. Se impacientó con el atraso.

impetuous *adj. (person)* lanzado/a, impulsivo/a

impolite *adj.* grosero/a

import *v.t.* importar

important *adj.* importante
be important (to) *v.i.* importar
It's (not) important that… (No) Es importante que…

importation *n.* importación *f.*

impossible *adj.* imposible
it's impossible es imposible

impostor *n.* impostor(a) *m., f.*

impoverish *v.t.* empobrecer

impression *n.* impresión *f.*
make a good/bad impression causar una buena/mala impresión

imprison *v.t.* encarcelar

improbable *adj.* improbable; inverosímil
it's improbable es improbable

improve *v.t.* mejorar

improvement *n.* mejora *f.*

impulsive *adj.* lanzado/a

in *prep.* en
in a jiffy *idiom* en un dos por tres; en un santiamén
in front of *prep.* delante de; enfrente

inaugurate *v.t.* inaugurar

inauguration *n.* inauguración *f.*

incomprehensible *adj.* incomprensible

inconceivable *adj.* inconcebible

inconvenience *n.* molestia *f.*

increase *n.* aumento *m.;* incremento *m.*
be on the increase estar en auge

increasing *adj.* creciente

incredible *adj.* increíble

independent *adj.* independiente
become independent independizarse

indescribable *adj.* inefable

indigenous *adj.* indígena

indigo *n., adj.* añil *m.*

individual *n., adj.* individuo *m. (may be pejorative:* **Who's that guy?** ¿Quién es ese individuo?); individual

individuality *n.* individualidad *f.*

inebriated *adj.* ebrio/a; embriagado/a

inequality *n.* desigualdad *f.*

inexperienced *adj.* novato/a

inexplicable *adj.* inexplicable

infection *n.* infección *f.*

influence *v.t.* influir en; influenciar
Darío's poems influenced other poets. Los poemas de Darío influyeron en otros poetas.

inform *v.t.* informar
inform oneself informarse

information *n.* información *f.*

ingest *v.t.* ingerir

ingestion *n.* ingestión *f.*

inherit *v.t.* heredar

inheritance *n.* herencia *f.*

inject *v.t.* inyectar

injection *n.* inyección *f.*

give an injection poner una inyección
injure v.t. (oneself) lastimarse
  injure one's (foot) lastimarse el (pie)
injured n., adj. herido/a m., f.
inn n. hostal m.
innovate v.i. innovar
innovation n. innovación f.
innovative adj. innovador(a)
innovator n. innovador(a) m., f.
insect n. insecto m.
inside adv. (a)dentro
insipid adj. insípido/a
insist (on + gerund) insistir (en + inf.)
  He insists on going. Insiste en ir.
insistence n. insistencia f.
insomnia n. insomnio m.
inspire v.t. inspirar
install v.t. (equipment) instalar
  install oneself instalarse
installment n. (payment) plazo m. (monthly payment) mensualidad f.
  pay in installments pagar a plazos
institution n. institución f.
instrument n. instrumento m.
insulate v.t. aislar
insulation n. aislante m.
insulin n. insulina f.
insult n. insulto m.; ofensa f.
insurance n. seguro m.
intake n. consumo m.
intelligent adj. inteligente
intend (to do something) v. pensar (+ inf.)
intentionally adv.

intencionalmente, adrede, a propósito
interest n. interés m.
interest v.t. interesar
  take an interest (in) interesarse (en) **He's only interested in the results.** Sólo se interesa en los resultados.
  be interested interesar
interesting adj. interesante
  be interesting to interesar
intermediate adj. intermedio/a
international adj. internacional
Internet n. Internet m.; red f.
interpreter n. intérprete m., f.
interpreting n. interpretación f.
interrupt v.t. interrumpir
intersection n. intersección f.
intervention n. intervención f.
interview n. entrevista f.
interview v.t. entrevistar
interviewer n. entrevistador(a) m., f.
intestine n. intestino m.
intolerant adj. intolerante
intrigue n. intriga f.
intrigued adj. intrigado/a
introduction n. presentación f.
invertebrate n., adj. invertebrado m.; invertebrado/a
invest v.t. invertir (e:ie)
investigator n. investigador(a) m., f.
invitation n. invitación f.
invite v.t. invitar
involuntary adj. involuntario/a
iron n. (metal) hierro m.; (clothes) plancha f.

iron *v.t.* planchar (la ropa)
ironic *adj.* irónico/a
irony *n.* ironía *f.*
irresponsible *adj.*
  irresponsable
irritating *adj.* antipático/a
isolate *v.t.* aislar
  isolate oneself aislarse
issue *n.* cuestión *f.*
Italian *n., adj.* italiano/a *m., f.;*
  (language) italiano
item *n.* artículo *m.*
itinerary *n.* itinerario *m.*
its su(s) *poss. adj.;*
  suyo(s)/suya(s) *poss. pron.*
ivy *n.* hiedra *f.*

J

jack *n. (playing cards)* jota *f.*
jacket *n.* chaqueta *f.;* abrigo;
  saco
jackknife *n.* navaja *f.*
jail *n.* cárcel *f.*
jail *v.t.* encarcelar
jam *n.* mermelada *f.*
January *n.* enero *m.*
Japanese *n., adj.* japonés *m.,*
  japonesa *f.; (language)*
  japonés
javelin throw *n.* lanzamiento
  m. de jabalina
jealous *adj.* celoso/a;
  envidioso/a
jealousy *n.* celos *m., pl.*
jeans *n.* (blue)jeans *(L.A.) m.,*
  pl.; vaqueros, tejanos *(Spain)*
  m., pl.
jellyfish *n.* medusa *f.*
jest: in jest en broma
jetty *n.* embarcadero *m.*

Jew *n.* judío/a *m., f.*
jeweler *n.* joyero/a *m., f.*
jewelry box *n.* joyero *m.*
jewelry store *n.* joyería *f.*
jewel *n.* joya *f.*
Jewish *adj.* judío/a
job *n.* empleo *m.;* puesto *m.;*
  trabajo *m.*
job application *n.* solicitud *f.*
  de trabajo
jog *v.i.* correr
joint *n. (anatomy)* articulación
  f.
joke *n.* broma *f.*
  as a joke en broma
  make jokes hacer bromas
  practical joke broma
  pesada; novatada *f.*
joker *n.* bromista *m., f.*
journalism *n.* periodismo *m.*
journalist *n.* periodista *m., f.;*
  reportero/a *m., f.*
joy *n.* alegría *f.*
  give joy dar alegría
joyful *adj.* alegre
jubilation *n.* algarabía *f.*
judge *n.* juez *m., f.*
judge *v.t.* juzgar
judgment *n.* juicio *m.*
juice *n.* jugo *(L.A.) m.;* zumo
  (Spain) m.
  fruit juice jugo/zumo de fruta
juicer *n.* exprimidor *m.*
juicy *adj.* jugoso/a
July *n.* julio *m.*
jump *n.* salto *m.*
jump *v.i.* saltar, brincar
June *n.* junio *m.*
jungle *n.* selva *f.,* jungla *f.*
jury *n.* jurado *m.*

just *adv.* apenas
justice *n.* justicia *f.*

K

kangaroo *n.* canguro *m.*
key *n.* llave *f.*
key chain *n.* llavero *m.*
keyboard *n.* teclado *m.*
kid *n.* niño/a *m., f.*
kid *v.i.* bromear
  kid someone *idiom* tomarle
  el pelo a alguien
kidnap *v.t. (people)* secuestrar
kidnapping *n.* secuestro *m.*
kidney *n.* riñón *m.*
kill *v.t.* matar (a alguien)
  kill two birds with one stone
  loc. matar dos pájaros de un
  tiro
kilometer *n.* kilómetro *m.*
kind *adj.* amable
  That's very kind of you.
  (Eres/Es usted) Muy amable.
kingdom *n.* reino *m.*
kiss *n.* beso *m.*
  give a kiss dar un beso
kiss *v.t.* besar; *(each other)*
  besarse
kitchen *n.* cocina *f.*
kitchenware *n.* artículos *m., pl.*
  de cocina
knee *n.* rodilla *f.*
knife *n.* cuchillo *m.*
knit *v.i.* hacer punto
knitted *adj.* de punto
knitwear *n.* artículos *m., pl.* de
  punto
know *v.t.* saber; conocer
  know how (to) saber
know-it-all *n., adj.*

  sabihondo/a *m., f.*
known *adj.* conocido/a

L

laboratory *n.* laboratorio *m.*
lack *n.* falta *f.;* carencia *f.*
lack *v.t.* faltar
lack of understanding *n.*
  incomprensión *f.*
ladle *n.* cucharón *m.*
lake *n.* lago *m.*
lamb *n.* cordero *m.*
lame *adj.* cojo/a
lamp *n.* lámpara *f.*
land *n.* tierra *f.; (parcel)*
  terreno *m.*
land *v.t.* aterrizar
landing *n.* aterrizaje *m.*
landing strip *n.* pista *f.* de
  aterrizaje
landlord *n.* dueño/a *m., f.*
landscape *n.* paisaje *m.*
lane *n. (highway)* carril *m.*
language *n.* lengua *f.;* idioma
  m.
  foreign languages *n., pl.*
  lenguas *f., pl.* extranjeras
lap *n. (sports)* vuelta *f.*
laptop (computer) *n.*
  computadora *f.* portátil
large *n., adj. (clothing size)*
  talla *m.* grande; grande,
  (quantity) elevado/a **You**
  notice a large quantity of fat
  in the food. Se nota una
  cantidad elevada de grasa
  en la comida.
large intestine *n.* intestino *m.*
  grueso
larva *n.* larva *f.*

larynx *n.* laringe *f.*
last *adj.* pasado/a; último/a
last *v.i.* durar
   last week la semana pasada
   last year el año pasado
last night *adv.* anoche
lasting *adj.* duradero/a
late *adv.* tarde
   be late llegar tarde;
   retrasarse **be late (in)** tardar
   en **The bus was late (in
   arriving).** El autobús tardó en
   llegar.
lately *adv.* últimamente
later *adv.* más tarde
   at the very latest a más
   tardar **Bring it to me on
   Thursday at the very latest.**
   Tráemelo el jueves a más
   tardar.
Latin *n., adj.* latino/a *m., f.;*
   (language) latín *m.*
laugh *v.i.* reír, reírse (e:i)
laughed *p.p.* reído *(of* reír)
launch *n.* lanzamiento *m.*
launch *v.t.* lanzar **NASA
   launched a rocket to Saturn.**
   La NASA lanzó un cohete a
   Saturno.
laundromat *n.* lavandería *f.*
law *n.* ley *f.*
lawn *n.* pasto *m.*
lawn mower *n.* cortacésped *f.*
lawyer *n.* abogado/a *m., f.*
laziness *n.* pereza *f.*
lazy *adj.* perezoso/a; flojo/a
lead *n.* plomo *m.* **a lead pipe**
   un tubo de plomo
lead *v.t.* liderar
leader *n.* líder *m., f.*

leadership *n.* liderazgo *m.*
leaf *n.* hoja *f.*
leak *n.* *(gas, water)* fuga *f.*
learn *v.t.* aprender (a + *inf.*)
learned *adj.* sabio/a
learning *n.* enseñanza *f.*
lease *n.* contrato *m.*
least: at least por lo menos
leather *n.* piel *f.*
   made of leather de piel
leather goods *n., pl.* artículos
   m., pl. de piel
leave *v.i.* salir; irse; partir;
   dejar
   leave a message dejar un
   mensaje/recado
   leave alone dejar
   leave (behind) dejar
   leave for *(a place)* salir
   para...
   leave from salir de
lecture *n.* conferencia *f.*
lecture hall *n.* aula (el) *f.*
   main lecture hall aula
   magna
left *adj., n.* izquierdo/a *m., f.*
   be left over quedar, sobrar
   to the left (of) a la izquierda
   (de)
leftovers *n., pl.* restos *m., pl.;*
   sobras *f., pl.*
leg *n.* pierna *f.*
legacy *n.* legado *m.*
legal *adj.* legal
legalize *v.t.* legalizar
legend *n.* leyenda *f.*
leisure time *n.* ocio *m.*
lemon *n.* limón *m.*
lemon tree *n.* limonero *m.*
lemonade *n.* limonada *f.*

lend *v.t.* prestar
lengthwise section *n. (Tech.)* corte *m.* longitudinal
lentil *n.* lenteja *f.*
leopard *n.* leopardo *m.*
less *adv.* menos
  less . . . than menos… que
  less than + *(number)* menos de + *(number)*
lesson *n.* lección *f.*
let *v.t.* dejar
  let go soltar
  let up *(pain)* aliviarse
letter *n.* carta *f.; (alphabet)* letra *f.*
  put a letter in the mailbox echar una carta al buzón
lettuce *n.* lechuga *f.*
level *n.* nivel *m.*
lever *n.* palanca *f.*
liar *n.* mentiroso/a *m., f.*
liberal *n., adj.* liberal *m., f.*
liberation *n.* liberación *f.*
liberty *n.* libertad *f.*
librarian *n.* bibliotecario/a *m., f.*
library *n.* biblioteca *f.*
license *n. (driver's)* licencia *f.* de manejar/conducir
license plate *n.* (placa *f.* de) matrícula *f.*
lid *n.* tapa *f.*
lie *n.* mentira *f.*
lie *v.i.* mentir
lie down (in the sun) *v.* tumbarse (al sol)
life *n.* vida *f.*
  in my life en mi vida
life expectancy *n.* esperanza *f.* de vida

life imprisonment *n.* cadena *f.* perpétua
life jacket *n.* salvavidas *m., sing.*
life sentence *n.* cadena *f.* perpétua
lifeguard *n.* salvavidas *m., f., sing.*
lifestyle: lead a healthy lifestyle llevar una vida sana
lift *v.t.* levantar
  lift weights levantar pesas
light *n., adj.* luz *f.;* liviano/a; ligero/a
light aircraft *n.* avioneta *f.*
light green *n., adj.* verde *m.* claro
lighter *n.* encendedor *m.*
lightning bolt *n.* rayo *m.;* relámpago *m.*
lightning rod *n.* pararrayos *m., sing.*
like *prep.* como
  What's . . . like? ¿Cómo es…?
like *v.t.* gustar
  Do you like . . . ? ¿Te gusta(n)…?
  I like . . . very much. Me encanta…
  I would like to introduce… to you. Te presento a…
  would like to tener ganas de (+ *inf.*) **I would like to visit Diamantina.** Tengo ganas de visitar Diamantina.
  Would you like to? ¿Te gustaría?
  Like father, like son. *loc.* De tal palo, tal astilla.
like this *adv.* así

likeable *adj.* simpático/a
likely: be likely that *(something will happen)* ser probable que (+ *subj.*) **It's likely that they won't arrive on time.** Es probable que no lleguen a tiempo.
likewise *adv.* igualmente
lily *n.* lirio *m.*
limb *n.* *(body)* miembro *m.*
limit *v.t.* limitar
limousine *n.* limusina *f.*
line *n.* línea *f.;* cola *f.* **There is a long line at the cinema.** Hay una larga cola en el cine.
   stand in/on line hacer cola
   line up hacer cola
linen *adj.* de hilo
linguist *n.* lingüista *m., f.*
linguistic *adj.* lingüístico/a
linguistics *n.* lingüística *f.*
lion *n.* león *m.*
lipstick *n.* lápiz *m.* labial; pintalabios *m., sing.*
liqueur *n.* licor *m.*
liquid *n., adj.* líquido *m.;* líquido/a
listen (to) *v.t.* escuchar
   listen to music escuchar música
   listen to the radio escuchar la radio
   Listen! *(command)* ¡Oye! *fam., sing.;* ¡Oigan! *form., pl.*
listener *n.* oyente *m., f.; (radio)* radioyente *m., f.*
literature *n.* literatura *f.*
little *adj.* pequeño/a; *adv.* poco/a

little bit *n.* pizca *f.*
Little Dipper *n.* Osa *f.* Menor
live *v.i.* vivir; residir
   live by begging vivir de limosnas
lively *adj.* vivo/a
liver *n.* hígado *m.*
living being *n.* ser *m.* vivo
living room *n.* sala *f.*
lizard *n.* lagarto *f.*
loaf (of bread) *n.* barra *f.* (de pan) *(Spain)*
loan *n.* préstamo *m.*
loan *v.* prestar
lobster *n.* langosta *f.*
located *adj.* situado/a
   be located quedar
locker room *n.* vestuario *m.*
locomotive *n.* locomotora *f.*
lodge *v.t.* alojar
lodging *n.* alojamiento *m.;* parador *m.*
log *n.* *(wood)* tronco *m.,* leño *m.*
long *adj.* *(length)* largo/a
   long-distance race *n.* carrera *f.* de fondo
   long jump *n.* salto *m.* de longitud *(Spain);* salto *m.* largo *(L.A.)*
long for *v.* ansiar
   long for (someone) añorar (a alguien)
longevity *n.* longevidad *f.*
longing *n.* ansia *f.*
look after oneself *v.* cuidarse
look at *v.* mirar; *(a topic)* enfocar **The program looks at the problem of homelessness.** El programa

enfoca el problema de la
falta de vivienda.
look for *v.* buscar
look good *v.* lucir
look in *v. (reference)* consultar
I'll look in the dictionary.
Consultaré el diccionario.
look up *v. (word)* buscar (en el
diccionario)
lose *v.t.* perder (e:ie)
lose weight adelgazar
lost *adj.* perdido/a
be lost estar perdido/a
lot *n.* terreno *m.*
lot (of), a *adj.* mucho/a
a lot *n.* sinfín *m.* **She still has
a lot of things to do.** Todavía
tiene un sinfín de cosas que
hacer.
a lot *adv.* muchas veces
loud *adj.* escandaloso/a
loudspeaker *n.* altavoz *m.*
lounge chair *n.* tumbona *f.*
love *n.* amor *m.*
in love (with) *adj.*
enamorado/a (de)
fall in love (with)
enamorarse (de)
love *v.t. (another person)*
querer (e:ie); *(things)*
encantar; fascinar
loyal *adj.* fiel
luck *n.* suerte *f.*
be lucky tener suerte
luggage *n.* equipaje *m.*
lunch *n.* almuerzo *m.*
have lunch almorzar (o:ue);
comer
lung *n.* pulmón *m.*
luxurious *adj.* lujoso/a

luxury *n.* lujo *m.*
lying *adj.* mentiroso/a

M

ma'am *n.* señora *f.* (Sra.)
machine *n.* máquina *f.*
answering machine
contestadora *f.*
mad *adj.* enojado/a
be hopping mad *idiom* echar
chispas
madness *n.* locura *f.*
magazine *n.* revista *f.*
magic *n.* magia *f.*
magical *adj.* mágico/a
magician *n.* mago/a *m., f.*
magma *n.* magma *m.*
magna cum laude *(grade)*
matrícula de honor
magnesium *n.* magnesio *m.*
magnet *n.* imán *m.*
magnificent *adj.* magnífico/a
magnifying glass *n.* lupa *f.*
mail carrier *n.* cartero/a *m., f.*
mail *n.* correo *m.* **I sent it in
the mail.** Lo mandé por
correo.; correspondencia *f.*
You got a lot of mail.
Recibiste mucha
correspondencia.
mail carrier cartero *m.*
mail *v.t.* enviar, mandar (por
correo); echar una carta al
buzón
mailbox *n.* buzón *m.*
main *adj.* principal
maintain *v.t.* mantener
major *n.* especialización *f.*
majority *n.* mayoría *f.*
make *v.t.* hacer; *(coffee)* colar

make a living *idiom* ganarse la vida **Mario makes his living writing soap opera scripts.** Mario se gana la vida escribiendo guiones de telenovela.

make a long story short *loc.* en resumidas cuentas

make one's mouth water *idiom.* hacérsele agua la boca **It smells good. It makes my mouth water.** ¡Qué bien huele! Se me hace agua la boca.

make sure *v.* asegurarse

make up *v.* maquillar

make up one's mind *v.* decidirse

makeup *n.* maquillaje *m.*

put on makeup *v.* maquillarse; pintarse

makeup artist *n.* maquillador(a) *m., f.*

male *n.* macho *m.*

malignant *adj.* maligno/a

mall *n.* centro *m.* comercial

mammal *n.* mamífero *m.*

man *n.* hombre *m.*

manage *v.t. (business)* administrar

management *n.* administración *f.*

manager *n.* gerente *m., f.*

manicure *n.* manicura *f.*

mannequin *n.* maniquí *m.*

manufacture *n.* fabricación *f.*

manufacture *v.t.* fabricar

manufacturer *n.* fabricante *m., f.*

manure *n.* estiércol *m.*

many *adj.* muchos/as

a great many *n.* sinfín *m.*

map *n.* mapa *m.*

city map *n.* plano *m.*

road map mapa *m.* de carreteras

marathon *n.* maratón *m.*

marble *n.* mármol *m.*

March *n.* marzo *m.*

margarine *n.* margarina *f.*

marital status *n.* estado *m.* civil

mark *n.* marca *f.; (imprint)* huella *f.; (grade)* nota *f.*

market *n.* mercado *m.;* supermercado *m.*

open-air market mercado al aire libre

street market *n.* mercadillo *m.*

marriage *n.* matrimonio *m.*

married *adj.* casado/a

marrow *n.* médula *f.*

marry: get married (to) *v.* casarse (con)

marsh *n.* pantano *m.*

martial arts *n., pl.* artes *f., pl.* marciales

marvelous *adj.* maravilloso/a

marvelously *adv.* maravillosamente

mask *n.* máscara *f.;* mascarilla *f.;* antifaz *m.*

mass produce *v.t.* fabricar en serie

mass production *n.* fabricación *f.* en serie

massage *n.* masaje *m.*

masseur *n.* masajista *m.*

masseuse *n.* masajista *f.*

master *v.t.* dominar

I am far from mastering Spanish. Estoy lejos de dominar el español.

Master's degree *n.* maestría *(L.A.) f.*

pursue a Master's degree hacer una maestría

masterpiece *n.* obra *f.* maestra

match *n.* cerilla *f.;* fósforo *m.; (sports)* partido *m.*

match (with) *v.t.* hacer juego (con)

match up *v.i.* coincidir

mate n. compañero/a *m., f.*

materialistic *adj.* materialista

maternal *adj. (relative)* materno/a

mathematician *n.* matemático/a *m., f.*

mathematics *n.* matemáticas *f., pl.*

matriculation *n.* matrícula *f.*

matter *n.* cuestión *f.* **She's an expert in matters of medieval history.** Es una experta en cuestiones de historia medieval.

matter *v.t.* importar

mattress *n.* colchón *m.*

foam mattress colchón de espuma

sprung mattress colchón de muelles

mature *adj.* maduro/a

maturity *n.* madurez *f.*

maximum *n., adj.* máximo *m.;* máximo/a

May *n.* mayo *m.*

maybe *adv.* tal vez; quizás

mayonnaise *n.* mayonesa *f.*

mayor *n.* alcalde *m.,* alcaldesa *f.*

mayor's office *n.* alcaldía *f.*

me: It's me./That's me. Soy yo.

meal *n.* comida *f.*

mean *adj. (person)* malo/a

means of communication *n., pl.* medios *m., pl.* de comunicación

means: by no means de ninguna manera, de ningún modo

measles *n.* sarampión *m.*

measure *v.t.* medir

measurement *n.* medición *f.;* medida *f.*

meat *n.* carne *f.*

mechanic *n.* mecánico/a *m., f.*

mechanic's workshop *n.* taller *m.* de mecánica

mechanic's repair shop taller mecánico

mechanism *n.* mecanismo *m.*

medal *n.* medalla *f.*

media *n.* medios *m., pl.* de comunicación

medical *adj.* médico/a

medical insurance *n.* seguro *m.* médico

medication *n.* medicamento *m.*

medicine *n.* medicina *f.*

medicine cabinet *n.* botiquín *m.*

mediocre *adj.* mediocre

meditate *v.i.* meditar

meditation *n.* meditación *f.*

medium *adj.* mediano/a

meet *v.t.* encontrar; conocer; *(each other)* encontrarse; conocerse

Where shall we meet?
¿Dónde nos encontramos?
They met in Paris. Se
conocieron en París.
meeting *n.* reunión *f.; (political)*
n. mitin *m.*
megaphone *n.* megáfono *m.*
melon *n.* melón *m.*
melt *v.t.* derretir **The heat will
melt the butter.** El calor
derritirá la mantequilla.*; v.i.*
derretirse **The ice cream
melted.** El helado se derritió.
member *n.* miembro *m.*
membrane *n.* membrana *f.*
memorize *v.t.* memorizar
memory *n.* memoria *f.*
menopause *n.* menopausia *f.*
mental disorder *n.* trastorno *m.*
mental
mental hospital *n.* manicomio
m.
mentality *n.* mentalidad *f.*
menu *n.* menú *m.*
mercury *n.* mercurio *m.*
merit *n.* mérito *f.*
**mess around: Don't mess
around on the way to school.**
No te entretengas camino a
la escuela.
message *n.* mensaje *m.;
(telephone)* recado *m.*
messy *adj.* desarreglado/a
metabolism *n.* metabolismo *m.*
metabolize *v.t.* metabolizar
metal *n.* metal *m.*
metamorphosis *n.*
metamorfosis *f.*
metaphor *n.* metáfora *f.*
metaphoric *adj.* metafórico/a

meteorite *n.* meteorito *m.*
meteorologist *n.*
meteorólogo/a *m., f.*
meteorology *n.* metereología *f.*
method *n.* método *m.*
methodical *adj.* metódico/a
Mexican *n., adj.* mexicano/a
m., f.
Mexico *n.* México *m.*
microphone *n.* micrófono *m.*
microscope *n.* microscopio *m.*
microwave *n.* microonda *f.*
microwave oven *n.* horno *m.*
de microondas
middle age *n.* madurez *f.*
middle school *n.* escuela *f.*
secundaria
midnight *n.* medianoche *f.*
mild *adj. (taste)* suave
mile *n.* milla *f.*
milk *n.* leche *f.*
Milky Way *n.* Vía Láctea *f.*
mill *n.* molino *m.*
million (of) *n.* millón (de) *m.*
mind *n.* mente *f.*
  keep in mind tener en
  cuenta
mine *n.* mina *f.*
mine mío(s)/mía(s) *poss. pron.*
miner *n.* minero/a *m., f.*
mineral *n.* mineral *m.*
mining industry *n.* minería *f.*
miniskirt *n.* minifalda *f.*
minister *n. (government)*
ministro/a *m., f.*
minority *n.* minoría *f.*
mint *n.* menta *f.*
minute *adj.* minúsculo/a
minute *n.* minuto *m.*
minute *adj. (object)* diminuto/a

mirror *n.* espejo *m.*
misbehave *v.* portarse mal
miscarriage *n.* aborto *m.* espontáneo
  have a miscarriage abortar
mischief *n.* travesura *f.*
mischievous *adj.* travieso/a
miser *n.* avaro/a *m., f.*
misfortune *n.* desgracia *f.*
Miss *n.* señorita *f.* (Srta.)
miss *v.* perder (e:ie)
  miss someone *v.t.* añorar a alguien
missile *n.* misil *m.;* proyectil *m.*
missing *adj.* desaparecido/a
mistake *n.* equivocación *f.*
  make a mistake equivocarse
mistaken *adj.* equivocado/a
  be mistaken equivocarse
  You are mistaken in thinking that. Te equivocas si piensas eso.
mister *n.* señor *m.*
mix *v.t.* mezclar
mixer *n.* batidora *(Spain) f.*
mobile *adj.* móvil
mobility *n.* movilidad *f.*
modem *n.* módem *m.*
modern *adj.* moderno/a
modernize *v.t.* modernizar
modest *adj. (person)* modesto/a; *(simple)* sencillo/a
modify *v.t.* modificar
moisturizer *n.* crema *n.* hidratante; humectante *m.*
molar *n.* muela *f.*
mold *n.* moho *m.*
mom *n.* mamá *f.,* mami *f.*
moment *n.* momento *m.*

monarch *n.* monarca *m., f.*
monarchy *n.* monarquía *f.*
monastery *n.* monasterio *m.*
Monday *n.* lunes *m., sing.*
money *n.* dinero *m.*
  paper money billete *m.*
money order *n.* giro *m.* postal
monitor *n.* monitor *m.*
monk *n.* monje *m.*
monkey *n.* mono *m.*
monologue *n.* monólogo *m.*
month *n.* mes *m.*
monument *n.* monumento *m.*
mood: in a good/bad mood de buen/mal humor
moon *n.* luna *f.*
mop *n.* fregona *(Spain) f.;* trapeador *(L.A.) m.*
mop (the floor) *v.t.* trapear (el piso) *(L.A.);* fregar (el suelo) *(Spain)*
moral *n.* moral *f.*
morality *n.* moralidad *f.*
more *adj., adv.* más
  more . . . than más… que
  more than (+ number) más de (+ *number*)
moribund *adj.* moribundo/a
morning *n.* mañana *f.*
  in the morning de la mañana; por la mañana
morphology *n.* morfología *f.*
mortality *n.* mortalidad *f.*
mortality rate *n.* índice *m.* de mortalidad
mortgage *n.* hipoteca *f.*
mortgage *v.t.* hipotecar
mosque *n.* mezquita *f.*
mosquito net *n.* mosquitero *m.*
mother *n.* madre *f.*

mother-in-law n. suegra f.

motor n. motor m.

motorboat n. lancha f.

motorcycle n. moto f.; motocicleta f.

   go by motorcycle ir en motocicleta

motorcycling n. motociclismo m.

motorcyclist n. motociclista m., f.

motorist n. automovilista m., f.

mountain n. montaña f.

mountain range n. cordillera f. (montañosa)

mountainside n. ladera f.

mouse n. ratón m.

moustache n. bigote(s) m. (pl.)

mouth n. boca f.; (river) desembocadura f.

mouth-to-mouth resuscitation n. respiración f. boca a boca

move n. mudanza f.

move v.i. (from one house to another) mudarse; (from one place to another) desplazarse

move forward v.i. avanzar

movement n. desplazamiento m.

movie n. película f.

   see movies ver películas

moviemaker n. cineasta m., f.

movie star n. estrella m., f. de cine

movie theater n. cine m.

movies n. cine m.

mow the lawn v.t. cortar el pasto

Mr. n. señor m. (Sr.), don

Mrs. n. señora f. (Sra.)

much adj., adv. mucho/a

mud n. barro m.; fango m.

muffler n. (car) silenciador m.

mug n. taza f.

mug v.t. atracar

municipal n. municipal m.

murder n. asesinato m.; crimen m.

murderer n. asesino/a m., f.

muscle n. músculo m.

muscular adj. musculoso/a

museum n. museo m.

mushroom n. champiñón m.

music n. música f.

   play loud music poner la música muy alta

musical adj. musical

musician n. músico/a m., f

Muslim n., adj. musulmán m., musulmana f.

mussel n. mejillón m.

must deber (+ inf.)

   It must be… Debe ser…

mustard n. mostaza f.

mute adj. mudo/a

my mi(s) poss. adj.

myopia n. miopía f.

myopic adj. miope

mysterious adj. enigmático/a; misterioso/a

mystery n. misterio m.; enigma m.

   a mystery novel una novela de misterio

N

nail n. clavo m.; (finger, toe) uña f.

   hit the nail on the head

idiom dar en el clavo
nail file *n.* lima *f.*
name *n.* nombre *m.*
  be named llamarse
  in the name of a nombre de
  last name apellido *m.*
  My name is . . . Me llamo…
  What's your name? *fam.*
  ¿Cómo te llamas (tú)?, *form.*
  ¿Cómo se llama usted?
name *v.t.* ponerle nombre a
nap *n. (afternoon)* siesta *f.*
napkin *n.* servilleta *f.*
narrator *n.* narrador(a) *m., f.*
nasty *adj.* antipático/a
national *adj.* nacional
nationalism *n.* nacionalismo *m.*
nationalist *adj.* nacionalista
nationality *n.* nacionalidad *f.*
native *adj.* indígena
natural *adj.* natural
nature *n.* naturaleza *f.*
nature reserve *n.* parque *m.*
  natural
naughty *adj.* travieso/a
nausea *n.* náusea *f.*
nauseate *v.t.* asquear,
  repugnar, dar asco
nauseated *adj.* mareado/a
nauseating *adj.* asqueroso/a,
  repugnante
navel *n.* ombligo *m.*
navy blue *n., adj.* azul *m.*
  marino
near *prep.* cerca de
neaten *v.* arreglar
necessary *adj.* necesario/a
  It's (not) necessary that…
  (No) Es necesario que…
necessity *n.* necesidad *f.*

neck *n.* cuello *m.*
necklace *n.* collar *m.*
nectarine *n.* nectarina *f.*
need *v.t.* faltar; necesitar
needle *n.* aguja *f.*
negative *adj.* negativo/a
neighbor *n.* vecino/a *m., f.*
neighborhood *n.* barrio *m.*
neither *adv.* tampoco
  neither . . . nor *conj.* ni… ni
  I eat neither meat nor fish.
  No como ni carne ni
  pescado.
nephew *n.* sobrino *m.*
nerve *n.* nervio *m.;*
  atrevimiento *m.*
  You've got some nerve! ¡Qué
  cara más dura tienes!
nervous *adj.* nervioso/a
nervous breakdown *n.* crisis *f.*
  nerviosa
network *n.* red *f.*
neuron *n.* neurona *f.*
never *adv.* nunca; jamás
new *adj.* nuevo/a; novato/a
  What's new? ¿Qué hay de
  nuevo?
newlywed *n.* recién casado/a
  m., f.
news *n.* noticias *f., pl.;*
  actualidades *f., pl.*
newscast *n.* noticiero *m.*
newsletter *n.* boletín *m.*
  informativo
newspaper *n.* periódico *m.;*
  diario *m.*
next *adj.* próximo/a
  next to *prep.* al lado de
nice *adj.* simpático/a; amable;
  agradable

nice person *idiom* buena gente
Nice to meet you. Mucho gusto.
nickname *n.* apodo *m.*
niece *n.* sobrina *f.*
nieces and nephews *n., pl.* sobrinos *m., pl.*
night *n.* noche *f.*
　at night *adv.* por la noche
　night stand *n.* mesita *f.* de noche
　night table mesa de noche
nightmare *n.* pesadilla *f.*
nine nueve
nine hundred novecientos/as
nineteen diecinueve
ninety noventa
ninth noveno *m.; adj.* noveno/a
nitrogen *n.* nitrógeno *m.*
no *adj.* ningún, ninguno/a(s)
　no one *pron.* nadie
no *adv.* no; ningún, ninguno/a(s) *adj.*
　no entry (*sign*) prohibido el paso
　no one *pron.* nadie
　no problem ningún problema
　no way de ninguna manera
nobody *pron.* nadie
noise *n.* ruido *m.*
noisy *adj.* ruidoso/a
none *adj.* ningún, ninguno/a(s)
non-fattening *adj.* que no engorda
non-resident *n.* transeúnte *m., f.*
noon *n.* mediodía *m.*
nor *conj.* ni
Nordic *adj.* nórdico/a

north *n.* norte *m.*
　to the north al norte
Northern European *n.* nórdico/a *m., f.*
nose *n.* nariz *f.*
not *adv.* no
　not any *adj.* ningún, ninguno/a(s)
　not anyone *pron.* nadie
　not anything *pron.* nada
　not bad at all nada mal
　not either *adv.* tampoco
　not ever *adv.* nunca; jamás
　Not very well. No muy bien.
note *n.* nota *f.*
notebook *n.* cuaderno *m.*
nothing *pron.* nada
　I've nothing to say. No tengo nada que decir.
nothingness *n.* nada *f.*
notice *v.t.* notar; advertir
noun *n.* sustantivo *m.*
November *n.* noviembre *m.*
now *adv.* ahora
nowadays *adv.* hoy día
nowhere a ninguna parte
nuclear *adj.* nuclear
nucleus *n.* núcleo *m.*
number *n.* número *m.; (figure)* cifra *f.*
nun *n.* monja *f.*
nunnery *n.* convento *m.*
nurse *n.* enfermero/a *m., f.*
nursery school *n.* guardería *f.*
nutcracker *n.* cascanueces *m., sing.*
nutrition *n.* nutrición *f.*
nutritionist *n.* nutricionista *m., f.*

o

o'clock: It's . . . o'clock. Son las...

  It's one o'clock. Es la una.

oak tree *n.* roble *m.*

oar *n.* remo *m.*

obese *adj.* obeso/a

obesity *n.* obesidad *f.*

obey *v.t.* obedecer (c:zc)

objective *adj.* objetivo/a

objective *n.* meta *f.*, objetivo *m.*

obligation *n.* deber *m.*

observant *adj.* observador(a)

observation *n.* observación *f.*

observatory *n.* observatorio *m.*

observe *v.t.* observar

obstacle course carrera de obstáculos

obtain *v.t.* conseguir (e:i); obtener (e:ie)

obvious *adj.* obvio

  it's obvious es obvio

occasion *n.* tiempo *m.*

occupation *n.* ocupación *f.*

occur *v.i. (happen)* ocurrir, suceder, pasar, realizarse; *(come to mind)* ocurrir

ocean *n.* mar *m., f.;* océano *m.*

ocean liner *n.* transatlántico *m.*

ocher *n.* ocre *m.*

October *n.* octubre *m.*

octopus *n.* pulpo *m.*

odor *n.* olor *m.*

of *prep.* de

  of course claro que sí; por supuesto; *(idiom)* desde luego

offend *v.t.* ofender

offer *n.* oferta *f.*

offer *v.t.* ofrecer (c:zc)

offering *n.* ofrenda *f.*

office *n.* oficina *f.; (medical)* consultorio *m.*

often *adv.* a menudo

Oh! *interj.* ¡Ay!

oil *n.* aceite *m.;* petróleo *m.*

OK! *interj.* ¡Vale! *(Spain)*; de acuerdo

okay *adj.* regular

  It's okay. Está bien.

old *adj.* viejo/a; antiguo/a

  be . . . years old tener... años

  How old are you? ¿Cuántos años tienes?

  become old hacerse viejo/a

  grow old envejecer

old age *n.* vejez *f.*

older *adj.* mayor

  older brother/sister *n.* hermano/a mayor *m., f.*

oldest *adj.* el/la mayor

old-fashioned *adj.* anticuado/a

olive *n.* aceituna *f.*

Olympic *adj.* olímpico/a

Olympic Games *n., pl.* Juegos *m., pl.* Olímpicos

omelet *n.* tortilla (de huevo) *(Spain)* f.

on *prep.* en; sobre

  on the dot en punto

  on (the) one hand. . . on the other hand. . . por un lado... por otro lado...

  on the other hand en cambio

on top of *prep.* encima de

once *adv.* una vez

oncologist *n.* oncólogo/a *m., f.*

one un, uno/a *m., f., sing. pron.*
  one of these days un día de estos
one hundred cien(to)
our nuestro(s)/nuestra(s) *poss. adj.; poss. pron.*
one thousand mil
one-way *n. (travel)* ida *f.*
onion *n.* cebolla *f.*
only *adj.* único/a
only *adv.* sólo, solamente
opaque *adj.* opaco/a
open *adj.* abierto/a
open *v.t.* abrir
  in the open air al aire libre
open-air dance *n.* verbena *f.*
opened *p.p.* abierto (*of* abrir)
opener *n.* abridor *m.*
opera *n.* ópera *f.*
operating room *n.* quirófano *m.*
operation *n.* operación *f.;* intervención *f.* quirúrgica
ophthalmologist *n.* oftalmólogo/a *m., f.*
opinion *n.* opinión *f.*
  express an opinion opinar
  in my opinion en mi opinión
opponent *n.* contrincante *m., f.*
opposite *prep.* en frente de
optimist *n.* optimista *m., f.*
optimistic *adj.* optimista
or *conj.* o
orange *adj.* anaranjado/a
orange *n.* naranja *f.*
orange tree *n.* naranjo *m.*
orchard *n.* huerta *f.*
orchestra *n.* orquesta *f.*
order *n.* orden *m.;* (commercial) encargo *m.*
  in order to (+ *inf.*) *prep.* para

(+ *inf.*) ; a fin de (+ *inf.*)
  out of order descompuesto/a *(L.A.);* averiado/a *(Spain);* (sign) no funciona
order *v.t.* mandar; *(food)* pedir (e:i); encargar
orderly *adj.* ordenado/a
ordinal *adj.* ordinal
oregano *n.* orégano *m.*
organ *n.* órgano *m.*
organic *adj.* orgánico/a; *(food)* ecológico/a
organization *n.* organización *f.*
organize *v.t.* organizar
original *adj.* original
originality *n.* originalidad *f.*
ostrich *n.* avestruz *m.*
other *adj.* otro/a
ounce *n.* onza *f.*
our nuestro(s)/nuestra(s) *poss. adj.; poss pron.*
out *adv.* fuera, afuera
out of stock *adj.* agotado/a
outline *v.t.* delinear
outrageous *adj.* escandaloso/a
outside *adv.* (a)fuera
outskirts *n., pl.* afueras *f., pl.;* alrededores *m., pl.* **on the outskirts of Barcelona** en los alrededores de Barcelona
outstanding *adj.* sobresaliente, extraordinario, excepcional
oven *n.* horno *m.*
over *prep.* sobre
overcome *v.t.* superar
oversleep *v.i.* quedarse dormido
owl *n.* búho *m.*
own *adj.* propio/a
own *v.t.* poseer

owner *n.* dueño/a *m., f.*
oxygen *n.* oxígeno *m.*
oyster *n.* ostra *f.*

P

p.m. en la tarde, de la tarde
pacemaker *n.* marcapasos *m., sing.*
pacifist *n., adj.* pacifista *m., f.*
pack (one's suitcases) *v.t.* hacer las maletas; empacar
package *n.* paquete *m.*
padded *adj.* acolchado/a
page *n.* página *f.*
pain *n.* dolor *m.*
　have a pain in the (knee) tener dolor de (rodilla)
　What pain! ¡Qué dolor!
paint *v.t.* pintar
painter *n.* pintor(a) *m., f.*
painting *n.* pintura *f.*
pair *n.* par *m.*
　a pair of shoes un par de zapatos
pajamas *n., pl.* pijama *(Spain) m.;* piyama *(L.A.) m.*
palace *n.* palacio *m.*
palate *n.* paladar *m.*
paleontologist *n.* paleontólogo/a *m., f.*
paleontology *n.* paleontología *f.*
palm tree *n.* palmera *f.*
pan *n. (frying)* sartén *f.*
pancreas *n.* páncreas *m.*
panic attack *n.* ataque *m.* de nervios
panties *n., pl.* bragas *(Spain) f., pl.;* pantaletas *(Venezuela) f., pl.;* calzones *(L.A.) m., pl.*
pantry *n.* despensa *f.*

pants *n., pl.* pantalones *m., pl.*
pantyhose *n., pl.* medias *f., pl.*
paper *n.* papel *m.; (report)* informe *m.; (school essay)* trabajo *m.*
paperback *n.* libro *m.* de bolsillo
parachute *n.* paracaídas *m.*
parachuting *n.* paracaidismo *m.*
parachutist *n.* paracaidista *m., f.*
parade *n.* desfile *m.*
paragraph *n.* párrafo *m.*
parakeet *n.* perico *m.;* periquito *m.*
Paralympics *n., pl.* Juegos *m., pl.* Paralímpicos
parasite *n.* parásito *m.*
Pardon me. Perdón.; *(May I?)* Con permiso.
parents *n., pl.* padres *m., pl.;* papás *m., pl.*
park *n.* parque *m.*
park *v.t.* estacionar(se)
parking lot *n.* estacionamiento *m.*
parking *n.* estacionamiento *m.*
parking space *n.* estacionamiento *m.*
parole *n.* libertad *f.* condicional
parrot *n.* loro *m.*
parsley *n.* perejil *m.*
participate *v.i.* participar; *(contest)* concursar
participation *n.* participación *f.;* intervención *f.*
partner *n.* compañero/a *m., f.; (business)* socio/a *m., f. (marriage, romance, sport)* pareja *f.*

partnership *n.* asociación *f.*
party *n.* fiesta *f.; (political)* partido *m.* (*político*)
  throw a party hacer una fiesta
party pooper *n.* aguafiestas *m., f., sing.*
pass *v.t.* pasar; *(test)* aprobar
  He passed the test. Aprobó el examen.
  no passing *(traffic sign)* prohibido adelantar
  pass (a vehicle) adelantar (a un vehículo)
pass away *v.* fallecer
pass on *v. (illness)* contagiar
passed *p.p.* pasado/a (*of pasar*)
passenger *n.* pasajero/a *m., f.*
passer-by *n.* transeúnte *m., f.*
passing grade *n.* aprobado *m.*
passport *n.* pasaporte *m.*
past *n., adj.* pasado *m.;* pasado/a
pastime *n.* pasatiempo *m.*
pastry shop *n.* pastelería *f.*
paternal *adj. (relative)* paterno/a
path *n.* camino *m.;* sendero *m.; (of an object)* trayectoria *f.*
patience *n.* paciencia *f.*
patient *n., adj.* paciente *m., f.*
patio *n.* patio *m.*
patterned *adj. (fabric)* estampado/a
pay *v.t.* pagar
  pay attention atender; prestar atención
  pay in cash pagar en efectivo; pagar al contado

  pay in installments pagar a plazos
  pay the bill pagar la cuenta
pea *n.* arveja *(L.A.) f.;* chícharo *(Mexico) m.;* guisante *(Spain) m.*
peace *n.* paz *f.*
peach *n.* durazno *(L.A.) m.;* melocotón *(Spain) m.*
peak *n.* (mountain) cumbre *m.,* cima *f.;* auge *m.*
pear *n.* pera *f.*
pedagogical *adj.* pedagógico/a
pedagogue *n.* pedagogo/a *m., f.*
pedagogy *n.* pedagogía *f.*
pedal *n.* pedal *m.*
pedantic *adj.* pedante
pedestrian *n.* peatón *m.*
pedicure *n.* pedicura *f.*
peel *v.t.* pelar
peeler *n.* pelapapas *m., sing.*
pen *n.* pluma *f.;* bolígrafo *m.*
pencil *n.* lápiz *m.*
penguin *n.* pingüino *m.*
penicillin *n.* penicilina *f.*
peninsula *n.* península *f.*
penitentiary *n.* penitenciaría *f.*
penknife *n.* navaja *f.*
pensioner *n.* pensionista *m., f.*
people *n., pl.* gente *f., sing.*
pepper *n. (black)* pimienta *f.; (bell)* pimiento *m.*
percent por ciento
percentage *n.* porcentaje *m.*
perfect *adj.* perfecto/a
perfectionist *adj.* perfeccionista; detallista
perforate *v.t.* perforar
perform *v.t.* interpretar

perfume n. perfume m.
perfume shop n. perfumería f.
perhaps adv. quizás; tal vez
perimeter n. perímetro m.
period n. periodo m.; (limited time) plazo m., (punctuation) punto m.
permission n. permiso m.; consentimiento m.
permit v.t. permitir; consentir
persecution n. persecución f.
  He suffered persecution for his ideas. Sufrió persecuciones por sus creencias.
persist v.i. persistir
persistent adj. persistente
person n. persona f.
personality n. personalidad f.
perspiration n. transpiración f.
perspire v.i. transpirar
pessimist n. pesimista m., f.
pessimistic adj. pesimista
pesticide n. pesticida m.
petal n. pétalo m.
petrified adj. petrificado/a
Ph.D. n. doctorado m.; (title) Dr. m., Dra. f.
pharmacy n. farmacia f.
pharynx n. faringe f.
pheasant n. faisán m.
phenomenal adj. espectacular, extraordinario; increíble; fenomenal
phenomenon n. fenómeno m.
philately n. filatelia f.
philologist n. filólogo/a m., f.
philology n. filología f.
philosopher n. filósofo/a m., f.
philosophize v.i. filosofar

philosophy n. filosofía f.
phonetics n. fonética f.
phonology n. fonología f.
photocopier n. fotocopiadora f.
photocopy v.t. fotocopiar
photograph n. foto(grafía) f.
  take photos tomar/sacar fotos
photosynthesis n. fotosíntesis f., sing.
physical (exam) n. chequeo m. (médico), revisión f. médica; examen m. médico
physician n. doctor(a) m., f., médico/a m., f.
physicist n. físico/a m., f.
physics n. física f.
physique n. tipo m.
pick up v.t. recoger
pick up boys/girls v.i. ligar
pickup truck n. camioneta f.
picture n. cuadro m.; pintura f.
picturesque adj. pintoresco/a
pie n. pastel m.
pig n. cerdo m.; puerco m.
pilgrim n. peregrino/a m., f.
pilgrimage n. peregrinación f.
pill n. pastilla f.; píldora f.
pillow n. almohada f.
pimple n. grano m.
pinch n. (quantity) pizca f.
pine forest n. pinar m.
pine tree n. pino m.
pineapple n. piña f.
pink adj. rosado/a
pipe n. tubo m., caño m.; cañería f., tubería f.
pit n. (fruit) hueso m.
pitcher n. jarra f.
pity n. lástima f.

place *n.* lugar *m.*
place *v.t.* poner; colocar
placing *n.* colocación *f.*
plagiarism *n.* plagio *m.*
plagiarize *v.t.* plagiar
plaid *adj.* de cuadros
plan (to do something) *v.* pensar *(+ inf.)*
plan *n.* plan *m.*
have plans tener planes
plane *n.* avión *m.*
planet *n.* planeta *m.*
planetarium *n.* planetario *m.*
plant *n.* planta *f.*
climbing plant enredadera *f.*
plantain *n.* plátano *m.*
plastic *n.* plástico *m.*
made of plastic de plástico
plate *n.* plato *m.*
license plate placa *f.*
plateau *n.* meseta *f.*
platter *n.* fuente *f.*
platter of fried food *n.* fuente de fritada
play *n.* drama *m.;* comedia *f.*
play *v.t.* jugar (u:ue);
play (a musical instrument) tocar (un instrumento musical)
play hooky hacer novillos *(Spain)*
play sports practicar deportes
play the role (of) hacer el papel (de)
player *n.* jugador(a) *m., f.*
playwright *n.* dramaturgo/a *m., f.*
plead *v.i.* rogar (o:ue), suplicar
pleasant *adj.* agradable

please *interj.* por favor
be pleased (with) contentarse (con)
Pleased to meet you. Mucho gusto.; Encantado/a (de conocerle).
pleasing: be pleasing to gustar
pleasure *n.* gusto *m.;* placer *m.*
It's a pleasure to . . . Gusto de *(+ inf.)*
It's been a pleasure. Ha sido un placer.
The pleasure is mine. El gusto es mío.
What a pleasure to . . . ! ¡Qué gusto (+ *inf.).*..
plot *n. (story)* argumento *m.; (land)* terreno *m.*
plot *v.t.* tramar
pluck *v. (eyebrows)* depilarse
plum *n.* ciruela *f.*
plumber *n.* fontanero/a *(Spain) m., f.;* plomero/a *(L.A.) m., f.*
plumbing *n.* fontanería *(Spain) f.;* plomería *(L.A.) f.*
pluralism *n.* pluralismo *m.*
plurality *n.* pluralidad *f.*
pocket *n.* bolsillo *m.*
podium *n.* podio *m.*
poem *n.* poema *m.*
poet *n.* poeta *m., f.*
poetry *n.* poesía *f.*
point *n.* punto *m.*
polemical *adj.* polémico/a
police *n. (force)* policía *f.*
police officer *n.* policía *m.,* mujer *f.* policía
police station *n.* comisaría *f.* (de policía)
polish *n. (shoe)* brillo *m.* (para

zapatos); *(floor)* abrillantador
m. (para pisos/suelos)
polish *v.t.* abrillantar; encerar
polite *adj.* educado/a
political *adj.* político/a
politician *n.* político/a *m., f.*
politics *n.* política *f.*
polka dot *n.* lunar *m.*
polka-doted *adj.* de lunares
poll *n.* encuesta *f.*
pollen *n.* polen *m.*
pollinate *v.t.* polinizar
pollute *v.t.* contaminar
polluted *adj.* contaminado/a
  be polluted estar
  contaminado/a
pollution *n.* contaminación *f.*
  air/water pollution
  contaminación del aire/del
  agua
pomegranate *n.* granada *f.*
pond *n. (man-made)* estanque
  m.; (natural) charca *f.*
pony tail *n.* cola *f.* de caballo
pool: swimming pool *n.*
  piscina *f.;* alberca *(Mexico) f.*
  indoor pool piscina
  climatizada
poor *adj.* pobre
  become poor empobrecerse
  make poor empobrecer
poppy *n.* amapola *f.*
populate *v.t.* poblar
population *n.* población *f.*
porch *n.* porche *m.*
pork *n.* cerdo *m.*
pork chop *n.* chuleta *f.* de
  cerdo
port *n.* puerto *m.*
portable *adj.* portátil

portable computer *n.*
  computadora *f.* portátil
porter *n.* portero/a *m., f.*
position *n. (job)* puesto *m.*
possession *n.* posesión *f.*
possessive *adj.* posesivo/a
possible *adj.* posible
  it's (not) possible (no) es
  posible
post office *n.* correo *m.;*
  correos *(Spain) m., pl.*
postcard *n.* postal *f.;* tarjeta *f.*
  postal
poster *n.* cartel *m.*
postpone *v.t.* aplazar
postponement *n.* aplazamiento
  m.
pot *n. (cooking)* olla *f.*
potato *n.* papa *(L.A.) f.;* patata
  (Spain) f.
potato omelet *n.* tortilla *f.* de
  patatas
potter *n.* ceramista *m., f.*
pottery *n.* cerámica *f.*
pound *n.* libra *f.*
pour *v.i.* llover a cántaros
poverty *n.* pobreza *f.*
power *n.* poder *m.;* potencia *f.*
power failure *n.* apagón *m.*
power steering *n.* dirección *f.*
  asistida
powerful *adj.* poderoso/a
practice *n.* práctica *f.*
practice *v.t.* practicar;
  entrenarse
prairie *n.* llanura *f.*
praise *n.* elogio *f.*
praise *v.t.* elogiar
prank *n.* travesura *f.*
prawn *n.* langostino *m.*

pray *v.i.* rezar
predator *n.* depredador *m.*
predatory *adj.* depredador(a)
prefabricate *v.t.* prefabricar
prefabricated *adj.*
   prefabricado/a
prefer *v.t.* preferir (e:ie)
pregnant *adj.* embarazada
premiere *n. (film, play)* estreno
   m.
preparations *n., pl.*
   preparativos *m., pl.*
prepare *v.t.* preparar
preposition *n.* preposición *f.*
prescribe *v.t.* recetar
prescription *n.* receta *f.*
present *n. (gift)* regalo *m.;*
   (time) presente *m.*
present *v.t.* presentar
presenter *n.* presentador(a) *m.,*
   f.
press *n.* prensa *f.*
pressure *n.* presión *f.*
   be under (a lot of) pressure
   sufrir (muchas) presiones
pressure cooker *n.* olla *f.* a
   presión
pretend *v.t./v.i.* fingir; disimular
pretentious *adj.* pretencioso/a
pretty *adj.* bonito/a; bastante
   adv.
prevent *v.t.* prevenir; impedir;
   evitar
prevention *n.* prevención *f.*
prey *n.* presa *f.*
price *n.* precio *m.*
   What is the price? ¿Qué
   precio tiene?
pride *n.* orgullo *m.*
priest *n.* padre *m.*

primitive *adj.* primitivo/a
print *adj.* estampado
print *v.t.* imprimir
printer *n. (machine)* impresora
   f.
prison *n.* prisión *f.;* cárcel *f.*
prisoner *n.* preso/a *m., f.*
privacy *n.* intimidad *f.*
private *adj.* privado/a;
   particular; individual
prize *n.* premio *m.;* galardón *m.*
probable *adj.* probable
   it's (not) probable (no) es
   probable
problem *n.* problema *m.*
prodigy *n.* prodigio/a *m., f.*
produce *n.* frutas *f., pl.* y
   verduras *f., pl.*
produce *v.t.* fabricar
product *n.* producto *m.*
profession *n.* profesión *f.*
professor *n.* profesor(a) *m., f.;*
   catedrático/a *m., f.*
program *n.* programa *m.*
programmer *n.* programador(a)
   m., f.
prohibit *v.t.* prohibir
prohibited *p.p.* prohibido (*of*
   prohibir)
project *v.t.* proyectar
projection *n.* proyección *f.*
prolific *adj.* prolífico/a
promise *v.* prometer
promote *v.i. (work)* ascender
promotion *n. (career)* ascenso
   m.
prone to *adj.* propenso/a a
pronoun *n.* pronombre *m.*
proof *n.* demostración *f.*
proposal *n.* propuesta *f.*

propose *v.t.* proponer
protect *v.t.* proteger
protection *n.* protección *f.*
protein *n.* proteína *f.*
protest *n.* protesta *f.*
protest *v.t.* protestar
Protestant *n., adj.* protestante *m., f.*
proud *adj.* orgulloso/a
prove *v.t.* demostrar
provided (that) *conj.* con tal (de) que
provisions *n., pl.* provisiones *f., pl.;* víveres *m., pl.*
provocation *n.* provocación *f.*
provocative *adj. (dress)* atrevido/a
provoke *v.t.* provocar
psychiatrist *n.* (p)siquiatra *m., f.*
psychiatry *n.* (p)siquiatría *f.*
psychologist *n.* (p)sicólogo/a *m., f.*
psychology *n.* (p)sicología *f.*
puberty *n.* pubertad *f.*
public school *n.* escuela *f.* pública
publish *v.t.* publicar
Puerto Rican *n., adj.* puertorriqueño/a *m., f.*
Puerto Rico *n.* Puerto Rico *m.*
pull *v.t.* halar *(L.A.),* jalar *(L.A.);* tirar *(Spain)*
  pull an all-nighter *idiom* quemarse las pestañas
  pull out all the stops *loc.* echar la casa por la ventana
  pull someone's leg *idiom* tomarle el pelo a alguien
pumpkin *n.* calabaza *f.*

punchbowl *n.* ponchera *f.*
punctual *adj.* puntual
punish *v.t.* castigar
punishment *n.* castigo *m.*
pupil *n. (eye)* pupila *f.; (student)* pupilo/a *m., f.;* alumno/a *m., f.*
purchase *n.* compra *f.,* adquisición *f.*
purchase *v.t.* comprar, adquirir
pure *adj.* puro/a
purple *n., adj.* morado *m.;* morado/a
purpose *n.* propósito *m.*
  on purpose *adv.* adrede; a propósito
purse *n.* bolsa *f.*
pursue *v.t.* perseguir
pursuit *n.* persecución *f.* **The police took off in pursuit of the fugitive.** La policía salió en persecución del fugitivo.; búsqueda *f.* **the pursuit of truth** la búsqueda de la verdad
push *v.t.* empujar
put *v.t.* poner; colocar
  put in a cast escayolar *(Spain);* enyesar *(L.A.)*
put *p.p.* puesto *(of* poner*)*
put off *v.* aplazar
put on *v. (a performance)* presentar; *(clothing)* ponerse
put out *v.t.* sofocar; extinguir **The firefighters put out the blaze.** Los bomberos extinguieron el incendio.
put something over (on somebody) *idiom* dar gato por liebre

put up *v.t.* *(give lodging)* alojar
put up with *v.* aguantar
puzzle, (jigsaw) *n.*
 rompecabezas *m., sing.*
pyramid *n.* pirámide *f.*

Q

quail *n.* codorniz *f.*
qualify *v.t./v.i.* calificarse
quality *n.* calidad *f.*
quarrel *n.* pelea *f.*
quarrel *v.i.* pelearse; discutir
 **They always quarrel over
 money.** Siempre se pelean
 por el dinero.
quarter *n.* trimestre *m.;* cuarto
 m.
 quarter after *(time)* y cuarto;
 y quince **It's quarter after
 three.** Son las tres y
 cuarto/quince.
 quarter to menos cuarto;
 menos quince **It's quarter to
 five.** Son las cinco menos
 cuarto/quince.
queen *n.* reina *f.*
question *v.t.* cuestionar
question *n.* pregunta *f.*
quickly *adv.* rápido
quiet *adj.* tranquilo/a; callado/a
quit (doing something) *v.t.*
 (habit) dejar de (+ *inf.*); dejar
quiz *n.* prueba *f.*

R

rabbi *n.* rabino/a *m., f.*
rabbit *n.* conejo *m.*
race *n.* *(sport)* carrera *f.;*
 (people) raza *f.*
racecar *n.* carro *m.* de
 carreras
racism *n.* racismo *m.*
racist *adj.* racista
racket *n.* *(sport)* raqueta *f.*
radio *n.* *(medium)* radio *f.; (set
 receiver)* radio *m.*
radish *n.* rábano *m.*
railroad *n.* ferrocarril *m.*
railroad crossing *n.* paso *m.* a
 nivel
rain *n.* lluvia *f.*
rain *v.imp.* llover (o:ue)
 It's raining. Llueve.
 rain cats and dogs *idiom*
 llover a cántaros
rain forest *n.* bosque *m.*
 tropical
rainbow *n.* arco *m.* iris
raincoat *n.* impermeable *m.*
raise *n.* *(salary)* aumento *m.* de
 sueldo
raise *v.t.* *(children, animals)*
 criar; *(money)* recaudar
 (fondos)
raisin *n.* pasa *f.*
rake *n.* rastrillo *m.*
rancher *n.* ganadero/a *m., f.*
ranching *n.* ganadería *f.*
randomly *adv.* al azar
 at random *adv.* al azar
ranger *n.* guarda *m., f.* forestal
raspberry *n.* frambuesa *f.*
rate *n.* índice *m.*
rather *adv.* bastante
rattlesnake *n.* serpiente *f.* de
 cascabel
raw *adj.* *(food)* crudo/a
razor *n.* máquina *f.* de afeitar;
 rasuradora *f.*
reach *n.* alcance

within arm's reach al alcance de la mano

reach *v.t.* alcanzar; llegar a; contactar, ponerse en contacto con

reach a conclusion llegar a una conclusión

reach an agreement llegar a un acuerdo

How can I reach you? ¿Cómo puedo ponerme en contacto contigo?

react *v.i.* reaccionar

reaction *n.* reacción *f.*

read *v.t.* leer

read e-mail/a newspaper/a magazine leer correo electrónico/un periódico/una revista

read *p.p.* leído (*of* leer)

reader *n.* lector(a) *m., f.*

ready *adj.* listo/a

be ready estar listo/a

get ready prepararse; arreglarse **He takes forever getting ready.** Tarda mucho en arreglarse.

real *adj.* auténtico/a

real estate *n.* bienes raíces *m., pl.*

realistic *adj.* verosímil **His characters aren't realistic.** Sus personajes no son verosímiles.

realize *v.t.* darse cuenta de (que) **Gustavo realized he was alone.** Gustavo se dio cuenta de que estaba solo.

reap the benefits (of) *v.t.* disfrutar (de)

rearview mirror *n.* retrovisor *m.*

reason *n.* razón *f.*

reason *v.i.* razonar

rebellious *adj.* rebelde

receive *v.t.* recibir

receptionist *n.* recepcionista *m., f.; (hotel)* conserje *m., f.*

recess *n.* recreo *m.*

recipe *n.* receta *f.*

recital *n.* recital *m.*

recognition *n.* reconocimiento *m.*

recognize *v.t.* reconocer

recommend *v.t.* recomendar (e:ie)

record *n. (sport)* marca *f.;* récord *m.*

record *v.t.* grabar

recreation *n.* diversión *f.*

rectangle *n.* rectángulo *m.*

rectify *v.t.* rectificar

recycle *v.t.* reciclar

recycling *n.* reciclaje *m.*

red *n., adj.* rojo *m.;* rojo/a

Red Cross *n.* Cruz *f.* Roja

reddish *adj.* rojizo/a

red-hair *adj.* pelirrojo/a

red-headed *adj.* pelirrojo/a

reduce *v.t.* reducir

reduce stress/tension aliviar el estrés/la tensión

reduced *adj.* de rebaja

reef *n.* arrecife *m.*

referee *n.* árbitro/a *m., f.*

reference book *n.* libro *m.* de consulta

reflect *v.t. (light)* reflejar; *v.i.* **(on something)** reflexionar (sobre algo)

reform *n.* reforma *f.*

reform *v.t.* reformar
refreshing *adj.* refrescante
refrigerate *v.t.* refrigerar
refrigerator *n.* refrigerador *m.*
refund *n.* devolución *f.*
refusal *n.* negación *f.*
refuse *v.i.* negarse; *v.t.* negarse a (+ *inf.*)
  He refused to answer. Se negó a contestar.
regarding to (con) respecto a
regards *n., pl.* recuerdos *m., pl.*; saludos *m., pl.*
  Lila sends her regards. Lila manda saludos.
region *n.* región *f.*
register *v.i. (school)* matricularse; inscribirse **She intends to register for the astronomy class.** Pretende inscribirse en la clase de astronomía.
registration *n.* inscripción *f.; (education)* matrícula *f.*
registration number *n. (car)* matrícula *f.*
regret *v.t.* arrepentirse (de) (e:ie); lamentar; sentir (e:ie)
regular (customer) *n.* asiduo/a *m., f.*
regularization *n.* regularización *f.*
regulate *v.t.* regular; *(temperature, etc.)* graduar
rehearsal *n.* ensayo *m.*
rehearse *v.t.* ensayar
reign *v.i.* reinar
reinforce *v.t.* reforzar
reinforcement *n.* refuerzo *m.*
reject *v.t.* rechazar

rejection *n.* rechazo *m.*
rejoicing *n.* algarabía *f.*
rejuvenate *v.i.* rejuvenecer
rejuvenation *n.* rejuvenecimiento *m.*
relationship *n.* relación *f.*
relative *adj., n.* relativo/a; pariente *m., f.*
relatives *n.* familiares *m., pl.*; parientes *m., pl.*
relax *v.i.* relajarse
relaxation *n.* relajación *f.*
relay race *n.* carrera *f.* de relevos
release *v.t.* liberar; soltar; poner en libertad
relief *n.* alivio *m.*
relieve *v.t. (pain)* aliviar
religion *n.* religión *f.*
religious *adj.* religioso/a
remain *v.i.* quedarse
remember *v.t./v.i.* recordar (o:ue); acordarse (de) (o:ue)
remembrance *n.* conmemoración *f.*
remote *adj.* alejado/a; lejano/a
remote control *m.* control *m.* remoto
Renaissance *adj.* renacimento *m.*
Renaissance artist *n.* renacentista *m., f.*
renew *v.t.* renovar
renewal *n.* renovación *f.*
rent *n. (payment)* alquiler *m.*
rent *v.t.* alquilar
repeat *v.t.* repetir (e:i)
repellent *n.* repelente *m.*
replace *v.t.* reemplazar; sustituir **They replaced the**

sugar with honey.
Sustituyeron el azúcar por la miel.

report *n.* informe *m.;* reportaje *m.;* boletín *m.;* denuncia *f.*

report *v.t. (crime)* denunciar

reporter *n.* reportero/a *m., f.*

representative *n.* representante *m., f.*

repress *v.t.* reprimir

repression *n.* represión *f.*

reprimand *v.t.* regañar

reproduce *v.t.* reproducir **It's difficult to reproduce the results.** Es difícil reproducir los resultados.; *(biology)* reproducirse **Rabbits reproduce quickly.** Los conejos se reproducen rápidamente.

reptile *n.* reptil *m.*

reputation *n.* reputación *f.;* fama *f.*
  have a good/bad reputation tener buena/mala fama
  have a reputation for tener fama de

request *v.t.* pedir (e:i); solicitar

rescue *n.* rescate *m.;* salvamento *m.*

rescue *v.t.* rescatar

research *v.t.* investigar
  do research documentarse

researcher *n.* investigador(a) *m., f.*

resentful *adj.* rencoroso/a

resentment *n.* rencor *m.*

reservation *n.* reservación *f.*

reserved *adj.* reservado/a

reservoir *n.* embalse *m.;*

pantano *m.*

reside *v.i.* residir

residence *n.* residencia *f.*

resident *n., adj.* residente *m., f.*

resign (from) *v.i.* renunciar (a)

resign *v.i.* dimitir

resignation *n.* dimisión *f.*

resist *v.t.* resistir

resistance *n.* resistencia *f.*

resolve *v.t.* resolver (o:ue)

resolved *p.p.* resuelto *(of* resolver*)*

resort *n. (coastal)* balneario *m.*

resource *n.* recurso *m.*
  natural resource recurso natural

respect *n.* respeto *m.*

respect *v.t.* respetar

respiration *n.* respiración *f.*

respiratory failure *n.* crisis *f.* respiratoria

responsibility *n.* responsabilidad *f.* ; deber *m.*

responsible *adj.* responsable

rest *n.* reposo *m.;* descanso *m.*

rest *v.i.* descansar; reposar **He had to rest for several weeks after the operation.** Tuvo que reposar por varias semanas después de la operación.
  the rest *n.* lo/los/las demás

restaurant *n.* restaurante *m.*

restore *v.t.* restaurar

restrain oneself *v.refl.* dominarse

result *n.* resultado *m.*

résumé *n.* currículum *m.* (vitae); hoja *f.* de vida *(Colombia)*

retire (from work) *v.i.* jubilarse

retired person *n.* pensionista *m., f.;* jubilado/a *m., f.*

retirement pension *n.* pensión *f.*

return *n. (object)* devolución *f.*

return *v.i.* regresar; volver (o:ue); *v.t. (object)* devolver (o:ue)

return trip *n.* vuelta *f.*

returned *p.p.* vuelto *(of* volver)

rewind *v.t.* rebobinar

rewind button *n.* botón *m.* de rebobinado

  push the rewind button apriete el botón de rebobinado

rhetoric *n.* retórica *f.*

rhetorical *adj.* retórico/a

rheumatism *n.* reumatismo *m.*

rhinoceros *n.* rinoceronte *m.*

rhythm *n.* ritmo *m.;* compás *m.*

rib *n.* costilla *f.*

ribbon *n.* cinta *f.*

rice *n.* arroz *m.*

rich *adj.* rico/a

  get rich enriquecerse

  make rich enriquecer

riddle *n.* adivinanza *f.*

ride *v.* pasear

ride bikes/a bike *v.i.* andar/pasear en bicicleta

ridiculous *adj.* ridículo/a

  It's ridiculous (that…) Es ridículo (que…)

right *n., adj. (direction)* derecha *f.;* derecho *m.;* derecho/a; correcto/a

  be right tener razón

  right? *interj.* ¿no?; ¿verdad?

right away *adv.* enseguida; en el acto

right here/there aquí/allí mismo

right now ahora mismo

to the right (of) a la derecha de

rights *n., pl.* derechos *m., pl*

  human rights derechos humanos

ring *n.* anillo *m.;* sortija *f.; (boxing)* cuadrilátero *m.*

  wedding ring anillo de bodas

ring *v.t. (bell)* sonar (o:ue)

rise *n. (advance)* ascenso *m.*

rise *v.i.* ascender

river *n.* río *m.*

road *n.* camino *m.*

roar *n.* rugido *m.*

roar *v.i.* rugir

roast *n.* asado *m.*

  roast chicken *n.* pollo *m.* asado

  roast lamb *n.* asado de cordero

roasted *p.p.* asado/a *(of* asar)

rob *v.t.* robar

robber *n.* ladrón *m.,* ladrona *f.*

robbery *n.* atraco *m.;* robo *m.*

robe *n.* bata *f.*

rock *n.* roca *f.,* piedra *f.*

rock *v.t.* mecer

rocket *n.* cohete *m.*

rocking chair *n.* mecedora *f.*

role *n. (movie, theater)* papel *m.*

  leading role papel principal

  supporting role papel secundario

roller skating *n.* patinaje *m.*

sobre ruedas

rollerblade *v.* patinar en línea

Roman *n., adj.* romano/a *m., f.*

Romanesque *adj.* románico/a

romantic *n., adj.* romántico/a *m., f.*

Romanticism *n.* romanticismo *m.*

room *n.* cuarto *m.;* habitación *f.;* sala *f.*

  double room habitación doble

  single room habitación individual

roommate *n.* compañero/a *m., f.* de cuarto

rooster *n.* gallo *m.*

root *n.* raíz *f.*

rope *n.* cuerda *f.*

rose *n.* rosa *f.*

rosebush *n.* rosal *m.*

rosemary *n.* romero *m.*

rough *adj. (surface, skin)* áspero/a; *(person)* grosero/a

roulette *n.* ruleta *f.*

roundtrip *n., adj.* de ida y vuelta

  roundtrip ticket *n.* pasaje *m.* de ida y vuelta

route *n.* ruta *f.*

routine *n.* rutina *f.*

row *n.* hilera *f.;* fila *f.*

row *v.i.* remar

rower *n.* remero/a *m., f.*

royal *adj.* real

royalty *n.* realeza *f.*

rubber *adj.* de goma

ruby *n.* rubí *m.*

rude *adj.* maleducado/a; grosero/a

rug *n.* alfombra *f.*

rugged *adj. (terrain)* accidentado/a

rule *v.t.* gobernar

rum *n.* ron *m.*

rumor *n.* rumor *m.*

run *v.t.* correr; *v.i. (business)* administrar

  run a red light *v. pron.* pasarse (el alto/el semáforo en rojo)

run away *v.* fugarse

run into *v. (have an accident)* chocar (con); *(meet accidentally)* darse con; *(each other)* encontrarse (o:ue)

run out *v. (supplies)* agotar(se)

run over *v.* derramarse

run over (someone with a vehicle) *v.* atropellar (a alguien con un vehículo)

rural *adj.* rural; campestre

rush *v.i.* apurarse; darse prisa

rust *n.* óxido *m.*

rust *v.i.* oxidarse

S

sacred *adj.* sagrado/a

sad *adj.* triste

  It's sad (that…) Es triste (que…)

sadness *n.* tristeza *f.*

safe *n.* seguro *m.*

safe *adj.* seguro/a

saffron *n.* azafrán *m.*

saga *n.* saga *f.*

sage *n. (herb)* salvia *f.*

said *p.p.* dicho *(of* decir*)*

sail *n.* vela *f.*

sailboat *n.* velero *m.*
sailing *n.* vela *f.*
sake: for the sake of por
 for the sake of love por amor
salad *n.* ensalada *f.*
salad bowl *n.* ensaladera *f.*
salary *n.* salario *m.;* sueldo *m.*
sale *n.* rebaja *f.*
salesperson *n.* vendedor(a) *m.,*
 f.
salmon *n.* salmón *m.*
salt *n.* sal *f.*
salt shaker *n.* salero *m.*
salty *adj.* salado/a
same *adj.* mismo/a; igual
 be all the same dar lo mismo
 **It's all the same to me if she
 comes or not.** Me da lo
 mismo si viene o no.
sand *n.* arena *f.*
sandal *n.* sandalia *f.*
sandwich *n.* sándwich *m.*
sap *n.* savia *f.*
sardine *n.* sardina *f.*
Saturday *n.* sábado *m.*
sauce *n.* salsa *f.*
sauna *n.* sauna *f.*
sausage *n.* salchicha *f.*
sauté *v.t.* saltear, sofreír
save *v.t. (on a computer)*
 guardar; *(money)* ahorrar
 (dinero); salvar
savings *n.* ahorros *m., pl.*
savings account *n.* cuenta *f.*
 de ahorros
saw *n.* sierra *f.*
saw *v.t.* serrar
say *v.t.* decir (e:i); declarar
 You don't say! ¡No me
 diga(s)!

say good-bye (to) despedirse
 (de) (e:i)
saying *n.* dicho *m.;* refrán *m.*
scale *n.* balanza *f.;* báscula *f.*
scallop *n.* vieira *f.*
scalpel *n.* bisturí *m.*
scapula *n.* omoplato *m.*
scar *v.i.* cicatrizar
scarcely *adv.* apenas
 He can scarcely talk.
 Apenas sabe hablar.
scared: be scared (of) tener
 miedo (de)
scarf *n.* bufanda *f.*
scent *n.* aroma *m.*
schedule *n.* horario *m.*
scheme *v.i.* tramar
scholarship *n.* beca *f.*
school *n.* escuela *f.*
school report *n.* boletín *m.* de
 notas
science *n.* ciencia *f.*
science-fiction *n.* ciencia *f.*
 ficción; ...de ciencia ficción
scientist *n.* científico/a *m., f.*
scissors *n.* tijeras *f., pl.*
scold *v.t.* regañar
scoreboard *n.* marcador *m.*
scorpion *n.* escorpión *m.*
scream *v.i.* gritar
screen *n.* pantalla *f.*
screenplay *n.* guión *m.*
screenwriter *n.* guionista *m., f.*
screw *n.* tornillo *m.*
screwdriver *n.* destornillador
 m.
script *n.* guión *m.*
scriptwriter *n.* guionista *m., f.*
scuba dive *v.* bucear
sculpt *v.t./v.i.* esculpir

sculptor *n.* escultor(a) *m., f.*
sculpture *n.* escultura *f.*
sea *n.* mar *m.*; océano *m.*
seafood *n.* mariscos *m., pl.*
   assorted seafood mariscada
   f.
seal *n.* foca *f.*
seaquake *n.* maremoto *m.*
search *n.* búsqueda *f.*
season *n.* estación *f.*;
   temporada *f.*
season *v.t. (salad)* aderezar,
   aliñar
seasoning *n.* aderezo *m.*; aliño
   m.
seat *n.* silla *f.*; asiento *m.*
seat belt *n.* cinturón *n.* de
   seguridad
seaweed *n.* alga (el) *f.*
second *n., adj.* segundo *m.*;
   segundo/a
secretary *n.* secretario/a *m., f.*
security guard *n.* guardia *m., f.*
   de seguridad
sedentary *adj.* sedentario/a
sediment *n.* sedimento *m.*
sedimentation *n.*
   sedimentación *f.*
seduce *v.t.* seducir
seducer *n.* seductor(a) *m., f.*
seductive *adj.* seductor(a)
seductress *n.* seductor(a) *m., f.*
see *v.t.* ver; mirar
   let's see a ver; veamos
   See you. Nos vemos.
   see (you) again volver a
   ver(te/lo/la)
   See you later. Hasta la vista.;
   Hasta luego.
   See you soon. Hasta pronto.

   See you tomorrow. Hasta
   mañana.
see-through *adj.* transparente
seed *n.* semilla *f.*; grano *m.*
seem *v.i.* parecer
seen *p.p.* visto/a (*of* ver)
select *adj.* selecto/a
select *v.t.* seleccionar
self-employed worker *n.*
   autónomo/a *m., f.*
self-portrait *n.* autorretrato *m.*
self-taught *adj.* autodidacta
selfish *adj.* egoísta
selfishness *n.* egoísmo *m.*
sell *v.t.* vender
semantics *n.* semántica *f.*
semester *n.* semestre *m.*
seminar *n.* seminario *m.*
senate *n.* senado *m.*
send *v.t.* enviar, mandar
sense *n.* sentido *m.*
   common sense sentido
   común
sense of order *n.* sentido *m.*
   del orden
sensible *adj.* sensato/a
sensitive *adj.* sensible
sensitivity *n.* sensibilidad *f.*
sensory organs *n., pl.* órganos
   m., pl. de los sentidos
sentimental *adj.* sentimental
separate (from) *v.* separarse
   (de)
separated *adj.* separado/a
September *n.* septiembre *m.*
sequence *n.* secuencia *f.*
series circuit *n.* circuito *m.* en
   serie
serious *adj.* serio/a; *(illness,
   wound)* grave

serve *v.t./v.i.* servir (e:i)
service *n.* servicio *m.*
serving *n.* porción *f.*
set *adj. (price)* fijo/a
set *n. (theater)* decorado *m.*
set *v.t.* poner, colocar
  set the table poner la mesa
set (a world record) *v.*
  establecer (una marca
  mundial)
settle *v.i.* instalarse **He settled**
  in front of the TV and didn't
  budge. Se instaló ante la tele
  y no se movió.
settlement *n.* colonización *f.;*
  (agreement) resolución *f.*
settler *n.* colono/a *m., f.*
seven siete
seven hundred setecientos/as
seventeen diecisiete
seventh séptimo *m.; adj.*
  séptimo/a
seventy setenta
sew *v.t./v.i.* coser
sewer *n.* cloaca *f.*
sewing machine *n.* máquina *f.*
  de coser
sexism *n.* sexismo *m.*
shame *n.* lástima *f.;* vergüenza
  f.
  It's a shame (that…) Es una
  lástima (que…)
shame *v.t.* avergonzar
shameful *adj.* vergonzoso/a
shampoo *n.* champú *m.*
shape *n.* forma *f.*
  be in good shape estar en
  buena forma
  stay in shape mantenerse en
  forma

share *v.t.* compartir
shark *n.* tiburón *m.*
sharp *adv. (time)* en punto **It**
  starts at 4:00 sharp. Empieza
  a las cuatro en punto.
sharp curve *n.* curva *f.*
  peligrosa
shave *v.i.* afeitarse; *(legs)*
  depilarse
shaving cream *n.* crema *f.* de
  afeitar
shawl *n.* chal *m.*
shed *n.* cobertizo *m.*
sheep *n.* oveja *f.*
sheet *n.* sábana *f.; (paper)* hoja
  f.
shellfish *n.* mariscos *m. pl.*
sherry *n.* jerez *m.*
shift *n. (work)* turno *m.*
shift gears *v.t.* cambiar de
  marcha
shine *v.i.* brillar
ship *n.* barco *m.*
  go by ship ir en barco
shirt *n.* camisa *f.*
shiver *n.* escalofrío *m.*
shiver *v.i.* temblar; tener
  escalofríos
shock *n.* choque *m.,* impacto
  m.
shock absorber *n.*
  amortiguador *m.*
  electric shock *n.* descarga *f.*
  (eléctrica)
shoe *n.* zapato *m.*
  put one's shoes on calzarse
shoe size *n.* número *m.*
  take (wear) a shoe size
  calzar
shoe store *n.* zapatería *f.*

shoelace *n.* cordón *m.*

shoes *n.* calzado *m.*

shoot *v.t.* disparar; *(movies)* rodar

shooting *n.* rodaje *m.*

shooting star *n.* estrella *f.* fugaz

shop *n.* tienda *f.*

shop window *n.* escaparate *(Spain) m.;* vitrina *(L.A.) f.*

shopping mall/center *n.* centro *m.* comercial

shore *n.* orilla *f.* **The house is on the seashore.** La casa está a orillas del mar.

short *adj. (height)* bajo/a; *(length)* corto/a

  in short *loc.* en resumidas cuentas

short circuit *n.* cortocircuito *m.*

short cut *n.* atajo *m.*

short story *n.* cuento *m.*

shortage *n.* carencia *f.*

shortcoming *n.* deficiencia *f.*

shorts *n., pl.* pantalones *m., pl.* cortos

shot *n.* disparo *m.;* tiro *m.*

shotput *n. (sport)* lanzamiento *m.* de bala *(L.A.);* lanzamiento *m.* de peso *(Spain)*

should *(do something)* deber (+ *inf.*)

shoulder *n.* hombro *m.*

shoulder bag *n.* bolso *m.*

shovel *n.* pala *f.*

show *n.* espectáculo *m.*

show *v.t.* mostrar (o:ue); enseñar

shower *n.* ducha *f.*

shower *v.i.* ducharse, *v.t.* bañarse

shrewd *adj.* astuto/a

shrimp *n.* camarón *(L.A.)m.;* gamba *(Spain) f.*

  marinated shrimp ceviche *m.* de camarón *m.*

shrub *n.* arbusto *m.*

shy *adj.* tímido/a

sick *adj.* enfermo/a

  be sick estar enfermo/a

  get sick enfermarse

side *n.* lado *m.*

sideburn *n.* patilla *f.*

sight *n. (senses)* vista *f.*

sight *v.t.* divisar

sightseeing: go sightseeing hacer turismo

sign *n. (board)* letrero *m.;* señal *f.*

sign *v.t.* firmar

signature *n.* firma *f.*

silence *n.* silencio *m.*

silk *n., adj.* seda *f.;* de seda

silky *adj.* sedoso/a

silly *adj.* tonto/a

silver *n., adj.* plata *f.;* plateado/a

silverware *n.* cubiertos *m., pl.*

similar *adj.* similar; semejante

simmer *v.t.* cocer a fuego lento

simple *adj.* sencillo/a, simple

sinagogue *n.* sinagoga *f.*

since *prep.* desde

sing *v.t.* cantar

singer *n.* cantante *m., f.*

single *adj. (unmarried)* soltero/a

single room *n.* habitación *f.* individual

singles *n. (sports)* individual *m.*

sink n. (bathroom) lavabo m.; lavamanos m.; (kitchen) fregadero (de la cocina) m.

sip n. sorbo m.

sir n. señor m. (Sr.); don

sister n. hermana f.
younger sister hermana menor

sister-in-law n. cuñada f.

sit down v. sentarse (e:ie)

sitting: related to sitting sedentario/a adj.

six seis

six hundred seiscientos/as

sixteen dieciséis

sixth sexto m.; adj. sexto/a

sixty sesenta

size n. talla f.
What size do you take? ¿Qué talla lleva/usa?

skate v.i. patinar
skate in-line patinar en línea

skateboard v.t. andar en patineta

skating n. patinaje m.

skating rink n. pista f. de patinaje

skeleton n. esqueleto m.

ski v.i. esquiar

ski cap n. gorro m. de lana

ski slope n. pista f. de esquí

skier n. esquiador(a) m., f.

skiing n. esquí m.

skill n. habilidad f.

skillful adj. hábil

skimmed adj. (dairy products) descremado/a; desnatado/a

skin n. cutis m.; piel f.; (on boiled milk) nata f.

skinny adj. flaco/a

skirt n. falda f.

skull n. calavera f.; cráneo m.

sky n. cielo m.

sky blue n., adj. (color) azul m. celeste

skylight n. tragaluz m.

skyscraper n. rascacielos m., sing.

sleep n. sueño m.

sleep v.i. dormir (o:ue)
fall asleep dormirse (o:ue)
I couldn't fall asleep last night. No pude dormirme anoche.
go to sleep dormirse (o:ue)

sleepy: be sleepy tener sueño

sleeping bag n. saco m. de dormir

sleeve n. manga f.

slender adj. (person) delgado/a, esbelto/a

slice n. trozo m.; rebanada f. **a slice of bread** una rebanada de pan; rodaja f. **sliced onions** rodajas de cebolla

slice v.t. cortar

slide n. (photo.) diapositiva f.

slim down v. adelgazar

slippers n., pl. pantuflas f., pl.

slope n. ladera f. **The group ascended the northern slope.** El equipo subió por la ladera norte.

slot machine n. tragaperras (Spain) f., sing.; tragamonedas (L.A.) f., sing.

sloth n. perezoso m.

slow adj. lento/a; adv. despacio

slowly adv. despacio

small *adj.* pequeño/a
small intestine *n.* intestino *m.* delgado
smallpox *n.* viruela *f.*
smart *adj.* listo/a
smell *n. (sense)* olfato *m.;* olor *m.* **The smell of gasoline makes me sick.** El olor a gasolina me da asco.
smell (like) *v.i.* oler (a) **It smells like smoke here.** Huele a humo aquí.
smile *n.* sonrisa *f.*
smile *v.i.* sonreír (e:i)
smiled *p.p.* sonreído (*of* sonreír)
smoggy: It's (very) smoggy. Hay (mucha) contaminación.
smoke *n.* humo *m.*
smoke *v.t./v.i.* fumar
smoking section *n.* sección *f.* de fumar
non smoking section sección de no fumar
not to smoke no fumar
smother *v.t.* *(fire)* sofocar
snack *n. (in the afternoon)* merienda *f.; (at a bar)* tapa *f.*
snack *v.i.* merendar
have an afternoon snack merendar
snail *n.* caracol *m.*
snake *n.* serpiente *f.;* culebra *f.;* víbora *f.*
sneakers *n., pl.* zapatos *m., pl.* de tenis
sneeze *v.i.* estornudar
snob *n.* esnob *m., f.*
snobbery *n.* esnobismo *m.*
snobby *adj.* esnob

snore *n.* ronquido *m.*
snore *v.i.* roncar
snorkel *n.* esnórkel *m.*
snow *n.* nieve *f.*
snow *v.imp.* nevar (e:ie) **It's snowing.** Nieva.
so *adv.* tan; *(in such a way)* así **It's so big.** Es tan grande.
and so on y así sucesivamente
so much *adv.* tanto
so so *adv.* así así; regular; más o menos
so that *conj.* para que
soap *n.* jabón *m.*
soap dish *n.* jabonera *f.*
soap opera *n.* telenovela *f.*
sob *n.* sollozo *m.*
sob *v.i.* sollozar
sober *adj.* sobrio/a
sobriety test *n.* prueba *f.* de la alcoholemia
soccer *n.* fútbol *m.*
soccer field *n.* campo *m.* de fútbol
soccer player *n.* futbolista *m., f.*
sociable *adj.* sociable
socialize *v.i.* socializar
society *n.* sociedad *f.*
sociologist *n.* sociólogo/a *m., f*
sociology *n.* sociología *f.*
sock *n.* calcetín *m.*
soda *n.* refresco *m.*
sodium *n.* sodio *m.*
sofa *n.* sofá *m.*
soft *adj. (to the touch)* suave; esponjoso/a
soft drink *n.* refresco *m.*
software *n.* programa *m.* de computación

soil *n.* tierra *f.*
solar *adj.* solar
solarium *n.* solario *m.*
soldier *n.* soldado *m., f.*
solution *n. (to a problem)* resolución *f.;* solución *f.*
solve *v.t.* resolver (o:ue); solucionar
some *pron., adj.* algún, alguno/a(s); unos/as, *m., f., pl., indef. art.*
somebody *pron.* alguien
someone *pron.* alguien
somersault *n.* salto *m.* mortal; voltereta *f.*
something *pron.* algo
  something like that algo por el estilo
sometimes *adv.* a veces
son *n.* hijo *m.*
son-in-law *n.* yerno *m.*
song *n.* canción *f.*
soon *adv.* pronto
  as soon as en cuanto; tan pronto como
  as soon as possible lo antes posible
soprano *n.* soprano *m., f.*
sorbet *n.* sorbete *m.*
sore *adj.* adolorido/a
sorry: be sorry sentir(se) (e:ie); arrepentirse
  I'm extremely sorry. Mil perdones.
  I'm sorry. Lo siento.
soul *n.* alma (el) *f.*
soup *n.* sopa *f.; (broth)* caldo *m.*
  beef soup caldo de patas
sour *adj.* agrio/a
south *n.* sur *m.*

  to the south al sur
South American *n., adj.* sudamericano/a *m., f.*
souvenir *n.* recuerdo *m.*
spa *n.* balneario *m.*
space shuttle *n.* transbordador *m.*
spaghetti *n.* espagueti *m.*
Spain *n.* España *f.*
Spaniard *n.* español(a) *m., f.*
Spanish *n., adj.* español(a) *m., f.; (language)* español
spare time *n.* ratos *m., pl.* libres; tiempo *m.* libre
spare tire *n.* rueda *f.* de recambio/repuesto
spark plug *n.* bujía *f.*
sparkling wine *n.* cava *m.*
sparrow *n.* gorrión *m.*
spatula *n.* espátula *f.*
speak *v.i.* hablar
Special Olympics *n., pl.* Olimpiadas *f., pl.* Especiales
specialist *n.* especialista *m., f.*
specialization *n.* especialización *f.*
specialize (in something) *v.i.* especializarse (en algo)
species *n.* especie *f.*
  protected species *n.* especie *f.* protegida
spectacular *adj.* espectacular
spectator *n.* espectador(a) *m., f.*
speech *n.* discurso *m.*
speed *n.* velocidad *f.*
  speed limit *n.* velocidad *f.* máxima
speed *v.* ir a exceso de velocidad

spelling *n., adj.* ortografía *f.;* ortográfico/a
spend *v.t. (money)* gastar
  spend time pasar tiempo
sphere *n.* esfera *f.*
spicy *adj.* picante
spider *n.* araña *f.*
spiderweb *n.* telaraña *f.*
spill *v.t.* derramar
spill over *v.* derramarse
spinach *n.* espinaca *f.*
spinal column *n.* columna *f.* vertebral
spine *n.* columna *f.* vertebral
spleen *n.* bazo *m.*
spoiled (child) *n. (niño/a)* m., f. mimado/a/consentido/a
spokesperson *n.* portavoz *m., f.*
sponge *n.* esponja *f.*
spongy *adj.* esponjoso/a
sponsor *n.* patrocinador(a) *m., f.*
sponsor *v.t.* patrocinar
spontaneous *adj.* espontáneo/a
spoon *n.* (*table or large*) cuchara *f.*
sport *n.* deporte *m.*
  sports-loving *adj.* deportivo/a
  sports-related *adj.* deportivo/a
sporting *adj.* deportista
sporting goods *n., pl.* artículos *m., pl.* de deporte
sports car *n.* carro *m.* deportivo
sports center *n.* polideportivo *m.*
sports facilities *n., pl.* instalaciones *f., pl.*

deportivas
sports-loving *adj.* deportivo/a
sportswear *n.* ropa *f.* deportiva
spouse *n.* esposo/a *m., f.*
sprain *n.* esguince
sprain (an ankle) *v.t.* torcerse (el tobillo)
sprained *adj.* torcido/a
  be sprained estar torcido/a
spread *v.t. (information)* divulgar; propagar **Some papers spread rumors.** Algunos periódicos propagan rumores.; propagarse **The rumor was spreading rapidly.** El rumor se propagaba rápidamente.; *(butter, etc.)* untar
spreading *n. (news, ideas)* divulgación *f.*
spring *n. (season)* primavera *f.; (coil)* muelle *m.,* resorte *m.; (water)* manantial *m.*
sprinkle *v.t. (sugar, etc.)* espolvorear
square *n.* cuadrado *m.*
square: city or town square *n.* plaza *f.*
squat *v.i.* agacharse
squid *n.* calamar *m.*
squirrel *n.* ardilla *f.*
stable *n.* establo *m.*
stack *v.t.* apilar
stadium *n.* estadio *m.*
stage *n.* etapa *f.; (theater)* escenario *m.*
  the stages of life las etapas de la vida
stained-glass window *n.* vidriera *f.* (de colores)

stainless steel n. acero m. inoxidable

stair n. escalón m.; peldaño m.

stairs n. escalera f.

stairway n. escalera f.

stammer v.i. tartamudear

stamp n. estampilla (L.A.) f.; sello (Spain) m.

stamp collecting n. filatelia f.

stand v.i. (person) estar parado (L.A.); estar de pie

stand in line v. hacer cola

stand out v. sobresalir

stand somebody up v. dejar a alguien plantado/a

star n. estrella f.

starry adj. estrellado/a

start v.t. (vehicle) arrancar; (begin) empezar (e:ie), comenzar (e:ie)

state n. estado m.

station n. (train, bus) estación f.

statue n. estatua f.

status: marital status estado m. civil

stay n. estancia f. **Our stay in La Coruña was magnificent.** Nuestra estancia en La Coruña fue magnífica.

stay v.i. quedarse; (hotel) alojarse

stay up all night v. trasnochar

steady adj. fijo/a

steak n. bistec m.

steal v.t. robar

steam n. vapor m.

steel n. acero m.

steering wheel n. volante m.

step n. etapa f.; paso m.; (stair) escalón m., peldaño m.

stepbrother n. hermanastro m.

stepdaughter n. hijastra f.

stepfather n. padrastro m.

stepmother n. madrastra f.

stepsister n. hermanastra f.

stepson n. hijastro m.

stereo n. estéreo m.

sterile adj. estéril

sterilize v.t. esterilizar

stethoscope n. estetoscopio m.

stew n. guiso m.

stick v.t. pegar

stifling adj. (heat) sofocante, agobiante **The heat is stifling.** Este calor es agobiante.

still adv. todavía, aún, ya

stingy adj. tacaño/a

stir v.t. remover

stockbroker n. bolsista m., f.; corredor(a) m., f. de bolsa

stockings n. medias f., pl.

stomach n. estómago m. f. **get an upset stomach** empacharse

stomach disorder n. trastorno m. estomacal

stone n. piedra f.

stool n. taburete m.

stop v.i. parar(se)

stop (doing something) v. dejar de (+ inf.)

stop sign n. señal m. de alto

storage n. almacenamiento m.

store n. tienda f.

store v.t. almacenar

stork n. cigüeña f.

storm n. tormenta f.

story n. cuento m.; historia f.

stove n. estufa f.; cocina (Spain) f.

straight adj. derecho/a; recto/a; (hair) lacio/a

straight adv. derecho
  straight ahead (todo) derecho

straighten up v. arreglar

strain v.t. colar

strange adj. extraño/a
  It's strange (that…) Es extraño (que…)

straw n. paja f.; (drinking) pajita f., popote m.
  That's the last straw! loc. ¡Esto es el colmo!

strawberry n. fresa f., frutilla (Ecuador) f.

stream n. riachuelo m.

streamer n. serpentina f.

street n. calle m.
  street light n. semáforo m.

stress n. estrés m.; tensión f.
  under stress adj. estresado/a

stress v.t. destacar, enfatizar, recalcar

stressful adj. estresante

stretch v.t. estirar

stretcher n. camilla f.

stretching n. estiramiento m.
  do stretching exercises hacer ejercicios m., pl. de estiramiento

strike n. (labor) huelga f.

striker n. huelguista m., f.

stripe n. raya f.

striped adj. de rayas

stroke n. (swimming) estilo m.

stroll v.i. pasear

strong adj. fuerte

struggle (for/against; to + inf.) v. luchar (por/contra; para + inf.)

stubborn adj. testarudo/a

student n., adj. estudiante m., f.; estudiantil
  student desk n. pupitre m.

studious adj. estudioso/a

study v.t./v.i. estudiar

stuff v.t. (culinary) rellenar

stuff oneself v. hartarse

stuffed adj. relleno/a
  I love stuffed chilies. Adoro los chiles rellenos.

stuffed-up adj. congestionado/a

stuffing n. relleno m.

stunned adj. atontado/a

stupendous adj. estupendo/a

stutter v.i. tartamudear

style n. estilo m.

subject matter n. temática f.

subject n. (university) disciplina f.; tema m.

subjective adj. subjetivo/a

submarine n. submarino m.

substance n. sustancia f.

substitute n. sustituto/a m., f.

substitute v.t. sustituir
  He substituted coffe for tea. Sustituyó el café por el té.

subterranean adj. subterráneo/a

suburbs n. afueras f., pl.

subway n. metro m.
  go by subway ir en metro

subway station n. estación f. del metro

succeed v.i. triunfar

success n. éxito m.

be successful tener éxito
successively *adv.*
sucesivamente
such as [tal(es)] como
She used words such as justice and freedom. Usó palabras (tales) como justicia y libertad.
suddenly *adv.* de repente
suffer *v.t.* sufrir
suffer an illness sufrir una enfermedad
suffer from *v. (disease)* padecer de **He suffers from heart problems.** Padece del corazón.
suffering *n.* padecimiento *m.*
sufficient *adj.* bastante
suffocation *n.* sofoco *m.*
sugar *n.* azúcar *m.*
sugar bowl *n.* azucarero *m.*
suggest *v.t.* sugerir (e:ie)
suggestion *n.* sugerencia *f.*
suicide *n.* suicidio *m.*
commit suicide suicidarse
suit *n.* traje *m.*
suit *v.t. (clothes)* sentar
That jacket suits you. Esa chaqueta te sienta bien.
suitable *adj.* apto/a
suitcase *n.* maleta *f.*
summer *n.* verano *m.*
summer *v.i.* veranear
She summers in the mountains. Veranea en las montañas.
summit *n.* cima *f.*
sumptuous *adj.* suntuoso/a
sun *n.* sol *m.*
sunbathe *v.i.* tomar el sol;

tumbarse al sol
Sunday *n.* domingo *m.*
sunflower *n.* girasol *m.*
sunglasses *n., pl.* lentes *m., pl.* de sol; gafas *f., pl.* oscuras/negras/de sol
sunny *adj.* soleado/a
It's (very) sunny. Hace (mucho) sol.
sunrise *n.* salida *f.* del sol
sunset *n.* puesta *f.* de(l) sol
sunshade *n.* sombrilla *f.*
suntan lotion *n.* bronceador *m.*
sun-tanned *adj.* bronceado/a
supermarket *n.* supermercado *m.*
superstition *n.* superstición *f.*
superstitious *adj.* supersticioso/a
supervise *v.t.* supervisar
supper *n.* cena *f.*
supplier *n.* suministrador(a) *m., f.*
supplies *n., pl.* provisiones *f., pl.;* víveres *m., pl.*
supply *n.* suministro *m.*
supply *v.t.* suministrar
support *v.t.* apoyar; sostener; soportar; respaldar
suppose *v.t.* suponer
Supreme Court *n.* Corte *f.* Suprema *(L.A.);* Tribunal *m.* Supremo *(Spain)*
sure *adj.* seguro/a
be sure estar seguro/a
surf (the Internet) *v.i.* navegar (en Internet)
surgeon *n.* cirujano/a *m., f.*
surgery *n.* cirugía *f.*
surprise *n.* sorpresa *f.*

What a surprise! ¡Qué sorpresa!
surprise *v.t.* sorprender
 be surprised sorprenderse
 He was surprised to see me. Se sorprendió al verme.
surrounding area *n.* alrededores *m., pl.*
survey *n.* encuesta *f.*
survival *n.* supervivencia *f.*
survivor *n.* superviviente *m., f.*
suspect *v.t.* sospechar
suspenders *n., pl.* tirantes *m., pl.*
suspense: in suspense *adj.* intrigado/a
suspension bridge *n.* puente *f.* colgante
suspicion *n.* sospecha *f.*
suspicious *adj.* sospechoso/a
swallow *v.t./v.i.* tragar
swamp *n.* pantano *m.;* ciénaga *f.*
swan *n.* cisne *m.*
swear *v.t.* jurar
sweat *v.i.* sudar
sweater *n.* suéter *m.*
sweaty *adj.* sudado/a
sweep (the floor) *v.t.* barrer (el piso/suelo)
sweet *adj.* dulce
sweets *n., pl.* dulces *m., pl.*
swim *v.i.* nadar
swimmer *n.* nadador(a) *m., f.*
swimming *n.* natación *f.*
 synchronized swimming natación sincronizada
swimming pool *n.* piscina *f.;* alberca *(Mexico)* *f.*
swimming suit *n.* traje *m.* de baño

symbiosis *n.* simbiosis *f.*
symbolize *v.t.* simbolizar
symphonic *adj.* sinfónico/a
symphony *n.* sinfonía *f.*
symphony orchestra *n.* sinfónica *f.*
symptom *n.* síntoma *m.*
synonym *n.* sinónimo *m.*
synonymous *adj.* sinónimo/a
syntax *n.* sintaxis *f.*
syringe *n.* jeringa *f.*
syrup *n.* almíbar *m.*
system *n.* sistema *f.*

T

table *n.* mesa *f.*
tablecloth *n.* mantel *m.*
tablespoon *n.* cuchara *f.*
tablet *n. (pill)* pastilla *f.*
tactful *adj.* diplomático/a
tactless *adj.* indiscreto/a
tail *n.* cola *f.*
tailor *n.* sastre *m.*
take *v.t.* llevar; tomar; traer
 take a bath *v. pron.* bañarse
 take a shower *v. pron.* ducharse
 take a trip *v.* hacer un viaje
 take someone somewhere llevar
take advantage of *v.* aprovecharse de
take back *v.t.* devolver
take care of cuidar
 take care of oneself cuidarse
 take care of clients *v.i.* atender a los clientes
take off *v. (clothes)* quitarse; *(airplane, rocket)* despegar

take off one's shoes descalzarse

take-off *n.* despegue *m.*

take offense *v.* ofenderse

take out (the trash) *v.* sacar (la basura)

take out (walk) the dog sacar al perro a pasear

take the risk *v.* arriesgarse

take up *v. (hobby)* aficionarse

talented *adj.* talentoso/a

talk *v.i.* hablar; conversar

talk show *n.* programa *m.* de entrevistas

talkative *adj. (person)* hablador(a); charlatán, charlatana

tall *adj.* alto/a

tan *v.t.* broncear; *v.i.* broncearse

tangerine *n.* mandarina *f.*

tangy *adj.* ácido/a

tank *n.* depósito *m.;* tanque *m.*

tanned *adj.* moreno/a

tantrum *n.* berrinche *m.*
  throw tantrums hacer berrinches

tape *n.* cinta *f.*

tape recorder *n.* grabadora *f.*

tapestry *n.* tapiz *m.*

target shooting *n.* tiro *m.* al blanco

tart *adj.* ácido/a

taste *n. (senses)* gusto *m.*

taste *v.t.* probar (o:ue)

tasteless *adj.* soso/a

tasty *adj.* rico/a, sabroso/a

tax *n.* impuesto *m.*

taxi(cab) *n.* taxi *m.*
  go by taxi ir en taxi

tea *n.* té *m.*
  herbal tea *n.* infusión *f.* (de hierbas)

teabag *n.* bolsita *f.* de té

teach *v.t.* enseñar

teacher *n.* profesor(a) *m., f.; (elementary school)* maestro/a *m., f.*

team *n.* equipo *m.*
  technical team equipo de técnicos

teapot *n.* tetera *f.*

tear *n.* lágrima *f.*

tear gas *n.* gas *m.* lacrimógeno

technician *n.* técnico/a *m., f.*

teddy bear *n.* osito *m.* de peluche

telecommuting *n.* teletrabajo *m.*

teleconference *n.* videoconferencia *f.*

telephone *n.* teléfono *m.*
  cellular telephone teléfono celular
  by phone por teléfono

telescope *n.* telescopio *m.*

television *n.* televisión *f.; (set)* televisor *m.*

tell *v.* decir; contar

temperament *n.* temperamento *m.*

temperature *n.* temperatura *f.*
  take (someone's) temperature tomar la temperatura (a alguien)

temple *n.* templo *m.*

ten diez

tendency *n.* tendencia *f.*

tender *adj. (meat; loving)* tierno/a

tendon *n.* tendón *m.*

tennis *n.* *(sport)* tenis *m.*;
(sneakers) tenis *m.*

tennis court *n.* pista *f.* de tenis

tennis player *n.* tenista *m., f.*

tennis shoes *n.* zapatillas *f., pl.*
de deporte; zapatos *m., pl.* de
tenis

tenor *n.* tenor *m.*

tension *n.* tensión *f.*

tent *n.* tienda *f.* (de campaña)

tenth décimo *m.*; *adj.* décimo/a

terrace *n.* terraza *f.*

terrible *adj.* terrible
  It's terrible (that…) Es
  terrible (que…)

terrific *adj.* genial, fantástico,
estupendo, chévere

terrorist *n., adj.* terrorista *m., f.*

terrorist attack *n.* atentado *m.*
terrorista

test *n.* examen *m.*; prueba *f.*;
evaluación *f.*
  placement test prueba de
  nivel
  aptitude test prueba de
  aptitud

test *v.t.* evaluar

thanks *interj.* gracias
  Thank you. Gracias.
  Thank you very much.
  Muchas gracias.
  Thank you very, very much.
  Muchísimas gracias.
  Thanks (a lot). (Muchas)
  gracias.
  Thanks again. Gracias una
  vez más.
  Thanks for everything.
  Gracias por todo.

that (one) ése, esa, eso *pron.*;

ese, esa *adj.*

that (over there) aquél,
aquélla, aquello *pron.*; aquel,
aquella *adj.*

that *conj.* que

that which *conj.* lo que

that's why por eso

theater *n.* teatro *m.*; auditorio

theft *n.* robo *m.*

their su(s) *poss. adj.*;
suyo(s)/suya(s) *poss. pron.*

thematic *adj.* temático/a

theme *n.* tema *m.*

then *adv.* *(afterward)* después
(de); *(as a result)* entonces;
(next) luego, pues

theorize *v.i.* teorizar

theory *n.* teoría *f.*

therapeutic *adj.* terapéutico/a

therapy *n.* terapia *f.*

there *adv.* allí
  There is/are… Hay…
  There is/are not… No hay…

therefore *adv.* por eso; por lo
tanto

thermostat *m.* termostato

these estos, estas *adj.*; éstos,
éstas *pron.*

thesis *f.* tesis

thief *n.* ladrón *m.*, ladrona *f.*

thigh *n.* muslo *m.*

thin *adj.* delgado/a

thing *n.* cosa *f.*

think *v.t.* pensar (e:ie);
(believe) creer
  What do you think? *form.*
  ¿Qué le/les parece?
  think about *v.* pensar en

third tercio *m.*; *adj.* tercer,
tercero/a

third-world country n. país m. tercermundista

thirst n. sed f.

be thirsty tener sed

thirsty adj. sediento/a

thirteen trece

thirty treinta; (minutes past the hour) y treinta, y media

It's six thirty. Son las seis y treinta/media.

this este, esta adj.; éste, ésta, esto pron.

This is he/she. (on the phone) Con él/ella habla.

thorn n. espina f.

those esos, esas adj.; ésos, ésas pron.

thread n. hilo m.

threat n. amenaza f.

threaten v.t. amenazar

three tres

three hundred trescientos/as

thrilled adj. ilusionado/a

throat n. garganta f.

through prep. por; a través de

throw n. lanzamiento m.

throw v.t. echar; tirar; lanzar

throw away v.t. (leftovers) desechar, tirar

thunder n. trueno m.

Thursday n. jueves m., sing.

thus adv. así

thyme n. tomillo m.

ticket n. (show) boleto (L.A.) m.; entrada (Spain) f.; (trip) pasaje; (fine) multa f.

tidal wave n. maremoto m.

tidy adj. arreglado/a

tie n. (clothing) corbata f.; (sports) empate m.; (bond)

lazo m., vínculo m

family ties lazos familiares

tie v.t. atar; (sports) empatar

tiger n. tigre m.

tile n. (ceramic) azulejo m.; (floor) baldosa f.; (roof) teja f.

time n. tiempo m.; (occasion) vez f.

We have time. Tenemos tiempo.

We had a great time. Lo pasamos de película/super bien.

What time is it? ¿Qué hora es?

ahead of time con anticipación

full-time tiempo completo

many times muchas veces

on time a tiempo

one more time una vez más

one time una vez

part-time tiempo parcial

time trial n. carrera n. contra reloj

timid adj. tímido/a

tinfoil n. papel m. de aluminio

tiny adj. minúsculo/a

tip n. propina f.

leave a tip dejar una propina

tire n. llanta f.; neumático m.

tire oneself out v. cansarse

tired adj. cansado/a

be tired estar cansado/a

tissue n. (anat.) tejido m.; pañuelo m. de papel

title n. título m.

to prep. a

toad n. sapo m.

toast n. pan m. tostado;

tostada *f.; (drinking)* brindis *m.*

toast *v.t.* tostar; *(drinking)* brindar (por)

toasted *adj.* tostado/a
toasted bread pan tostado

toaster *n.* tostadora *f.*

today *adv.* hoy
Today is… Hoy es…

toe *n.* dedo *m.* (del pie)

together *adj.* juntos/as

toilet *n.* inodoro *m.*

toiletry kit *n.* neceser *m.*

toilet paper *n.* papel *m.* higiénico

tolerance *n.* tolerancia *f.*

tolerant *adj.* tolerante

tolerate *v.t.* tolerar

tomato *n.* tomate *m.*

tomorrow *adv.* mañana

tongs *n., pl.* tenazas *f., pl.*

tonight *adv.* esta noche

tonsil *n.* amígdala *f.*

too *adv.* también

too much *adv.* demasiado; en exceso

tool *n.* herramienta *f.*

tooth *n.* diente *m.; (back)* muela *f.*
pull a tooth sacar una muela
I had a tooth pulled. Me sacaron una muela.

toothbrush *n.* cepillo *m.* de dientes

toothpaste *n.* pasta *f.* de dientes

toothpick *n.* mondadientes *m., sing.;* palillo *m.* (de dientes)

top *n.* cima *f.*

torch *n.* antorcha *f.*

tornado *n.* tornado *m.*

tortilla *n.* tortilla *f.*

toss *v.t.* tirar; mezclar

touch *n. (sense)* tacto *m.*

touch *v.t.* tocar

tour *n.* visita *f.* turística; viaje *m.*
go on a tour hacer una excursión
tour around an area excursión *f.*

tourism *n.* turismo *m.*

tourist *adj.* turístico/a

tourist *n.* turista *m., f.*

toward *prep.* hacia

towel *n.* toalla *f.*

towel bar *n.* toallero *m.*

tower *n.* torre *f.*

town *n.* pueblo *m.*

town square *n.* plaza *f.* mayor

toy *n.* juguete *m.*

toy store *n.* juguetería *f.*

track *n.* pista *f.; (sport)* pista de atletismo; *(railroad)* vía *f.*
indoor track *n.* pista *f.* cubierta

track and field *n.* atletismo *m.*

trade *n.* oficio *m.*

tradition *n.* tradición *f.*

traffic *n.* circulación *f.;* tráfico *m.*

traffic (in) *v.t.* traficar (en)

traffic jam *n.* atasco *m.;* embotellamiento *m.* (de tráfico) *(Spain)*

traffic sign *n.* señal *f.* de tráfico

traffic signal *n.* semáforo *m.*

tragedy *n.* tragedia *f.*

tragic *adj.* trágico/a

trail *n.* sendero *m.*

trailer *n.* caravana *f.*

trailhead *n.* sendero *m.*

train *n.* tren *m.*

  go by train ir en tren

train station estación *f.* de tren

train *v.i.* entrenarse

trainer *n.* entrenador(a) *m., f.;* monitor(a) *m., f.*

training *n.* entrenamiento *m.;* capacitación *f.*

traitor *n.* traidor(a) *m., f.*

trajectory *n.* trayectoria *f.*

transfer *n.* transferencia *f.*

transfusion *n.* transfusión *f.*

translate *v.t.* traducir

translation *n.* traducción *f.*

translator *n.* traductor(a) *m., f.*

transparent *adj.* transparente

transplant *n.* transplante *m.*

transport *v.t.* transportar

transportation *n.* transporte *m.*

trapshooting *n.* tiro *m.* al plato

trash *n.* basura *f.*

travel *v.i.* viajar; desplazarse

travel agency *n.* agencia *f.* de viajes

travel agent *n.* agente *m., f.* de viajes

travel document *n.* documento *m.* de viaje

traveler *n.* viajero/a *m., f.*

traveler's check *n.* cheque *m.* de viajero

treacherous *adj.* traicionero/a, traidor(a); peligroso/a

treachery *n.* traición *f.*

treadmill cinta caminadora

treason *n.* traición *f.*

treasure *n.* tesoro *m.*

tree *n.* árbol *m.*

trendy: be trendy ir a la moda

trial *n.* juicio *m.*

triangle *n.* triángulo *m.*

tribute *n.* homenaje *m.*

tricycle *n.* triciclo *m.*

trigger *n. (firearm)* gatillo *m.*

trigonometry *n.* trigonometría *f.*

trimester *n.* trimestre *m.*

trip *n.* viaje *m.;* desplazamiento *m.*

  go on/take a trip hacer un viaje

tripod *n.* trípode *m.*

triviality *n.* trivialidad *f.*

trivialize *v.t.* trivializar

trout *n.* trucha *f.*

truck *n.* camión *m.*

truck driver *n.* camionero/a *m., f.*

true *adj.* verdadero/a; cierto

  it's (not) true (no) es verdad

true-to-life *adj.* verosímil

trunk *n.* baúl *m.; (car)* maletero *(Spain) m.; (live tree)* tronco *m.*

truth *n.* verdad *f.*

try *n.* intento *m.*

try *v.t.* intentar; probar (o:ue); *(to do something)* tratar de (+ *inf.*)

try hard *v.* esforzarse

try on *v. (clothes)* probarse (o:ue)

try out *v.t./v.i.* experimentar

t-shirt *n.* camiseta *f.*

tube *n.* tubo *m.*

tuberculosis *n.* tuberculosis *f.*

Tuesday *n.* martes *m., sing.*

tulip *n.* tulipán *m.*

tuna *n.* atún *m.*
tune up *v.t.* afinar
  out of tune *adj.* desafinado/a
tunnel *n.* túnel *m.*
turbine *n.* turbina *f.*
turkey *n.* pavo *m.*
turn *n.* giro *m.;* turno *m.;* vuelta *f.*
turn *v.t./v.i.* doblar; girar;
  dar(se) la vuelta **Turn left at
  the next corner.** Gira
  a la izquierda en la próxima
  esquina.
turn off *v.t.*
  (electricity/appliance)
  apagar
turn on *v.t.*
  (electricity/appliance) poner,
  encender; prender
turn over *v.t. (tortilla, cup)*
  voltear *(L.A.)*
turn signal *n. (car)* intermitente
  m
turquoise *n.* turquesa *f.*
turtle *n.* tortuga *f.*
tutor *n.* profesor(a) *m., f.*
  particular
tweezers *n., pl.* pinzas *f., pl.*
  (para depilar)
twelve doce
twenty veinte
twenty-eight veintiocho
twenty-five veinticinco
twenty-four veinticuatro
twenty-nine veintinueve
twenty-one veintiún, veintiuno/a
twenty-seven veintisiete
twenty-six veintiséis
twenty-three veintitrés
twenty-two veintidós
twice *adv.* dos veces

twin *n.* gemelo/a *m., f.;*
  mellizo/a *m., f.*
twisted *adj.* torcido/a
  be twisted estar torcido/a
two dos
  two times dos veces
two hundred doscientos/as
two weeks *n., pl.* quincena *f.*
type *n.* especie *f.*
type *v.i.* escribir a máquina;
  teclear
typewriter *n.* máquina *f.* de
  escribir
typist *n.* mecanógrafo/a *m., f.*

U

**UFO (Unidentified Flying
  Object)** *n.* OVNI *m.* (Objeto
  Volador No Identificado)
ugly *adj.* feo/a
umbrella *n.* paraguas *m.*
umbrella stand *n.* paragüero *m.*
umpire *n.* árbitro/a *m.*
unbearable *adj.* insoportable
unblock *v.t.* desatascar
uncertainty *n.* incertidumbre *f.*
uncle *n.* tío *m.*
under *adv.* bajo, debajo (de)
undergo *v.t. (test, examination)*
  someterse a
underground *adj.*
  subterráneo/a
underlined *adj.* subrayado/a
understand *v.t.* comprender;
  entender (e:ie)
understanding *n.* comprensión
  f.
underwear *n.* ropa *f.* interior
  long underwear *n.*
  calzoncillos *m., pl.* largos

undress *v.i.* desvestirse
unemployment *n.* desempleo *m.*
unexpected *adj.* inesperado/a
unfair *adj.* injusto/a
unfavorable *adj.* desfavorable
unforgettable *adj.* inolvidable
unfortunate *adj.* desgraciado/a
unfortunately *adv.* desafortunadamente; desgraciadamente
unfriendly *adj.* antipático/a; arisco/a
ungrateful *adj.* desagradecido/a
unhappy *adj.* infeliz; desgraciado/a
United States *n., pl.* Estados *m., pl.* Unidos
universe *n.* universo *m.*
university *n.* universidad *f.*
unkempt *adj. (appearance)* desarreglado/a
unless *adv.* a menos que
unlikely *adj.* improbable, poco probable
   be unlikely that *(something will happen)* ser poco probable que (+ *subj.*) **It's unlikely that they will arrive on time.** Es poco probable que lleguen a tiempo.
unmarried *adj.* soltero/a
unnoticed *adj.* inadvertido/a
unpack *v.t.* desempacar
unpleasant *adj.* desagradable; *(person)* antipático/a
unresolved *adj.* pendiente
unsociable *adj.* insociable
unsuccessful *adj.* fracasado/a

unthinkable *adj.* impensable
until *adv.* hasta (que)
until *prep.* hasta
   until now hasta ahora
unusual *adj.* inusual, poco corriente; insólito/a
unwillingly *adv.* de mala gana
up *adv.* arriba
   up to date al día, al corriente
   bring someone up to date *idiom* poner a uno al día/al corriente
upset enojado/a; molesto/a
urgent *adj.* urgente
   It's (not) urgent that… (No) Es urgente que…
urinate *v.i.* orinar
urine *n.* orina *f.*
use *v.t.* usar
   make good use of aprovechar
useful *adj.* útil; práctico/a
usually *adv.* soler (o:ue) +*inf.*
   I usually study at night. Suelo estudiar por la noche.
utensil *n.* utensilio *m.*
uterus *n.* útero *m.*

V

vacation *n.* vacaciones *f., pl.*
   be on vacation estar de vacaciones
   go on vacation ir(se) de vacaciones
vacationer *n. (summer)* veraneante *m., f.*
vacuum *v.i.* pasar la aspiradora
vacuum cleaner *n.* aspiradora *f.*
vain *adj.* presumido/a

valley *n.* valle *m.*
value *n.* valor *m.*
value *v.t.* valorar
vanilla *n.* vainilla *f.*
vapor *n.* vapor *m.*
variation *n.* variación *f.*
varied *adj.* variado/a
variety *n.* surtido *m.*
various *adj.* varios/as
vary *v.i.* variar
vase *n.* florero *m.;* jarrón *m.*
VCR *n.* videocasetera *f.*
veal *n.* ternera *f.*
vegetables *n., pl.* verduras *f., pl.*
vegetation *n.* vegetación *f.*
vehicle *n.* vehículo *m.*
vein *n.* vena *f.*
velodrome *n.* velódromo *m.*
velvet *n.* terciopelo *m.*
verb *n.* verbo *m.*
verisimilitude *n.* verosimilitud *f.*
vermillion *n.* bermellón *m.*
vermouth *n.* vermut *m.*
versatile *adj.* versátil
vertebra *n.* vértebra *f.*
vertebrate *n., adj.* vertebrado *m.;* vertebrado/a
very *adv.* muy
  Very good, thank you. Muy bien, gracias.
very well *adv.* muy bien
very much *adv.* muchísimo/a
vest *n.* chaleco *m.*
veterinarian *n.* veterinario/a *m., f.*
veterinary science *n.* veterinaria *f.*
vibrate *v.i.* vibrar

vibration *n.* vibración *f.*
video *n.* video *(L.A.) m.;* vídeo *(Spain) m.*
video(cassette) *n.* video(casete) *m.*
video camera *n.* cámara *f.* de video
videoconference *n.* videoconferencia *f.*
visor n. visera f.
view *n.* vista *f.*
village *n.* aldea *f.*
vinegar *n.* vinagre *m.*
violence *n.* violencia *f.*
visit *v.t.* visitar
  visit monuments visitar monumentos
visiting team *n. (sports)* equipo *m.* visitante
visitor *n.* visitante *m., f.*
visor *n.* visera *f.*
vitamin *n.* vitamina *f.*
vocational training *n.* formación *f.* profesional
volcano *n.* volcán *m.*
volleyball *n.* vóleibol *m.*
volume *n.* volumen *m.*
voluntary *adj.* voluntario
volunteer *n.* voluntario/a *m., f.*
vomit *v.i.* vomitar
vote *n.* voto *m.*
vote *v.i.* votar
vulture *n.* buitre *m.*

W

wage *n.* sueldo *m.*
waist *n.* cintura *f.*
wait (for) *v.i.* esperar
  be waiting estar pendiente

I'm waiting for Woody to call me. Estoy pendiente de que Woody me llame.

waiter n. camarero m.; mesero m.; mozo m. (L.A.)

waitress n. camarera f.; mesera f.; moza f. (L.A.)

wake up v.i. despertarse (e:ie)

walk v.i. caminar
  go for a walk dar un paseo
  take a walk pasear
  walk around the city/the town pasear por la ciudad/el pueblo

walking stick n. bastón m.

Walkman n. walkman m.

wall n. pared f.; muro m.

wallet n. cartera f.

walnut n. nuez f.

walnut tree n. nogal m.

want v.t. querer (e:ie)
  I don't want to. No quiero.

war n. guerra f.

wardrobe n. ropero m.; vestuario m.

warm (oneself) up v. calentarse (e:ie)

warranty n. garantía f.

wart n. verruga f.

wash v.t. lavar; v.ref. (oneself) lavarse
  wash one's face/hands lavarse la cara/las manos
  wash the floor lavar el piso

washing machine n. lavadora f.

wasp n. avispa f.

waste v.t. malgastar

wastebasket n. papelera f.

watch n. reloj m.

watch v.t./v.i. mirar; ver
  watch television mirar (la) televisión

watch out interj. cuidado

water n. agua (el) f.
  drinking water agua potable
  fresh water agua dulce
  holy water agua bendita
  mineral water agua mineral
  salt water agua salada

water v.t. (plants) regar

water park n. parque m. acuático

water skiing n. esquí m. acuático

waterfall n. catarata f.

watering can n. regadera f.

watermelon n. sandía f.

waterproof adj. impermeable

waterskiing n. esquí m. acuático

wave n. (water) ola f.; (physics, radio) onda f.

wax n. cera f.

wax v.t. encerar; (legs) depilarse

way n. manera f.; camino m.

weak adj. débil

weapon n. arma (el) f.

wear v.t. llevar; usar; ponerse
  wear a costume disfrazarse de
  wear for the first time estrenar

wear oneself out v. fatigarse

weary adj. fatigado/a

weather n. tiempo m.
  It's nice/bad weather. Hace buen/mal tiempo.
  What's the weather like?

¿Qué tiempo hace?
weaving *n.* tejido *m.*
Web *n.* red *f.*
website *n.* sitio *m.* web
wedding *n.* boda *f.*
  wedding ring *n.* anillo *m.* de
  bodas
Wednesday *n.* miércoles *m.,*
  sing.
week *n.* semana *f.*
  next week semana entrante,
  semana que viene
weekdays, (on) entre semana
weekend *n.* fin *m.* de semana
weigh oneself *v.* pesarse
weight *n.* pesa *f.;* peso *m.*
weightless *adj.* ingrávido/a
weightlifting *n. (sport)*
  halterofilia *f.*
welcome *adj.* bienvenido/a(s)
  You're welcome.
  (responding to thanks) De
  nada; No hay de qué
weld *v.t.* soldar
welding *n.* soldadura *f.*
well *adv.* bien; pues; bueno
well *n.* pozo *m.*
well-being *n.* bienestar *m.*
well-known *adj.* conocido/a
  be well-known for tener
  fama de
well-mannered *adj.* educado/a
well-organized *adj.*
  ordenado/a
west *n.* oeste *m.*
  to the west al oeste
western *adj. (genre)* ...de
  vaqueros
  a western una (película) de
  vaqueros

wet *adj.* mojado/a
wet *v.t.* mojar
  get wet mojarse
whale *n.* ballena *f.*
wharf *n.* embarcadero *m.*
what *rel. pron.* lo que
what? *adj., pron.* ¿qué?
  What did you say? ¿Cómo?
  What's going on? ¿Qué
  pasa?
  What a . . . ! ¡Qué...!
  What a drag! *loc.* ¡Qué lata!
wheat *n.* trigo *m.*
wheel *n.* rueda *f.*
wheel chair *n.* silla *f.* de
  ruedas
wheelbarrow *n.* carretilla *f.*
when *adv., conj.* cuando
when? *adv.* ¿cuándo?
  when all's said and done
  loc. a fin de cuentas
where *prep.* donde
where? *adv. (destination)*
  ¿adónde?; *(location)* ¿dónde?
  Where are you from? *(fam.)*
  ¿De dónde eres?; *(form.)* ¿De
  dónde es Ud.?
  Where is . . . ? ¿Dónde
  está...?
which? *adj., pron.* ¿cuál(es)?;
  ¿qué?
  which one(s)? ¿cuál(es)?
while *adv.* mientras
whim *n.* antojo *m.;* capricho *m.*
whine *v.i.* lloriquear
whisk *v.t.* batir
whisk *n.* batidor *m.*
whistle *n.* silbato *m.*
whistle *v.i.* silbar
white *n., adj.* blanco *m.;*

blanco/a

who *pron.* que **Is there anyone who speaks English?** ¿Hay alguien que hable inglés?; quien(es)

who? *pron.* ¿quién(es)?
Who is . . . ? ¿Quién es...?
Who is calling? *(on telephone)* ¿De parte de quién?
Who is speaking? *(on telephone)* ¿Quién habla?

whole *adj.* todo/a

whole-wheat bread *n.* pan *m.* integral

whose? *adj., pron.* ¿de quién(es)?

why? *adv.* ¿por qué?

wicker *n.* mimbre *m.*

widow *adj.* viuda

widowed *adj.* viudo/a

widower *adj.* viudo

wife *n.* esposa *f.*

wig *n.* peluca *f.*

wild *adj. (animal)* salvaje; *(plant)* silvestre

willingly *adv.* de buena gana

win *v.t.* ganar; vencer

wind *n.* viento *m.*
It's (very) windy. Hace (mucho) viento.

window *n.* ventana *f.;* cristal *m.*

windshield *n.* parabrisas *m., sing.*

windshield wiper *n.* limpiaparabrisas *m., sing.*

wine *n.* vino *m.*
bottle of wine *n.* botella *f.* de vino

red/white wine vino tinto/blanco

wine cellar *n.* bodega *f.*

wineglass *n.* copa *f.*

wink (one's eye) *v.t.* guiñar(le) (el ojo) (a alguien)

winter *n.* invierno *m.*

wire netting *n.* tela *f.* metálica

wisdom *n.* sabiduría *f.*

wisdom tooth *n.* muela *f.* del juicio

wise *adj.* sabio/a

wise person *n.* sabio/a *m., f.*

wish *n.* deseo *m.*

wish *v.t.* desear; esperar
I wish (that) *interj.* Ojalá (que)

with *prep.* con
with me conmigo
with you *fam.* contigo
with regard to con respecto a

withdrawn *adj. (person)* retraído/a

within *prep.* dentro de

without *conj.* sin que

without *prep.* sin

withstand *v.t.* soportar, resistir, aguantar

witness *n.* testigo *m., f.*

wolf *n.* lobo *m.*

woman *n.* mujer *f.*

womanizer *n.* donjuán *m.;* mujeriego *m.*

womb *n.* útero *m.*

wool *n.* lana *f.*
made of wool de lana

wool cap *n.* gorro *m.* de lana

word *n.* palabra *f.*

work *n.* trabajo *m.; (of art,*

literature, music, etc.) obra f.
work *v.i.* trabajar; funcionar
 not working *adj.*
 descompuesto/a
work out *v.i.* hacer gimnasia
workshop *n.* taller *m.;*
 (mechanic's) taller de
 mecánica
world *n.* mundo *m.*
worldwide *adj.* mundial
worm *n.* gusano *m.*
worried (about) *adj.*
 preocupado/a (por);
 inquieto/a
worry (about) *v.* preocuparse
 (por); inquietar(se)
 Don't worry. No se/te
 preocupe/s.
worrysome *adj.* inquietante
worse *adj.* peor
worse than *adv.* peor que
worst *adj.* el/la peor, lo peor
 the worst *n.* el/la peor *m., f.*
 lo peor
worth *n.* valor
 be worth the trouble valer la
 pena
wound *n.* herida f.
wrap *v.t.* envolver
wretch *n.* desgraciado/a *m., f.*
wrist *n.* muñeca f.
write *v.t.* escribir
 write a letter/postcard/e-
 mail message escribir una
 carta/una (tarjeta) postal/un
 mensaje electrónico
writer *n.* escritor(a) *m., f.*
written *p.p.* escrito/a *(of*
 escribir)
wrong *adj.* equivocado/a

 be wrong no tener razón
 What's wrong? ¿Qué pasa?

X
X-ray *n.* radiografía f.

Y
yam *n.* ñame *m.*
yard *n.* jardín *m.;* patio *m.*
year *n.* año *m.*
yearning *n.* añoranza f.
yeast *n.* levadura f.
yellow *n., adj.* amarillo *m.;*
 amarillo/a
yellowish *adj.* amarillento/a
yes *interj.* sí
 Yes, sure! ¡Sí, vale!
yesterday *adv.* ayer
yet *adv.* todavía
yield (the right of way) *v.*
 ceder el paso
yoga *n.* yoga *m.*
yogurt *n.* yogur *m.*
young *adj.* joven
young person *n.* joven *m., f.;*
 chico/a *m., f.*
younger *adj.* menor
youngest *n.* el/la menor *m., f.*
your su(s) *poss. adj. form.;* tu(s)
 poss. adj. fam. sing.;
 vuestro(s)/vuestra(s) *poss.*
 adj. form. pl.; suyo(s)/suya(s)
 poss. pron. form.;
 tuyo(s)/tuya(s) *poss. fam.*
 sing.
youth *n.* juventud f.; joven *m., f.*
youth hostel *n.* albergue *m.*
 juvenil
youthful *adj.* juvenil

z

zebra *n.* cebra *f.*
zero *n.* cero *m.*
zipper *n.* cremallera *f.*
zoo *n.* zoológico *m.*
zoologist *n.* zoólogo/a *m., f.*

Useful Expressions

The *Useful Expressions* section of the **Vista Higher Learning Introductory Spanish Pocket Dictionary & Language Guide** puts at your fingertips a great variety of useful language organized according to situations similar to those in your textbook. This section of the dictionary provides numerous models of natural and expressive Spanish and covers all the conversational situations likely to come up as you progress through your book.

To use *Useful Expressions* for your class work, look for situations similar to those in the lesson you are studying, read through the section, copy out sentences and expressions that interest you, review them several times, and write new sentences modeled on them. Before you know it, you will find that you have acquired the new vocabulary, expressions, and language structures. This section can not only help you make yourself understood, it can help you express yourself, your opinions, and your personality in fluent and natural Spanish.

SALUDOS, PRESENTA-CIONES Y DESPEDIDAS	GREETINGS, INTRODUCTIONS, AND FAREWELLS
Buenos días.	Good morning.
¿Hay alguien?	Is anyone there?
¿Se puede pasar?	May I come in?
Pues claro, adelante.	Of course, come in.
Pasa./Pase./Pasen.	Come in.
Es (todo) un placer conocerle.	It's a (great) pleasure to meet you.
El placer es mío.	The pleasure is mine.
(Muchísimas) Gracias.	Thank you (very much).
Quiero presentarle a la Sra. Paredes.	I would like you to meet Mrs. Paredes.

ENCUENTROS	UPON MEETING
¡Cuánto tiempo sin verte/verlo/verla/verlos/verlas!	Long time no see!
¡Qué alegría volver a verte!	How nice to see you again!
¿Qué (te) cuentas?	What's going on?/What's up?
Ha pasado mucho tiempo.	What a long time it's been.
¡Cómo vuela el tiempo!	How time flies!
¿Cómo va la vida?	How's life?
Bien, muy bien.	Good, very good.
Todo va sobre ruedas.	Everything's going smoothly.
Y tú, ¿qué tal?	How are things with you?
No me puedo quejar.	I can't complain.
Me alegro de volver a verte.	I'm so glad to see you again.
Es estupendo verte otra vez.	It's great to see you again.

Igualmente.	Likewise./The same to you.
Lo mismo digo.	Same here.

EXPRESIONES CORTESES Y SERVICIALES

EXPRESSIONS OF COURTESY AND HELPFULNESS

Con permiso.	Excuse me.
Permítame.	Allow me.
¡A la orden!	At your service.
No hay de qué.	Don't mention it./You're welcome.
Con gusto.	With pleasure.
¡Para servirle!	At your service./You're welcome.
Perdone.	Pardon me./Excuse me.
Perdóneme.	Pardon me./Excuse me.
Sin falta.	By all means.
Ahora mismo.	Right away.
Al minuto.	Right away.
No faltaba más.	Of course./No problem.
¿Cómo no?	But of course./Sure.
Enseguida.	Right away.

EXPRESIONES DE TIEMPO

EXPRESSIONS OF TIME

¿A cuántos estamos? A doce de agosto.	What's the date? The twelfth of August.
¿A qué día estamos hoy? A seis.	What's the date today? The sixth.
¿Qué día es hoy? Miércoles veinticuatro.	What day is it? Wednesday, the twenty-fourth.
¡Uy, qué tarde es!	Oh, it's so late!
Se me ha hecho tarde.	I'm late.
¡Ya es mediodía!	It's already noon!

Tengo mucha prisa.	I'm in a big hurry.
¡Qué contratiempo! No tengo reloj.	What a nuisance! I don't have a watch.
¡Qué inconveniente!	How inconvenient!
Son las dos de la tarde.	It's two in the afternoon.
Son las tres de la madrugada.	It's three in the morning.
Es la una de la noche.	It's one in the morning.
Son las siete de la tarde.	It's seven in the evening.
¿Tiene (Ud.) hora, por favor?	Do you have the time, please?
¿Qué hora tiene?	What time do you have?
¿Me dice la hora?	Can you tell me the time?
¿Podría Ud. decirme qué hora es?	Could you please tell me what time it is?
Pasan diez minutos de las once.	It's ten minutes past eleven.
Llego justito.	I'm just in the nick of time.
Falta (un) cuarto para las dos.	It's (a) quarter to two.
Tengo tiempo de tomar un café.	I have time for a cup of coffee.
Es la una y media.	It's one thirty.
Aún es temprano.	It's still early.
Son las tres en punto.	It's three on the dot.
Aún falta una hora.	There's still an hour to go.
Son las seis menos cuarto.	It's a quarter to six.
No llego, no llego.	I'll never make it.
Se me/nos ha ido el día en tonterías.	I/We have fiddled away the entire day.
Son las cinco cuarenta y cinco.	It's five forty-five.
Ya llego tarde.	I'm already late.

¡Cómo vuela/pasa el tiempo!	How time flies!
El tiempo vuela.	Time flies.
¿Te das cuenta de lo rápido que pasa el tiempo?	Do you realize how fast time goes by?
¡Qué de prisa/despacio pasan las horas!	The hours pass so quickly/slowly!
Vamos, date prisa/apresúrate que llegamos tarde.	Let's go! Hurry up or we'll be late.
Siempre de prisa./Siempre con prisas.	Always in a hurry./Always in a rush.

DE VIAJE / TRAVELING

¡Por fin (nos) vamos de viaje!	At last we're going on a trip!
Nos vamos.	We're leaving.
Es hora de irse/partir.	It's time to leave.
¡Todos a bordo!	All aboard!
Vamos de excursión.	We're going on a field trip/day trip.
¡Vámonos!	Let's go!
Estamos listos.	We're ready.
Buen viaje.	Have a good trip!/Bon voyage!
¡Que (te/le/les) vaya bien!	Have a nice time!/Hope it goes well!
¡Que lo pases/pasen bien!	Have a nice time!/Hope it goes well!
¡Que disfrutes/disfrute/disfruten!	Enjoy yourself/yourselves!
Nada de despedidas.	No goodbyes.
Feliz viaje y hasta la vuelta.	Have a nice trip. See you when you get back.

217

Nos vemos a la vuelta.	We'll see each other when you/we/I return.
¡Que se divierta/diviertan!	Have fun!
No olviden mandar una postal.	Don't forget to send a postcard.
A ver si nos escribes unas líneas.	Drop a line.

DE REGRESO

BACK HOME

¡Estamos de vuelta!	We're back!
Aquí estamos, sanos y salvos.	Here we are, safe and sound.
Bienvenidos.	Welcome.
¡Qué alegría!	Great!/Wonderful!
¿Qué tal el viaje?	How was your trip?
Indescriptible. Inolvidable.	Indescribable. Unforgettable.
¿Cómo (te/le/les) fue?	How was it?
Lo pasé/pasamos en grande.	I/We had a great time.
Lo pasé/pasamos super bien.	I/We had a terrific time.
No hay nada como volver a casa.	There's no place like home./It's great to be home.
Me alegro de que estés/esté/estén de vuelta.	I'm glad you're back.
Me alegra volver a verte/verlo/verlos.	It's nice to see you again.
Ya te/los echaba de menos./Ya te/los extrañaba.	I missed you.
¿Me/Nos echaste de menos?/¿Me/Nos extrañaste?	Did you miss me/us?
Te/Los eché muchísimo de menos./Te/Los extrañé muchísimo.	I missed you a lot.

218

Pues claro que te/los extrané.	Of course I missed you.
Estamos impacientes por ver las fotos.	We can't wait to see the pictures.
Hogar, dulce hogar.	Home sweet home.
EN CLASE	IN CLASS
Buenos días, clase.	Good morning, class.
Ahora voy a pasar lista.	Now I'll take the roll/attendance.
A ver… ¿Adams?	Let's see, Adams?
Presente.	Present./Here.
Ahora, presten atención.	Now pay attention.
Fíjense bien.	Pay attention.
¡Qué profe tan estupendo/a!	What a terrific professor!
La profesora de historia del arte es buenísima.	The art history professor is great.
Sabe muchísimo y además explica muy bien.	She knows a lot and explains everything so well.
Sus clases son muy interesantes, y aprendo mucho.	Her classes are really interesting, and I learn a lot.
¡Qué profe tan pesado/a!	That professor is a pain in the neck!
Siempre habla de lo mismo.	He/She says the same thing over and over again.
¡Qué clase más/tan aburrida!	What a boring class!
El próximo semestre (no) voy a tomar geografía.	Next semester I'm (not) going to take geography.
Las fechas no son mi fuerte.	I don't have a head for dates.
Tengo ganas de que se acabe/termine el curso.	I can't wait until this course is over.

Yo también tengo ganas de ir de vacaciones.	I also want a vacation.
Tranquilo, hombre. Sólo faltan los exámenes finales.	Take it easy, man. Just the final exams are left.
Uf, no quiero ni pensarlo.	Ugh, I don't even want to think about it.
Tengo que presentar un trabajo el próximo martes.	I have to hand in a paper next Tuesday.
Es sobre la sociología de las masas.	It's on the sociology of the masses.
Tengo tanto/tantísimo trabajo.	I have so much work.
No sé por dónde empezar.	I don't know where to begin.
No te preocupes.	Don't worry.
Vas a sacar unas notas de fábula, como siempre.	You're going to get excellent grades, as always.
Ya lo verás.	You'll see.
Tú siempre apruebas todos los exámenes.	You always pass all your exams.
Y además con buena nota.	And with a good grade to boot.
DESPUÉS DE CLASE	*AFTER CLASS*
Ay, dormilón/dormilona, ¿de dónde sales?	Hey, sleepyhead, where have you been?
¿Dónde estabas esta mañana?	Where were you this morning?
¿Se te pegaron las sábanas?	Couldn't you drag yourself out of bed?
La clase de historia estuvo muy interesante; como siempre.	History class was very interesting, as always.
Anoche no pegué ojo.	I didn't sleep a wink last night.
Estoy/Voy atrasado/a en álgebra.	I'm behind in algebra.
Soy fatal para las matemáticas.	I'm lousy in math.

A mí se me dan muy bien las ciencias en general.	I do very well in science, in general.
Si necesitas ayuda, te hecho una mano.	If you need help, I'll give you a hand.
Laura es una sabihonda, ¡se cree que lo sabe todo!	Laura is a know-it-all; she thinks she knows everything!
Su nombre de pila es Eduardo; su apodo es Dudu.	His given name is Eduardo; his nickname is Dudu.
¿Por qué estudia tanto ese individuo?	Why does that guy study so much?
Quiere (llegar a) ser presidente.	He/she wants to be president (some day).
Tiene fama de ambicioso.	He/she has a reputation for being ambitious.
No me digas. ¿En serio? ¿Me tomas el pelo?	You don't say. Seriously? Are you pulling my leg?
¿Cómo te fue en el examen de química?… Fatal./Estupendo.	How was the chemistry exam?… Terrible./Great.
El examen fue pan comido.	The exam was a piece of cake.
Tengo que ponerme al día en biología.	I need to catch up in biology.
No quiero suspender otra vez.	I don't want to flunk again.
Los exámenes finales ya están cerca.	Final exams are getting close.
Sí, están a la vuelta de la esquina.	Yes, they're just around the corner.
No sé qué me pasa.	I don't know what's happening to me.
No me puedo concentrar.	I can't concentrate.
Estoy lleno/a de dudas.	I'm full of doubts.

No me gusta nada la computación.	I don't like computer science at all.
A mí tampoco.	Neither do I.
A mí se me dan muy bien los idiomas.	I do very well with languages.
¡Qué casualidad! A mí también.	What a coincidence! Me too.
¡Qué coincidencia! Compartimos el mismo interés por las lenguas.	What a coincidence! We share an interest for languages.
Tengo mucho interés en las lenguas clásicas.	I'm very interested in classical languages.
¡Genial! A mí me interesa muchísimo el latín.	Great! I'm really interested in Latin.
El único inconveniente es que no tengo con quién practicarlo.	The only drawback is that I don't have anyone to practice with.
¿Te importa dejarme tus apuntes de literatura?	Would you mind lending me your literature notes?
En absoluto./Pues claro que no./Aquí los tienes./Aquí están.	Not at all. /Of course not./Here you go./Here they are.
Espero que entiendas mi letra.	I hope you can read my writing.
Tengo una letra horrible/ilegible.	My handwriting is terrible/illegible.
Pero están muy completos.	But they're very complete.

LA FAMILIA

YOUR FAMILY

¿Todos bien?	Is everyone well?
Sí, todos bien, gracias a Dios.	Yes, everyone's well, thank goodness.
¿Tienes muchos hermanos/parientes/sobrinos?	Do you have a lot of brothers and sisters/relatives/nieces and nephews?
¿Dónde viven tus padres?	Where do your parents live?

¿Visitas muy a menudo a tus familiares/parientes?

Do you visit your family/relatives often?

¿Son tus padres muy mayores?

Are your parents very old?

¿Vives con tus padres?

Do you live with your parents?

¿Quién es mayor, tu padre o tu madre?

Who is older, your father or your mother?

¿A qué se dedica tu padre/madre?

What does your father/mother do for a living?

¿Qué estudia tu hermano mayor?

What does your older brother study?

¿Tienen bisnietos tus abuelos?

Do your grandparents have great-grandchildren?

¿Conoces a todos tus primos?

Do you know all your cousins?

¿Son tus padres de la misma nacionalidad?

Are your parents of the same nationality?

¿Hablan tus padres español?

Do your parents speak Spanish?

¿Te llevas bien con tus hermanos?

Do you get along well with your brothers and sisters?

¿Dónde se conocieron tus padres?

Where did your parents meet?

¿Tienes familiares en el extranjero?

Do you have relatives abroad?

¿Dónde nacieron tus padres?

Where were your parents born?

¡Qué dicha ver a toda la familia junta!

What good fortune to see the whole family together!

Con una familia tan grande, siempre hay de qué/con quién hablar.

With such a big family, there is always something to talk about/someone to talk to.

EL OCIO

¿Dónde vas a ir este sábado?

¿Vas a hacer algo especial el domingo?

¿Tienes algún pasatiempo favorito/preferido?

¿Cuál es tu pasatiempo favorito/preferido?

¿Qué vas a hacer después de clase?

¿Qué vas a hacer este fin de semana?

Creo que voy a ir al zoológico.

La entrada es gratuita los fines de semana.

¿Puedes creerlo?

Y tú, ¿qué? ¿Vas a ir al cine este fin de semana?

Bah, ya estoy harto/a de ir al cine.

No hay ninguna película interesante.

¿Ves mucho la televisión?

¡Que va! Es terrible. Siempre hacen lo mismo.

Me gusta divertirme sin gastar mucho dinero.

Me gustan las actividades que no cuestan dinero.

LEISURE

Where are you going this Saturday?

Are you going to do anything special on Sunday?

Do you have a favorite pastime?

What is your favorite pastime?

What are you doing after class?

What are you doing this week-end?

I think I'll go to the zoo.

Admission is free on weekends.

Can you believe it?

What about you? Are you going to go to the movies this week-end?

I'm tired/sick of going to the movies.

There aren't any interesting movies.

Do you watch a lot of television?

No way! It's awful. It's always the same thing.

I like to have fun without spending too much money.

I like activities that don't cost money.

Oye, ¿por qué no vienes conmigo al zoológico?	Hey, why don't you come to the zoo with me?
Estupendo. ¡Decidido, pues!	Great. It's decided, then!
El domingo vamos los dos al zoológico. ¡Y no se hable más!	On Sunday the two of us will go to the zoo. That's settled!
A partir de ahora voy a comprar la guía del ocio todas las semanas.	From now on I'm going to buy the city entertainment guide every week.
Quiero estar informado de todas las actividades que tienen lugar en la ciudad.	I want to know about all the activities that take place in the city.
No quiero perderme nada, sobre todo si es gratis.	I don't want to miss anything, especially if it's free.
Nos vemos en el zoológico.	We'll see each other at the zoo.
¡Que se diviertan en el zoológico!	Have a good time at the zoo!

EXPRESIONES DEL TIEMPO

WEATHER EXPRESSIONS

¡Qué buen día hace hoy!	What a nice day it is today!
Hoy hace un día espléndido.	It's a beautiful day today.
El cielo está totalmente despejado.	The sky is perfectly clear.
No hay ni una nube.	There's not a cloud in the sky.
El hombre del tiempo pronosticó lluvia para el fin de semana.	The weatherman predicted rain for the weekend.
Afortunadamente, ¡se equivocó!	Fortunately, he was wrong!
Me pregunto qué tiempo va a hacer mañana.	I wonder what the weather will be like tomorrow.
¡Últimamente el tiempo es tan variable!	The weather has been so variable lately!
Sí, es imprevisible. No es fácil adivinar/predecir.	Yes, it's unpredictable. It's not easy to predict.

Mañana (dicen que) va a caer un aguacero.	Tomorrow (they say that) there will be a downpour.
Llueve a cántaros.	It's raining cats and dogs.
Y yo sin paraguas. ¡Qué contratiempo!	And me without an umbrella. How annoying!
No salgas sin paraguas.	Don't leave/go out without an umbrella.
Si llueve y hace sol, va a salir el arco iris.	If it rains and the sun comes out, there will be a rainbow.
¡Qué emoción! Me fascinan los arco iris.	Cool! I love rainbows.
A ver si vemos uno bien grande.	Maybe we'll see a nice big one.
¡Qué lunes tan horrible!	What a horrible Monday!
Hace viento y hace frío.	It's windy and it's cold.
¡Qué día tan feo! Es feo con ganas.	What an awful day! It's awful and then some.
Hay mucha niebla y no se ve nada.	There's a lot of fog and you can't see anything.
Hoy hace un día para no salir de casa/para quedarse en casa.	Today is a nice day to stay home.
¡Que pase/tenga un buen día!	Have a nice day!
Igualmente.	Same to you.

EN LA AGENCIA DE VIAJES — AT THE TRAVEL AGENCY

Bueno, ¡menos mal! Parece que hoy está abierto.	Okay, great! It looks like it's open today.
Quisiéramos dos pasajes para Octopulco, ida y vuelta.	We'd like two round-trip tickets to Octopulco.
En primera clase, por supuesto.	In first class, of course.
Cómo no.	But of course.

226

¿Para qué día?	For what day?
¿Cuándo quieren regresar?	When would you like to return?
Queremos hospedarnos en un hotel de cinco estrellas/hotel barato.	We'd like to stay in a five-star hotel/an inexpensive hotel.
¿Cuántos días van a quedarse?	How many days will you stay?
Nos vamos a quedar quince días.	We're going to stay two weeks.
¿Quieren alquilar un auto?	Do you want to rent a car?
No, no hace falta.	No, we don't need one.
La isla es pequeña. Podemos ir en bicicleta.	The island is small. We can get around by bike.
Aquí tienen sus pasajes.	Here are your tickets.

EN EL AEROPUERTO / AT THE AIRPORT

¿Dónde está la aerolínea Gavilán?	Where is Gavilán Airlines?
Vuelo 8778	Flight 8778
Destino Octopulco	Destination: Octopulco
¿Cancelado?… No, retrasado.	Canceled? . . . No, delayed.
Bueno, pues a esperar.	Okay, then we'll wait.
¡Estoy cansado/a de esperar en los aeropuertos!	I'm tired of waiting in airports!
¿Debemos facturar el equipaje ahora?	Should we check our luggage now?
Me olvidé el itinerario.	I forgot the itinerary.
Al menos es un vuelo directo, sin escalas.	At least it's a direct flight, without any stopovers.
¿Dónde está la tienda libre de impuestos?	Where is the duty-free shop?

Da igual. No tenemos tiempo. Ya vamos a embarcar.	It doesn't matter. We don't have time. We're going to board now.
Esta maleta pesa demasiado/es demasiado pesada.	This suitcase weighs too much/is too heavy.
Voy a buscar un carrito.	I'm going to look for a cart.
Yo prefiero viajar ligero de equipaje.	I prefer to travel light.
A la vuelta debemos pasar por la aduana.	On the way back we have to go through customs.
¿Algo que declarar?	Anything to declare?
No, nada.	No, nothing.

EN EL HOTEL

AT THE HOTEL

Bienvenidos al hotel Miramar.	Welcome to the Hotel Miramar.
Por fin llegamos.	Finally we're here.
¿Tuvieron un vuelo agradable?	Did you have a good flight?
¡Qué vuelo tan largo!	What a long flight!
Lo sentimos, pero el ascensor/el elevador no funciona hoy.	We're sorry, but the elevator is out of order today.
Deben subir por las escaleras.	You need to take the stairs.
Por suerte están Uds. en el primer piso.	Luckily you're on the second floor.
Ésta es la mejor habitación con vista(s) al mar.	This is the best room with an ocean view.
Esperamos que todo sea de su agrado.	We hope that everything will be to your liking.
Cualquier cosa que necesiten, llamen a recepción.	If you need anything, call the front desk.
Gracias por hospedarse en/elegir nuestro hotel.	Thank you for staying in/choosing our hotel.

Esperamos que tengan una estancia agradable.

We hope you have an enjoyable stay.

¡Que tengan una feliz estancia!

Have a nice stay!

EN LA PLAYA

AT THE BEACH

¡Qué belleza de paisaje!

What beautiful scenery!

Pues, espera a ver el atardecer.

Wait until you see the sunset.

Dicen que es de película.

They say it's fantastic.

¡Qué paz!

What peace!

¡Qué aire tan puro y fresco!

What pure, fresh air!

No hay nada como la brisa del mar.

There's nothing like a sea breeze.

¡Qué calor!

It's so hot!

Este verano no quiero quemarme.

This summer I don't want to get sunburned.

¡Cuánta gente!

What a lot of people!

Pensaba que veníamos a una isla desierta.

I though we were going to a desert island.

¡Qué tonto/a! Me olvidé el traje de baño.

How stupid! I forgot my bathing suit.

Hoy no me apetece hacer nada.

Today I'm not in the mood to do anything.

Voy a contemplar el paisaje y pasear por la orilla.

I'm going to contemplate the scenery and take a walk along the shore.

¿QUÉ ME PONGO PARA LA FIESTA DEL SÁBADO?

WHAT SHOULD I WEAR TO THE PARTY SATURDAY?

¡Qué problema!

What a problem!

No tengo nada que ponerme.

I don't have anything to wear.

Necesito renovar mi vestuario.

I need a new wardrobe.

No tengo nada que me guste.	I don't have anything that I like.
Estoy harta de ponerme siempre la misma ropa.	I'm tired of always wearing the same clothes.
Lo que necesitas es un cambio de imagen.	You need a new image.
Sí, tienes razón.	Yes, you're right.
Es justo lo que necesito.	It's just what I need.
¿Quieres ser mi asesor de imagen?	Would you like to be my image consultant?
Esta misma tarde voy a ir al centro (comercial) a ver qué encuentro.	This afternoon I'm going to the mall/downtown to see what I can find.
Esta semana hay unas rebajas espectaculares.	This week there are some great discounts.
No me gustan los mercados; odio regatear.	I don't like markets; I hate to haggle.

EN LA TIENDA DE ROPA PARA DAMAS

IN THE WOMEN'S CLOTHING STORE

¡Cuánta variedad! ¡Cuánto colorido!	What variety! So many colors!
Va a ser difícil decidir.	It's going to be hard to decide.
Quiero un vestido bien llamativo.	I want an attractive dress.
Señorita, ¿podría probarme este vestido?	Miss, may I try on this dress?
Naturalmente. El probador está al fondo a la derecha.	Of course. The fitting room is in the back to the right.
Uy, me queda un poco justo.	Aw, it's a little too small.
Necesito una talla más grande.	I need a bigger size.
¿Qué talla quiere?	What size do you want?
La mediana, por favor.	Medium, please.

230

Sí, éste me sienta bien/mejor.	Yes, this one fits me well/better.
¿Cuál te gusta más, el rojo o el negro?	Which do you like better, the red or the black?
El negro te va como anillo al dedo.	The black one suits you to a "T."
El color negro te favorece.	You look good in black.
Te ves más delgada.	It makes you look thinner.
Sí, el rojo no me sienta tan bien.	Yes, the red one doesn't fit me as well.
Te ves muy atractiva con ese vestido.	You look very attractive in that dress.
¡Y qué suave es!	And it's so soft!
¡Buena compra!	A good buy!
Ahora necesitas otro bolso.	Now you need another purse.
Ese bolso no va (bien) con el vestido.	This purse doesn't go (well) with this dress.
Y también unos zapatos a juego.	And also shoes to match.
Espérame, voy a pagar el vestido y nos vamos a una zapatería.	Wait, I'll pay for the dress, then we'll go to a shoe store.
¿Cuánto vale?	How much does it cost?
Uy, baratísimo.	Oh, really inexpensive/cheap.
¡Hoy es mi día de suerte!/¡Hoy estoy de suerte!	Today is my lucky day!
¿Vamos a la zapatería?	Shall we go to the shoe store?

EN LA TIENDA DE ROPA PARA CABALLEROS

IN THE MEN'S CLOTHING STORE

Necesito un traje bien elegante.	I need an elegant suit.
¿De qué color lo quiere?	What color would you like?

No sé… ¿Qué me sugiere Ud.?	I don't know . . . What would you suggest?
Un color oscuro le quedará/sentará bien.	You'd look good in a dark color.
Venga por aquí, joven.	Come over hear, young man.
¿Qué talla usa?	What size do you wear?
No sé, es mi primer traje.	I don't know. It's first suit.
Bueno, Ud. debe usar la talla 52 para la chaqueta… y la talla 32 para los pantalones.	Well, you should wear a size 52 jacket . . . and size 32 pants.
A ver, pruébese este traje azul marino… ¿Qué tal?	Let's see. Try on this dark blue suit. What do you think?
Le queda perfecto.	It fits you perfectly.
Parece hecho a su medida.	It looks like it was made for you.
Ahora necesita una bonita camisa.	Now you need a nice shirt.
¿La prefiere blanca o azul?	Would you like white or blue?
¿Blanca?	White?
Muy bien. Tenga, pruébese ésta.	Okay. Here you are. Try on this one.
Es la talla 16.	It's size 16.
Sí, me gusta…¡Qué tela más fina!	Yes, I like it. . . . What nice material!
Ahora sólo falta el último toque… ¡la corbata!	Now all you need is the last touch . . .a tie!
¿Qué tal esta roja?	How about this red one?
Ni hablar… demasiado llamativa.	Don't even suggest it . . . too flashy.
Necesitamos un color más suave.	We need a more muted color.

232

Azul celeste… Confíe en mí.	Light blue . . . trust me.
Mire, pruébese ésta… Es de seda italiana.	Look, try this one on. It's Italian silk.
Está Ud. impecable.	You are impeccable.
Pues sí, parezco otra persona.	Yes, I look like another person.
No sabía que era tan guapo.	I didn't know I was so handsome.
Muchísimas gracias por su ayuda.	Thanks so much for your help.
¿Cuánto le debo?	How much do I owe you?

LA RUTINA DIARIA
DAILY ROUTINE

¿Necesitas simplificar tu vida?	Do you need to simplify your life?
¿A qué hora te levantas?	What time do you get up?
¿Qué es lo primero que haces al levantarte?	What's the first thing you do when you get up?
¿Desayunas en casa?	Do you have/eat breakfast at home?
¿Qué desayunas? ¿Tostadas con mantequilla?	What do you have/eat for breakfast? Toast with butter?
¿Desayunas lo mismo todos los días?	Do you have/eat the same thing for breakfast every day?
¿Te vistes antes de desayunar o desayunas primero y luego te vistes?	Do you get dressed before breakfast or do you eat breakfast first and then get dressed?
¿A qué hora sales de casa?	What time do you leave the house?
¿Cuánto tiempo necesitas para prepararte por la mañana?	How much time do you need to get ready in the morning?
¿Te gusta ir de prisa o te tomas las cosas con calma?	Do you like to be quick or do you take your time?
¿A qué hora almuerzas?	What time do you eat lunch?

¿Dónde? ¿Con quién?	Where? With whom?
¿Te gusta almorzar solo o acompañado/a?	Do you like to eat lunch alone or with other people?
¿Estudias, trabajas o haces las dos cosas?	Are you studying, working, or both?
¿Qué haces de las 3 a las 5 de la tarde?	What do you do from 3:00 to 5:00 in the afternoon?
¿Qué haces después de las clases/después del trabajo?	What do you do after class/after work?
¿A qué hora regresas a casa?	What time do you get home?
¿Llegas muy tarde a casa por la noche?	Do you get home very late at night?
¿Qué es lo primero que haces al llegar a casa?	What's the first thing you do when you get home?
¿A qué hora cenas?	What time do you eat/have dinner?
¿Qué haces después de cenar?	What do you do after dinner?
¿Cuántas veces al día te lavas los dientes?	How many times a day do you brush your teeth?
¿A qué hora te vas a dormir/te acuestas?	What time do you go to sleep/to bed?
¿Qué es lo último que haces antes de acostarte?	What is the last thing you do before going to bed?
¿Cuántas horas duermes?	How many hours do you sleep?
¿Crees que duermes pocas horas?	Do you think you don't get enough sleep?
¿Es necesaria la rutina?	Is routine necessary?
¿Estás contento/a con tu rutina?	Are you happy with your routine?
¿Pierdes mucho tiempo por las mañanas?	Do you waste a lot of time in the morning?

¿Cuál es tu secreto para ganar tiempo libre?	What is your secret for finding free time?

EN EL RESTAURANTE

AT THE RESTAURANT

¿Mesa para dos?	Table for two?
¡Qué ambiente más selecto!	What an exclusive place!
Este lugar es muy acogedor.	This place is very cozy.
Está decorado con mucho gusto.	This place is decorated in very good taste.
Sin duda es el restaurante más caro de la ciudad.	Without a doubt, this is the most expensive restaurant in the city.
Tiene fama de ser excelente… y de ser carísimo.	It is supposed to be excellent . . . and very expensive.
Todo el mundo habla muy bien de este sitio.	Everyone speaks very well of this place.
Los cubiertos son de plata.	The silverware is real silver.
A ver el menú.	Let's look at the menu.
Aquí tienen el menú.	Here's the menu.
Mmm, se me hace la boca agua.	Mmm, it makes my mouth water.
No sé qué pedir.	I don't know what to order.
¿Qué nos sugiere?	What do you suggest?
Pidan lo que más les guste.	Order whatever you like the best.
Todo es exquisito, sin excepción.	Everything is superb, without exception.
Esta carne está en su punto.	This meat is just right.
¡Qué ensalada más original!	What an original salad!
Sí, combina frutas y verduras.	Yes, it combines fruit and vegetables.
El aderezo/aliño es divino.	The dressing is divine.

¿Nos trae la carta de vinos, por favor?

Would you bring us the wine list, please?

No me gusta el vino tinto; prefiero el vino blanco.

I don't like red wine; I prefer white wine.

Yo no puedo tomar vino de ningún color; enseguida me emborracho.

I can't drink wine of any color; it goes right to my head.

Tenemos una selección de postres que les va a encantar.

You're going to love our dessert selection.

¡Qué carta de postres más creativa!

What a creative dessert menu!

Tiremos la casa por la ventana.

Let's go all out.

Probémoslos todos.

Let's try everything.

Camarero/a, nos trae la cuenta (cuando pueda), por favor.

Waiter, please bring us the check (when you can).

¿Cuánto se debe?

How much is it?

Quédese con el cambio.

Keep the change.

Nos quedamos sin plata/dinero.

We're broke.

¡Qué velada más/tan agradable!

What a pleasant evening!

¿A quién vamos a recomendar este restaurante?

To whom are we going to recommend this restaurant?

EL ALMUERZO

LUNCH

¡A comer!

Lunch is ready!

¿Qué hay para comer?

What is there/do we have to eat?

¡Qué hambre tengo!

I'm so hungry!

Estoy muerto/a de hambre./Me muero de hambre.

I'm starved.

Tengo un hambre feroz.

I'm famished./I could eat a horse.

Yo me lo como todo.

I'll eat anything.

Pues yo no. Estoy harto/a de lentejas.	Well, not me. I'm tired of lentils.
¿Otra vez lo mismo?	The same thing again?
No tengo (nada de) hambre.	I'm not hungry (at all).
¡Mmm, qué bien huele!	Mmm, it smells good!
Este estofado sabe a gloria.	This casserole tastes heavenly.
Esta sopa quema.	This soup is burning hot.
¡Pues sopla!	So blow on it!
Por favor, ¿me pasas la sal?	Please pass the salt.
¿Qué es esto rojo?	What's this red stuff?
Esta carne no me la como, está cruda.	I won't eat this meat, it's raw.
No me gusta este pescado, tiene muchas espinas.	I don't like this fish, it has lots of bones.
Esta salsa es demasiado picante/pica demasiado.	This sauce is too spicy.
¿Qué hay de postre?	What's for dessert?
Yo estoy lleno/a.	I'm full.
Claro, te comiste todo el pan.	Of course, you ate all the bread.
Voy a explotar.	I'm going to explode.
Mejor dejo el postre para la noche.	I'd better leave dessert until later tonight.
¡Coman, coman!	Eat up!
¡Buen provecho!/¡Que aproveche!	Enjoy your meal!

CELEBRACIONES

¡Estamos de fiesta!	Let's celebrate!
¿Qué se celebra?	What is being celebrated?

CELEBRATIONS

EL NACIMIENTO DE NUESTRO HIJO

Mi esposa dio a luz a nuestro tercer hijo.

¿Cuándo nació?

El 1º de enero.

¡Enhorabuena! ¡Felicidades!

¡Es un niño precioso!

THE BIRTH OF OUR SON

My wife gave birth to our third child/son.

When was he born?

January first.

Congratulations!

What a beautiful child!

EL CUMPLEAÑOS DE MI HERMANO JORGE

¿Cuántos años cumple?

Dieciocho. Ya es mayor de edad.

¡Cuántos amigos y amigas tiene tu hermano!

En esta fiesta no cabe ni un alfiler.

¡Muchísimas felicidades, Jorge!

¡Y que cumplas muchos más!

MY BROTHER JORGE'S BIRTHDAY

How old is he?

Eighteen. He's of legal age now.

Your brother has so many friends!

This party is packed.

Best wishes, Jorge!

And may you have many more!

LA GRADUACIÓN DE MARGARITA

Es nuestra hija más pequeña.

Se acaba de graduar en geología.

Estamos muy orgullosos de ella.

¡Felicidades!

¡Por un futuro brillante!

MARGARITA'S GRADUATION

She's our youngest daughter.

She's just graduated with a degree in geology.

We're very proud of her.

Congratulations!

To a bright future!

EL ANIVERSARIO DE BODAS DE MIS PADRES

¿Cuántos años hace que se casaron?

MY PARENTS' ANNIVERSARY

How many years have they been married?

Cincuenta. Celebran sus bodas de oro.	Fifty. They are celebrating their golden anniversary.
Y aún se quieren como cuando eran recién casados.	They still love each other as much as they did when they were newlyweds.
¡Qué maravilla!	How wonderful!
¡Feliz aniversario!	Happy anniversary!
¡Y que celebren muchos más!	May you have many more!

LA BODA DE MI TÍA CAROLINA	*MY AUNT CAROLINA'S WEDDING*
¡Qué dicha!	What good fortune!
¡Que sean muy felices!	May they be very happy!
¡Que se besen los novios!	A kiss!
Un brindis por los recién casados.	A toast to the newlyweds.
¡Vivan los novios!	Long live the newlyweds!

DAR EL PÉSAME — GIVING CONDOLENCES

Estamos de luto.	We're in mourning.
¡Qué desgracia!	How unfortunate!
Murió Roberto.	Roberto died.
¡Qué lástima!	What a shame!
Pobre Roberto, era tan joven.	Poor Roberto, he was so young.
Estamos todos muy apenados/tristes.	We're all very sad.
Le acompaño en el sentimiento.	My thoughts are with you.
Reciba nuestro más sincero pésame.	Our deepest sympathies.
No sé qué decir.	I don't know what to say.
Sólo puedo llorar.	I can only cry.

Lo vamos a echar mucho de menos.	We're going to miss him very much.

EN EL CONSULTORIO

IN THE DOCTOR'S OFFICE

¡Me duele todo el cuerpo!	My whole body aches!
¿Cuál es el problema?	What is the problem?
¿Qué le pasa?	What's the matter?
¿Dónde le duele?	Where does it hurt?
¿Qué síntomas tiene?	What are your symptoms?
¿Cuáles son sus síntomas?	What are your symptoms?
¿Cómo se encuentra hoy?	How are you feeling today?
Mejor./Peor.	Better./Worse.
Doctor, parece que no mejoro.	Doctor, it seems like I'm not getting better.
¿Se encuentra mejor hoy?	Are you feeling better today?
Al contrario, cada día estoy peor.	No, just the opposite, every day I'm worse.
¿Qué dicen los resultados de los análisis?	What do the test results show?
Tiene Ud. el colesterol muy alto/por las nubes.	Your cholesterol is very high/sky-high.
¿(Le) Duele?	Does it hurt?
Sólo va a notar un pinchazo.	You'll only feel a pinch.
¿Me va a doler, doctor?	Will it hurt, doctor?
Esto le va a doler un poco.	This will hurt a little.
Ay, creo que me voy a desmayar.	Oh, I think I'm going to faint.
Me aterran las agujas.	I'm afraid of needles.
No va a sentir ningún dolor.	You won't feel any pain.

Le vamos a operar con anestesia local/general.	We'll operate with local/general anesthesia.
¡Qué valiente es Vicente!	Vicente is so brave!
¿Hay que operar?	Do you have to operate?
¿Me quedará cicatriz?	Will I have/it leave a scar?
¿Podré volver a caminar/andar?	Will I be able to walk again?
¿Cuánto dura el tratamiento?	How long will the treatment last?
Doctor, ¿puede recetarme algo para el dolor?	Doctor, can you prescribe me something for the pain?
Inyecciones no, por favor.	Please, no shots.
¿No hay otra solución?	There's no other solution?
Le recomiendo que siga el tratamiento al pie de la letra.	I recommend that you follow the treatment to the letter.
¿Qué efectos secundarios tiene este medicamento?	What are the side effects of this medication?
Produce vómito y somnolencia.	It causes vomiting and drowsiness.
¿Qué opciones tengo?	What options do I have?
¿Va a tomarme la presión?	Are you going to take my blood pressure?
Tiene Ud. la presión/tensión muy alta/baja.	You have very high/low pressure.
¿Cuándo empezó a fumar?	When did you start smoking?
¿Cuántos años hace que fuma?	How many years have you been smoking?
Debe dejar de fumar YA.	You must stop smoking NOW.
Le aconsejo que deje de fumar cuanto antes.	I advise you to stop smoking immediately.
El tabaco perjudica la salud.	Tobacco jeopardizes your health.

Durante el embarazo no debe fumar ni consumir alcohol.	While you're pregnant, you shouldn't smoke or drink alcohol.
Debe Ud. ver a un especialista.	You need to see a specialist.
Es una enfermedad muy grave.	It's a very serious illness.
Conocemos los síntomas, pero no las causas.	We are familiar with the symptoms, but not the causes.
El pronóstico es grave/favorable.	The prognosis is serious/good.
Lo que yo necesito es reposo indefinido.	What I need is a prolonged rest.

LA COMUNICACIÓN TELEFÓNICA

TELEPHONING

¿Con quién hablo?	With whom am I speaking?
Soy el vecino de al lado…	I'm the next-door neighbor.
¿Quién es? ¿Quién?	Who is it? Who?
Hable más fuerte. No oigo./No oigo nada.	Please, speak up. I can't hear you/a thing.
Soy Juan, tu vecino.	It's Juan, your neighbor.
¿Te importaría bajar el volumen del radio, por favor?	Would you mind turning the radio down, please?
¿Podría hablar con el director?	May I speak with the director?
Por favor, me pone con el Sr. Ramos.	May I speak with Mr. Ramos, please?
¿De parte de quién? ¿Quién lo llama?	May I tell him/ask who's calling?
Dígale que lo llama Ruti, su primo.	Tell him that his cousin Ruti is calling.
Espere un momentito, ahora pongo.	Just a minute, here he is.
No cuelgue por favor, ahora paso.	Don't hang up, please; here he is.

Oiga, el Sr. Ramos salió a almorzar.	Oh, Mr. Ramos is out to lunch.
¿Quiere dejar un mensaje?	Would you like to leave a message?
No, yo vuelvo a llamar mañana.	No, I'll call back tomorrow.
Dígale que me llame, por favor.	Tell him to call me, please.
¿Quiere que le devuelva la llamada cuando regrese?	Would you like me to have him call you when he gets back?
Pues sí. Gracias.	Yes, thanks.
Mire, mi número es el 001-1100.	My number is 001-1100.
¿Es éste el 010-0110?	Is this 010-0110?
Lo siento, se ha equivocado de número.	I'm sorry, you have the wrong number.
Disculpe.	Oh, excuse me./I'm sorry.
Vuelva a marcar.	Try dialing again.
Estoy esperando una llamada importante.	I'm expecting an important call.
¡Ese teléfono no para de sonar!	That phone won't stop ringing/is ringing off the hook!
¿Quieres hacer el favor de contestar el teléfono?	Would you please answer the phone?
¿Cómo? ¿No tienes contestador automático?	What? You don't have an answering machine?
Señora, tiene una llamada a cobro revertido. ¿Acepta Ud. la llamada?	Ma'am, you have a collect call. Will you accept the call?
Hago un sinfín de llamadas de larga distancia e internacionales.	I make a ton of long distance and international calls.

La factura del teléfono me cuesta cada mes una fortuna/un dineral.	My phone bill costs a fortune each month.
Ring, riiiing,… riiiiiiing. No contestan.	Ring, ring, riiiing. No answer.
Parece que la línea está ocupada.	It seems that the line is busy.
Llama/e a la operadora.	Call the operator.
¿A qué número llama?	What number are you calling?
Ay, olvidé el número.	Oh, I forgot the number.
Llame a información. Marque el 003.	Call information. Dial 003.
Para más información, llame al 1-800-289-1948.	For more information, call 1-800-289-1948.
Las líneas están abiertas 24 horas al día, siete días a la semana.	The lines are open 24 hours a day, seven days a week.

LOS APARATOS

MECHANICAL DEVICES

¿Cómo funciona esto?	How does this thing work?
¿Y me preguntas a mí?	You're asking me?
¡Qué sé yo!	What do I know?
¿Y a mí me lo preguntas?	You're asking me?
No tengo ni (la más mínima) idea.	I have no idea./I haven't the foggiest idea.
Las máquinas me asustan.	Machines frighten me.
Las instrucciones me aburren.	Instructions bore me.
¿No hay una versión abreviada?	Isn't there a shorter version?
¿Cuándo viene el técnico a arreglar la antena?	When is the repair man coming to fix the antenna?

Hace semanas que no funciona el televisor.	It's been weeks since the television worked.
Me vuelvo loco/a sin la caja tonta.	I'm going crazy without the idiot box.
Creo que quiero una computadora portátil.	I think I want a laptop.
Están de moda.	They are in style.
Son prácticas, ¿no?	They're practical, aren't they?
¿Cómo se pone en marcha este trasto?	How do you get this thing/piece of junk to work?
Esta máquina de coser funciona a las mil maravillas.	This sewing machine works like a dream.
No sé qué haría sin ella.	I don't know what I would do without it.
En fin, ¿qué más?	So, what else?

LOS AUTOMÓVILES

CARS

¿Necesito carro?	Do I need a car?
A lo mejor me compro uno de segunda mano.	Maybe I should get a used one.
Cuanto más barato sea, mejor, ¿no?	The cheaper the better, no?
Total, ¿qué más da? Se va a estropear/descomponer igual.	Bah, what does it matter? It will break down just the same.
Al menos si me cuesta barato, no me preocupo tanto.	At least if it's cheap, I won't worry too much.
Un carro puede durar muchos años si lo cuidas bien.	A car can last many years if you take good care of it.
Creo que voy a vender mi carro viejo y me voy a comprar uno nuevo.	I think I'll sell my old car and buy a new one.

Pero no puedo tomar una decisión sin ton ni son.	But I can't make a decision willy nilly.
Esto es un asunto serio.	This is a serious matter.
Debo pensarlo bien.	I should think it over well.
A ver, ¿qué tipo de carro me conviene más?	Let's see, what kind of car is best for me?
¿Uno automático o uno de marchas?	An automatic or manual transmission?
¿Uno deportivo o uno familiar?	A sports car or a family car?
¿Uno de lujo o uno todo terreno?	A luxury car or an all-terrain vehicle?
¿Cuánto dinero me quiero gastar?	How much money do I want to spend?
¿Qué es lo más importante a la hora de comprar un carro?	What is the most important thing when it comes time to buy a car?
¿Cuál es mi máxima necesidad/prioridad?	What is my top priority?
¿Una carretera sin baches?	A road without potholes?
Pero pensándolo bien/mejor, ¿para qué necesito yo un carro?	But, on second thought, what do I need a car for?
¿Qué sé yo de mecánica?	What do I know about mechanics?

LAS AVERÍAS

BREAKDOWNS

Otra vez al mecánico.	To the mechanic again.
Este carro es un tremendo dolor de cabeza.	This car is a big headache.
Se estropea/descompone cada dos por tres.	It breaks down all the time.
Cuando no es una cosa es otra.	If it's not one thing, it's another.
El mes pasado eran los frenos.	Last month it was the brakes.

Hace dos meses, el cambio de marchas.	Two months ago, the gear shift.
Ayer, el intermitente delantero izquierdo.	Yesterday, the front left directional signal.
Ya te digo, me da más problemas que alegrías/satisfacciones.	I'm telling you, it's more trouble than it's worth.
Cada reparación me cuesta una fortuna/un ojo de la cara.	Every repair costs a fortune/an arm and a leg.
Además, es dificilísimo encontrar un buen mecánico en quien poder confiar.	And it's so hard to find a good, trustworthy mechanic.
Encontrar un buen mecánico es como buscar una aguja en un pajar.	Finding a good mechanic is like finding a needle in a haystack.
Ahora llevo el tubo de escape colgando y, cuando llueve, no hay quien lo ponga en marcha.	Now my exhaust pipe is hanging, and when it rains the car won't start.

EN LA CARRETERA

ON THE HIGHWAY

Iba yo conduciendo tan tranquilo/a y me paró la policía.	I was just driving along and the police pulled me over.
Me paró un policía de tráfico…	A traffic cop stopped me…
Aparentemente, por ir demasiado despacio.	Apparently, for driving too slowly.
La velocidad límite era de 65 millas por hora.	The speed limit was 65 miles per hour.
Yo iba a 15 millas por hora.	I was going 15 miles per hour.
Le dije que no tenía gasolina.	I told him that I didn't have gas.
El policía se hizo el sordo y me puso una multa.	The policeman didn't listen and gave me a fine.
Fue inútil discutir.	It was pointless to argue about it.

Me pregunto quién la va a pagar.	I'm wondering who is going to pay it.
¿Dónde hay una estación de servicio?	Where is there a service station?
Necesito llenar el tanque/el depósito.	I need to fill the tank.

UNA VIVIENDA DESASTROSA

A DISASTROUS HOUSE

¡Esta casa es un desastre!	This house is a disaster!
¡Qué casa, madre mía! Un frigorífico en invierno y un horno en verano.	What a house! A refrigerator in the winter and an oven in the summer.
Las luces se encienden y se apagan cuando les da la gana.	The lights turn on and off when they feel like it.
¿Electrodomésticos? ¿Para qué?	Appliances? For what?
Por la noche hay que tener las velas preparadas.	At night we have to have candles ready.
Siempre hay que estar prevenido (por lo que pueda pasar).	You always have to be prepared (for what may happen).
Ninguna puerta cierra bien; ninguna ventana abre bien.	None of the doors close tight; none of the windows open easily.
Las paredes son de papel.	The walls are paper thin.
No existe la intimidad.	There is no privacy.
El gato que tenía se ha mudado.	The cat I had has moved.
La ropa sale de la lavadora tal y como estaba.	The clothes come out of the washing machine the same as they went in.
Las goteras inundan el altillo.	The leaks flood the attic.
El día que llueve es todo un espectáculo.	When it rains, it's a show.

No queda pintura en la fachada.

There's no paint left on the outside.

Y esta escalera de caracol es una pesadilla a cualquier hora del día.

And this spiral staircase is a nightmare at any time of day.

Las sorpresas no faltan viviendo en tal casa.

We have no lack of surprises living in such a house.

¿Por qué no vienen Uds. mañana?

Why don't you come over tomorrow?

LA VIVIENDA PERFECTA

THE PERFECT HOUSE

¡Qué ilusión me hace tener una casa!

How I'd love to own a house!

Una casa bien grande, con jardín y con terraza.

A fairly large house, with a garden and a patio.

Siempre he querido ser ama de casa.

I have always wanted to be a housewife.

Limpiar, ordenar y lavar a todas horas del día.

Cleaning, straightening up, and washing at all hours of the day.

Cantar y cantar mientras preparo la comida.

Singing and singing while I prepare the meals.

Tener una cocina moderna y práctica a la vez.

I'd have a kitchen that was both modern and practical.

Tener electrodomésticos de todos los colores y tamaños.

I'd have appliances of all shapes and colors.

Pues no son sólo trastos; algunos te echan una mano.

They're not just pieces of junk; some help you out.

Y con un lavaplatos, todo está limpio y ordenado.

And with a dishwasher, all is clean and organized.

¡Qué maravilla! ¡Qué sueño de vida!

How wonderful! What a dream of a life!

MEDIO AMBIENTE Y ECOLOGÍA

ENVIRONMENT AND ECOLOGY

Parece que la contaminación del aire crece a un ritmo alarmante.

It seems that air pollution is growing at an alarming rate.

El dióxido de carbono es cada vez más abundante en la atmósfera.

There is more and more carbon dioxide in the atmosphere.

La sequía es un grave problema en muchos países de África.

Drought is a serious problem in many African countries.

Las aguas de los ríos, océanos y mares están cada vez más contaminadas.

Rivers, oceans, and seas are becoming more and more polluted.

El agujero de la capa de ozono sigue creciendo.

The hole in the ozone layer keeps growing.

Los incendios forestales y las inundaciones están a la orden del día.

Forest fires and floods are everyday events.

PREGUNTAS SOBRE ECOLOGÍA

ENVIRONMENTAL QUESTIONS

¿Está en peligro la vida en la Tierra?

Is life on earth in danger?

¿A quién afecta la destrucción del medio ambiente?

Who does the destruction of the environment affect?

¿Qué predicen los científicos para dentro de cincuenta años?

What do scientists predict for the next fifty years?

¿Qué consecuencias puede tener el calentamiento global de la Tierra?

What can the consequences of global warming be?

¿Es posible que se deshielen los casquetes polares?

Is it possible that the polar caps will melt?

250

¿Crees que hay solución a los problemas actuales de contaminación?

Do you think there's a solution to the current pollution problems?

¿Cuáles son las condiciones medioambientales óptimas que garantizan la existencia de los seres vivos en la Tierra?

What are the optimal environmental conditions that guarantee the existence of living beings on earth?

¿Qué medidas se pueden tomar para poner marcha atrás al problema de la contaminación atmosférica? ¿Y de la contaminación del agua?

What measures can be taken to reverse the problem of atmospheric pollution? And of water pollution?

¿Qué medidas generales se pueden adoptar para conservar la naturaleza?

What general measures can be adopted to conserve nature?

¿Qué países producen más basura? ¿Cuáles consumen más recursos naturales?

What countries produce the most garbage? Consume more natural resources?

¿Perteneces a alguna organización dedicada a la conservación del medio ambiente?

Do you belong to an organization dedicated to environmental conservation?

¿Crees que son exagerados los datos sobre el calentamiento global del planeta?

Do you think the global warming data is exaggerated?

¿Crees que es todo una farsa? ¿Una exageración de los Verdes?

Do you think it is all a farce? An exaggeration of the Green Party?

¿Cómo afecta la tala de árboles al ecosistema?

How does the cutting of trees affect the ecosystem?

¿Cuáles son en tu opinión las principales causas del creciente deterioro medioambiental?

In your opinion, what are the main causes of the increasing environmental degradation?

¿De qué modo colaboras tú en la conservación de la naturaleza?

In what way do you help in the conservation of nature?

¿Quién tiene la culpa del deterioro medioambiental? ¿Hay algún culpable?

Whose fault is environmental degradation? Is anyone at fault?

DAR Y PEDIR DIRECCIONES

GIVING AND ASKING FOR DIRECTIONS

¿Por dónde se va al centro?

How do I get downtown?

Sigan todo recto/derecho hasta el final de esta calle.

Keep going straight until you get to the end of this street.

Luego doblen/giren a la derecha.

Then turn right.

Sigan tres cuadras y ya están en pleno centro.

Go three blocks and you'll be right downtown.

Señor, ¿sabe cómo llegar al Museo Nacional de Arte Contemporáneo?

Sir, do you know how to get to the National Museum of Contemporary Art?

Está en la otra punta de la ciudad.

It's on the other side of the city.

Está demasiado lejos para ir caminando.

It's too far to walk.

Tienen que tomar el metro.

You need to take the subway.

Tomen la línea roja en dirección Colinas.

Take the red line towards Colinas.

Deben bajarse en la última parada.

You should get off at the last stop.

Luego deben tomar la línea amarilla en dirección Paseo Coral.

Then you need to take the yellow line towards Paseo Coral.

Y bajarse en la penúltima parada.

Get off at the next-to-last stop.

Todo el trayecto les tomará casi una hora y cuarto.

The whole trip should take you about an hour and a quarter.

Al salir del metro verán el Museo Nacional justo enfrente.	When you get out of the subway, you'll see the National Museum right in front of you.
Señora, ¿le importaría decirnos cómo llegar al Ayuntamiento?	Ma'am, would you mind telling us how to get to City Hall?
Es que somos turistas y queremos verlo todo.	We're tourists and we want to see everything.
Es mejor que no vayan caminando.	It's better not to walk.
Les recomiendo que tomen un taxi.	I recommend that you take a taxi.
¡Qué paciencia tiene con nosotros la gente de esta ciudad!	The people in this city are so patient with us!
Creo que debemos dejar de preguntar.	I think we should stop asking questions.
Esta ciudad es monstruosa, gigantesca y complicada.	This city is monstrous, gigantic, and complicated.
Y una de dos, o compramos un mapa o tomamos un autobús turístico.	One or the other: do we buy a map or take a tour bus?
Si es que queremos llegar a algún sitio.	If we want to get anywhere.
¿Qué opinas?	What do you think?
Me parece buena la idea del autobús turístico.	I think the tour bus idea is a good idea.

PREGUNTAS SOBRE NUTRICIÓN

QUESTIONS ABOUT NUTRITION

¿Cuántas calorías tiene este plato preparado?	How many calories does this prepared meal have?
¿Qué porcentaje de sodio tiene una lata de frijoles?	What percentage of sodium does a can of beans have?

¿Cuántos gramos de azúcar suele tener más o menos un jugo envasado?

How many grams of sugar, more ore less, does a container of juice have?

¿Qué alimentos son ricos en Vitamina A?

What foods are rich in Vitamin A?

¿Es verdad que el aceite de hígado de bacalao contiene Vitamina D?

Is it true that cod liver oil has Vitamin D?

¿Es verdad que la falta de hierro en la sangre causa anemia?

Is it true that a lack of iron in the blood causes anemia?

¿Para qué es importante la Vitamina C?

What is Vitamin C important for?

¿Por qué necesita el cuerpo vitaminas y minerales?

Why does the body need vitamins and minerals?

¿Es bueno ingerir fibra para evitar el estreñimiento?

Is it good to eat fiber to avoid constipation?

¿Por qué es mejor comer pan integral que pan blanco?

Why is it better to eat whole-wheat bread than white bread?

¿Qué alimentos son esenciales para llevar una dieta equilibrada?

What foods are essential to a balanced diet?

¿Qué alimentos deben ingerirse diariamente?

What foods should you eat daily?

¿Qué alimentos deben consumirse con moderación?

What foods should you eat in moderation?

¿Qué desventajas tiene la dieta vegetariana?

What drawbacks does a vegetarian diet have?

¿Qué ventajas tiene la dieta mediterránea?

What advantages does a Mediterranean diet have?

¿Qué alimentos constituyen la base de la dieta mediterránea?

What are the basic foods in a Mediterranean diet?

¿Qué dieta proporciona mayores ventajas para la salud?

What diet offers the most health advantages?

¿Qué es el colesterol?	What is cholesterol?
¿Qué alimentos son ricos en colesterol?	What foods are high in cholesterol?
¿Qué alimentos contienen elevados índices de colesterol?	What foods have high amounts of cholesterol?
¿Cuáles son los inconvenientes de la comida rápida?	What are the drawbacks of fast food?
¿Qué tipo de alimentación favorece el buen funcionamiento del organismo?	What kind of nutrition promotes the proper functioning of the body?
¿Qué sustancias son perjudiciales para la salud?	What substances are harmful to your health?
¿Qué comían nuestros antepasados?	What did our ancestors eat?
¿Cómo han evolucionado los hábitos alimenticios a lo largo de la historia?	How have nutritional habits evolved throughout history?

PREGUNTAS SOBRE LA FORMA FÍSICA Y MENTAL

QUESTIONS ABOUT PHYSICAL AND MENTAL WELL-BEING

¿Es el estar en forma una moda o un estilo de vida?	Is being in shape a fashion or a lifestyle?
¿Hasta qué punto es importante estar en forma?	How important is it to be in shape?
¿Qué es aconsejable hacer para mantenerse en forma?	What activities are advisable for staying in shape?
¿Qué es recomendable hacer para perder peso?	What is recommended for losing weight?
¿Hasta qué punto es importante mantener un peso adecuado?	How important is it to maintain an adecuete weight?
¿Por qué es aconsejable realizar algún tipo de actividad física?	Why is it advisable to keep up some kind of physical activity?

¿Es la obesidad una cuestión estética o un grave problema de salud?

Is obesity an issue of appearance or a serious health problem?

¿Qué inconvenientes presenta para la salud el estilo de vida de los países industrializados?

What disadvantages does the lifestyle of industrialized countries have to health?

¿Qué es el estrés?

What is stress?

¿Qué papel juega el estrés en la salud de la sociedad actual?

What role does stress play in the health of society today?

¿En qué medida puede afectar el medio ambiente a la salud?

To what extent can the environment affect health?

¿Qué condiciones medioambientales son perjudiciales para la salud?

What environmental conditions are hazardous to our health?

¿Debo preocuparme por lo que como/bebo?

Should I worry about what I eat/drink?

¿Qué puedo hacer para mantenerme en forma?

What can I do to stay in shape?

¿Debo vigilar mi peso?

Should I watch my weight?

¿Soy un fanático/una fanática de la nutrición?

Am I a nutrition fanatic?

¿Qué me preocupa más, el número de calorías que ingiero al día o el valor nutritivo de los alimentos que tomo?

What should I worry about more, the number of calories I take in every day or the nutritional value of the foods I eat?

¿Quiero vivir cien años? ¿Por qué?

Do I want to live a hundred years? Why?

PREGUNTAS SOBRE EL FUTURO LABORAL

QUESTIONS ABOUT YOUR FUTURE IN THE WORKPLACE

¿Qué piensas hacer cuando te gradúes?

What do you think you'll do after you graduate?

¿Piensas en el futuro o vives al día?	Do you think about the future, or do you live day to day?
¿Has pensado seriamente en tu futuro?	Have you thought seriously about your future?
¿De qué color lo ves?	And how do you see it?/What do you think it will be like?
¿Eres optimista o pesimista?	Are you an optimist or a pessimist?
¿Te gustan los retos?	Do you like challenges?
¿Te interesa correr riesgos?	Are you interested in taking risks?
¿Cuál es tu trabajo/profesión ideal?	What is your ideal job/ profession?
¿Qué buscas en un trabajo? ¿Y en un jefe o jefa?	What do you look for in a job? And in a boss?
¿Qué alicientes crees que ofrece el mundo del trabajo?	What incentives/attractions do you think the working world offers?
¿Quieres ganar mucho dinero?	Do you want to earn a lot of money?
¿Podrías vivir sin dinero?	Could you live without money?
¿Qué tipo de trabajo buscas?	What kind of job are you looking for?
¿En qué tipo de ambiente laboral piensas?	What kind of work atmosphere are you thinking about?
¿Estás impaciente por salir de la universidad e incorporarte al mundo laboral?	Are you eager to leave school and enter the working world?
¿Eres una persona responsable?	Are you a responsible person?
¿Crees que trabajar es más interesante que estudiar?	Do you think working is more interesting than studying?

257

¿Has asistido ya a alguna entrevista de trabajo?	Have you gone on a job interview yet?
¿Cuáles consideras tus puntos fuertes?	What do you consider your strong points to be?
¿Cuáles crees que son tus puntos débiles?	What do you think your weak points are?
¿Buscas un trabajo creativo, de atención al público o de dirección?	What kind of job are you looking for, a creative one, one where you have to work with the public, or a managerial one?
¿Buscas un trabajo vocacional o uno puramente lucrativo?	Are you looking for a job you love, or just one that will make a lot of money?
¿Para qué tipo de trabajo crees que estás mejor preparado?	For what type of job do you think you are best prepared?
¿Qué crees que puedes ofrecer?	What do you think you have to offer?
¿Qué esperas recibir a cambio?	What do expect to get in return?
¿Cuál es tu meta u objetivo principal?	What is your main goal or objective?
¿Hasta dónde quieres llegar?	How far do you want to go?
¿Qué estás dispuesto/a a arriesgar para conseguirlo?	What are you willing to risk to get there?
¿Qué precio estás dispuesto/a a pagar?	What price are you willing to pay?
¿Cuáles serían tus prioridades?	What would your priorities be?
¿Estarías interesado/a en trabajar horas extras?	Would you be interested in working extra hours?
En caso afirmativo, ¿esperarías algo a cambio?	If so, would you expect something in return?
¿Por qué cualidades te gustaría ser recordado?	For what qualities would you like to be remembered?

258

¿Cómo te gustaría pasar a la historia?

How would you like to go down in history?

¿O prefieres vivir tranquilo/a y pasar desapercibido/a?

Or do you prefer to live quietly and go unnoticed?

LAS ARTES

THE ARTS

¿Para qué sirve el arte?

What is art for?

¿Qué significa el término artista?

What does the term "artist" mean?

¿Para qué usa el arte el/la "artista"?

What does an artist use art for?

¿Cuál es la misión del/de la artista?

What is the artist's mission?

¿Son los artistas egocentristas?

Are artists egocentric/self-centered?

¿Son realistas los artistas?

Are artists realists?

¿Envidias la vida del/de la artista?

Do you envy the life of an artist?

¿Tienes tú madera de artista?

Do you have what it takes to be an artist?

¿Qué significa la expresión "trabajar por amor al arte"?

What does the expression "to work for the love of art" mean?

¿Por qué llaman al cine el séptimo arte?

Why do they call film the seventh art?

¿Crees que una imagen vale más que mil palabras?

Do you think a picture is worth a thousand words?

¿Te gusta ver películas extranjeras en versión original subtitulada?

Do you like to see foreign films in the original language with subtitles?

¿Cómo expresas lo que piensas, lo que sientes, lo que quieres, lo que te gusta?

How do you express what you think, feel, want, and like?

¿Eres aficionado/a a la pintura?

Are you a painting aficionado?

¿Estás familiarizado/a con el surrealismo? ¿Y con el cubismo?

Are you familiar with surrealism? With cubism?

¿Qué otras tendencias artísticas conoces? ¿Cuáles te interesan más? ¿Por qué?

What other artistic movements do you know about? Which ones interest you the most? Why?

¿Te gusta o te gustaría coleccionar objetos de arte?

Do you or would you like to collect works of art?

¿Pagarías cincuenta millones de dólares por un original de Picasso?

Would you pay fifty million dollars for a Picasso original?

¿Eres amante de la música?

Are you a music lover?

¿A qué sentidos seduce la música?

Which senses does music affect?

¿Qué se necesita para disfrutar del arte?

What do you need to enjoy art?

¿Hace falta un sexto sentido?

Do you need a sixth sense?

¿Sin cuál de los cinco sentidos no podrías vivir?

Which of the five senses could you not live without?

¿Qué tipo de música está de moda entre la juventud actual?

What kind of music is popular with today's youth?

Y por último, la pregunta del millón, ¿Beatles o Rolling Stones?

And finally, the million-dollar question, the Beatles or the Rolling Stones?

PREGUNTAS SOBRE LAS ACTUALIDADES

QUESTIONS ABOUT CURRENT EVENTS

¿Estás al día?

Are you up to date?

¿Qué dicen hoy los periódicos?

What do the newspapers say today?

¿Has leído las últimas noticias?

Have you read the latest news?

¿Te interesa la política? ¿Por qué?	Are you interested in politics? Why?
¿Estás al día de lo que pasa en tu país? ¿Y en el resto del mundo?	Are you up to date with what's happening in your country? And in the rest of the world?
¿Qué temas sociales y políticos te preocupan?	What social and political topics concern you?
Si fueras político/a, ¿qué medidas tomarías para solucionar los problemas actuales del medio ambiente?	If you were a politician, what measures would you take to solve the current environmental problems?
¿Sigues de cerca la actualidad (política)?	Do you follow current events (politics) closely?
¿Lees las noticias internacionales?	Do you read international news?
¿Te interesa la política exterior?	Does foreign politics interest you?
¿(Te) Crees todo lo que lees en los periódicos?	Do you believe everything you read in the newspapers?
¿Te consideras una persona bien informada?	Do you consider yourself well-informed?
¿Crees que estamos bien informados?	Do you think we are well-informed?
¿Cómo es posible digerir tanta información?	How can one take in so much information?
En tu opinión, ¿qué cualidades debe tener un buen político/una buena política?	In your opinion, what qualities should a good politician have?
¿Qué harías si fueras presidente de los Estados Unidos?	What would you do if you were president of the United States?
¿Cuáles crees que son las causas principales de la violencia?	What do you think the principal causes of violence are?

¿Qué opinas de las campañas electorales/publicitarias?	What do you think of electoral/publicity campaigns?
¿Crees que los políticos tienen demasiado poder?	Do you think politicians have too much power?
¿Crees que el poder corrompe?	Do you think that power corrupts?
¿Qué opinas de la sociedad actual?	What do you think about present-day society?
¿Cómo valoras los últimos avances de la tecnología?	What do you think of/How do you rate the latest technology advances?
¿Ha avanzado el ser humano al mismo ritmo que la tecnología?	Have human beings advanced at the same rate as technology?
¿Qué avances positivos se lograron a lo largo del siglo XX?	What positive advances were made over the course of the 20th century?
¿Qué cuestiones te gustaría ver resueltas en el siglo XXI?	What issues would you like to see resolved in the 21st century?
¿Confías en los líderes políticos de tu país?	Do you trust the political leaders of your country?
¿Qué papel crees que juega el dinero en la sociedad actual?	What role do you think money plays in present-day society?
¿Hasta qué punto crees que los medios de comunicación influyen en la visión que tenemos del mundo?	To what extent do you think that the media influence our world view?
¿Crees que está bien repartida la riqueza del planeta?	Do you think the wealth of the planet is well distributed?
¿Hay problemas de discriminación en tu ciudad y/o país?	Are there discrimination problems in your city and/or country?
¿Crees que vivimos en un mundo justo y solidario?	Do you think we live in a just and supportive world?

¿Qué medidas tomarías para que el mundo fuera un lugar mejor para todos?

What measures would you take so that the world would be a better place for everyone?

¿Quién tiene la última palabra?

Who has the last word?

Verb conjugation tables

The verb lists

The list of verbs below and the model-verb tables that start on page 270 show you how to conjugate every verb taught in **VISTAS, AVENTURAS,** and **INVITACIONES.** Each verb in the list is followed by a model verb that is conjugated according to the same pattern. The number in parentheses indicates where in the tables you can find the conjugated forms of the model verb. If you want to find out how to conjugate **divertirse,** for example, look up number 33, **sentir,** the model for verbs that follow the e:ie stem-change pattern.

abrazar (z:c) like cruzar (37)

abrir like vivir (3) *except* past participle is abierto

aburrir(se) like vivir (3)

acabar de like hablar (1)

acampar like hablar (1)

aceptar like hablar (1)

acompañar like hablar (1)

aconsejar like hablar (1)

acordarse (o:ue) like contar (24)

acostarse (o:ue) like contar (24)

adelgazar (z:c) like cruzar (37)

afeitarse like hablar (1)

ahorrar like hablar (1)

alegrarse like hablar (1)

aliviar like hablar (1)

almorzar (o:ue) like contar (24) *except* (z:c)

alquilar like hablar (1)

andar like hablar (1) *except* preterite stem is anduv-

anunciar like hablar (1)

apagar (g:gu) like llegar (41)

aplaudir like vivir (3)

apreciar like hablar (1)

aprender like comer (2)

apurarse like hablar (1)

armar like hablar (1)

arrancar (c:qu) like tocar (43)

arreglar like hablar (1)

asistir like vivir (3)

aumentar like hablar (1)

ayudar(se) like hablar (1)

bailar like hablar (1)

bajar(se) like hablar (1)

bañarse like hablar (1)

barrer like comer (2)

beber like comer (2)

besar(se) like hablar (1)

borrar like hablar (1)

brindar like hablar (1)

bucear like hablar (1)

buscar (c:qu) like tocar (43)

caber (4)

caer(se) (5)

calentarse (e:ie) like pensar (30)

calzar (z:c) like cruzar (37)

cambiar like hablar (1)

caminar like hablar (1)

cantar like hablar (1)

casarse like hablar (1)

castigar like hablar (1)

cazar (z:c) like cruzar (37)

celebrar like hablar (1)

cenar like hablar (1)

How to use the verb tables

In the tables you will find the infinitive, present and past participles, and all the simple forms of each model verb. The formation of the compound tenses of any verb can be inferred from the table of compound tenses, pages 270–271, either by combining the past participle of the verb with a conjugated form of **haber** or by combining the present participle with a conjugated form of **estar**.

cepillarse like hablar (1)

cerrar (e:ie) like pensar (30)

chocar (c:qu) like tocar (43)

cobrar like hablar (1)

cocinar like hablar (1)

colorear like hablar (1)

comenzar (e:ie) (z:c) like empezar (26)

comer (2)

compartir like vivir (3)

comprar like hablar (1)

comprender like comer (2)

comprometerse like comer (2)

comunicarse (c:qu) like tocar (43)

conducir (c:zc) (6)

confirmar like hablar (1)

conocer (c:zc) (35)

conseguir (e:i)
like seguir (32)

conservar like hablar (1)

consumir like vivir (3)

contaminar like hablar (1)

contar (o:ue) (24)

controlar like hablar (1)

correr like comer (2)

cortar like hablar (1)

costar (o:ue) like contar (24)

creer (y) (36)

cruzar (z:c) (37)

cubrir like vivir (3) *except* past participle is cubierto

cuidar(se) like hablar (1)

cumplir like vivir (3)

dañar like hablar (1)

dar(se) (7)

deber like comer (2)

decidir like vivir (3)

decir (e:i) (8)

declarar like hablar (1)

dejar like hablar (1)

depositar like hablar (1)

desarrollar like hablar (1)

desayunar like hablar (1)

descansar like hablar (1)

descargar like hablar (1)

descomponer(se) like poner(se) (15)

describir like vivir (3) *except* past participle is descrito

descubrir like vivir (3) *except* past participle is descubierto

desear like hablar (1)

despedirse (e:i) like pedir (29)

despertarse (e:ie)
like pensar (30)

destruir (y) (38)

dibujar like hablar (1)

dirigir (g:j) like vivir (3) *except* (g:j)

discutir like vivir (3)

disfrazar(se) like hablar (1)
disfrutar like hablar (1)
divertirse (e:ie) like sentir (33)
divorciarse like hablar (1)
doblar like hablar (1)
doler (o:ue) like volver (34) *except* past participle is regular
dormir(se) (o:ue) (25)
ducharse like hablar (1)
dudar like hablar (1)
durar like hablar (1)
echar like hablar (1)
elegir (e:i) like pedir (29) *except* (g:j)
embarazarse like hablar (1)
emitir like vivir (3)
empezar (e:ie) (z:c) (26)
empujar like hablar (1)
enamorarse like hablar (1)
encantar like hablar (1)
encontrar(se) (o:ue) like contar (24)
enfermarse like hablar (1)
engordar like hablar (1)
enojarse like hablar (1)
enseñar like hablar (1)
ensuciar like hablar (1)
entender (e:ie) (27)
entrar like hablar (1)
entregar like hablar (1) *except* (g:gu)
entrenarse like hablar (1)
entrevistar like hablar (1)
enviar (envío) (39)
escalar like hablar (1)
escoger (g:j) like proteger (42)
escribir like vivir (3) *except* past participle is escrito
escuchar like hablar (1)
esculpir like vivir (3)
esperar like hablar (1)
esquiar (esquío) like enviar (39)
establecer (c:zc) like conocer (35)
estacionar(se) like hablar (1)
estar (9)
estornudar like hablar (1)
estudiar like hablar (1)

evitar like hablar (1)
explicar (c:qu) like tocar (43)
explorar like hablar (1)
faltar like hablar (1)
fascinar like hablar (1)
firmar like hablar (1)
frenar like hablar (1)
fumar like hablar (1)
funcionar like hablar (1)
ganar like hablar (1)
gastar like hablar (1)
grabar like hablar (1)
graduarse (gradúo) (40)
guardar like hablar (1)
gustar like hablar (1)
haber (hay) (10)
hablar (1)
hacer (11)
iluminar like hablar (1)
importar like hablar (1)
imprimir like vivir (3)
informar like hablar (1)
insistir like vivir (3)
interesar like hablar (1)
invertir (e:ie) like sentir (33)
invitar like hablar (1)
ir(se) (12)
jubilarse like hablar (1)
jugar (u:ue) (g:gu) (28)
juntar(se) like hablar (1)
lastimarse like hablar (1)
lavar(se) like hablar (1)
leer (y) like creer (36)
levantar(se) like hablar (1)
limpiar like hablar (1)
llamar(se) like hablar (1)
llegar (g:gu) (41)
llenar like hablar (1)
llevar(se) like hablar (1)
llover (o:ue) like volver (34) *except* past participle is regular
luchar like hablar (1)
mandar like hablar (1)
manejar like hablar (1)
mantener(se) (e:ie) like tener (20)

maquillarse like hablar (1)
mejorar like hablar (1)
merendar (e:ie) like pensar (30)
mirar like hablar (1)
molestar like hablar (1)
montar like hablar (1)
morir (o:ue) like dominar (25) *except* past participle is muerto
mostrar (o:ue) like contar (24)
mudarse like hablar (1)
nacer (c:zc) like conocer (35)
nadar like hablar (1)
navegar (g:gu) like llegar (41)
necesitar like hablar (1)
negar (e:ie) like pensar (30) *except* (g:gu)
nevar (e:ie) like pensar (30)
obedecer (c:zc) like conocer (35)
obtener (e:ie) like tener (20)
ocurrir like vivir (3)
odiar like hablar (1)
ofrecer (c:zc) like conocer (35)
oír (13)
olvidar like hablar (1)
pagar (g:gu) like llegar (41)
parar(se) like hablar (1)
parecer (c:zc) like conocer (35)
pasar(se) like hablar (1)
pasear like hablar (1)
patinar like hablar (1)
pedir (e:i) (29)
pegar like hablar (1) *except* (g:gu)
peinarse like hablar (1)
pelearse like hablar (1)
pensar(se) (e:ie) (30)
perder (e:ie) like entender (27)
pescar (c:qu) like tocar (43)
pintar(se) like hablar (1)
planchar like hablar (1)
poder (o:ue) (14)
ponchar(se) like hablar (1)
poner(se) (15)
portar(se) like hablar (1)
practicar (c:qu) like tocar (43)
preferir (e:ie) like sentir (33)

preguntar like hablar (1)
preocuparse like hablar (1)
preparar like hablar (1)
presentar like hablar (1)
prestar like hablar (1)
probar(se) (o:ue) like contar (24)
prohibir like vivir (3)
prometer like comer (2)
proteger (g:j) (42)
publicar (c:qu) like tocar (43)
quedar(se) like hablar (1)
quemar like hablar (1)
querer (e:ie) (16)
quitar(se) like hablar (1)
rasurar(se) like hablar (1)
recetar like hablar (1)
recibir(se) like vivir (3)
reciclar like hablar (1)
recoger (g:j) like proteger (42)
recomendar (e:ie) like pensar (30)
recordar (o:ue) like contar (24)
reducir (c:zc) like conducir (6)
regalar like hablar (1)
regañar like hablar (1)
regatear like hablar (1)
regresar like hablar (1)
reír(se) (e:i) (31)
relajarse like hablar (1)
renunciar like hablar (1)
repetir (e:i) like pedir (29)
resolver (o:ue) like volver (34)
respirar like hablar (1)
revisar like hablar (1)
rogar (o:ue) like contar (24) *except* (g:gu)
romper(se) like comer (2) *except* past participle is roto
saber (17)
sacar (c:qu) like tocar (43)
sacudir like vivir (3)
salir(se) (18)
saltar like hablar (1)
saludar(se) like hablar (1)
secar(se) (c:q) like tocar (43)
seguir (e:i) (32)

sentarse (e:ie) like pensar (30)
sentir(se) (e:ie) (33)
separarse like hablar (1)
ser (19)
servir (e:i) like pedir (29)
solicitar like hablar (1)
sonar (o:ue) like contar (24)
sonreír (e:i) like reír(se) (31)
sorprender like comer (2)

subir(se) like vivir (3)
sudar like hablar (1)
sufrir like vivir (3)
sugerir (e:ie) like sentir (33)
suponer like poner (15)
temer like comer (2)
tener (e:ie) (20)
terminar like hablar (1)
tocar (c:qu) (43)

tomar like hablar (1)

torcerse (o:ue) like volver (34)
except (c:z) and past participle is
regular; e.g. yo me tuerzo

toser like comer (2)

trabajar like hablar (1)

traducir (c:zc) like conducir (6)

traer (21)

transmitir like vivir (3)

tratar like hablar (1)

usar like hablar (1)

vender like comer (2)

venir (e:ie) (22)

ver (23)

vestirse (e:i) (44)

viajar like hablar (1)

visitar like hablar (1)

vivir (3)

volver (o:ue) (34)

votar like hablar (1)

Regular verbs: simple tenses

		INDICATIVE			
Infinitive	**Present**	**Imperfect**	**Preterite**	**Future**	
1 hablar	hablo	hablaba	hablé	hablaré	
	hablas	hablabas	hablaste	hablarás	
Participles:	habla	hablaba	habló	hablará	
hablando	hablamos	hablábamos	hablamos	hablaremos	
hablado	habláis	hablabais	hablasteis	hablaréis	
	hablan	hablaban	hablaron	hablarán	
2 comer	como	comía	comí	comeré	
	comes	comías	comiste	comerás	
Participles:	come	comía	comió	comerá	
comiendo	comemos	comíamos	comimos	comeremos	
comido	coméis	comíais	comisteis	comeréis	
	comen	comían	comieron	comerán	
3 vivir	vivo	vivía	viví	viviré	
	vives	vivías	viviste	vivirás	
Participles:	vive	vivía	vivió	vivirá	
viviendo	vivimos	vivíamos	vivimos	viviremos	
vivido	vivís	vivíais	vivisteis	viviréis	
	viven	vivían	vivieron	vivirán	

All verbs: compound tenses

PERFECT TENSES					
INDICATIVE					
Present Perfect		**Past Perfect**		**Future Perfect**	
he		había		habré	
has		habías		habrás	
ha	hablado	había	hablado	habrá	hablado
hemos	comido	habíamos	comido	habremos	comido
habéis	vivido	habíais	vivido	habréis	vivido
han		habían		habrán	

INDICATIVE	SUBJUNCTIVE		IMPERATIVE
Conditional	Present	Past	
hablaría	hable	hablara	
hablarías	hables	hablaras	habla (no hables)
hablaría	hable	hablara	hable
hablaríamos	hablemos	habláramos	hablemos
hablaríais	habléis	hablarais	hablad (no habléis)
hablarían	hablen	hablaran	hablen
comería	coma	comiera	
comerías	comas	comieras	come (no comas)
comería	coma	comiera	coma
comeríamos	comamos	comiéramos	comamos
comeríais	comáis	comierais	comed (no comáis)
comerían	coman	comieran	coman
viviría	viva	viviera	
vivirías	vivas	vivieras	vive (no vivas)
viviría	viva	viviera	viva
viviríamos	vivamos	viviéramos	vivamos
viviríais	viváis	vivierais	vivid (no viváis)
vivirían	vivan	vivieran	vivan

PERFECT TENSES

INDICATIVE	SUBJUNCTIVE	
Conditional Perfect	Present Perfect	Past Perfect
habría habrías habría habríamos habríais habrían } hablado comido vivido	haya hayas haya hayamos hayáis hayan } hablado comido vivido	hubiera hubieras hubiera hubiéramos hubierais hubieran } hablado comido vivido

PROGRESSIVE TENSES

INDICATIVE

Present Progressive		Past Progressive		Future Progressive	
estoy estás está estamos estáis estan	} hablando comiendo viviendo	estaba estabas estaba estábamos estabais estaban	} hablando comiendo viviendo	estaré estarás estará estaremos estaréis estarán	} hablando comiendo viviendo

Irregular verbs

	Infinitive	INDICATIVE			
		Present	Imperfect	Preterite	Future
4	caber Participles: cabiendo cabido	**quepo** cabes cabe cabemos cabéis caben	cabía cabías cabía cabíamos cabíais cabían	**cupe** **cupiste** **cupo** **cupimos** **cupisteis** **cupieron**	**cabré** **cabrás** **cabrá** **cabremos** **cabréis** **cabrán**
5	caer(se) Participles: **cayendo** **caído**	**caigo** caes cae caemos caéis caen	**caía** **caías** **caía** **caíamos** **caíais** **caían**	**caí** **caíste** **cayó** **caímos** **caísteis** **cayeron**	caeré caerás caerá caeremos caeréis caerán
6	conducir (c:zc) Participles: conduciendo conducido	**conduzco** conduces conduce conducimos conducís conducen	conducía conducías conducía conducíamos conducíais conducían	**conduje** **condujiste** **condujo** **condujimos** **condujisteis** **condujeron**	conduciré conducirás conducirá conduciremos conduciréis conducirán

PROGRESSIVE TENSES

	SUBJUNCTIVE	
Conditional Progressive	Present Progressive	Past Progressive
estaría estarías estaría estaríamos estaríais estarían } hablando comiendo viviendo	esté estés esté estemos estéis estén } hablando comiendo viviendo	estuviera estuvieras estuviera estuviéramos estuvierais estuvieran } hablando comiendo viviendo

	SUBJUNCTIVE		IMPERATIVE
Conditional	Present	Past	
cabría cabrías cabría cabríamos cabríais cabrían	quepa quepas quepa quepamos quepáis quepan	cupiera cupieras cupiera cupiéramos cupierais cupieran	cabe (no quepas) quepa quepamos cabed (no quepáis) quepan
caería caerías caería caeríamos caeríais caerían	caiga caigas caiga caigamos caigáis caigan	cayera cayeras cayera cayéramos cayerais cayeran	cae (no caigas) caiga caigamos caed (no caigáis) caigan
conduciría conducirías conduciría conduciríamos conduciríais conducirían	conduzca conduzcas conduzca conduzcamos conduzcáis conduzcan	condujera condujeras condujera condujéramos condujerais condujeran	conduce (no conduzcas) conduzca conduzcamos conducid (no conduzcáis) conduzcan

		INDICATIVE			
	Infinitive	**Present**	**Imperfect**	**Preterite**	**Future**
7	dar	**doy**	daba	**di**	daré
		das	dabas	**diste**	darás
	Participles:	da	daba	**dio**	dará
	dando	damos	dábamos	**dimos**	daremos
	dado	dais	dabais	**disteis**	daréis
		dan	daban	**dieron**	darán
8	decir (e:i)	**digo**	decía	**dije**	**diré**
		dices	decías	**dijiste**	**dirás**
	Participles:	**dice**	decía	**dijo**	**dirá**
	diciendo	decimos	decíamos	**dijimos**	**diremos**
	dicho	decís	decíais	**dijisteis**	**diréis**
		dicen	decían	**dijeron**	**dirán**
9	estar	**estoy**	estaba	**estuve**	estaré
		estás	estabas	**estuviste**	estarás
	Participles:	**está**	estaba	**estuvo**	estará
	estando	estamos	estábamos	**estuvimos**	estaremos
	estado	**estáis**	estabais	**estuvisteis**	estaréis
		están	estaban	**estuvieron**	estarán
10	haber	**he**	había	**hube**	**habré**
		has	habías	**hubiste**	**habrás**
	Participles:	**ha**	había	**hubo**	**habrá**
	habiendo	**hemos**	habíamos	**hubimos**	**habremos**
	habido	habéis	habíais	**hubisteis**	**habréis**
		han	habían	**hubieron**	**habrán**
11	hacer	**hago**	hacía	**hice**	**haré**
		haces	hacías	**hiciste**	**harás**
	Participles:	hace	hacía	**hizo**	**hará**
	haciendo	hacemos	hacíamos	**hicimos**	**haremos**
	hecho	hacéis	hacíais	**hicisteis**	**haréis**
		hacen	hacían	**hicieron**	**harán**
12	ir	**voy**	iba	**fui**	iré
		vas	ibas	**fuiste**	irás
	Participles:	**va**	iba	**fue**	irá
	yendo	**vamos**	íbamos	**fuimos**	iremos
	ido	**vais**	ibais	**fuisteis**	iréis
		van	iban	**fueron**	irán
13	oír (y)	**oigo**	oía	**oí**	oiré
		oyes	oías	**oíste**	oirás
	Participles:	**oye**	oía	**oyó**	oirá
	oyendo	oímos	oíamos	**oímos**	oiremos
	oído	oís	oíais	**oísteis**	oiréis
		oyen	oían	**oyeron**	oirán

	SUBJUNCTIVE		IMPERATIVE
Conditional	**Present**	**Past**	
daría	dé	diera	
darías	des	dieras	da (no des)
daría	dé	diera	dé
daríamos	demos	diéramos	demos
daríais	deis	dierais	dad (no deis)
darían	den	dieran	den
diría	diga	dijera	
dirías	digas	dijeras	di (no digas)
diría	diga	dijera	diga
diríamos	digamos	dijéramos	digamos
diríais	digáis	dijerais	decid (no digáis)
dirían	digan	dijeran	digan
estaría	esté	estuviera	
estarías	estés	estuvieras	está (no estés)
estaría	esté	estuviera	esté
estaríamos	estemos	estuviéramos	estemos
estaríais	estéis	estuvierais	estad (no estéis)
estarían	estén	estuvieran	estén
habría	haya	hubiera	
habrías	hayas	hubieras	
habría	haya	hubiera	
habríamos	hayamos	hubiéramos	
habríais	hayáis	hubierais	
habrían	hayan	hubieran	
haría	haga	hiciera	
harías	hagas	hicieras	haz (no hagas)
haría	haga	hiciera	haya
haríamos	hagamos	hiciéramos	hayamos
haríais	hagáis	hicierais	haced (no hayáis)
harían	hagan	hicieran	hayan
iría	vaya	fuera	
irías	vayas	fueras	ve (no vayas)
iría	vaya	fuera	vaya
iríamos	vayamos	fuéramos	vayamos
iríais	vayáis	fuerais	id (no vayáis)
irían	vayan	fueran	vayan
oiría	oiga	oyera	
oirías	oigas	oyeras	oye (no oigas)
oiría	oiga	oyera	oiga
oiríamos	oigamos	oyéramos	oigamos
oiríais	oigáis	oyerais	oíd (no oigáis)
oirían	oigan	oyeran	oigan

	Infinitive	INDICATIVE			
		Present	Imperfect	Preterite	Future
14	poder (o:ue)	puedo	podía	pude	podré
		puedes	podías	pudiste	podrás
	Participles:	puede	podía	pudo	podrá
	pudiendo	podemos	podíamos	pudimos	podremos
	podido	podéis	podíais	pudisteis	podréis
		pueden	podían	pudieron	podrán
15	poner	pongo	ponía	puse	pondré
		pones	ponías	pusiste	pondrás
	Participles:	pone	ponía	puso	pondrá
	poniendo	ponemos	poníamos	pusimos	pondremos
	puesto	ponéis	poníais	pusisteis	pondréis
		ponen	ponían	pusieron	pondrán
16	querer (e:ie)	quiero	quería	quise	querré
		quieres	querías	quisiste	querrás
	Participles:	quiere	quería	quiso	querrá
	queriendo	queremos	queríamos	quisimos	querremos
	querido	queréis	queríais	quisisteis	querréis
		quieren	querían	quisieron	querrán
17	saber	sé	sabía	supe	sabré
		sabes	sabías	supiste	sabrás
	Participles:	sabe	sabía	supo	sabrá
	sabiendo	sabemos	sabíamos	supimos	sabremos
	sabido	sabéis	sabíais	supisteis	sabréis
		saben	sabían	supieron	sabrán
18	salir	salgo	salía	salí	saldré
		sales	salías	saliste	saldrás
	Participles:	sale	salía	salió	saldrá
	saliendo	salimos	salíamos	salimos	saldremos
	salido	salís	salíais	salisteis	saldréis
		salen	salían	salieron	saldrán
19	ser	soy	era	fui	seré
		eres	eras	fuiste	serás
	Participles:	es	era	fue	será
	siendo	somos	éramos	fuimos	seremos
	sido	sois	erais	fuisteis	seréis
		son	eran	fueron	serán
20	tener (e:ie)	tengo	tenía	tuve	tendré
		tienes	tenías	tuviste	tendrás
	Participles:	tiene	tenía	tuvo	tendrá
	teniendo	tenemos	teníamos	tuvimos	tendremos
	tenido	tenéis	teníais	tuvisteis	tendréis
		tienen	tenían	tuvieron	tendrán

	SUBJUNCTIVE		IMPERATIVE
Conditional	Present	Past	
podría	pueda	pudiera	
podrías	puedas	pudieras	puede (no puedas)
podría	pueda	pudiera	pueda
podríamos	podamos	pudiéramos	podamos
podríais	podáis	pudierais	poded (no podáis)
podrían	puedan	pudieran	puedan
pondría	ponga	pusiera	
pondrías	pongas	pusieras	pon (no pongas)
pondría	ponga	pusiera	ponga
pondríamos	pongamos	pusiéramos	pongamos
pondríais	pongáis	pusierais	poned (no pongáis)
pondrían	pongan	pusieran	pongan
querría	quiera	quisiera	
querrías	quieras	quisieras	quiere (no quieras)
querría	quiera	quisiera	quiere
querríamos	queramos	quisiéramos	queramos
querríais	queráis	quisierais	quered (no queráis)
querrían	quieran	quisieran	quieran
sabría	sepa	supiera	
sabrías	sepas	supieras	sabe (no sepas)
sabría	sepa	supiera	sepa
sabríamos	sepamos	supiéramos	sepamos
sabríais	sepáis	supierais	sabed (no sepáis)
sabrían	sepan	supieran	sepan
saldría	salga	saliera	
saldrías	salgas	salieras	sal (no salgas)
saldría	salga	saliera	salga
saldríamos	salgamos	saliéramos	salgamos
saldríais	salgáis	salierais	salid (no salgáis)
saldrían	salgan	salieran	salgan
sería	sea	fuera	
serías	seas	fueras	sé (no seas)
sería	sea	fuera	sea
seríamos	seamos	fuéramos	seamos
seríais	seáis	fuerais	sed (no seáis)
serían	sean	fueran	sean
tendría	tenga	tuviera	
tendrías	tengas	tuvieras	ten (no tengas)
tendría	tenga	tuviera	tenga
tendríamos	tengamos	tuviéramos	tengamos
tendríais	tengáis	tuvierais	tened (no tengáis)
tendrían	tengan	tuvieran	tengan

		INDICATIVE			
Infinitive		Present	Imperfect	Preterite	Future
21 traer		**traigo**	**traía**	**traje**	traeré
		traes	**traías**	**trajiste**	traerás
Participles:		trae	**traía**	**trajo**	traerá
trayendo		traemos	**traíamos**	**trajimos**	traeremos
traído		traéis	**traíais**	**trajisteis**	traeréis
		traen	**traían**	**trajeron**	traerán
22 venir (e:ie)		**vengo**	venía	**vine**	**vendré**
		vienes	venías	**viniste**	**vendrás**
Participles:		**viene**	venía	**vino**	**vendrá**
viniendo		venimos	veníamos	**vinimos**	**vendremos**
venido		venís	veníais	**vinisteis**	**vendréis**
		vienen	venían	**vinieron**	**vendrán**
23 ver		**veo**	**veía**	**vi**	veré
		ves	**veías**	viste	verás
Participles:		ve	**veía**	vio	verá
viendo		vemos	**veíamos**	vimos	veremos
visto		veis	**veíais**	visteis	veréis
		ven	**veían**	vieron	verán

Stem-changing verbs

		INDICATIVE			
Infinitive		Present	Imperfect	Preterite	Future
24 contar (o:ue)		**cuento**	contaba	conté	contaré
		cuentas	contabas	contaste	contarás
Participles:		**cuenta**	contaba	contó	contará
contando		contamos	contábamos	contamos	contaremos
contado		contáis	contabais	contasteis	contaréis
		cuentan	contaban	contaron	contarán
25 dormir (o:ue)		**duermo**	dormía	dormí	dormiré
		duermes	dormías	dormiste	dormirás
Participles:		**duerme**	dormía	**dumió**	dormirá
durmiendo		dormimos	dormíamos	dormimos	dormiremos
dormido		dormís	dormíais	dormisteis	dormiréis
		duermen	dormían	**durmieron**	dormirán
26 empezar (e:ie) (c)		**empiezo**	empezaba	**empecé**	empezaré
		empiezas	empezabas	empezaste	empezarás
		empieza	empezaba	empezó	empezará
Participles:		empezamos	empezábamos	empezamos	empezaremos
empezando		empezáis	empezabais	empezasteis	empezaréis
empezado		**empiezan**	empezaban	empezaron	empezarán

	SUBJUNCTIVE		IMPERATIVE
Conditional	Present	Past	
traería	traiga	trajera	
traerías	traigas	trajeras	trae (no traigas)
traería	traiga	trajera	traiga
traeríamos	traigamos	trajéramos	traigamos
traeríais	traigáis	trajerais	traed (no traigáis)
traerían	traigan	trajeran	traigan
vendría	venga	viniera	
vendrías	vengas	vinieras	ven (no vengas)
vendría	venga	viniera	venga
vendríamos	vengamos	viniéramos	vengamos
vendríais	vengáis	vinierais	venid (no vengáis)
vendrían	vengan	vinieran	vengan
vería	vea	viera	
verías	veas	vieras	ve (no veas)
vería	vea	viera	vea
veríamos	veamos	viéramos	veamos
veríais	veáis	vierais	ved (no veáis)
verían	vean	vieran	vean

	SUBJUNCTIVE		IMPERATIVE
Conditional	Present	Past	
contaría	cuente	contara	
contarías	cuentes	contaras	cuenta (no cuentes)
contaría	cuente	contara	cuente
contaríamos	contemos	contáramos	contemos
contaríais	contéis	contarais	contad (no contéis)
contarían	cuenten	contaran	cuenten
dormiría	duerma	durmiera	
dormirías	duermas	durmieras	duerme (no duermas)
dormiría	duerma	durmiera	duerma
dormiríamos	durmamos	durmiéramos	durmamos
dormiríais	durmáis	durmierais	dormid (no durmáis)
dormirían	duerman	durmieran	duerman
empezaría	empiece	empezara	
empezarías	empieces	empezaras	empieza (no empieces)
empezaría	empiece	empezara	empiece
empezaríamos	empecemos	empezáramos	empecemos
empezaríais	empecéis	empezarais	empezad (no empecéis)
empezarían	empiecen	empezaran	empiecen

	Infinitive	INDICATIVE			
		Present	Imperfect	Preterite	Future
27	entender (e:ie)	**entiendo**	entendía	entendí	entenderé
		entiendes	entendías	entendiste	entenderás
		entiende	entendía	entendió	entenderá
	Participles:	entendemos	entendíamos	entendimos	entenderemos
	entendiendo	entendéis	entendíais	entendisteis	entenderéis
	entendido	**entienden**	entendían	entendieron	entenderán
28	jugar (u:ue)	**juego**	jugaba	**jugué**	jugaré
	(gu)	**juegas**	jugabas	jugaste	jugarás
		juega	jugaba	jugó	jugará
	Participles:	jugamos	jugábamos	jugamos	jugaremos
	jugando	jugáis	jugabais	jugasteis	jugaréis
	jugado	**juegan**	jugaban	jugaron	jugarán
29	pedir (e:i)	**pido**	pedía	pedí	pediré
		pides	pedías	pediste	pedirás
		pide	pedía	**pidió**	pedirá
	Participles:	pedimos	pedíamos	pedimos	pediremos
	pidiendo	pedís	pedíais	pedisteis	pediréis
	pedido	**piden**	pedían	**pidieron**	pedirán
30	pensar (e:ie)	**pienso**	pensaba	pensé	pensaré
		piensas	pensabas	pensaste	pensarás
		piensa	pensaba	pensó	pensará
	Participles:	pensamos	pensábamos	pensamos	pensaremos
	pensando	pensáis	pensabais	pensasteis	pensaréis
	pensado	**piensan**	pensaban	pensaron	pensarán
31	reír(se) (e:i)	**río**	reía	reí	reiré
		ríes	reías	reíste	reirás
	Participles:	**ríe**	reía	**rió**	reirá
	riendo	reímos	reíamos	reímos	reiremos
	reído	reís	reíais	reísteis	reiréis
		ríen	reían	**rieron**	reirán
32	seguir (e:i)	**sigo**	seguía	seguí	seguiré
	(gu)	**sigues**	seguías	seguiste	seguirás
		sigue	seguía	**siguió**	seguirá
	Participles:	seguimos	seguíamos	seguimos	seguiremos
	siguiendo	seguís	seguíais	seguisteis	seguiréis
	seguido	**siguen**	seguían	**siguieron**	seguirán
33	sentir (e:ie)	**siento**	sentía	sentí	sentiré
		sientes	sentías	sentiste	sentirás
	Participles:	**siente**	sentía	**sintió**	sentirá
	sintiendo	sentimos	sentíamos	sentimos	sentiremos
	sentido	sentís	sentíais	sentisteis	sentiréis
		sienten	sentían	**sintieron**	sentirán

	SUBJUNCTIVE		IMPERATIVE
Conditional	Present	Past	
entendería	**entienda**	entendiera	
entenderías	**entiendas**	entendieras	**entiende** (no **entiendas**)
entendería	**entienda**	entendiera	entienda
entenderíamos	entendamos	entendiéramos	entendamos
entenderíais	entendáis	entendierais	entended (no entendáis)
entenderían	**entiendan**	entendieran	**entiendan**
jugaría	**juegue**	jugara	
jugarías	**juegues**	jugaras	**juega** (no **juegues**)
jugaría	**juegue**	jugara	**juegue**
jugaríamos	**juguemos**	jugáramos	**juguemos**
jugaríais	**juguéis**	jugarais	jugad (no **juguéis**)
jugarían	**jueguen**	jugaran	**jueguen**
pediría	**pida**	**pidiera**	
pedirías	**pidas**	**pidieras**	**pide** (no **pidas**)
pediría	**pida**	**pidiera**	**pida**
pediríamos	**pidamos**	**pidiéramos**	**pidamos**
pediríais	**pidáis**	**pidierais**	pedid (no **pidais**)
pedirían	**pidan**	**pidieran**	**pidan**
pensaría	**piense**	pensara	
pensarías	**pienses**	pensaras	**piensa** (no **pienses**)
pensaría	**piense**	pensara	**piense**
pensaríamos	pensemos	pensáramos	pensemos
pensaríais	penséis	pensarais	pensad (no penséis)
pensarían	**piensen**	pensaran	**piensan**
reiría	**ría**	**riera**	
reirías	**rías**	**rieras**	**ríe** (no **rías**)
reiría	**ría**	**riera**	**ría**
reiríamos	**riamos**	**riéramos**	**riamos**
reiríais	**riáis**	**rierais**	reíd (no **riáis**)
reirían	**rían**	**rieran**	**rían**
seguiría	**siga**	**siguiera**	
seguirías	**sigas**	**siguieras**	**sigue** (no **sigas**)
seguiría	**siga**	**siguiera**	**siga**
seguiríamos	**sigamos**	**siguiéramos**	**sigamos**
seguiríais	**sigáis**	**siguierais**	seguid (no **sigáis**)
seguirían	**sigan**	**siguieran**	**sigan**
sentiría	**sienta**	**sintiera**	
sentirías	**sientas**	**sintieras**	**siente** (no **sientas**)
sentiría	**sienta**	**sintiera**	**sienta**
sentiríamos	**sintamos**	**sintiéramos**	**sintamos**
sentiríais	**sintáis**	**sintierais**	sentid (no **sintáis**)
sentirían	**sientan**	**sintieran**	**sientan**

		INDICATIVE			
Infinitive	**Present**	**Imperfect**	**Preterite**	**Future**	
34 volver (o:ue)	**vuelvo**	volvía	volví	volveré	
	vuelves	volvías	volviste	volverás	
Participles:	**vuelve**	volvía	volvió	volverá	
volviendo	volvemos	volvíamos	volvimos	volveremos	
vuelto	volvéis	volvíais	volvisteis	volveréis	
	vuelven	volvían	volvieron	volverán	

Verbs with spelling changes and reflexive verbs

		INDICATIVE			
Infinitive	**Present**	**Imperfect**	**Preterite**	**Future**	
35 conocer	**conozco**	conocía	conocí	conoceré	
(c:zc)	conoces	conocías	conociste	conocerás	
	conoce	conocía	conoció	conocerá	
Participles:	conocemos	conocíamos	conocimos	conoceremos	
conociendo	conocéis	conocíais	conocisteis	conoceréis	
conocido	conocen	conocían	conocieron	conocerán	
36 creer (y)	creo	creía	**creí**	creeré	
	crees	creías	**creíste**	creerás	
Participles:	cree	creía	**creyó**	creerá	
creyendo	creemos	creíamos	**creímos**	creeremos	
creído	creéis	creíais	**creísteis**	creeréis	
	creen	creían	**creyeron**	creerán	
37 cruzar (c)	cruzo	cruzaba	**crucé**	cruzaré	
	cruzas	cruzabas	cruzaste	cruzarás	
Participles:	cruza	cruzaba	cruzó	cruzará	
cruzando	cruzamos	cruzábamos	cruzamos	cruzaremos	
cruzado	cruzáis	cruzabais	cruzasteis	cruzaréis	
	cruzan	cruzaban	cruzaron	cruzarán	
38 destruir (y)	**destruyo**	destruía	destruí	destruiré	
	destruyes	destruías	destruiste	destruirás	
Participles:	**destruye**	destruía	**destruyó**	destruirá	
destruyendo	destruimos	destruíamos	destruimos	destruiremos	
destruido	destruís	destruíais	destruisteis	destruiréis	
	destruyen	destruían	**destruyeron**	destruirán	
39 enviar	**envío**	enviaba	envié	enviaré	
(envío)	**envías**	enviabas	enviaste	enviarás	
	envía	enviaba	envió	enviará	
Participles:	enviamos	enviábamos	enviamos	enviaremos	
enviando	enviáis	enviabais	enviasteis	enviaréis	
enviado	**envían**	enviaban	enviaron	enviarán	

	SUBJUNCTIVE		IMPERATIVE
Conditional	Present	Past	
volvería	**vuelva**	volviera	
volverías	**vuelvas**	volvieras	**vuelve** (no **vuelvas**)
volvería	**vuelva**	volviera	**vuelva**
volveríamos	volvamos	volviéramos	volvamos
volveríais	volváis	volvierais	volved (no volváis)
volverían	**vuelvan**	volvieran	**vuelvan**

	SUBJUNCTIVE		IMPERATIVE
Conditional	Present	Past	
conocería	**conozca**	conociera	
conocerías	**conozcas**	conocieras	conoce (no **conozcas**)
conocería	**conozca**	conociera	**conozca**
conoceríamos	**conozcamos**	conociéramos	**conozcamos**
conoceríais	**conozcáis**	conocierais	conoced (no **conozcáis**)
conocerían	**conozcan**	conocieran	**conozcan**
creería	crea	**creyera**	
creerías	creas	**creyeras**	cree (no creas)
creería	crea	**creyera**	crea
creeríamos	creamos	**creyéramos**	creamos
creeríais	creáis	**creyerais**	creed (no creáis)
creerían	crean	**creyeran**	crean
cruzaría	**cruce**	cruzara	
cruzarías	**cruces**	cruzaras	cruza (no **cruces**)
cruzaría	**cruce**	cruzara	**cruce**
cruzaríamos	**crucemos**	cruzáramos	**crucemos**
cruzaríais	**crucéis**	cruzarais	cruzad (no **crucéis**)
cruzarían	**crucen**	cruzaran	**crucen**
destruiría	**destruya**	**destruyera**	
destruirías	**destruyas**	**destruyeras**	**destruye** (no **destruyas**)
destruiría	**destruya**	**destruyera**	**destruya**
destruiríamos	**destruyamos**	**destruyéramos**	**destruyamos**
destruiríais	**destruyáis**	**destruyerais**	destruid (no **destruyáis**)
destruirían	**destruyan**	**destruyeran**	**destruyan**
enviaría	**envíe**	enviara	
enviarías	**envíes**	enviaras	**envía** (no **envíes**)
enviaría	**envíe**	enviara	**envíe**
enviaríamos	**enviemos**	enviáramos	enviemos
enviaríais	**enviéis**	enviarais	enviad (no enviéis)
enviarían	**envíen**	enviaran	**envíen**

	Infinitive	Present	Imperfect	Preterite	Future
40	graduarse (gradúo) Participles: graduando graduado	**gradúo** **gradúas** **gradúa** graduamos graduáis **gradúan**	graduaba graduabas graduaba graduábamos graduabais graduaban	gradué graduaste graduó graduamos graduasteis graduaron	graduaré graduarás graduará graduaremos graduaréis graduarán
41	llegar (gu) Participles: llegando llegado	llego llegas llega llegamos llegáis llegan	llegaba llegabas llegaba llegábamos llegabais llegaban	**llegué** llegaste llegó llegamos llegasteis llegaron	llegaré llegarás llegará llegaremos llegaréis llegarán
42	proteger (j) Participles: protegiendo protegido	**protejo** proteges protege protegemos protegéis protegen	protegía protegías protegía protegíamos protegíais protegían	protegí protegiste protegió protegimos protegisteis protegieron	protegeré protegerás protegerá protegeremos protegeréis protegerán
43	tocar (qu) Participles: tocando tocado	toco tocas toca tocamos tocáis tocan	tocaba tocabas tocaba tocábamos tocabais tocaban	**toqué** tocaste tocó tocamos tocasteis tocaron	tocaré tocarás tocará tocaremos tocaréis tocarán
44	vestirse (e:i) Participles: **vistiendo** vestido	**me visto** **te vistes** **se viste** nos vestimos os vestís **se visten**	me vestía te vestías se vestía nos vestíamos os vestíais se vestían	me vestí te vestiste **se vistió** nos vestimos os vestisteis **se vistieron**	me vestiré te vestirás se vestirá nos vestiremos os vestiréis se vestirán

	SUBJUNCTIVE		IMPERATIVE
Conditional	**Present**	**Past**	
graduaría	**gradúe**	graduara	
graduarías	**gradúes**	graduaras	**gradúa** (no **gradúes**)
graduaría	**gradúe**	graduara	**gradúe**
graduaríamos	graduemos	graduáramos	graduemos
graduaríais	**graduéis**	graduarais	graduad (no **graduéis**)
graduarían	**gradúen**	graduaran	**gradúen**
llegaría	**llegue**	llegara	
llegarías	**llegues**	llegaras	llega (no **llegues**)
llegaría	**llegue**	llegara	**llegue**
llegaríamos	**lleguemos**	llegáramos	**lleguemos**
llegaríais	**lleguéis**	llegarais	llegad (no **lleguéis**)
llegarían	**lleguen**	llegaran	**lleguen**
protegería	**proteja**	protegiera	
protegerías	**protejas**	protegieras	protege (no **protejas**)
protegería	**proteja**	protegiera	**proteja**
protegeríamos	**protejamos**	protegiéramos	**protejamos**
protegeríais	**protejáis**	protegierais	proteged (no **protejáis**)
protegerían	**protejan**	protegieran	**protejan**
tocaría	**toque**	tocara	
tocarías	**toques**	tocaras	toca (no **toques**)
tocaría	**toque**	tocara	**toque**
tocaríamos	**toquemos**	tocáramos	**toquemos**
tocaríais	**toquéis**	tocarais	tocad (no **toquéis**)
tocarían	**toquen**	tocaran	**toquen**
me vestiría	**me vista**	**me vistiera**	
te vestirías	**te vistas**	**te vistieras**	**vístete** (no te **vistas**)
se vestiría	**se vista**	**se vistiera**	**vístase**
nos vestiríamos	**nos vistamos**	**nos vistiéramos**	**vistámonos**
os vestiríais	**os vistáis**	**os vistierais**	vestíos (no os **vistáis**)
se vestirían	**se vistan**	**se vistieran**	**vístanse** Uds.

Sección de consulta
Reference Section

MATERIAS	ACADEMIC SUBJECTS
la administración de empresas	business administration
la agronomía	agriculture
el alemán	German
el álgebra	algebra
la anatomía	anatomy
la antropología	anthropology
la arqueología	archaeology
la arquitectura	architecture
el arte	art
la astronomía	astronomy
la biología	biology
la bioquímica	biochemistry
la botánica	botany
el cálculo	calculus
el chino	Chinese
las ciencias políticas	political science
la computación	computer science
las comunicaciones	communications
la contabilidad	accounting
la danza	dance
el derecho	law
la economía	economics
la educación	education
la educación física	physical education

la enfermería	nursing
el español	Spanish
la filosofía	philosophy
la física	physics
el francés	French
la geografía	geography
la geología	geology
el griego	Greek
el hebreo	Hebrew
la historia	history
la informática	computer science
la ingeniería	engineering
el inglés	English
el italiano	Italian
el japonés	Japanese
el latín	Latin
las lenguas clásicas	classical languages
las lenguas romances	romance languages
la lingüística	linguistics
la literatura	literature
las matemáticas	mathematics
la medicina	medicine
el mercadeo/la mercadotecnia	marketing
la música	music
los negocios	business
el periodismo	journalism

el portugués	Portuguese
la psicología	psychology
la química	chemistry
el ruso	Russian
los servicios sociales	social services
la sociología	sociology
el teatro	theater
la trigonometría	trigonometry
la zoología	zoology

LOS ANIMALES	**ANIMALS**
la abeja	bee
la araña	spider
la ardilla	squirrel
el ave (f.), el pájaro	bird
la ballena	whale
el burro	donkey
la cabra	goat
el caimán	alligator
el camello	camel
la cebra	zebra
el ciervo, el venado	deer
el cocodrilo	crocodile
el cochino, el cerdo, el puerco	pig
el conejo	rabbit
el coyote	coyote
la culebra, la serpiente,	snake

la víbora	
el elefante	elephant
la foca	seal
la gallina	hen
el gallo	rooster
el gato	cat
el gorila	gorilla
el hipopótamo	hippopotamus
la hormiga	ant
el insecto	insect
la jirafa	giraffe
el lagarto	lizard
el león	lion
el lobo	wolf
el loro, la cotorra, el papagayo, el perico	parrot
la mariposa	butterfly
el mono	monkey
la mosca	fly
el mosquito	mosquito
el oso	bear
la oveja	sheep
el pato	duck
el perro	dog
el pez	fish
la rana	frog

el ratón	mouse
el rinoceronte	rhinoceros
el saltamontes, el chapulín	grasshopper
el tiburón	shark
el tigre	tiger
el toro	bull
la tortuga	turtle
la vaca	cow
el zorro	fox

EL CUERPO HUMANO Y LA SALUD

THE HUMAN BODY AND HEALTH

EL CUERPO HUMANO

THE HUMAN BODY

la barba	beard
el bigote	mustache
la barriga, la panza, la guata	belly, tummy
la boca	mouth
el brazo	arm
la cabeza	head
la cadera	hip
la ceja	eyebrow
el cerebro	brain
la cintura	waist
el codo	elbow
el corazón	heart
la costilla	rib
el cráneo	skull

el cuello	neck
el dedo	finger
el dedo del pie	toe
la espalda	back
el estómago	stomach
la frente	forehead
la garganta	throat
el hombro	shoulder
el hueso	bone
el labio	lip
la lengua	tongue
la mandíbula	jaw
la mejilla	cheek
el mentón, la barba	chin
la muñeca	wrist
el músculo	muscle
el muslo	thigh
las nalgas, el trasero, las asentaderas	buttocks
la nariz	nose
el nervio	nerve
el oído	(inner) ear
el ojo	eye
el ombligo	navel, belly button
la oreja	(outer) ear
la pantorrilla	calf

el párpado	eyelid
el pecho	chest
la pestaña	eyelash
el pie	foot
la piel	skin
la pierna	leg
el pulgar	thumb
el pulmón	lung
la rodilla	knee
la sangre	blood
el talón	heel
el tobillo	ankle
el tronco	torso, trunk
la uña	fingernail
la uña del dedo del pie	toenail
la vena	vein

LOS CINCO SENTIDOS	THE FIVE SENSES
el gusto	taste
el oído	hearing
el olfato	smell
el tacto	touch
la vista	sight

LA SALUD	HEALTH
el accidente	accident
alérgico/a	allergic
el antibiótico	antibiotic

la aspirina	aspirin
el ataque cardiaco, el ataque al corazón	heart attack
el cáncer	cancer
la cápsula	capsule
la clínica	clinic
congestionado/a	congested
el consultorio	doctor's office
la curita	adhesive bandage
el/la dentista	dentist
el/la doctor(a), el/la médico/a	doctor
el dolor (de cabeza)	(head)ache, pain
embarazada	pregnant
la enfermedad	illness, disease
el/la enfermero/a	nurse
enfermo/a	ill, sick
la erupción	rash
el examen médico	physical exam
la farmacia	pharmacy
la fiebre	fever
la fractura	fracture
la gripe	flu
la herida	wound
el hospital	hospital
la infección	infection
la inyección	injection

el insomnio	insomnia
el jarabe	(cough) syrup
mareado/a	dizzy, nauseated
el medicamento	medication
la medicina	medicine
las muletas	crutches
la operación	operation
el/la paciente	patient
el/la paramédico/a	paramedic
la pastilla, la píldora	pill, tablet
los primeros auxilios	first aid
la pulmonía	pneumonia
los puntos	stitches
la quemadura	burn
el quirófano	operating room
la radiografía	X-ray
la receta	prescription
el resfriado	cold (illness)
la sala de emergencia(s)	emergency room
saludable	healthy, healthful
sano/a	healthy
el seguro médico	medical insurance
la silla de ruedas	wheelchair
el síntoma	symptom
el termómetro	thermometer
la tos	cough

la transfusión	transfusion
la vacuna	vaccination
la venda	bandage
el virus	virus
cortar(se)	to cut (oneself)
curar	to cure, to treat
desmayar(se)	to faint
enfermarse	to get sick
enyesar	to put in a cast
estornudar	to sneeze
guardar cama	to stay in bed
hinchar(se)	to swell
internar(se) en el hospital	to check into the hospital
lastimarse (el pie)	to hurt (one's foot)
mejorar(se)	to get better; to improve
operar	to operate
quemar(se)	to burn
respirar (hondo)	to breathe (deeply)
romperse (la pierna)	to break (one's leg)
sangrar	to bleed
sufrir	to suffer
tomarle la presión a alguien	to take someone's blood pressure
tomarle el pulso a alguien	to take someone's pulse
torcerse (el tobillo)	to sprain (one's ankle)
vendar	to bandage

EXPRESIONES ÚTILES PARA LA CLASE

USEFUL CLASSROOM EXPRESSIONS

PALABRAS ÚTILES

USEFUL WORDS

ausente	absent
el departamento	department
el dictado	dictation
la conversación, las conversaciones	conversation(s)
la expresión, las expresiones	expression(s)
el examen, los exámenes	test(s)
la frase	sentence
la hoja de actividades	activity sheet
el horario de clases	class schedule
la oración, las oraciones	sentence(s)
el párrafo	paragraph
la persona	person
presente	present
la prueba	quiz
siguiente	following
la tarea	homework

EXPRESIONES ÚTILES

USEFUL EXPRESSIONS

Abra(n) sus libros.	Open your book(s).
Cambien de papel.	Change roles.
Cierre(n) su(s) libro(s).	Close your books.
¿Cómo se dice ___ en español?	How do you say ___ in Spanish?
¿Cómo se escribe ___ en español?	How do you write ___ in Spanish?

296

¿Comprende(n)?	Do you understand?
(No) comprendo.	I (don't) understand.
Conteste(n) las preguntas.	Answer the questions.
Continúe(n), por favor.	Continue, please.
Escriba(n) su nombre.	Write your name.
Escuchen la cinta (el disco compacto).	Listen to the tape (compact disc).
Estudie(n) la lección tres.	Study lesson three.
Haga(n) la actividad (el ejercicio) número cuatro.	Do activity (exercise) number four.
Lea(n) la oración en voz alta.	Read the sentence aloud.
Levante(n) la mano.	Raise your hand(s).
Más despacio, por favor.	Slower, please.
No sé.	I don't know.
Páse(n)me los exámenes.	Pass me the tests.
¿Qué significa ___?	What does ___ mean?
Repita(n), por favor.	Repeat, please.
Siénte(n)se, por favor.	Sit down, please.
Siga(n) las instrucciones.	Follow the instructions.
¿Tiene(n) alguna pregunta?	Do you have any questions?
Vaya(n) a la página dos.	Go to page two.

COUNTRIES & NATIONALITIES

PAÍSES Y NACIONALIDADES (GENTILICIOS)

NORTH AMERICA	**NORTEAMÉRICA**	
Canada	**Canadá**	canadiense
Mexico	**México**	mexicano/a
United States	**Estados Unidos**	estadounidense
CENTRAL AMERICA	**CENTROAMÉRICA**	
Belize	**Belice**	beliceño/a
Costa Rica	**Costa Rica**	costarricense
El Salvador	**El Salvador**	salvadoreño/a
Guatemala	**Guatemala**	guatemalteco/a
Honduras	**Honduras**	hondureño/a
Nicaragua	**Nicaragua**	nicaragüense
Panama	**Panamá**	panameño/a
THE CARIBBEAN	**EL CARIBE**	
Cuba	**Cuba**	cubano/a
Dominican Republic	**República Dominicana**	dominicano/a
Haiti	**Haití**	haitiano/a
Puerto Rico	**Puerto Rico**	puertorriqueño/a
SOUTH AMERICA	**AMÉRICA DEL SUR**	
Argentina	**Argentina**	argentino/a
Bolivia	**Bolivia**	boliviano/a
Brazil	**Brasil**	brasileño/a
Chile	**Chile**	chileno/a
Colombia	**Colombia**	colombiano/a

Ecuador	**Ecuador**	**ecuatoriano/a**
Paraguay	**Paraguay**	**paraguayo/a**
Peru	**Perú**	**peruano/a**
Uruguay	**Uruguay**	**uruguayo/a**
Venezuela	**Venezuela**	**venezolano/a**
EUROPE	*EUROPA*	
Armenia	**Armenia**	**armenio/a**
Austria	**Austria**	**austríaco/a**
Belgium	**Bélgica**	**belga**
Bosnia	**Bosnia**	**bosnio/a**
Bulgaria	**Bulgaria**	**búlgaro/a**
Croatia	**Croacia**	**croata**
Czech Republic	**República Checa**	**checo/a**
Denmark	**Dinamarca**	**danés, danesa**
England	**Inglaterra**	**inglés, inglesa**
Estonia	**Estonia**	**estonio/a**
Finland	**Finlandia**	**finlandés, finlandesa**
France	**Francia**	**francés, francesa**
Germany	**Alemania**	**alemán, alemana**
Great Britain (United Kingdom)	**Gran Bretaña (Reino Unido)**	**británico**
Greece	**Grecia**	**griego/a**
Hungary	**Hungría**	**húngaro/a**
Iceland	**Islandia**	**islandés, islandesa**
Ireland	**Irlanda**	**irlandés, irlandesa**
Italy	**Italia**	**italiano/a**

Latvia	**Letonia**	**letón, letona**
Lithuania	**Lituania**	**lituano/a**
Netherlands (Holland)	**Países Bajos (Holanda)**	**holandés, holandesa**
Norway	**Noruega**	**noruego/a**
Poland	**Polonia**	**polaco/a**
Portugal	**Portugal**	**portugués, portuguesa**
Romania	**Rumania**	**rumano/a**
Russia	**Rusia**	**ruso/a**
Scotland	**Escocia**	**escocés, escocesa**
Serbia	**Serbia**	**serbio/a**
Slovakia	**Eslovaquia**	**eslovaco/a**
Slovenia	**Eslovenia**	**esloveno/a**
Spain	**España**	**español(a)**
Sweden	**Suecia**	**sueco/a**
Switzerland	**Suiza**	**suizo/a**
Ukraine	**Ucrania**	**ucranio/a, ucraniano/a**
Wales	**Gales**	**galés, galesa**
Yugoslavia	**Yugoslavia**	**yugoslavo/a**
ASIA	*ASIA*	
Bangladesh	**Bangladesh**	**bangladesí**
Cambodia	**Camboya**	**camboyano/a**
China	**China**	**chino/a**
India	**India**	**indio/a**
Indonesia	**Indonesia**	**indonesio/a**

Iran	**Irán**	iraní
Iraq	**Iraq, Irak**	iraquí
Israel	**Israel**	israelí
Japan	**Japón**	japonés, japonesa
Jordan	**Jordania**	jordano/a
Korea	**Corea**	coreano/a
Kuwait	**Kuwait**	kuwaití
Lebanon	**Líbano**	libanés, libanesa
Malaysia	**Malaisia**	malaisiano/a
Pakistan	**Pakistán**	pakistaní
Russia	**Rusia**	ruso/a
Saudi Arabia	**Arabia Saudí**	saudí
Singapore	**Singapur**	singapurés, singapuresa
Syria	**Siria**	sirio/a
Taiwan	**Taiwán**	taiwanés, taiwanesa
Thailand	**Tailandia**	tailandés, tailandesa
Turkey	**Turquía**	turco/a
Vietnam	**Vietnam**	vietnamita
AFRICA	*ÁFRICA*	
Algeria	**Argelia**	argelino/a
Angola	**Angola**	angolano/a
Cameroon	**Camerún**	camerunés, camerunesa
Congo	**Congo**	congolés, congolesa
Egypt	**Egipto**	egipcio/a
Equatorial Guinea	**Guinea Ecuatorial**	ecuatoguineano

Ethiopia	**Etiopía**	etíope
Ivory Coast	**Costa de Marfil**	ivoriano/a
Kenya	**Kenia, Kenya**	keniano/a
Libya	**Libia**	libio/a
Mali	**Malí**	malinqués, malinquesa
Morocco	**Marruecos**	marroquí
Mozambique	**Mozambique**	mozambicano
Nigeria	**Nigeria**	nigeriano/a
Rwanda	**Ruanda**	ruandés, ruandesa
Somalia	**Somalia**	somalí
South Africa	**Sudáfrica**	sudafricano/a
Sudan	**Sudán**	sudanés, sudanesa
Tunisia	**Tunicia, Túnez**	tunecino/a
Uganda	**Uganda**	ugandés, ugandesa
Zambia	**Zambia**	zambiano/a
Zimbabwe	**Zimbabue**	zimbabuense
AUSTRALIA AND THE PACIFIC	***AUSTRALIA Y EL PACÍFICO***	
Australia	**Australia**	australiano/a
New Zealand	**Nueva Zelanda**	neozelandés, neozelandesa
Philippines	**Filipinas**	filipino/a

MONEDAS DE LOS PAÍSES HISPANOS

PAÍS
Country

Country	Currency
Argentina	el peso
Bolivia	el boliviano
Chile	el peso
Colombia	el peso
Costa Rica	el colón
Cuba	el peso
Ecuador	el sucre, el dólar estadounidense
El Salvador	el colón, el dólar estadounidense
España	el euro
Guatemala	el quetzal, el dólar estadounidense
Honduras	el lempira
México	el peso
Nicaragua	el córdoba
Panamá	el balboa, el dólar estadounidense
Paraguay	el guaraní
Perú	el sol
Puerto Rico	el dólar estadounidense
República Dominicana	el peso
Uruguay	el peso
Venezuela	el bolívar

CURRENCIES OF SPANISH-SPEAKING COUNTRIES

MONEDA
Currency

303

EXPRESIONES Y REFRANES

EXPRESIONES Y REFRANES CON PARTES DEL CUERPO

A cara o cruz

A corazón abierto

A lo hecho, pecho

A ojos vistas

Al dedillo

¡Choca/Vengan esos cinco!

Codo con codo

Con las manos en la masa

Costar un ojo de la cara

De rodillas

Duro de oído

En cuerpo y alma

En la punta de la lengua

Darle a la lengua

En un abrir y cerrar de ojos

Entrar por un oído y salir por otro

Estar con el agua al cuello

Estar para chuparse los dedos

Hablar entre dientes

Hablar por los codos

Hacer la vista gorda

EXPRESSIONS & SAYINGS

EXPRESSIONS & SAYINGS WITH PARTS OF THE BODY

Heads or tails

Open heart

What's done is done./Don't cry over spilled milk.

Clearly, visibly

Like the back of one's hand

Put it there!/Give me five!

Very closely/Cheek by jowl

Red handed

To cost an arm and a leg

On one's knees

Hard of hearing

In body and soul

On the tip of one's tongue

To chatter/To gab

In a blink of the eye

In one ear and out the other

To be up to one's neck with/in

To be delicious/To be finger-licking good

To mutter/To speak under one's breath

To talk a lot

To turn a blind eye on something

Hombro con hombro	Shoulder to shoulder
Llorar a lágrima viva	To sob/To cry one's eyes out
Metérsele (a alguien) algo entre ceja y ceja	To put an idea in someone's head
Mirar por encima del hombro	To look over one's shoulder
No pegar ojo	Not to be able to sleep/To stay up all night
No tener corazón	Not to have a heart
No tener dos dedos de frente	Not to have an ounce of common sense
Ojos que no ven, corazón que no siente	Out of sight, out of mind
Perder la cabeza	To lose one's head
Quedarse con la boca abierta	To be thunderstruck
Romper el corazón	To break someone's heart
Tener buen/mal corazón	Have a good/bad heart
Tener un nudo en la garganta	Have a knot in your throat
Tomarse algo a pecho	To take something too seriously
Venir como anillo al dedo	To fit like a charm/To suit perfectly

EXPRESIONES Y REFRANES CON ANIMALES	*EXPRESSIONS & SAYINGS WITH ANIMALS*
A caballo regalado no le mires el diente.	Don't look a gift horse in the mouth.
Comer como un cerdo	To eat like a pig
Cuando menos se piensa, salta la liebre.	Things happen when you least expect it.
Es una mosquita muerta.	Butter wouldn't melt in his/her mouth.

Llevarse como el perro y el gato	To fight like cats and dogs
Perro ladrador, poco mordedor./Perro que ladra no muerde.	His/her bark is worse than his/her bite.
¿Quién le pone el cascabel al gato?	Who will bell the cat?
Ser una tortuga	To be a slowpoke

EXPRESIONES Y REFRANES CON ALIMENTOS	*EXPRESSIONS AND SAYINGS WITH FOOD*
Agua que no has de beber, déjala correr.	If you're not interested, don't ruin it for everybody else.
Al pan, pan y al vino, vino.	Not to mince words.
Como agua para chocolate	Ready to explode/At the boiling point
Con pan y vino se anda el camino.	Things never seem as bad after a good meal.
Contigo pan y cebolla.	You are all I need.
Dame pan y dime tonto.	I don't care what you say, as long as I get what I want.
Descubrir el pastel	To let the cat out of the bag
Dulce como la miel	Sweet as honey
Estar en el ajo	To be in the know
Estar en la higuera	To take the lid off something
Estar más claro que el agua	To be clear as a bell
Ganarse el pan	To earn a living/To earn one's daily bread
No hay miel sin hiel.	There's no rose without a thorn./There's always a catch.
No sólo de pan vive el hombre.	Man doesn't live by bread alone.

Pan con pan, comida de tontos.	Variety is the spice of life./All work and no play makes Jack a dull boy.
Ser agua pasada	To be water under the bridge
Ser más bueno que el pan	To be gorgeous
Temblar como un flan	To shake/tremble like a leaf

EXPRESIONES Y REFRANES CON COLORES

EXPRESSIONS AND SAYINGS WITH COLORS

Estar verde	To be inexperienced/wet behind the ears
Poner los ojos en blanco	To roll one's eyes
Ponerle a alguien un ojo morado	To give someone a black eye
Ponerse rojo de ira	To turn red with anger
Ponerse rojo	To turn red/To blush
Ponerse verde de envidia	To be green with envy
Quedarse en blanco	To go blank
Verlo todo de color de rosa	See the world through rose-colored glasses

REFRANES

SAYINGS

A buen entendedor, pocas palabras bastan.	A word to the wise is sufficient.
Ande o no ande, caballo grande.	Bigger is always better.
A quien madruga, Dios le ayuda.	The early bird catches the worm.
Cuídate, que te cuidaré.	Take care of yourself, and then I'll take care of you.
De tal palo tal astilla.	A chip off the old block.
Del dicho al hecho hay mucho trecho.	Easier said than done.

Dime con quién andas y te diré quién eres.	A man is known by the company he keeps.
El saber no ocupa lugar.	You can never know too much.
Lo que es moda no incomoda.	No discomfort is too great in the name of fashion.
Más vale maña que fuerza.	Brains is better than brawn.
Más vale prevenir que curar.	Prevention is better than cure.
Más vale solo que mal acompañado.	Better alone than with a bad companion.
Más vale tarde que nunca.	Better late than never.
Mucho ruido y pocas nueces.	All talk and no action.
No es oro todo lo que reluce.	All that glitters is not gold.
Poderoso caballero es don Dinero.	Money talks.
Por la boca muere el pez.	Talking too much can be dangerous.
Vale más una imagen que mil palabras.	A picture is worth a thousand words.

COMMON FALSE FRIENDS

False friends are Spanish words that look similar to English words but have very different meanings. While recognizing the English relatives of unfamiliar Spanish words you encounter is an important way of constructing meaning, there are some Spanish words whose similarity to English words is deceptive. Here is a list of some of the most common Spanish false friends.

actualmente ≠ actually

actualmente = nowadays, currently

actually = **de hecho, en realidad, en efecto**

aprobar ≠ approve

aprobar = to pass (an exam)

approve = **consentir, estar de acuerdo**

argumento ≠ argument

argumento = plot

argument = **discusión, pelea**

armada ≠ army

armada = navy

army = **ejército**

asistir ≠ assist

asistir = to attend, to go to

assist = **ayudar, colaborar**

balde ≠ bald

balde = pail, bucket

bald = **calvo/a**

batería ≠ battery

batería = drum set

battery = **pila**

bravo ≠ brave

bravo = wild, fierce

brave = **valiente**

cándido/a ≠ candid

cándido/a = innocent

candid = **sincero/a**

carbón ≠ carbon

carbón = coal

carbon = **carbono**

casual ≠ casual

casual = coincidental

casual = **informal, despreocupado/a**

casualidad ≠ casualty

casualidad = coincidence

casualty = **víctima**

colegio ≠ college

colegio = school

college = **universidad**

collar ≠ collar

collar = necklace

collar = **cuello (de camisa)**

comprensivo/a ≠ comprehensive

comprensivo/a = understanding

comprenhensive = **completo, extensivo**

constipado ≠ constipated

estar constipado/a = to have a cold

to be constipated = **estar estreñido/a**

crudo/a ≠ crude

crudo/a = raw, undercooked

crude = **burdo/a; grosero/a**

desgracia ≠ disgrace

desgracia = misfortune

disgrace = **deshonra, vergüenza**

divertir ≠ divert

divertirse = to enjoy oneself

to divert = **desviar**

educado/a ≠ educated

educado/a = well-behaved

educated = **culto/a, instruido/a**

embarazada ≠ embarrassed

estar embarazada = to be pregnant

to be embarrassed = **tener vergüenza**

eventualmente ≠ eventually

eventualmente = possibly

eventually = **finalmente, al final**

éxito ≠ exit

éxito = success

exit = **salida**

físico/a ≠ physician

físico/a = physicist

physician = **médico/a**

fútbol ≠ football

fútbol = soccer

football = **fútbol americano**

lectura ≠ lecture
lectura = reading
lecture = **conferencia**

librería ≠ library
librería = bookstore
library = **biblioteca**

máscara ≠ mascara
máscara = mask
mascara = **rímel**

molestar ≠ to molest
molestar = to bother, to annoy
molest = **abusar**

oficio ≠ office
oficio = trade, occupation
office = **oficina**

rato ≠ rat
rato = while
rat = **rata**

realizar ≠ realize
realizar = to do
to realize = **darse cuenta**

red ≠ red
red = net
red = **rojo**

remover ≠ remove
remover = to stir; to turn over
remove = **sacar, quitar**

revolver ≠ revolver
revolver = to stir; to rummage
through
revolver = **revólver**

sensible ≠ sensible
sensible = sentitive
sensible = **sensato/a, razonable**

suceso ≠ success
suceso = event
success = **éxito**

sujeto ≠ subject
sujeto = fellow, guy
subject = **tema, asunto**

LOS ALIMENTOS

FRUTAS

la aceituna	olive
el aguacate	avocado
el albaricoque, el damasco	apricot
la banana, el plátano	banana
la cereza	cherry
la ciruela	plum
el dátil	date
la frambuesa	raspberry
la fresa, la frutilla	strawberry
el higo	fig
el limón	lemon, lime
el melocotón, el durazno	peach
la mandarina	tangerine
el mango	mango
la manzana	apple
la naranja	orange
la papaya	papaya
la pera	pear
la piña	pineapple
el pomelo, la toronja	grapefruit
la sandía	watermelon
las uvas	grapes

FOODS

FRUITS

VEGETALES	*VEGETABLES*
la alcachofa	artichoke
el apio	celery
la arveja, el guisante	pea
la berenjena	eggplant
el brócoli	broccoli
la calabaza	squash, pumpkin
la cebolla	onion
el champiñón, la seta	mushroom
la col, el repollo	cabbage
la coliflor	cauliflower
los espárragos	asparagus
las espinacas	spinach
los frijoles, las habichuelas	beans
las habas	lima beans
las judías verdes, los ejotes	string beans, green beans
la lechuga	lettuce
el maíz, el choclo, el elote	corn
la papa, la patata	potato
el pepino	cucumber
el pimentón	bell pepper
el rábano	radish
la remolacha	beet
el tomate, el jitomate	tomato
la zanahoria	carrot

El pescado y los mariscos	*Fish and Shellfish*
la almeja	clam
el atún	tuna
el bacalao	cod
el calamar	squid
el cangrejo	crab
el camarón, la gamba	shrimp
la langosta	lobster
el langostino	prawn
el lenguado	sole, flounder
el mejillón	mussel
la ostra	oyster
el pulpo	octopus
el salmón	salmon
la sardina	sardine
la vieira	scallop

La carne	*Meat*
la albóndiga	meatball
el bistec	steak
la carne de res	beef
el chorizo	hard pork sausage
la chuleta de cerdo	pork chop
el cordero	lamb
los fiambres	cold cuts; food served cold
el filete	fillet
la hamburguesa	hamburger

el hígado	liver
el jamón	ham
el lechón	suckling pig; roasted pig
el pavo	turkey
el pollo	chicken
el puerco	pork
la salchicha	sausage
la ternera	veal
el tocino	bacon
OTRAS COMIDAS	*OTHER FOODS*
el ajo	garlic
el arroz	rice
el azúcar	sugar
el batido	milkshake
el budín	pudding
el cacahuete, el maní	peanut
el café	coffee
los fideos	noodles, pasta
la harina	flour
el huevo	egg
el jugo, el zumo	juice
la leche	milk
la mermelada	marmalade; jam
la miel	honey
el pan	bread
el queso	cheese

la sal	salt
la sopa	soup
el té	tea
la tortilla	omelet (Spain); tortilla (Mexico)
el yogur	yogurt

CÓMO DESCRIBIR LA COMIDA — *WAYS TO DESCRIBE FOOD*

a la plancha, a la parrilla	grilled
ácido/a	sour
al horno	baked
amargo/a	bitter
caliente	hot
dulce	sweet
duro/a	tough
frío/a	cold
frito/a	fried
fuerte	strong, heavy
ligero/a	light
picante	spicy
sabroso/a	tasty
salado/a	salty

DÍAS FESTIVOS	HOLIDAYS

ENERO

JANUARY

Año Nuevo (1) — New Year's Day

Día de los Reyes Magos (6) — Three Kings Day (Epiphany)

Día de Martin Luther King, Jr. — Martin Luther King, Jr. Day

FEBRERO

FEBRUARY

Día de San Blas (Paraguay) (3) — St. Blas Day (Paraguay)

Día de San Valentín, Día de los Enamorados (14) — Valentine's Day

Día de los Presidentes — Presidents' Day

Carnaval — Carnival (Mardi Gras)

MARZO

MARCH

Día de San Patricio (17) — St. Patrick's Day

Nacimiento de Benito Juárez (México) (21) — Benito Juárez's Birthday (Mexico)

ABRIL

APRIL

Semana Santa — Holy Week

Pésaj — Passover

Pascua — Easter

Declaración de la Independencia de Venezuela (19) — Declaration of Independence of Venezuela

Día de la Tierra (22) — Earth Day

MAYO	*MAY*
Día del Trabajo (1)	Labor Day
Cinco de Mayo (5) (Mexico)	Cinco de Mayo (May 5th)
Día de las Madres	Mother's Day
Independencia Patria (Paraguay) (15)	Independence Day (Paraguay)
Día Conmemorativo	Memorial Day

JUNIO	*JUNE*
Día de los Padres	Father's Day
Día de la Bandera (14)	Flag Day
Día del Indio (Perú) (24)	Native People's Day

JULIO	*JULY*
Día de la Independencia de los Estados Unidos (4)	Independence Day (United States)
Día de la Independencia de Venezuela (5)	Independence Day (Venezuela)
Día de la Independencia de la Argentina (9)	Independence Day (Argentina)
Día de la Independencia de Colombia (20)	Independence Day (Colombia)
Nacimiento de Simón Bolívar (24)	Simón Bolívar's Birthday
Día de la Revolución (Cuba) (26)	Revolution Day (Cuba)
Día de la Independencia del Perú (28)	Independence Day (Peru)

Agosto	*August*
Día de la Independencia de Bolivia (6)	Independence Day (Bolivia)
Día de la Independencia del Ecuador (10)	Independence Day (Ecuador)
Día de San Martín (Argentina) (17)	San Martín Day (anniversary of his death)
Día de la Independencia del Uruguay (25)	Independence Day (Uruguay)

Septiembre	*September*
Día del Trabajo (EE. UU.)	Labor Day (U. S.)
Día de la Independencia de Costa Rica, El Salvador, Guatemala, Honduras y Nicaragua (15)	Independence Day (Costa Rica, El Salvador, Guatemala, Honduras, Nicaragua)
Día de la Independencia de México (16)	Independence Day (Mexico)
Día de la Independencia de Chile (18)	Independence Day (Chile)
Año Nuevo Judío	Jewish New Year
Día de la Virgen de las Mercedes (Perú) (24)	Day of the Virgin of Mercedes (Peru)

Octubre	*October*
Día de la Raza (12)	Columbus Day
Noche de Brujas (31)	Halloween

NOVIEMBRE	*NOVEMBER*
Día de los Muertos (2)	All Souls Day
Día de los Veteranos (11)	Veterans' Day
Día de la Revolución Mexicana (20)	Mexican Revolution Day
Día de Acción de Gracias	Thanksgiving
Día de la Independencia de Panamá (28)	Independence Day (Panama)

DICIEMBRE	*DECEMBER*
Día de la Virgen (8)	Day of the Virgin
Día de la Virgen de Guadalupe (México) (12)	Day of the Virgin of Guadalupe (Mexico)
Januká	Chanukah
Nochebuena (24)	Christmas Eve
Navidad (25)	Christmas
Año Viejo (31)	New Year's Eve

NOTE: In Spanish, dates are written with the day first, then the month. Christmas Day is **el 25 de diciembre**. In Latin America and in Europe, abbreviated dates also follow this pattern. Halloween, for example, falls on 31/10. You may also see the numbers in dates separated by periods: 14.2.01. When referring to centuries, roman numerals are always used. The 16th century, therefore, is **el siglo XVI**.

PESOS Y MEDIDAS

LONGITUD

El sistema métrico
Metric system

milímetro	**= 0,001 metro**	
millimeter	= 0.0001 meter	
centímetro	**= 0,01 metro**	
centimeter	= 0.01 meter	
decímetro	**= 0,1 metro**	
decimeter	= 0.1 meter	
metro		
meter		
decámetro	**= 10 metros**	
dekameter	= 10 meters	
hectómetro	**= 100 metros**	
hectometer	= 100 meters	
kilómetro	**= 1.000 metros**	
kilometer	= 1,000 meters	

U.S. system
El sistema estadounidense

inch		
pulgada		
foot	= 12 inches	
pie	**= 12 pulgadas**	
yard	= 3 feet	
yarda	**= 3 pies**	
mile	= 5,280 feet	
milla	**= 5.280 pies**	

WEIGHTS & MEASURES

LENGTH

El equivalente estadounidense
U.S. equivalent

= 0.039 inch

= 0.39 inch

= 3.94 inches

= 39.4 inches

= 32.8 feet

= 328 feet

= .62 mile

Metric equivalent
El equivalente métrico

= 2.54 centimeters
= 2,54 centímetros

= 30.48 centimeters
= 30,48 centímetros

= 0.914 meter
= 0,914 metro

= 1.609 kilometers
= 1,609 kilómetros

REFERENCE

SUPERFICIE

El sistema métrico
Metric system

SURFACE AREA

El equivalente estadounidense
U.S. equivalent

metro cuadrado square meter		= 10.764 square feet
área	= **100 metros cuadrados**	
are	= **100 square meters**	= 0.025 acre
hectárea **hectare**	= **100 áreas** = **100 ares**	= 2.471 acres

U.S. system
El sistema estadounidense

Metric equivalent
El equivalente métrico

yarda cuadrada = 9 pies cuadrados = 0,836 metros cuadrados
square yard = 9 square feet = 0.836 square meters

acre = 4.840 yardas cuadradas = 0,405 hectáreas
acre = 4,840 square yards = 0.405 hectares

CAPACIDAD

El sistema métrico
Metric system

CAPACITY

El equivalente estadounidense
U.S. equivalent

mililitro milliliter	= **0,001 litro** = 0.001 liter	= 0.034 ounces
centilitro centiliter	= **0,01 litro** = 0. 01 liter	= 0.34 ounces
decilitro deciliter	= **0,1 litro** = 0.1 liter	= 3.4 ounces
litro liter		= 1.06 quarts
decalitro dekaliter	= **10 litros** = 10 liters	= 2.64 gallons

hectolitro	**= 100 litros**	
hectoliter	= 100 liters	= 26.4 gallons
kilolitro	**= 1.000 litros**	
kiloliter	= 1,000 liters	= 264 gallons

U.S. system	*Metric equivalent*
El sistema estadounidense	*El equivalente métrico*

ounce		= 29.6 milliliters
onza		= 29,6 mililitros
cup	= 8 ounces	= 236 milliliters
taza	**= 8 onzas**	**= 236 mililitros**
pint	= 2 cups	= 0.47 liters
pinta	**= 2 tazas**	**= 0,47 litros**
quart	= 2 pints	= 0.95 liters
cuarto	**= 2 pinta**	**= 0,95 litros**
gallon	= 4 quarts	= 3.79 liters
galón	**= 4 cuartos**	**= 3,79 litros**

PESO   *WEIGHT*

El sistema métrico	*El equivalente estadounidense*
Metric system	*U.S. equivalent*

miligramo	**= 0,001 gramo**	
milligram	**= 0.001 gram**	
gramo		
gram		= 0.035 ounce
decagramo	**= 10 gramos**	
dekagram	= 10 grams	= 0.35 ounces
hectogramo	**= 100 gramos**	
hectogram	= 100 grams	= 3.5 ounces
kilogramo	**= 1.000 gramos**	
kilogram	= 1,000 grams	= 2.2 pounds

tonelada (métrica)	**= 1.000 kilo-gramos**	
metric ton	= 1,000 kilo-grams	= 1.1 tons

U.S. system
El sistema estadounidense

Metric equivalent
El equivalente métrico

ounce		= 28.35 grams
onza		*= 28,35 gramos*
pound	= 16 ounces	= 0.45 kilograms
libra	**= 16 onzas**	*= 0,45 kilogramos*
ton	= 2,000 pounds	= 0.9 metric tons
tonelada	**= 2,000 libras**	*= 0,9 toneladas métricas*

TEMPERATURA

Grados centígrados
Degrees Celsius

To convert from Celsius to Fahrenheit, multiply by 9/5 and add 32.

TEMPERATURE

Grados Fahrenheit
Degrees Fahrenheit

To convert from Fahrenheit to Celsius, subtract 32 and multiply by 5/9.

Centígrados
Celsius

°C °F

Fahrenheit
Fahrenheit

°C	°F
50°	122°
45°	113°
40°	104°
37°	98.6°
35°	95°
30°	86°
25°	75°
20°	68°
15°	59°
10°	50°
5°	41°
0°	32°
-5°	23°
-10°	14°

NOMBRES DE PILA ESPAÑOLES

SPANISH PERSONAL NAMES

Note: Not all Spanish names have English equivalents.

NOMBRES FEMENINOS	**WOMEN'S NAMES**
Alba	Elba
Alicia	Alice, Alicia
Amanda	Amanda
Ana	Ann, Anne
Araceli (Celi)	
Asunción (Asun)	
Asunta	
Aurora	Aurora, Dawn
Beatriz (Bea, Beti, Biata)	Beatrice
Belén	
Berta	Bertha
Blanca	Blanche
Carlota	Charlotte
Carolina (Carol)	Caroline
Catarina (Cati)	Catherine, Catharine
Cecilia	Cecile
Celia	Celia
Claudia	Claudia
Consuelo	
Diana	Diane
Dorotea	Dorothy
Elena	Helen, Ellen

Elia	
Elvira	Elvira
Emilia	Emily
Encarna	
Ester	Esther
Estrella	Stella, Estelle
Eva	Eve
Gemma	
Gertrudes	Gertrude
Gloria	Gloria
Inés	Inez
Irene	Irene
Isabel	Elizabeth
Josefa	
Josefina (Pepi, Fina)	Josephine
Juana	Joan, Joanne, Jane
Judith	Judith
Julia	Julia, Julie
Julieta	Juliet, Juliette
Laura	Laura
Leonor	Leonore
Lidia	Lydia
Lourdes	
Luisa	Louise
Manuela (Manola, Manoli)	
Margarita (Marga)	Margaret

María	Mary, Marie
Marta	Martha
Mercedes (Merche)	
Mónica	Monica, Monique
Montserrat (Montse)	
Noelia	
Norma	Norma
Olga	Olga
Paloma	
Patricia (Pati)	Patricia
Paula	Paula
Raquel	Rachel
Rocío	
Rosa	Rose
Rosalía	Rosalie
Rosana	Rosana, Roseanne
Rosario	
Sandra	Sandra
Sara	Sarah
Silvia	Sylvia
Sofía	Sophia
Sonia	Sonya
Susana (Susi)	Susan
Teresa	Theresa
Verónica	Veronica
Victoria (Vicki)	Victoria

Violeta	Violet
Zoe	Zoe
Nombres masculinos	*Men's names*
Alberto	Albert
Alejandro	Alexander
Álex	Alex
Alfonso	Alphonse
Alfredo	Alfred
Andrés	Andrew
Ángel	
Antonio (Toni)	Anthony
Aquiles	Achilles
Arturo	Arthur
Augusto	August
Bernardo	Bernard
Camilo	
Carlos	Charles
César	
Cristiano	Christian
Cristóbal	Christopher
Damián	Damian
David	David
Diego	James
Eduardo	Edward
Emilio	Emil
Enrique	Henry, Eric

Ernesto	Ernest
Esteban	Stephen
Eugenio	Eugene
Evaristo	
Federico (Fede)	Frederick
Felipe	Philip
Fernando	
Francisco (Paco)	Francis
Gerardo	Gerard
Gregorio	Gregory
Guillermo	William
Gustavo	Gustav
Ignacio (Nacho)	Ignatius
Jaime	James
Javier (Javi)	Xavier
Jeremías	Jeremiah, Jeremy
Jesús	
Joaquín	
Jorge	George
José (Pepe)	Joseph
Juan	John
Julián	Julian
Julio	Julius
Justino	Justin
León	Leo, Leon
Leonardo	Leonard

Lucas	Luke
Luis	Louis
Manolo	
Manuel	
Marcelo	Marcel
Marcos	Mark
Mariano	
Miguel	Michael
Oscar (Óscar)	Oscar
Pablo	Paul
Patricio	Patrick
Pedro	Peter
Rafael (Rafa)	Raphael
Raimundo	Raymond
Ramón	Raymond
Ricardo	Richard
Roberto	Robert
Santiago	James
Sebastián	Sebastian
Sergio	Serge
Simón	Simon
Sixto	
Teodoro	Theodore
Tomás	Thomas
Vicente	Vincent

COMPOUND WOMEN'S NAMES

In Spanish-speaking countries women frequently have names that are a combination of **María** and another name, as in **María Dolores** or **Ana María**, for example. Women with such names are rarely known as **María** but are addressed using the second name in the combination or a nickname derived from both names. **María del Carmen**, therefore, might be called **Carmen** or perhaps **Maricarmen**. Below are listed common combinations with **María**, followed by nicknames derived from them.

Note: **María** is not strictly a woman's name in the Spanish-speaking world. Some men's names contain **María**. **José María**, for example, is a common name.

María Ana (Ana, Mariana)

María Antonia (Antonia, Tonia, Toñi)

María Concepción (Concha)

María Cristina (Cristina, Cris, Tina)

María de los Ángeles (Ángeles, Mariángeles)

María del Carmen (Carmen, Maricarmen, Mámen)

María del Mar (Marimar)

María Dolores (Dolores, Mariló, Loles, Lola, Lolita)

María Elena (Elena)

María Eugenia (Eugenia, Maru, Genia)

María Inmaculada (Inma)

María Isabel (Isabel, Isa, Maribel, Mabel)

María Luisa (Luisa, Marilú)

María Nieves (Nieves, Marinieves)

María Pilar (Pilar, Pili, Maripili, Mapi)

María Reyes (Reyes, Marirreyes)

María Rosa (Marisa)

María Soledad (Marisol)

María Teresa (Teresa, Tere, Maritere, Maite)

Ana María (Ana, Anamari)

Ángela María (Ángela)

Eva María (Eva)

Rosa María (Rosa, Rosamari)

COMPOUND MEN'S NAMES

José Manuel (Josema)

José María (Josema, Chema)

José Miguel

Juan Antonio

Juan Carlos (Juanca)

Juan José (Juanjo)

Juan Luis (Juanlu)

Juan Manuel (Juanma)

Juan Pablo (Juanpa)

Miguel Ángel

NÚMEROS

NÚMEROS ORDINALES

primero/a	**1º/1ª**
segundo/a	**2º/2ª**
tercero/a	**3º/3ª**
cuarto/a	**4º/4ª**
quinto/a	**5º/5ª**
sexto/a	**6º/6ª**
séptimo/a	**7º/7ª**
octavo/a	**8º/8ª**
noveno/a	**9º/9ª**
décimo/a	**10º/10ª**

FRACCIONES

$\frac{1}{2}$	**un medio, la mitad**
$\frac{1}{3}$	**un tercio**
$\frac{1}{4}$	**un cuarto**
$\frac{1}{5}$	**un quinto**
$\frac{1}{6}$	**un sexto**
$\frac{1}{7}$	**un séptimo**
$\frac{1}{8}$	**un octavo**
$\frac{1}{9}$	**un noveno**
$\frac{1}{10}$	**un décimo**
$\frac{2}{3}$	**dos tercios**
$\frac{3}{4}$	**tres cuartos**
$\frac{5}{8}$	**cinco octavos**

NUMBERS

ORDINAL NUMBERS

first	1st
second	2nd
third	3rd
fourth	4th
fifth	5th
sixth	6th
seventh	7th
eighth	8th
ninth	9th
tenth	10th

FRACTIONS

one half
one third
one fourth (quarter)
one fifth
one sixth
one seventh
one eighth
one ninth
one tenth
two thirds
three fourths (quarters)
five eighths

DECIMALES		*DECIMALS*	
un décimo	0,1	one tenth	0.1
un centésimo	0,01	one hundredth	0.01
un milésimo	0,001	one thousandth	0.001

OCUPACIONES	OCCUPATIONS
el/la abogado/a	lawyer
el actor, la actriz	actor
el/la administrador(a) de empresas	business administrator
el/la agente de bienes raíces	real estate agent
el/la agente de seguros	insurance agent
el/la agricultor(a)	farmer
el/la arqueólogo/a	archaeologist
el/la arquitecto/a	architect
el/la artesano/a	artisan
el/la auxiliar de vuelo	flight attendant
el/la basurero/a	garbage collector
el/la bibliotecario/a	librarian
el/la bombero/a	firefighter
el/la cajero/a	bank teller, cashier
el/la camionero/a	truck driver
el/la cantinero/a	bartender
el/la carnicero/a	butcher
el/la carpintero/a	carpenter
el/la científico/a	scientist
el/la cirujano/a	surgeon

el/la cobrador(a)	bill collector
el/la cocinero/a	cook, chef
el/la comprador(a)	buyer
el/al consejero/a	counselor, advisor
el/la contador(a)	accountant
el/la corredor(a) de bolsa	stockbroker
el/la diplomático/a	diplomat
el/la diseñador(a) (gráfico/a)	(graphic) designer
el/la electricista	electrician
el/la empresario/a de pompas fúnebres	funeral director
el/la especialista en dietética	dietician
el/la fotógrafo/a	photographer
el/la higienista dental	dental hygienist
el hombre/la mujer de negocios	businessperson
el/la ingeniero/a en computación	computer engineer
el/la intérprete	interpreter
el/la juez	judge
el/la maestro/a	elementary school teacher
el/la marinero/a	sailor
el/la obrero/a	manual laborer
el/la oficial de prisión	prision guard
el/la obrero/a de la construcción	construction worker
el/la optometrista	optometrist
el/la panadero/a	baker
el/la paramédico/a	paramedic

el/la peluquero/a	hairdresser
el/la piloto	pilot
el/la pintor(a)	painter
el/la plomero/a	plumber
el/la político/a	politician
el/la programador(a)	computer programer
el/la psicólogo/a	psychologist
el/la quiropráctico/a	chiropractor
el/la redactor(a)	editor
el/la reportero/a	reporter
el/la sastre	tailor
el/la secretario/a	secretary
el/la supervisor(a)	supervisor
el/la técnico/a (en computación)	(computer) technician
el/la fisioterapeuta	physical therapist
el/la vendedor(a)	sales representative
el/la veterinario/a	veterinarian